# Moral
# Formation
### according to Paul

# Moral Formation

## according to Paul

The Context and Coherence of Pauline Ethics

James W. Thompson

**Baker Academic**

a division of Baker Publishing Group
Grand Rapids, Michigan

© 2011 James W. Thompson

Published by Baker Academic
a division of Baker Publishing Group
P.O. Box 6287, Grand Rapids, MI 49516-6287
www.bakeracademic.com

Printed in the United States of America

Library of Congress Cataloging-in-Publication Data
Thompson, James, 1942–
    Moral formation according to Paul : the context and coherence of Pauline ethics / James W. Thompson.
        p.   cm.
    Includes bibliographical references and index.
    ISBN 978–0–8010–3902–7 (pbk.)
    1. Bible. N.T. Epistles of Paul—Criticism, interpretation, etc. 2. Ethics in the Bible. I. Title.
BS2655.E8T56  2011
241.5—dc23                                                              2011020294

Unless otherwise indicated, Scripture quotations are the author's own translation.

Scripture quotations labeled ASV are from the American Standard Version of the Bible.

Scripture quotations labeled ESV are from The Holy Bible, English Standard Version® (ESV®), copyright © 2001 by Crossway, a publishing ministry of Good News Publishers. Used by permission. All rights reserved. ESV Text Edition: 2007.

Scripture quotations labeled KJV are from the King James Version of the Bible.

Scripture quotations labeled NEB are from *The New English Bible*. Copyright © 1961, 1970, 1989 by The Delegates of Oxford University Press and The Syndics of the Cambridge University Press. Reprinted by permission.

Scripture quotations labeled NIV are from the Holy Bible, New International Version®. NIV®. Copyright © 1973, 1978, 1984, 2011 by Biblica, Inc.™ Used by permission of Zondervan. All rights reserved worldwide. www.zondervan.com

Scripture quotations labeled NRSV are from the New Revised Standard Version of the Bible, copyright © 1989, by the Division of Christian Education of the National Council of the Churches of Christ in the United States of America. Used by permission. All rights reserved.

Scripture quotations labeled RSV are from the Revised Standard Version of the Bible, copyright 1952 [2nd edition, 1971] by the Division of Christian Education of the National Council of the Churches of Christ in the United States of America. Used by permission. All rights reserved.

11   12   13   14   15   16   17        7   6   5   4   3   2   1

Gewidmet der Familie Schauer

in Dankbarkeit für ihre

Gastfreundschaft

# Contents

# Preface

In *Pastoral Ministry according to Paul* I argued that moral formation was the goal of Paul's missionary work among his churches. His work as a missionary was never complete, for his ambition was to present "blameless" churches to God at the parousia (cf. 2 Cor. 1:14; 11:1–4; 1 Thess. 3:13). Both the results of the earlier book and the contemporary conversation about spiritual formation have left unanswered questions that I will explore in the following pages. What is formation in actual practice? What are the specific qualities of moral formation? Does Paul have a coherent vision of what he expects of all of his churches?

The revolution in Pauline studies has also stimulated my investigation of the apostle's moral instruction. Whereas earlier interpreters assumed that Paul's doctrine of freedom from the law precluded the Old Testament as a source of his ethic, recent works on Paul have shown that it had a continuing relevance for his work of shaping new communities. These developments have led me to explore the continuing role of the law as a source of his instruction.

Although I hope that this book has contemporary relevance, my primary task is not to ask the hermeneutical questions about the many moral dilemmas that now confront us, but to grasp the specific shape and inner logic of Paul's moral instructions. Writing to house churches that were far removed from the public square, Paul addressed the issues that were vital for the moral formation of his communities. I am convinced that Paul's address to minority communities in a pre-Christian world has continuing relevance for Christian communities in a post-Christian world.

I am grateful to the many who provided support and guidance as I completed this work. My wife, Carolyn, devoted many hours to copyediting and bibliographic research. My graduate assistant, Joel Brown, also aided with research and proofreading. Editors at Baker Academic, especially James Ernest and Brian Bolger, offered numerous suggestions to improve this book. Robert and Kay Onstead established the endowed chair that provided the resources for research and writing. This book is dedicated to Gerda and Josef Schauer of Tübingen, Germany, in gratitude for their friendship and hospitality for more than three decades.

# Abbreviations

## General

| | | | |
|---|---|---|---|
| ch(s). | chapter(s) | passim | here and there |
| frag(s). | fragment(s) | p(p). | page(s) |
| ibid. | in the same source | rev. | revised |
| idem | by the same author | v(v). | verse(s) |
| par. | parallel | | |

## Ancient Texts, Text Types, and Versions

| | |
|---|---|
| LXX | Septuagint |

## Modern Versions

| | | | |
|---|---|---|---|
| ASV | American Standard Version | NIV | New International Version |
| ESV | English Standard Version | NRSV | New Revised Standard |
| KJV | King James Version | | Version |
| NEB | The New English Bible | RSV | Revised Standard Version |

## Papyri

| | |
|---|---|
| P.Oxy. | Oxyrhynchus Papyri |

## Apocrypha and Septuagint

| | | | |
|---|---|---|---|
| Bar. | Baruch | Tob. | Tobit |
| 1–4 Macc. | 1–4 Maccabees | Wis. | Wisdom of Solomon |
| Sir. | Sirach | | |

## Old Testament Pseudepigrapha

| | | | |
|---|---|---|---|
| 2 Bar. | 2 Baruch (Syriac Apocalypse) | 2 En. | 2 Enoch (Slavonic Apocalypse) |
| 1 En. | 1 Enoch (Ethiopic Apocalypse) | Jos. Asen. | Joseph and Aseneth |
| | | Jub. | Jubilees |

| Odes Sol. | Odes of Solomon | T. Iss. | Testament of Issachar |
| Ps.-Phoc. | Sentences of | T. Jos. | Testament of Joseph |
| | Pseudo-Phocylides | T. Jud. | Testament of Judah |
| Pss. Sol. | Psalms of Solomon | T. Levi | Testament of Levi |
| Sib. Or. | Sibylline Oracles | T. Naph. | Testament of Naphtali |
| T. Ash. | Testament of Asher | T. Reub. | Testament of Reuben |
| T. Benj. | Testament of Benjamin | T. Sim. | Testament of Simeon |
| T. Dan | Testament of Dan | T. Zeb. | Testament of Zebulon |
| T. Gad | Testament of Gad | | |

## Dead Sea Scrolls and Related Texts

| 1QS | Rule of the Community |
|---|---|

## Apostolic Fathers

| Barn. | Barnabas | Ign. Pol. | Ignatius, To Polycarp |
| 1–2 Clem. | 1–2 Clement | Pol. Phil. | Polycarp, To the |
| Did. | Didache | | Philippians |

## Greek and Latin Authors

**AESCHYLUS**
　Sept.　　　　　Septem contra Thebas (Seven against Thebes)

**ARISTOPHANES**
　Thesm.　　　　Thesmophoriazusae

**ARISTOTLE**
　Eth. nic.　　　Ethica nicomachea (Nicomachean Ethics)
　Eth. eud.　　　Ethica eudemia (Eudemian Ethics)
　Pol.　　　　　Politica (Politics)

**CICERO**
　Clu.　　　　　Pro Cluentio
　Nat. d.　　　　De natura deorum
　Tusc.　　　　　Tusculanae Disputationes

**DIO CHRYSOSTOM**
　Orations
　　Or. 5　　　　Libycus mythos
　　Or. 7　　　　Venator
　　Or. 14　　　De servitute et libertatei
　　Or. 32　　　Ad Alexandrinos
　　Or. 38　　　Ad Nicomedienses
　　Or. 39　　　Ad Nicaeenses
　　Or. 48　　　In contione
　　Or. 49　　　Recusatio magistratus

**DIOGENES LAERTIUS**
　Vit.　　　　　Vitae philosophorum (Lives of Eminent Philosophers)

DIONYSIUS OF HALICARNASSUS
   *Ant. rom.*        *Antiquitates romanae*

EPICTETUS
   *Diatr.*        *Diatribai (Dissertationes)*

EURIPIDES
   *El.*        *Electra*
   *Iph. aul.*        *Iphegenia aulidensis (Iphegenia at Aulis)*

HERODOTUS
   *Hist.*        *Historiae (Histories)*

IRENAEUS
   *Haer.*        *Adversus haereses (Against Heresies)*

JOSEPHUS
   *Ag. Ap.*        *Against Apion*
   *J.W.*        *Jewish War*

PHILO
   *Abraham*        *On the Life of Abraham*
   *Alleg. Interp.*        *Allegorical Interpretation*
   *Cher.*        *On the Cherubim*
   *Creation*        *On the Creation of the World*
   *Decalogue*        *On the Decalogue*
   *Dreams*        *On Dreams*
   *Embassy*        *On the Embassy to Gaius*
   *Flaccus*        *Against Flaccus*
   *Flight*        *On Flight and Finding*
   *Giants*        *On Giants*
   *Good Person*        *That Every Good Person Is Free*
   *Joseph*        *On the Life of Joseph*
   *Moses*        *On the Life of Moses*
   *Names*        *On the Change of Names*
   *Posterity*        *On the Posterity of Cain*
   *Providence*        *On Providence*
   *QE*        *Questions and Answers on Exodus*
   *QG*        *Questions and Answers on Genesis*
   *Rewards*        *On Rewards and Punishments*
   *Sacrifices*        *On the Sacrifices of Cain and Abel*
   *Sobriety*        *On Sobriety*
   *Spec. Laws*        *On the Special Laws*
   *Virtues*        *On the Virtues*

PHOTIUS
   *Frag. Gal.*        *Fragmenta in epistulam ad Galatas*

PLATO
   *Apol.*        *Apologia*
   *Leg.*        *Leges*
   *Phaed.*        *Phaedo*

| Phaedr. | Phaedrus |
| Resp. | Respublica (Republic) |
| Symp. | Symposium |
| Theaet. | Theaetetus |

PLINY THE YOUNGER
| Ep. | Epistulae |

PLUTARCH
| Ag. Cleom. | Agis et Cleomenes |
| Amat. | Amatorius |
| Conj. praec. | Conjugalia Praecepta |
| Frat. amor. | De fraterno amore |
| Is. Os. | De Iside et Osiride |
| Lyc. | Lycurgus |
| Mor. | Moralia |
| Stoic. rep. | De Stoicorum repugnantiis |
| Ti. C. Gracch. | Tiberius et Caius Gracchus |

PSEUDO-PLATO
| Def. | Definitiones (Definitions) |

PSEUDO-PLUTARCH
| Lib. ed. | De liberis educandis |

SENECA
| Ep. | Epistulae morales |

SOPHOCLES
| Aj. | Ajax |
| Oed. col. | Oedipus coloneus |
| Oed. tyr. | Oedipus tyrannus |
| Trach. | Trachiniae |

STOBAEUS
| Ecl. | Eclogae |

THEOCRITUS
| Id. | Idylls |

XENOPHON
| Oec. | Oeconomicus |
| Symp. | Symposium |

## Secondary Sources

BDAG   Bauer, W., F. W. Danker, W. F. Arndt, and F. W. Gingrich. *Greek-English Lexicon of the New Testament and Other Early Christian Literature.* 3rd ed. Chicago, 1999

EDNT   *Exegetical Dictionary of the New Testament.* Edited by H. Balz and G. Schneider. 3 vols. Grand Rapids, 1990–1993

LCL    Loeb Classical Library

LSJ    Liddell, H. G., R. Scott, and H. S. Jones. *A Greek-English Lexicon*. 9th ed. with revised supplement. Oxford, 1996

*NIDB*    *New International Dictionary of the Bible*. Edited by J. D. Douglas and M. C. Tenney. Grand Rapids, 1987

*SVF*    *Stoicorum veterum fragmenta*. H. von Arnim. 4 vols. Leipzig, 1903–1924

*TDNT*    *Theological Dictionary of the New Testament*. Edited by G. Kittel and G. Friedrich. Translated by G. W. Bromiley. 10 vols. Grand Rapids, 1964–1976

*TLNT*    *Theological Lexicon of the New Testament*. C. Spicq. Translated and edited by J. D. Ernest. 3 vols. Peabody, MA, 1994

# Introduction

## Paul's Moral Teaching in Context:
## Living Worthily of the Gospel

For generations of interpreters, the central Pauline message is the human plight in sin and God's unconditional acceptance. Both evangelists and theologians have maintained that justification by faith is the center of Paul's theology and the culmination of the journey from plight to solution. Rudolf Bultmann, for example, organized Pauline theology according to this narrative, placing the Pauline message under two headings: "Man prior to the Revelation of Faith" and "Man under Faith."[1] Prior to the revelation of faith, the individual is subject to flesh and the power of sin. The solution to the plight is the new existence effected by the individual's experience of the righteousness of God by faith in Jesus Christ. Bultmann, like many others, interprets justification by faith as the individual's initial acceptance by God, the culmination of the narrative.[2]

Paul's letters indicate, however, that the readers stand not at the end of the story, but in the middle. The readers stand within a corporate narrative between their original conversion and the end. Paul consistently reminds his readers of both their new beginning in Christ (cf. Rom. 6:1–4; 1 Cor. 1:26–2:5; 2 Cor. 1:18–20; Gal. 3:1–5; Phil. 1:6; 1 Thess. 1:5) and the final day (cf. Rom. 2:5, 16; 13:2; 1 Cor. 3:13; 5:5; 2 Cor. 1:14; Phil. 1:6, 10; 2:16; 1 Thess. 5:2, 4). Thus his concern is not only to evoke faith and to baptize, but to complete the narrative of the community's existence.

1. Bultmann, *Theology of the New Testament*, 1:190, 270.
2. See Stuhlmacher, *Revisiting Paul's Doctrine of Justification*, 60.

1

Paul envisions a day when believers are "changed" (1 Cor. 15:52), "conformed to the image of [God's] son" (Rom. 8:29; cf. Phil. 3:21), sanctified (1 Thess. 5:23), and "blameless" (3:13). The success or failure of his ministry depends on whether they will reach this goal. His communities will be his "boast" (2 Cor. 1:14; Phil. 2:16–18; 1 Thess. 2:19–20) at the day of Christ. He is the anxious father of the bride who hopes to present the church as a "pure virgin to Christ" (2 Cor. 11:2) and the priestly servant (*leitourgos*) who presents the gentile converts to God "sanctified in the Holy Spirit" (Rom. 15:16). If he fails, he will have "run in vain" (Gal. 2:2; 4:11; Phil. 2:16).

If the transformation of believers is the ultimate goal of Paul's work, it is also the focal point of his theology,[3] as his letters indicate. He frequently employs the language of formation to describe the moral progress of the converts. Recognizing that his converts will be "conformed to the image of the Son" (Rom. 8:29; cf. Phil. 3:20–21) at the final day only if they are "being transformed into the same image" (2 Cor. 3:18), he describes himself as the mother about to give birth, addressing the Galatians as "my little children, with whom I am in the pangs of childbirth, until Christ is formed (*morphōthē*) in you" (Gal. 4:19). Introducing the section on moral conduct in Romans, he says, "Do not be conformed to this world, but be transformed (*metamorphousthe*) by the renewing of your mind" (12:2). Thus Paul provides the vocabulary for what would later be called spiritual formation. He envisions moral transformation—a metamorphosis—in the present as a prelude to the ultimate transformation at the end. Thus he writes letters to ensure that his goal is fulfilled.

Morna Hooker has described this transformation as "interchange" in which Christ "became what we are in order that we might become what he is."[4] Although the language comes from Irenaeus (*Haer.* 5, praefatio), it accurately describes the consistent theme of Paul's letters. He summarizes this theme in the creedal statement in 2 Corinthians 5:21: "For our sake he made him to be sin who knew no sin, so that in him we might become the righteousness of God." Similarly, he writes to the Romans, "For God has done what the law, weakened by the flesh, could not do: by sending his own son in the likeness of sinful flesh, and to deal with sin, he condemned sin in the flesh, so that the just requirement of the law might be fulfilled in us" (Rom. 8:3–4 NRSV).

Paul's understanding of transformation is evident in his letters. As the introduction to the moral advice in Romans 12:2 indicates, to be "transformed by the renewal of [the] mind" is to live according to the moral advice that

3. See Schnelle, "Transformation und Partizipation," 58–75.

4. Hooker, "Interchange in Christ and Ethics," 5. Hooker explains that the metaphor comes from the "interchange" of roads at a busy intersection. When the car breaks down and is towed in a new direction, interchange occurs. This provides the metaphor for the Christ event, in which Christ leads humans in a new direction. See also Thompson, *Pastoral Ministry according to Paul*, 24.

follows (12:3–15:13). In describing himself as the mother giving birth, Paul introduces his instructions for appropriate conduct in Galatians by describing his labor pains until Christ is "formed" among the readers (Gal. 4:19). Paul never uses the word "ethics" but speaks instead of being transformed (Rom. 12:2), living "worthily of the gospel" (Phil. 1:27; cf. 1 Thess. 2:12, "worthily of God"), walking in the Spirit (Gal. 5:16), and doing the will of God (Rom. 12:2; 1 Thess. 4:3).

The central place of moral transformation for Paul is reflected in the shape of his letters, all of which contain instructions for appropriate conduct. Contrary to popular interpretation, this instruction is neither the appendix nor the application of Paul's theological discourse, but his primary concern. His ethical advice is not limited to a separate section at the end of the letters. As Paul Schubert demonstrated long ago and rhetorical critics have reaffirmed, Paul sets the agenda for his writing in the opening thanksgiving of the letters.[5] In 1 Corinthians he expresses the hope that the community will be "blameless at the day of Christ" (1 Cor. 1:8). He gives thanks for the Thessalonians' "work of faith," "labor of love," and "steadfastness of hope" (1 Thess. 1:3). He prays to God that the Philippians will be "blameless" at the end and that the Thessalonians will be "blameless in holiness" (1 Thess. 3:13) at the final day. Thus the moral instructions are the means toward the transformation of the community.[6]

This metamorphosis in conduct will set the community apart from its surroundings, creating a moral counterculture. Paul resocializes his converts into a group ethos consisting of shared behavioral norms and conduct that maintain the cohesion of the house church. Transformation occurs when believers are "not conformed to this age" (Rom. 12:2). Paul even writes to gentile communities, encouraging them not to behave "like the gentiles who do not know God" (1 Thess. 4:5). When he discovers incest in the Corinthian church, he shames his readers, declaring that they are engaged in a vice that is not even practiced among the gentiles (1 Cor. 5:1). Those who do God's will are "blameless and pure, children of light in the midst of a crooked and perverse generation," among whom they "shine as lights in the world" (Phil. 2:15). With his low view of gentile morality (1 Thess. 4:5; cf. Rom. 1:18–32), Paul describes a sharp break in the conduct of believers, who have been rescued

---

5. Schubert, *Form and Function of the Pauline Thanksgivings*, 27.

6. Paul frequently uses forms of the Greek word *morphē* ("form"). Jesus takes the path from the form (*morphē*) of God (Phil. 2:6) to the form (*morphē*) of a slave (Phil. 2:7). Paul describes himself as "being conformed (*symmorphizomenos*) to his death" (Phil. 3:10) and assures his readers that "we . . . are being transformed" (*metamorphoumetha*, 2 Cor. 3:18). He encourages them, "Be transformed" (*metamorphousthe*, Rom. 12:2), anticipating the time when all will be "conformed" (*symmorphous*, Rom. 8:29; cf. Phil. 3:21) to the image of the Son. Current usage of terms like "Christian formation" and "spiritual formation" ultimately traces back to Paul's language of formation and transformation.

from the power of sin (cf. Rom. 6:1–23). Thus Paul indicates that those who are being transformed practice a distinctive morality.

## The Coherence of Paul's Moral Instruction

Although the moral transformation of the churches is the most consistent feature of Paul's catechetical instruction and letters, discovering the coherence of his theology and ethics remains a challenge.

First, Paul's moral instruction has been a problem for those who place the doctrine of justification by faith at the center of his thought;[7] that is, if God offers salvation without human deeds, why does God make ethical demands? If God is at work in believers "to will and to do" the good (Phil. 2:13), why does Paul encourage them to "work out [their] own salvation" (Phil. 2:12)? Why does Paul declare that God offers salvation apart from works (cf. Gal. 2:16; Rom. 4:2), but give thanks for the Thessalonians' "work of faith" (1 Thess. 1:3)? If salvation is by grace, why does Paul indicate that we shall stand before the judgment seat of God to give an account for our deeds (2 Cor. 5:10)? Paul declares that God has delivered believers from the power of sin (Rom. 6:1–11), but encourages them not to let sin reign in their bodies (Rom. 6:12). Rudolf Bultmann shaped the discussion of Pauline ethics in the twentieth century with his suggestion that the indicative—God's righteousness revealed in Christ—and the imperative stand in a paradoxical relationship in Paul's writings.[8] The demand is at the same time the gift of God's grace empowered by the Spirit. The paradox is present in Paul's exhortation, "If we live by the Spirit, let us walk in the Spirit" (cf. Gal. 5:25).[9] Bultmann insists that this righteousness is not the transformation of the believer's moral quality. There is no new content to the moral life that distinguishes believers from others. The demands placed on the justified person "consist only of what is good and pleasing and perfect, what may be included among praiseworthy things" (Rom. 12:2; Phil. 4:8).[10]

Although Bultmann's dialectic of indicative and imperative has dominated the study of Paul's ethics, becoming for many the organizing principle, subsequent scholarship has either modified or rejected it.[11] Recent studies have shown that this dialectic is reductionistic and inconsistent with the wide range of Paul's instruction.[12] The imperatives in Paul are not always clearly connected with the indicative of God's saving grace, for Paul appeals to a range

7. Zimmermann, "Jenseits von Indikativ und Imperativ," 260.

8. Bultmann, "Das Problem der Ethik bei Paulus," 132–40; idem, "The Problem of Ethics in Paul," 195–216.

9. Ibid., 140 ("Ethics in Paul," 216).

10. Ibid., 138–39 ("Ethics in Paul," 213–14).

11. On the numerous modifications to the indicative-imperative schema, see Zimmermann, "Jenseits von Indikativ und Imperativ," 262.

12. See ibid., 264.

of motivations in his exhortations. Nor does Bultmann acknowledge the corporate nature of Paul's instructions and the role of specific moral duties. Thus this dialectic is inadequate for demonstrating the coherence of Paul's moral instruction.

Second, Paul insists that believers conduct themselves "worthily of the gospel" (Phil. 1:27), but he gives no comprehensive ethical theory to guide their conduct. Although ethical lists appear in 1 and 2 Corinthians (1 Cor. 5:10; 6:9–10; 2 Cor. 12:20), Galatians (5:19–23), Philippians (2:1–4; 4:6–8), and the disputed Pauline letters (cf. Eph. 5:3–6:9; Col. 3:5–4:1), they are scarcely a comprehensive description of the life that is worthy of the gospel. Paul gives extensive oral catechetical instruction that is not available to us (cf. Gal. 5:21), but not a comprehensive code of conduct for his communities.[13] Alongside advice on traditional ethical concerns such as marriage and sexuality, he includes instructions for regular prayer and worship. Thus Paul's major goal for his communities is to ensure their moral formation, but he provides few details on the shape of this life. Ethics, as defined by the philosophers, is not a clearly delineated category in Paul. Hence Wayne Meeks prefers to speak of morality rather than ethics,[14] and W. Schrage and S. Schulz, both of whom have written books on Pauline ethics, have suggested that one use quotation marks in speaking of Paul's "ethics."[15]

Paul's moral instructions in the letters share common themes, but they are limited almost exclusively to matters of sexuality and other relationships within the community. Because he writes to minority communities about their concerns, he says little about civic life, family life, or other issues that were the topics of ethical discourse. Thus he offers no guidance on matters of public concern. When he addresses concerns about poverty and economic justice, he addresses only those issues that involve the church (cf. 2 Cor. 8:1–15; Philemon). In contrast to the Torah and the Pharisaic tradition, he does not offer regulations that attempt to cover every situation in life. Nor does he mention the common themes of the ancient moralists, including matters of civic life and duties to one's country, household, or friends.[16] Thus one who looks to Paul for moral guidance today is likely to be perplexed that Paul makes no explicit comment on specific issues such as abortion, the environment, or other issues that confront us. Paul offers amazingly few specific instructions that could be a code of conduct.

13. Meeks, *Origins of Christian Morality*, 69: "The earliest Christian lists are neither systematic nor comprehensive. Clearly their function is not to name *all* the wicked things one should eschew or all the good traits one ought to cultivate. Neither do they suggest a rationale of interconnectedness among the virtues or the vices."

14. Ibid., 3.

15. Schrage, *Ethik des Neuen Testaments*, 13; idem, *The Ethics of the New Testament*, 5; Schulz, *Neutestamentliche Ethik*, 350.

16. For the topoi of ancient ethical discourse, see Malherbe, *Moral Exhortation*, 86–105.

Third, although Paul insists that the moral conduct of his communities not "be conformed to this world" (Rom. 12:2) and distinguishes the conduct required of them from that observed in others (1 Thess. 4:5), one may ask what is distinctive about Paul's ethic. The focus of the literature on Pauline ethics in the twentieth century has been on the parallels to Paul's moral instructions, and scholars have mined both Greco-Roman and Jewish texts, identifying the parallels to Paul's instructions, leaving scarcely any ethical concept that may be described as distinctively Christian.[17] Indeed, as Teresa Morgan points out, many values are common to all societies. "People cannot live together until they have agreed not to murder each other (and agreed what counts as murder); they cannot farm until they have agreed not to steal from one another; they cannot decide who belongs to an ongoing group without deciding who breeds with whom."[18] Thus, while Paul insists on a countercultural morality, one is not likely to find instructions that are without parallels in antiquity.

Fourth, Paul insists that believers are not "under law" (Rom. 6:14) and will not be vindicated by "works of the law" (Gal. 2:16), yet instructs believers to "keep the commandments" (1 Cor. 7:19). He writes that both he and his readers "died to the law" (Gal. 2:19; Rom. 7:4), yet reminds them that he is under the law of Christ (1 Cor. 9:21) and that they may "fulfill the law of Christ" (Gal. 6:2; cf. Rom. 8:4). His moral instructions for gentile communities do not mention the Jewish boundary markers of circumcision, food laws, or the Sabbath. He writes to the Romans that "nothing is common or unclean" (Rom. 14:14). However, while he does not require those commandments of the Torah that are badges of Jewish identity, his instructions for gentile converts correspond to the commandments of the Torah, which was written "for our instruction" (Rom. 15:4).

Fifth, he shows extraordinary pessimism concerning the human potential to do the good apart from Christ, but equally extraordinary optimism concerning the possibilities for his communities to fulfill the will of God. His categorical claim that "no one is righteous" (3:10) is without parallel in both the philosophical tradition and Jewish literature. However, he assures his communities that if they walk by the Spirit they will not be overcome by the desire of the flesh (Gal. 5:16), and he assumes that his readers will keep the commandments.

With these tensions in mind, my task in this book is to explore Paul's moral instruction to determine what, if anything, gives coherence to his teaching. Inasmuch as the coherence of Paul's thought remains an open question, this study will contribute to the resolution of that problem by placing Paul's instruction within the larger context of his role as pastor and theologian. What was the relationship between the theoretical foundation of Paul's ethics and

17. Wolter, "Identität und Ethos bei Paulus," 126: "For every ethical instruction and every ethical value that we find in Paul, there are parallels outside the New Testament. What is not in pagan environment can be found in Judaism."

18. Morgan, *Popular Morality in the Early Roman Empire*, 3.

the specific instructions? By what criteria did he determine the character of the life that was worthy of the gospel? Did Paul offer moral instructions ad hoc in response to problems in his churches, or was he consistent in his requirement for the churches? Can we determine the center of his moral demands? Did he offer moral requirements that were distinctively Christian? Or did he shape his communities according to existing models in philosophy, popular folk morality, or the Jewish tradition? Recognizing that Paul did not answer many of the questions that we ask, I will follow the logic of his moral instructions as they relate to the issues involved in the formation of his communities.

## The Context of Paul's Moral Instructions

Paul's moral instruction is especially noteworthy within the context of the ethical teaching of the ancient moralists—which would have influenced the communities he established—and that of the Jewish heritage based on Scripture.[19] Both traditions offered coherent approaches to moral instruction, but they differed significantly.

### The Greek Heritage

Long before Paul, the Greeks had placed ethics alongside logic and physics as a division within philosophy.[20] As the first to reflect on ethics systematically,[21] Socrates offers an important point of comparison to Paul. Socrates devoted himself to the question how one should live, maintaining that the *eudaimonia* of the individual was the foundation of the good life.[22] The Socratic question led to wider self-determination, according to which one should care for one's soul rather than seek fame, wealth, or honor (Plato, *Apol.* 29c–d, 36c). The path to *eudaimonia* is virtue (*aretē*), which he associates with knowledge of the good.[23] With his focus on knowledge, Socrates gave to ethics a strong rational approach that was appropriated consistently among Greek thinkers.[24] Thus, according to Socrates, no one willingly does falsely, but only because of intellectual error, for bad behavior is the result of misinformation.[25]

Plato develops the schema of four cardinal virtues: wisdom (*sophia* or *phronēsis*), courage (*andreia*), self-control (*sōphrosynē*), and justice (*dikaiosynē*),

19. For the view that Pauline ethics is a synthesis of the Greek ethic of autonomy and self-control and the biblical ethic of command, see Theissen, "Urchristliches Ethos," 209–22.

20. Xenocrates, *Testimonia*, frag. 82; Inwood, "Ethics," 83.

21. Inwood, "Ethics," 82.

22. *Eudaimonia* can be rendered as "prosperity," "good fortune," or "happiness." LSJ 708.

23. Lohse, *Theological Ethics of the New Testament*, 16.

24. According to Dihle, the rational knowledge of human nature and the human environment became the basis for ethics throughout the Hellenistic world ("Ethik," 648).

25. Inwood, "Ethik," 162.

a theme to which he returns frequently (*Resp.* 427d–e; 442b–d; *Phaed.* 69c; *Leg.* 631c; 963a). Although later writers occasionally substituted for one of the four cardinal virtues, this schema shaped subsequent ethical reflection. Aristotle continued the development of a coherent theory of ethics in his *Nicomachean Ethics* and the *Eudemian Ethics*, maintaining that virtue consists of living according to our own nature.[26] Offering a comprehensive ethics, he expanded the list of four cardinal virtues and elaborated on each, maintaining that each virtue was the mean between two extremes. In addition to the four cardinal virtues, in the *Nicomachean Ethics* he also addressed such topics as friendship, liberality, proper speech, and gentleness.

Like Aristotle, the Stoics recognized the presence of irrational impulses in humankind but insisted that reason can overcome the destructive passions (Cicero, *Tusc.* 4.26=SVF 3.427; Seneca, *Ep.* 75.11=SVF 3.428). They also maintained the four cardinal virtues and offered a coherent ethical system, according to which the good life consists of living according to nature (cf. Diogenes Laertius, *Vit.* 7.87). Like Socrates, the Stoics argued that the good life consists not of material things but of virtue.

Although the Greek philosophers approached ethics variously, they also had points in common, which will be important in a comparison with Pauline ethics. They were individualistic, attending to human flourishing (*eudaimonia*).[27] They all assumed that the context for individual *eudaimonia* was the Greek polis, or city-state, in which the harmony of the larger community was essential.[28] Consequently, Plato put justice at the head of the virtues, Aristotle associated justice with the concern for others (*Eth. nic.* 5.1.1129b), and the Stoics insisted on the good of others within the context of the ancient city-state.[29] These philosophers assumed that correct behavior is derived from proper insight. Consequently, they assumed that through knowledge humankind could overcome destructive impulses and do the good.[30]

### The Heritage of Scripture

In contrast to the Greek ethical tradition, that of the Jews was based on submission to the command of God as stated in the Law, the Prophets, and the Writings—the three parts of Scripture. Before the Torah was gathered in written form, the prophets summoned Israel to obey God's commands. Micah summons Judah to do what the Lord requires: "to do justice, love mercy, and walk humbly with your God" (Mic. 6:8). The narrative literature indicates

26. Ibid., 163.

27. Dihle, "Ethik," 652.

28. Meeks, *Origin of Christian Morality*, 7. According to Aristotle, the human is a political animal designed by nature to live in an ordered community (*Eth. nic.* 9.9.3).

29. See Engberg-Pedersen, "Paul, Virtues, and Vices," 610.

30. Dihle, "Ethik," 649.

that certain things are "not done in Israel" (2 Sam. 13:12; cf. Gen. 34:7; Judg. 20:6, 10).[31] According to the psalmist,

> Good and upright is the Lord; therefore he instructs sinners in the way.
> He leads the humble in what is right, and teaches the humble his way.
> All the paths of the Lord are steadfast love and faithfulness,
> for those who keep his covenant and his decrees. (Ps. 25:8–10 NRSV)

The psalmist asks, "Who may dwell on your [God's] holy hill?" He answers,

> Those who walk blamelessly, and do what is right,
> and speak the truth from their heart;
> who do not slander with their tongue,
> and do no evil to their friends,
> nor take up a reproach against their neighbors;
> in whose eyes the wicked are despised,
> but who honor those who fear the Lord;
> who stand by their oath even to their hurt;
> who do not lend money at interest,
> and do not take a bribe against the innocent. (15:2–5 NRSV)

The Torah was God's gift to the covenant people and the expression of God's will. The legislation in the Pentateuch is comprehensive, covering the full range of obligations toward God and others who compose the community of Israel as well as foreigners who dwell among them. As epitomized in the Ten Commandments, the vertical relationship to God required that the Israelites obey God's law (Exod. 20:3), while the horizontal relationship promoted peace among the Israelites by eliminating causes of friction among them.[32] The legislators placed before Israel the choice between good and evil without questioning the potential of the Israelites to keep the law.[33] The developing rabbinic tradition attempted to interpret the Torah as a living document, appealing to it to cover all situations. While Jews in the Diaspora were united in their loyalty to the Torah, they did not produce a body of literature that offered a comprehensive ethics.

## The Content of Paul's Ethics in Previous Study

If the believer is not under law, what provides the source and coherence of Paul's instruction? The literature of the past century has provided a variety of answers. Many scholars maintain that Paul's moral instructions lack a coherent

31. Lohse, *Theological Ethics of the New Testament*, 11–12.
32. Mafico, "Ethics (OT)."
33. Lohse, *Theological Ethics of the New Testament*, 13.

organizing principle. Some argue that Paul's soteriology is the coherent center, while others find the focus in the love command.

### Alternatives to the Law as a Source of Guidance

Martin Dibelius insisted that Paul's eschatological consciousness was so intense that he gave no thought to a coherent set of ethical principles. As hopes for the eschaton diminished, Paul co-opted the ethical guidelines of Greek and Jewish moralists without laying a theoretical foundation.[34] Dibelius described the moral instruction as "paraenesis," which he regarded as unconnected ethical advice. Although some interpreters have challenged Dibelius's view, a major alternative in the understanding of Paul's ethics is to regard the specific instructions as independent both from the theology of the letter and from each other.

Numerous others have indicated that Paul followed the conventional morality of his day without including any specifically Christian dimension to his instruction. Scholars in the past century have focused on the affinities between his ethical instruction and the teaching of the moral philosophers, a familiar topic among the church fathers, who acknowledged similarities between the Christian and the Greek (especially Stoic) moral tradition.[35] Rudolf Bultmann maintained that Paul's ethic introduced nothing new, for he demanded nothing other than what was recognized as good in the judgment of the gentiles.[36] Scholars have explored the relationship between the ethical teachings of Dio Chrysostom,[37] Plutarch,[38] Musonius,[39] and Epictetus[40] on the one hand and those of the New Testament on the other. Others have examined the relationship between lists of vices and virtues, the household codes, lists of sufferings (peristasis catalogs), and other topics and the New Testament, maintaining that Paul's ethical instruction is indebted to these traditions. According to Abraham Malherbe, "Christians borrowed extensively from whatever school happened to meet their immediate needs."[41] According to this view, the needs of the community determined the ethic. "The contents of this instruction are for the most part determined by traditions that were already in circulation, taken over from the environment and reformulated so that they now correspond to the Christian way of life and become a vehicle for its communication."[42] Troels

34. Dibelius, *From Tradition to Gospel*, 239.
35. See Malherbe, "Hellenistic Moralists and the New Testament," 267–68.
36. Bultmann, "Das Problem der Ethik bei Paulus," 138 ("Ethics in Paul," 213).
37. Moxnes, "The Quest for Honor and the Unity of the Community."
38. Peterman, "Marriage and Sexual Fidelity."
39. Van der Horst, "Musonius Rufus and the New Testament," 306–15. Klassen, "Musonius Rufus, Jesus and Paul"; Ward, "Musonius and Paul on Marriage," 281–89.
40. See Thorsteinsson, "Paul and Roman Stoicism," 157.
41. Malherbe, "Hellenistic Moralists and the New Testament," 269.
42. Lohse, *Theological Ethics of the New Testament*, 83.

Engberg-Pedersen has compared the ethics of the Stoics with Paul's ethics in several works,[43] concluding that they share a deep structure, according to which the individual progresses from self-centeredness to a concern for others.

Numerous studies have shown parallels between Paul's instruction on specific topics and the instructions of ancient moralists. Will Deming argued for the Stoic background to Paul's instructions on marriage.[44] Hans Dieter Betz commented on the vice list of Galatians 5:19–25 that Paul merely summarizes the conventional morality of the time, but concedes that such lists might have been adapted from Hellenistic Jewish texts.[45] In commenting on the catalog of vices and virtues in 5:19–23, Betz remarks that, "with the exception of *agapē*, all of the concepts are common in Hellenistic philosophy."[46] He adds, "The individual concepts are not in any way specifically 'Christian,' but represent the conventional morality of the time."[47] Much the same can be said of the maxims (*sententiae*) in 5:25–6:10:

> With regard to the content of the *sententiae*, there is little that is specifically Christian. . . . The Christian is addressed as an educated person. He is expected to do no more than what would be expected of any other educated person in the Hellenistic culture of the time. In a rather conspicuous way, Paul conforms to the ethical thought of his contemporaries.[48]

But despite the formal connections that scholars have observed, major differences between Pauline ethics and the ethics of the Hellenistic moralists suggest the limitations of Hellenistic morality as a consistent source of Pauline ethics or as the basis for the coherence of Paul's ethical instructions. In contrast to the focus on individual flourishing (*eudaimonia*) within the city-state in Greek ethics, Paul speaks to communities, insisting on practices that are consistent within the subculture of the house churches. His focus on sexual vices has little analogue in Hellenistic ethics. Similarly, Paul never refers to the four cardinal virtues; the term *aretē* appears only once (Phil. 4:8). The dominant place of faith, hope, and love in Paul's ethical instruction has few parallels in the Hellenistic moral tradition. Moreover, Paul's emphasis on humility (*tapeinophrosynē*) transforms a Hellenistic vice into a positive quality.

According to many interpreters, Paul is a contextual ethicist for whom the only absolute is the command to love. Rudolf Bultmann, for example, argues that the absolute nature of the love command makes impossible "every ethic

43. Engberg-Pederson, *Paul and the Stoics*; Thorsteinsson, "Paul and Roman Stoicism"; Engberg-Pedersen, "Paul's Stoicizing Politics in Romans 12–13."
44. Deming, *Paul on Marriage and Celibacy*.
45. Betz, *Galatians*, 282.
46. Ibid., 281.
47. Ibid., 282.
48. Ibid., 292.

which tries to give an answer to the question, what shall I do? It therefore absolves the individual of the need for an answer."[49] Christians must know what love demands. In the encounter with the neighbor, those who love recognize how to respond, for the concrete demands become matters for the individual conscience.[50] According to H. Preisker, the demand for love makes all lists of virtues superfluous.[51] Similarly, Georg Strecker maintains that concrete norms would violate Paul's message of freedom. One discovers the demand of God in the situation and recognizes the good and the evil from the realm of ethical concepts in the larger culture.[52] According to William Doty,

> One of the most important reclamation projects in the history of biblical research was the reclaiming of Paul as a situational or contextualist theologian and ethicist rather than as a dogmatic moralist. Instead of visualizing Paul as an abstract thinker spinning webs of ethical and moral duties, modern interpreters see him as involved with his addressees in the process of dialogic piecing-together of concrete ethical responses in each situation.[53]

Robin Scroggs indicates that "Paul's ethical stance is close to a view in ethical discussion today called situation ethics." He argues that for Paul "there are no rules and regulations which predetermine a person's action." Paul listens to the concrete situation and then gives advice in each case.[54] He adds that "the believer is free to follow his or her own best judgment about actions, as long as these actions do not impinge upon the well-being of the other person." Wolfgang Schrage finds coherence in the Pauline ethic in the place he gives to four primary values: freedom, peace, love, and upbuilding of the other.[55]

In discussing the place of love in the Pauline ethic, however, scholars have failed to recognize both the literary and historical context of Paul's numerous appeals to love. He does not advocate love generically, but always assumes the communal context of the house church. When he employs the verb *agapan*, he employs the direct object "one another" (cf. Gal. 5:14; 1 Thess. 4:9–11), expanding on the nature of love in great detail. That Paul gives specific instructions in his letters suggests that love was not the only criterion for behavior. The extended descriptions of loving action (cf. 1 Cor. 8:1–13; Rom. 14:1–15:13) indicate the need to practice love.[56] While Paul argues that the law is "fulfilled"

---

49. Bultmann, *Glaube und Verstehen*, 1.234–35. See Schrage, "The Formal Ethical Interpretation of Pauline Paraenesis," 302. See also idem, *Die konkreten Einzelgebote*, 9.

50. Bultmann, *Glaube und Verstehen*, 2.70. Cited in Schrage, *Die konkreten Einzelgebote*, 10.

51. Preisker, *Das Ethos des Urchristentums*, 76.

52. Strecker, "Autonome Sittlichkeit," 871.

53. Doty, *Letters in Primitive Christianity*, 37.

54. Scroggs, *Paul for a New Day*, 70.

55. Schrage, *Die konkreten Einzelgebote*, 71–95.

56. Holtz, "The Question of the Content of Paul's Instructions," 70. Original publication, "Zur Frage der inhaltlichen Weisungen bei Paulus," *Theologische Literaturzeitung* 106 (1981): 385–400.

(Gal. 5:14; 6:2) in the love command, he never indicates that it renders other commands superfluous.[57]

Others have maintained that the guidance of the Spirit provides the norm for Christian action. Udo Schnelle insists that Paul's virtue and vice catalogs were consistent with the common moral values of the time and that Paul proceeds on the basis of what was generally considered ethical; moral instructions are valid not because they appear in Torah but because they are a fruit of the Spirit.[58] James D. G. Dunn maintains that the Spirit gave direction for ethical decisions:

> He must therefore have been envisaging a life-style and choice of conduct options which constantly referred to that inner consciousness of the Spirit's presence and which sought to bring the life of the Spirit to expression in daily life. The repeated contrast with the law implies an inward rather than an outward point of reference in matters of ethical decision. This is presumably what Paul had in mind when he spoke elsewhere of discerning God's will by means of a renewed mind, of being given discernment to approve what was best in any particular situation (Rom. 12:1–2; Phil 1:9–10). Paul was claiming in effect that the inner, spontaneous knowledge of God's will for which Jeremiah had looked as a feature of the new covenant (Jer. 31:31–34) was now a reality in the experience of those who had received the Spirit.[59]

Although the Spirit plays a decisive role in Paul's ethics, Paul never indicates that the Spirit guides believers in the ethical decisions of daily living, or even that the Spirit provides special insight into the issues facing Paul's communities.[60] The Spirit is the divine power that equips believers to keep the commands rather than a guide to consult in making decisions.

Because the imitation of Christ undoubtedly played a role in Paul's ethics, interpreters have maintained that Paul's instruction is based primarily on following the path of Jesus.[61] Paul expresses gratitude that the Thessalonians became imitators of himself and the Lord (1 Thess. 1:6) as well as imitators of the churches in Judea (1 Thess. 2:14). He models his own existence after the crucified Christ, describing his own self-denial (1 Cor. 4:9–12; 9:1–23) and identification with the sufferings of Christ (cf. 2 Cor. 4:10–11; Phil. 3:10). He challenges his readers to imitate him as he imitates Christ (1 Cor. 4:16; 11:1). He frequently bases his ethical advice on the example of Christ. He challenges the Romans not to please themselves, because "Christ did not please himself" (Rom. 15:3). He encourages the Corinthians to participate in the collection because "Christ being rich became poor" (2 Cor. 8:9). The Christ who humbled

---

57. Schrage, *Die konkreten Einzelgebote*, 12.
58. Schnelle, *Apostle Paul*, 552.
59. Dunn, *Theology of Paul's Letter to the Galatians*, 107.
60. Deidun, *New Covenant Morality in Paul*, 219.
61. Schürmann, "'Das Gesetz des Christus,' (Gal 6,2)," 58–59.

himself is the example in Paul's exhortation that believers ought to act with humility, counting others better than themselves (Phil. 2:3).

Richard Hays recognizes the significance of the cross as one of three "focal images" that give coherence to Paul's ethic, the other two being community and new creation. These three images are inseparable in Paul's understanding, for the cross is the eschatological event that ushered in the new community and new creation. Consequently, the path of the cross leads to selfless conduct and the building up of the eschatological community.[62] Paul was an ad hoc theologian, applying these focal images to the situations that emerged in the church. According to Hays, Paul derived his norms for ethical behavior not from a rule book but from Christ as the ultimate paradigm; following him, believers can discern appropriate conduct.[63]

While the focal images are undoubtedly principles guiding moral instruction for Paul, they do not exhaust it. He commonly adds specific deeds and prohibitions in his description of the life that is worthy of the gospel. Indeed, he appeals only to the example of the selflessness of Jesus in giving up the privileges of the preexistent state (2 Cor. 8:9; Phil. 2:6) and to Jesus's path to the cross, but never to Jesus's deeds on earth, asking, "What would Jesus do?"[64] Paul challenges his readers to imitate Christ not in concrete deeds but as a pattern of selflessness in all of their conduct. He also instructs his community in detail concerning the shape of the life that is worthy of the gospel.

### The Law as a Source of Moral Guidance

Attempts to focus on freedom, love, conventional Greek morality, and the Spirit as the guiding principles of Paul's ethic are consistent with the view that Paul's negative assessment of the law as a means of salvation for gentiles extended to its role as moral guide, leading to other sources of moral guidance. According to Victor Furnish,[65] "Paul never quotes the Old Testament *in extenso* for the purpose of developing a pattern of conduct" and makes little use of the Decalogue. He looks to sources other than the law to provide moral guidance. Andreas Lindemann, having surveyed the moral instructions of 1 Corinthians, concludes that the Torah played no role in Paul's instructions on marriage and community life.[66] Udo Schnelle is struck by the absence of appeals to the Old Testament in the moral instruction of both 1 Thessalonians and the Corinthian correspondence.[67]

62. Hays, *Moral Vision of the New Testament*, 193–205.
63. Ibid., 43.
64. Deidun, *New Covenant Morality*, 219.
65. Furnish, *Theology and Ethics in Paul*, 33.
66. Lindemann, "Die biblischen Toragebote und die paulinische Ethik," 243–61.
67. Schnelle, "Die Ethik des 1. Thessalonicherbriefes," 301. According to Schnelle, Paul never appeals explicitly to the OT in 1 Thessalonians. When one notices where he could have appealed to the OT (1 Thess. 4:5/Ps. 79:6; 1 Thess. 4:6/Ps. 94:2; 1 Thess. 4:8/Ezek. 36:27; 1 Thess. 4:9/Jer.

While Lindemann and Schnelle may correctly observe both Paul's insistence on freedom from the law and the paucity of direct citations from the Old Testament in ethical discourse as evidence that the law is not a source of moral guidance, their argument fails to recognize that Paul's appeal to the Old Testament is not limited to specific citations. Indeed, Hellenistic Jewish literature frequently appealed to the contents of the law without specific citation, as I will demonstrate in chapter 1. Nor do Lindemann and Schnelle take account of Paul's specific statements about the place of the Scripture for ethical guidance. In the context of moral guidance, Paul claims that the Scripture was written "for our instruction" (Rom. 15:4; cf. 1 Cor. 9:9–10) after citing a passage of Scripture. Moreover, as Peter Tomson has shown, Paul addresses the varied issues at Corinth within the framework of the Torah and the Jewish halakic tradition.[68] Michael Wolter cites an imaginary letter from the man whom Paul condemns for living with his father's wife in which the gentile convert asks, "How can you judge me according to Jewish standards? What gives you the right to evaluate my relationship with Chariklea according to the law of the Jews?"[69] Markus Bockmuehl argues that New Testament writers, including Paul, found a framework for ethical instruction to gentile churches in the Noachide Commandments.[70] Although Paul insisted that gentiles are not subject to the established boundary markers (circumcision, Sabbath, and food laws), his ethical instructions are consistent with the moral instruction of the Torah.

The revolution in Pauline studies in the past generation has resulted in a recognition of the complexity of Paul's view of the law. Recent studies have also shown that the sharp distinctions between the Hellenistic and Jewish backgrounds are no longer tenable in our study of Paul. In his moral instructions, Paul undoubtedly depended on both Hellenistic and Jewish sources while at the same time omitting those aspects of both traditions that were not consistent with his gospel. Indeed, the two traditions overlapped in numerous ways in their concepts of life in harmony with others. However, just as one may ask about the coherence of Paul's theology, my task is to examine the coherence of Paul's instructions within the context of his theology, calling, and predecessors.

Among Paul's predecessors was a Greek-speaking Jewish tradition that had attempted to be loyal to the Jewish law while communicating it with the terminology of the Greek ethical tradition. Attempting to maintain Jewish identity while adapting to a majority culture, they interpreted the law in summaries that focused not on the sacrificial system or the Jewish boundary markers but on an ethic that was reasonable to the larger audience. For these

---

31:34–35; 1 Thess. 5:22/Job 11:8) as the basis of his paraenesis, the absence of OT references is striking. Cf. also Schnelle, *Apostle Paul*, 638–39.

68. Tomson, *Paul and the Jewish Law*.

69. Wolter, "Der Brief des sogenannten Unzuchtsünders," 188.

70. Bockmuehl, *Jewish Law in Gentile Churches*, 169–73.

Jews of the Diapora, "There is no such thing as Torah as such, but always and only the interpreted, the historically applied Torah."[71] As he established and shaped minority communities within the larger society in such a way that they demarcated themselves from that society while coexisting with it, Paul faced a task similar to that of his predecessors in Hellenistic Judaism.[72] This study will explore the relationship between the paraenetic tradition of Diaspora Judaism and Paul's instructions to new converts in a similar situation.

Recent study of the background of Paul's ethics has not adequately examined Hellenistic Jewish texts and Paul's appropriation of them. According to Abraham Malherbe, "It is astonishing that we have paid relatively little attention to Hellenistic Jewish texts in exploring the philosophic moral context of early Christianity."[73] While Tomson and others have pointed to contacts between Paul and halakic traditions, their work is limited to a few texts. I propose that a study of Hellenistic Jewish ethics may provide the necessary background for the study of Paul's ethics.

Since Jewish writers of the Diaspora faced a situation analogous to that of Paul, chapter 1 will explore the moral instructions of Greek-speaking Judaism that demarcated the Jews from their surroundings. Summaries of the law played an important role in both catechetical and apologetic contexts, indicating the parts of the Torah that were especially relevant in the Diaspora situation. Chapter 1 examines the role of moral instructions for maintaining the Jewish identity and ethos.

Ethical instruction in the Diaspora was inseparable from the establishment of Jewish identity. This identity protected Jewish communities from assimilation by demarcating them from the surrounding society. This identity requires a distinctive symbolic world, myth, and rituals. Communities express their distinctive identity with a code of conduct that distinguishes them from others.[74] Through all of Paul's letters he weaves a thread of terminology that establishes a shared identity among converts who come from a variety of backgrounds. He appeals to this identity as the basis for his instructions. Since ethics is the expression of our identity, in chapter 2 I will examine Paul's establishment of a new identity for his gentile converts as the basis for his moral instructions.

The relationship between identity and ethics is especially evident in 1 Thessalonians, Paul's first letter. As a pastoral and paraenetic letter that repeats much of Paul's original catechesis (cf. 1 Thess. 4:1–2), 1 Thessalonians offers a window into Paul's moral instruction, which consisted largely of directions on how to walk "worthily" of God (1 Thess. 2:12). Since Paul is apparently responding to no crisis in 1 Thessalonians, his moral instructions probably provide a summary of his teaching in all of the churches. Chapter 3 will

71. Holtz, "The Question of the Content of Paul's Instructions," 70.
72. Wolter, "Die ethische Identität christlicher," 64.
73. Malherbe, "Hellenistic Moralists and the New Testament," 332.
74. See Horrell, *Solidarity and Difference*, 121–69.

examine the ethical teaching in Paul's earliest letter as the basis for observing the continuity between his basic catechesis and the ethical instruction in those letters that he wrote to a contingent situation.

Paul's catechesis includes other items that are not mentioned in 1 Thessalonians but were probably the common property of Paul's converts in numerous communities. New converts received lists of vices and virtues, which were easily committed to memory (cf. Gal. 5:21). While some items in the lists may be in response to a local situation, the presence of common themes among the lists indicates that they belong to Paul's basic catechesis. They contain the most important themes of Paul's ethical teaching for establishing a common ethos. In chapter 4 I will place the lists of vices and virtues within their larger context in Judaism and the Greco-Roman world.

What role did the law play in the ethical instructions for new converts? These lists were common throughout antiquity, but rare in the Old Testament. Although Paul does not cite the law frequently, the lists of vices and virtues cohere with the Old Testament and the Jewish tradition. Furthermore, Paul's moral guidance contains echoes of the Torah, and he declares that Scripture is useful for moral instruction (Rom. 15:3–4). Chapter 5 will examine the role of the law in formulating instructions for new converts.

Nothing is more consistent in Paul's moral instructions than the list of sexual vices and the demand that the people overcome the "passion of lust" (cf. 1 Thess. 4:5). In common with ancient moralists and Jewish writers in the Diaspora, Paul insisted that the moral life involved the overcoming of the destructive passions of the flesh (cf. Rom. 1:18–32). Unlike his contemporaries, he argued that no one can keep the law or overcome the passions without the intervention of divine power. In chapter 6 I shall examine Paul's view of the human capacity to do the will of God.

Just as Paul's vice lists regularly mention sexual offenses, his lists of positive qualities consistently place love at the center. However, he does not merely place love above all virtues, but elaborates at length on the meaning of love in actual practice. Paul never mentions the Greek word *philanthrōpia*, but insists on *agapē* for others within the community of faith. In the extended sections on love in 1 Corinthians and Romans, he describes the meaning of love in actual practice. Chapter 7 will explore the role of love in Paul's response to the concrete circumstances of his churches.

Interpreters frequently distinguish the ethic of undisputed letters from that of those that are either disputed or pseudepigraphical (Colossians, Ephesians, the Pastoral Epistles), insisting on a loss of Paul's major themes in the second generation and a turn to the conventional morality of the environment. In chapter 8 I shall compare these letters with the undisputed letters to determine the continuity of the former with the latter.

In the conclusion, I shall summarize the results of the preceding chapters to determine both the coherence and the logic of Paul's ethical instructions.

The task involves recognizing that, like his peers in Hellenistic Judaism, Paul was indebted to both the Greco-Roman and Jewish traditions, but appropriated these traditions to correspond with his own theology. This chapter will explore the basic convictions that guided Paul in his adaptation of the values of his own time. I shall conclude with reflections on the relevance of Paul's approach for the contemporary church.

# 1

# Ethics in Hellenistic Judaism

## Maintaining Jewish Identity in the Diaspora

Paul's challenge to gentiles to "turn to God from idols to serve the living and true God" (1 Thess. 1:9) resulted in the formation of communities that had rejected the majority culture's worldview and way of life. His first task, therefore, was to maintain a group not bound by familial or ethnic ties as a minority community within the larger society. This group would inevitably be confronted by the religious, social, and philosophical values of the majority culture. Thus, like all minority communities, Paul's churches would survive only if they distinguished themselves from the larger society by a group identity and shared ethos.[1] Paul created a "group ethos" to unite the community.[2]

Jewish communities of the Diaspora had faced a similar challenge prior to Paul's ministry. Although some Jews assimilated to the larger culture, the literature of Hellenistic Judaism demonstrates the urgency with which Jewish leaders attempted to maintain Jewish identity by sustaining the boundary markers between them and the larger society. Although these writers did not create a comprehensive code like the Mishnah, they shared a commitment

---

1. Cf. Volf, "Christliche Identität und Differenz," 359: "Every social unit that is not identical with the entire society . . . must distinguish itself by great or small differences from the surrounding culture, in order to exist. . . . They must exercise 'boundary maintenance.'"
2. See Schmeller, "Neutestamentliches Gruppenethos," 120.

to the law, which they interpreted for their own context. The law provided their symbolic world and identity as God's chosen people. Thus, just as the Pentateuch required Israelites to confirm their identity by not doing "as they do in the land of Egypt" (Lev. 18:3), the writers of the Diaspora distinguished sharply between the morality of Israel and that of the majority culture. According to the *Letter of Aristeas*, in giving the law to Israel, God "surrounded [the people] with unbroken palisades and iron walls to prevent [them] from mixing with any of the other peoples in any matter" (139). The Third Sibyl accuses the Greeks and other nations of idolatry, homosexuality, and other offenses (599–600). Wisdom distinguishes sharply between the righteous and the ungodly (1:15–16)—between the readers of this work and their enemies (12:22). The latter commit the outrageous offenses described in Wisdom 13–14. A common theme is the difference between the morality of those who keep the law and the immorality of the surrounding nations.

Although Diaspora Jews were diverse in many ways, they shared a commitment to the law. They expressed this commitment selectively in order to meet the needs of the communities. Philo's *Hypothetica* and Josephus's *Against Apion* summarized the law in remarkably similar ways. Interpreters have observed the extensive parallels between these summaries and the poem *Sentences of Pseudo-Phocylides*, which was undoubtedly written by a Jew under the name of the ancient Greek writer. This poem echoes the law at numerous points without overtly citing it. The parallels of these three works are evident in table 1.1 and the listed commands.[3] These writers, and other Hellenistic Jews as well, took their summaries of the law primarily from the Holiness Code (Lev. 17–26) and the Decalogue (Exod. 20:2–17; Deut. 5:6–21). Indeed, the laws of Leviticus 19 parallel the Decalogue at many points.[4] Laws also appear that are not explicitly in the Torah, but interpret and actualize the Torah for the circumstances of the readers. Some laws show concern about marriage and family life (table 1.2); others for the oppressed and the weak and for animals and birds (table 1.3); still others about drunkenness and the need for self-control (table 1.4).

Table 1.1. Proscribed Sexual Behaviors in Philo, Josephus, and *Sentences of Pseudo-Phocylides*

|  | *Hypothetica* 7 | *Ag. Ap.* 2 | *Ps.-Phoc.* | Torah |
|---|---|---|---|---|
| homosexual practices | 7.1 (pederesty) | 199, 215 | 3, 190–91 | Lev. 18:22; 20:13 |
| adultery | 7.1 | 201, 215 | 178 | Exod. 20:14; Lev. 18:20; 20:10 |
| rape | 7.1 | 201, 215 | 198 | Deut. 22:23–29 |

3. Table 1.1 adapts the work of Niebuhr, *Gesetz und Paränese*, 45–46.
4. Weber, *Das Gesetz im hellenistischen Judentum*, 284. Lev. 19:11–12 contains laws against stealing, false witness, and profaning the name of Yahweh.

| | Hypothetica 7 | Ag. Ap. 2 | Ps.-Phoc. | Torah |
|---|---|---|---|---|
| bestiality | 7.7 | 213 | 188 | Exod. 22:19; Lev. 18:23; 20:15–16; Deut. 27:21 |
| purification after intercourse | | 203 | | Lev. 15:18 |
| sexual relations with relatives | | 200 | 179–83 | Lev. 18:7–18; 20:11–21 |
| abortion | 7.7 | 202 | 184–85 | |
| violating a virgin | | | 198 | Exod. 22:16; Deut. 22:23–30 |
| inappropriate intercourse with wife | | | 186, 193–96 | |

Table 1.2. Marriage and Family Life in Philo, Josephus, and *Sentences of Pseudo-Phocylides*

| | Hypothetica 7 | Ag. Ap. 2 | Ps.-Phoc. | Torah |
|---|---|---|---|---|
| submission of wives | 7.3–4 | 201 | | |
| raising of children | 7.3 | | 207–16 | |
| honoring of parents and the aged | 7.2 | 206 | 221 | Exod. 20:12; Deut. 5:16 |
| treatment of slaves | 7.2 | | 223–27 | |

Table 1.3. The Oppressed and Animals in Philo, Josephus, and *Sentences of Pseudo-Phocylides*

| | Hypothetica 7 | Ag. Ap. 2 | Ps.-Phoc. | Torah |
|---|---|---|---|---|
| protection of birds | 7.9 | 213 | | Deut. 22:6 |
| protection of animals | 7.9 | 213 | | Exod. 23:4; Deut. 22:1–4 |
| unjust scales | 7.8 | 216 | | Lev. 19:35–36; Deut. 25:13–16 |
| bribing of judges | | 207 | | Exod. 23:8; Lev. 19:15; Deut. 16:19 |
| care of strangers | | 210 | | Exod. 22:21; 23:9; Lev. 19:33–34 |

Table 1.4. Drunkenness and Self-Control in Philo, Josephus, and *Sentences of Pseudo-Phocylides*

| | Hypothetica 7 | Ag. Ap. 2 | Ps.-Phoc. | Torah |
|---|---|---|---|---|
| lies and the tongue | | | 48–50 | |
| drunkenness (*metrō piein*) | | | 69 | |

| | Hypothetica 7 | Ag. Ap. 2 | Ps.-Phoc. | Torah |
|---|---|---|---|---|
| envy (phthonos) | | | 70–71 | |
| rage (thymos) | | | 63 | |
| dissension (eris) | | | 75, 78 | |
| gluttony (metrō edein) | | | 69 | |
| anger (orgē) | | | 64 | |

These summaries both refer to the Torah and add to it with common emphases. All three emphasize sexual matters, prohibiting homosexual practices, adultery, rape, and bestiality. They also include matters of family life (submission of wives, raising of children, honor to parents). All three prohibit abortion. Matters of social justice also play a major role. The dominant Old Testament passage in the summaries comes from the Holiness Code (Lev. 17–26). These summaries are also notable for what they do not include. They do not refer to circumcision, the Sabbath, the food laws, or laws exclusively determining Israelite national identity.[5]

The function of the law in maintaining Jewish identity in the Diaspora is also evident in works that appeal to the law in urging appropriate conduct but do not summarize the law. In such works as Tobit, 4 Maccabees, the Wisdom of Solomon, and the *Testaments of the Twelve Patriarchs*, the authors indicate which parts of the law are important in maintaining Jewish identity. Here the degree of openness to other sources of ethics varies among the authors.

## Ethics of Tobit

The book of Tobit describes the challenges of living in the Diaspora. Through the medium of the novella, the author describes the ideal of the pious man of the Diaspora who is firmly rooted in the Jewish tradition.[6] In the first section of this work, the aged Tobit describes his life of obedience to the Torah (1:1–3:6). In his youth, before the deportation from Judea, he sacrificed in the temple (1:4) and attended the festivals (1:6–8). Living in the Diaspora, he avoided the bread of the gentiles (1:10–11), gave alms to the poor (1:16), and fed the hungry and clothed the naked (1:17).[7] He expresses many of the same values in the testament he gives his son Tobias before dying. He urges his son not to transgress God's commandments (4:5) and offers a summary of the statutes that Tobias should keep. Two major themes dominate the testament: social obligations within the community and sexual purity. Tobit expresses his

---

5. Weber, *Gesetz im hellenistischen Judentum*, 285.
6. Niebuhr, *Gesetz und Paränese*, 204.
7. See Niebuhr, "Tora ohne Tempel," 438.

concern about social obligations by his instruction that his son must bury his mother and father properly and honor his mother all of her life (4:3–4; cf. Exod. 20:12). He also echoes numerous passages from the Old Testament on social justice and care for the poor (4:11, 14, 16; cf. Exod. 22:21–27; Lev. 19:9–10). He instructs Tobias, "Love your kindred" (*agapa tous adelphous*, 4:13), elaborating on the command with the counsel not to marry a non-Israelite. Tobias must express this love by marrying within the covenant community (4:13). Tobit states these obligations in negative terms with an apparent paraphrase of Leviticus 19:18: "And what you hate, do not do to anyone" (4:15 NRSV). He echoes the warnings against excessive drinking (4:15) from the Wisdom literature (cf. Prov. 20:1; 23:29–35; Sir. 31:28–29). Tobit's concern with sexual purity appears in his warning against fornication (4:12). The story of Tobias and Sarah illustrates the value of both love for kindred and chastity as Tobias seeks a woman from among his people, praying, "I now am taking this kinswoman of mine, not because of lust, with sincerity" (8:7 NRSV). Like the summaries of the law described above, Tobit focuses on the law's demands for protection of Jewish identity, social justice, and sexual purity within the Diaspora situation.

## Ethics of 4 Maccabees

Ethical instruction is a central concern of 4 Maccabees, a work written in Greek by an unknown author who was both firmly rooted in the Jewish tradition and open to the influences of Greek culture.[8] The author recasts the story of the Maccabean martyrs, employing the language of Hellenistic ethics to describe their struggle with tyranny and edify his audience, as the opening line indicates. The work consists of two major sections framed by an *exordium* (1:1–12) and a *peroratio* (17:7–18:24).[9] The first section (1:13–3:18) contains the theoretical basis for the thesis, which the author announces in 1:1: "Devout reason (*ho eusebēs logismos*) rules the emotions (*pathē*)." Here he states both the genus (*philosophōtatos logos*) and the content and purpose of his work.[10] This claim becomes the refrain for the entire book (1:1, 5–7, 9, 13–14, 19, 29; 2:4, 7, 9, 15, 24; 3:1, 5; 6:31; 7:1, 16; 13:1; 15:23; 16:1). In some instances, the author attributes the control of the passions to "pious reason," as in 1:1 (cf. 6:31; 7:16; 13:1; 15:23; 16:1; 18:2), while in other instances he attributes this power only to reason. He sometimes alters the refrain, claiming that reason (*logismos*) rules over the appetites (*orexeis*, 1:33), anger (*thymos*, 2:19–20), and desires (*epithymiai*, 1:4; 3:2). The true philosophy, therefore, has an ethical orientation, for ethics is concerned with the control of various emotions

---

8. Niebuhr, *Gesetz und Paränese*, 216.
9. Klauck, "Die Bruderliebe bei Plutarch und im vierten Makkabäerbuch," 91.
10. Weber, *Gesetz im hellenistischen Judentum*, 214.

and desires. Those who control the passions exhibit the cardinal virtues of justice (*dikaiosynē*), courage (*andreia*), temperance (*sōphrosynē*), and wisdom (*phronēsis*, 1:6, 18).

The author begins to develop the thesis in 1:2, indicating the relationship among three Hellenistic concepts. The true philosophy that reason (*logismos*) rules the passions is necessary for knowledge (*epistēmē*), and it includes praise of the highest virtue (*aretē*), rational judgment (*phronēsis*). He expands the thesis statement in 1:3–5, associating *phronēsis* with the reason that rules the passions that prevent the practice of the cardinal virtues of self-control (*sōphrosynē*, 1:3), justice (*dikaiosynē*, 1:4), and courage (*andreia*, 1:4, 6).

*Logismos* occurs seventy-three times in 4 Maccabees, primarily as a restatement of the thesis of 1:1.[11] In 1:15–18, the author brings together the Jewish and Greek traditions to elaborate on his thesis and to clarify the nature of reason (*logismos*). Reason is the equivalent of the mind (*nous*) that employs "sound logic" (*orthos logos*) to lead a life of wisdom (*sophia*), the knowledge of divine and human matters (1:15–16). In 1:18, the author defines the types of wisdom by listing the cardinal virtues of rational judgment (*phronēsis*), justice (*dikaiosynē*), courage (*andreia*), and self-control (*sōphrosynē*).

### The Passions

In the theoretical foundation for his thesis in chapters 1–3, the author delineates the nature of the passions that hinder the development of the cardinal virtues before portraying the martyrdoms of Eleazar, the seven brothers, and their mother as examples of the ethical life controlled by reason in 4:1–17:6. As the thesis suggests, the author portrays the ethical life in agonistic terms, describing the conflict between two powers. On the one hand, the passions (*pathē*) and desires (*epithymiai*) can enslave (3:2). Negative emotions hinder the development of each of the cardinal virtues, as the vice lists indicate. Gluttony (*gastrimargia*) and lust (*epithymia*) hinder self-control (1:3; cf. 2:7). Malice (*kakoētheia*) hinders justice, while anger (*thymos*), fear (*phobos*), and pain (*ponos*) prevent courage (1:4). For example, Joseph was at the age when "a frenzy of the passions" (*epithymiai*, 2:3 NRSV) tempted him to take another man's wife, and David was "tormented and . . . consumed" by an irrational desire for water in the enemy's territory (3:11 NRSV). Only *logismos* can preserve the cardinal virtues.

In addition to the basic desire for sex in the story of Joseph and the irrational thirst in the story of David, the catalog of vices and virtues describes the impulses that, when ungoverned by reason, inhibit the development of the cardinal virtues and take control. Indeed, the author indicates that humans are subject to two types of passions: those of the body and those of the soul.

---

11. Reddit, "The Concept of *Nomos* in Fourth Maccabees," 258.

According to 1:3, gluttony (*gastrimargia*) and lust (*epithymia*) head the list of the passions of the body. In the vice list of 1:27 (NRSV), "indiscriminate eating (*pantophagia*), gluttony (*laimargia*), and solitary gormandizing (*monophagia*)" are the vices of the body. According to the vice list of 2:7, in the absence of control, the person becomes a "solitary gormandizer (*monophagos*), a glutton (*gastrimargos*), and a drunkard (*methysos*)." Anticipating the story that follows, in which the martyrs die rather than eat forbidden foods, the author expresses a special interest in the desire for food. He speaks of the cravings for "seafood and fowl and animals and all sorts of foods that are forbidden" (1:34 NRSV) as temptations belonging to common experience that can be controlled by reason. This claim anticipates Eleazar's defense of Jewish food laws in his conversation with Antiochus (5:25–27).

The passions of the soul (*psyche*, 1:20) are anger (*thymos*), fear (*phobos*), and pain (*ponos*, 1:4). The author gives special attention to anger (*thymos*). In the soul is "boastfulness (*alazoneia*), love of money (*philargyria*), thirst for honor (*philodoxia*), rivalry (*philoneikia*), and malice (*baskania*)" (1:26). He lists these vices also in 2:15, adding arrogance (*megalauchia*). Because the author's focus lies elsewhere, he does not speak of these vices in great detail. Anticipating the later argument, he even claims that reason controls the emotions of affection for parents, love for one's wife, love for children, and the relationship of friends (2:11–13; cf. 13:19–14:1).

Maintaining a dialogue with both his ancestral religion and the Hellenistic environment, the author appeals to the Torah as the source of the lists of vices and virtues. In his condemnation of gluttony, he appeals to the prohibition of unclean foods, but he adds other food-related vices not derived from the Torah but belonging to paraenetic traditions in Hellenistic Judaism. Gluttony (*gastrimargia, gastrimargos*, 1:3; 2:7) appears nowhere else in the Septuagint, but appears fifteen times in Philo. Solitary eating (*monophagia*, 1:27; 2:7) appears also in the *Testament of Issachar* 7:5. The inclusion of drunkenness belongs to the Wisdom literature and to Jewish paraenesis.

The praise of Joseph for sexual self-control both reflects the Torah's condemnation of adultery and appeals to the tenth commandment, which the author quotes ("you shall not covet your neighbor's wife") but then abbreviates by omitting the direct object, making it a prohibition of all desire (*epithymia*, 2:6). Here he undoubtedly equates coveting with the general concept of *epithymia*. This extended meaning of the tenth commandment of the Decalogue is also attested in Philo (*Decalogue* 142, 150, 173). According to the *Apocalypse of Abraham* 24:8, coveting/*epithymia* is the head of all lawlessness.[12]

Love of money (*philargyria*) appears in the Septuagint (hereafter LXX) only in 2 and 4 Maccabees (cf. 2 Macc. 10:20; 4 Macc. 1:26; 2:8), but appears

---

12. Niebuhr, *Gesetz und Paränese*, 219.

frequently in Philo's vice lists.[13] Love of glory (*philodoxia*) appears only in 4 Maccabees and Esther (4:17d LXX), but appears in Philo.[14] *Philoneikia* (rivalry) appears only in Ezekiel (3:7, "hard forehead" NRSV), Proverbs (10:12), and 2 and 4 Maccabees (4 Macc. 1:26; 8:26; cf. 2 Macc. 4:4). *Baskan-* (malice) appears only in 4 Maccabees and the Wisdom literature (Wis. 4:12, "fascination of wickedness" NRSV; Prov. 8:22, "a miserly man"; Prov. 28:22; Sir. 18:18, "grudging given" NRSV; 37:11 "miser"). "Vainglory" (*kenodoxia*) appears only in Wisdom (14:14) and 4 Maccabees (2:15; 8:19; 14:14). The other vices play little role in the Old Testament. Boastfulness (1:26; 2:15; 8:19) is a major theme only in the Wisdom literature (Prov. 25:6; Wis. 5:8; 17:7). Anger and strife are also major themes in the Wisdom literature (Prov. 27:4; Wis. 19:1; Sir. 25:15; 28:8–10; 40:4–5), but not elsewhere in the LXX. Thus the vice lists indicate the significance of the Wisdom literature for the paraenesis within Hellenistic Judaism.

According to the theoretical analysis in chapters 1–3, the God who planted the passions in the body and the soul also provided the power to place them under control, as the thesis statement (1:1) and the consistent refrain of the book indicate. Reason (*logismos*) is the sovereign (*autokratōr*, 1:7, 13, 30; 16:1; *autodespotēs*, 1:1; 13:1) and master (*despotēs*, 2:24; *kyrios*, 2:7) of the emotions. Reason does not destroy the emotions, but provides the means so that no one will give way to them (1:7). It is like a gardener "who does not uproot the emotions but is their antagonist" (3:5 NRSV), who "tames the jungle of habits and emotions" (1:29 NRSV). It bridles the impulses (1:29), and it rules (*kratei*, 2:6, 15, 20; *epikratei*, 3:1) and controls (*epikratei*, 1:33–35) the emotions.

This knowledge comes from the "education in the law" (1:17 NRSV). Those who are faithful to the law exhibit the cardinal virtues (1:18). Joseph, for example, was the "temperate (*sōphrōn*) Joseph," as he lived in accordance with the tenth commandment (2:2 NRSV). One who is educated in the law overcomes the negative emotion of love of money (2:8–9) and displays justice (2:6) by canceling debts in the seventh year and not gleaning the harvest or eating the last grapes. The "one who lives subject to this will rule a kingdom that is temperate, just, good, and courageous" (2:23 NRSV). Thus the Torah plays a decisive role in the acquisition of the cardinal virtues and constraint of passion, for it is the source of knowledge (*epistēmē*, 1:2; 5:35), which trains the person in virtue.

Closely related to the Torah are the concepts of religion (*eusebeia*) and virtue (*aretē*). The word group *euseb-* appears 64 times in 4 Maccabees (the noun 47 times, the adjective *eusebēs* 11 times, the verb *eusebein* 5 times), while it appears only 40 times in the remainder of the Septuagint.[15] In 4 Maccabees

---

13. *Giants* 37.5; *Posterity* 116.6; *Good Person* 21.4; *Spec. Laws* 1.281; 2.78; *Joseph* 218.3; *Names* 226; *Flaccus* 60; *Providence* 2; *QG* 4.33.

14. *Abraham* 24, 104; 221; *Giants* 37; *Posterity* 116; *Good Person* 21; *Spec. Laws* 1.281; *QG* 4.33.

15. Weber, *Gesetz im hellenistischen Judentum*, 226.

it can be associated with philosophy (1:1; 7:21–23), reason (e.g., 5:31), and law (*nomos*, 5:18, 31; 6:21–22; 7:15–18; 9:4, 6–7, 23–24, 29–30; 11:20; 12:11; 14:6; 15:1–5, 12, 14; 16:13–17; 17:7). Its association with reason is evident in the claim that one overcomes the emotions not only through reason, but also through *eusebeia* (7:22).

Of the 33 occurrences of virtue (*aretē*) in the LXX, 17 are in 4 Maccabees. Just as the Greek ideal assumed that virtue could be taught, 4 Maccabees associates Torah with education (*paideia*).[16] To learn the law (1:17) is to learn virtue. Corresponding to Plato's claim that virtuous behavior results from *paideia*, the author of 4 Maccabees maintains that *paideia* in the law is the source of virtue (cf. 13:22). Those who suffer for the law also suffer for the sake of virtue (7:22; 9:18; 11:2) and religion (*eusebeia*, 13:27).

This theoretical foundation lays the basis for the narrative of the martyrs, who demonstrate the cardinal virtues and a willingness to suffer and die for the law and for virtue. The heroes have been educated in the law (5:21–25; 13:22), and thus they will not transgress it (5:16–34) by eating forbidden foods (5:25), but will keep (9:2, 5; 11:5) and protect it (9:15). They fight for the ancestral law (6:21, 30; 9:15; 11:27; 13:13; 15:29, 32; 16:16) and die for it (6:27, 30; 13:9, 13; 15:10). They suffer (10:10) and are tortured for the sake of *aretē* (11:2) and die for piety (*eusebeia*, 7:16; 9:16–24, 29–30; 11:20; 13:12; 14:3; 15:3, 14, 32; 16:13–14, 23; 18:3). They fulfilled their *eusebeia* to God as contestants for virtue (*aretē*).

The narrative indicates how reason controls the passions. Eleazar maintains his reason in the context of torture (5:31; 6:7), dies nobly because of reason (6:31–7:1, 4, 14, 16–17), and is followed in this by the sons (9:14–16; 15:1) and their mother (15:11, 23), all of whom exhibit the cardinal virtues. The narrator concludes that the martyrs were "righteous and self-controlled and brave and magnanimous" (15:10 NRSV). In response to the tyrant, Eleazar declares that the practice of the law teaches self-control, courage, justice, and piety (5:23–24). In observing the law, the martyrs become the exemplars of courage (*andreia*) and self-control (*sōphrosynē*). The author says that "the wise and courageous are the masters of their emotions" (7:23 NRSV). The mother was "more courageous than the males" (15:30), and the tyrant saw the courage of their virtue. Seeing this courage and also their endurance under the tortures, he made them an example for his own soldiers to follow (17:23).

The martyrs exemplify other virtues as well as the cardinal ones. According to 15:10, they were magnanimous (listed with three other virtues). They are exemplars of the Hellenistic virtue of goodness (*kalokagathia*), the "epitome of Greek anthropology and ethics."[17] The word appears six times in the LXX, all in 4 Maccabees. Just as the martyrs died for the law, they

16. Ibid., 228.
17. Ibid., 230.

died for the sake of goodness (1:10). According to 3:18 reason (*logismos*) is determined by *kalokagathia*. It is characteristic of the martyr's death (5:31; 6:7; 7:4, 12; 9:17; 11:27). It comes as a result of training in the law (13:24). Indeed, zeal for *kalokagathia* and *aretē* are parallel to zeal for the law/religion (1:8, 10; 6:21, 22, 27, 30; 7:16, 22; 9:6–7, 18, 23, 29–30; 12:14–15; 14:6, 8; 15:10, 12; 18:3), inasmuch as the law is virtuous.[18] Thus, according to Weber, "4 Maccabees restricted and isolated the concept of *kalokagathia*, giving it a special content that is Jewish as he associates *kalokagathia* and *nomos* in the face of martyrdom."[19]

In 13:25, goodness (*kalokagathia*) stands in association with brotherly love (*philadelphia*), which the martyrs also exemplify. Of the six instances of forms of *philadelphia* in the LXX, five are in 4 Maccabees (13:21, 23, 26; 14:1; 15:10). The author has employed a common topos of Hellenistic ethics to support his view that training in the law results in the acquisition of the Greek virtues.[20] The oldest of the brothers challenges his brothers not to "renounce [their] courageous family ties" (*tēn tēs eupsychias adelphotēta*). Then the author offers physiological data corresponding to ancient knowledge of nature to describe the origins of *philadelphia*: conception, growth in the mother's womb, birth, breast-feeding. The brothers were shaped in this way. God's providence implanted in them "the affection of family ties" (13:19 NRSV), implanting them in their mother's womb (13:19), where they were formed by the same blood and they spent the same length of time. When they were born, "they drank milk from the same fountains" (13:21 NRSV). *Philadelphia* originated from this common nurture and companionship, and then it grew as the brothers were educated in the same law (13:22–23). As a result, the brothers "were the more sympathetic to one another" (13:23 NRSV), loving each other "all the more" (13:24 NRSV), as religion strengthened their brotherly love. Their nobility of character (*kalokagathia*) strengthened their good will (*eunoia*) and concord (*homonoia*). They could make their brotherly love more fervent because of their religion (13:26). Thus the brothers are models of the Greek virtue of brotherly love.

Although the author employs the common Greek topos of *philadelphia* to describe the brothers' conformity to the Greek ideal (13:19–26), his primary concern is to show that the brothers surpassed the Greek ideal and proved his thesis (1:1). Brotherly love is an emotion implanted by nature (*physis*) and augmented by companionship (*synētheia*) and habit (*ethos*); it is nevertheless a human emotion to be controlled by reason. Therefore, *philadelphia* was not strong enough to defeat their fidelity to the law.[21] *Philadelphia* is one of the emotions that reason controls. Because the brothers mastered the emotions

18. Ibid., 231.
19. Ibid.
20. Klauck, "Bruderliebe," 94.
21. Ibid., 96.

of brotherly love, they were able to encourage one another to face tortures (13:27–14:1).

### Nature, Family, and the Ethical Life

The ideal of family life in accordance with Torah is stated in the testimony of the mother of the seven brothers, who recalls her own fidelity to the ancestral ways:

> I was a pure virgin and did not go outside my father's house; but I guarded the rib from which woman was made. No seducer corrupted me on a desert plain, nor did the destroyer, the deceitful serpent, defile the purity of my virginity. In the time of my maturity I remained with my husband, and when these sons had grown up their father died. A happy man was he, who lived out his life with good children, and did not have the grief of bereavement. (4 Macc. 18:6–9 NRSV)

This life conformed to the law. To live according to the ethical ideal of the law and the cardinal virtues is to live according to nature. *Physis* is mentioned eight times in 4 Maccabees. According to 1:20, nature gave emotions of body and soul. Nature provided family affection (13:27; 15:13, 25; 16:3). The author indicates the connection between the natural order and the law in the theoretical section in 2:21–23, when the author recalls the creation story. "When God fashioned human beings, he planted in them emotions and inclinations, but at the same time he enthroned the mind among the senses as a sacred governor over them all. To the mind he gave the law; and one who lives subject to this will rule a kingdom that is temperate, just, good, and courageous."

The encounter between Antiochus and Eleazar suggests the author's understanding of the rationality of the law and its association with nature (5:5–38). Antiochus claims rationality for his own case in demanding that Eleazar eat forbidden food, describing the food as "what nature has granted us" (5:8–9). It would be irrational (*anoētos*) to "spurn the gifts of nature" (5:9–10 NRSV). He describes the Jewish food laws as the result of "futile reasonings" (5:11 NRSV). Eleazar responds, arguing that the law is not irrational, but that it teaches self-control, courage, and justice. He adds, "In the nature of things the Creator of the world in giving us the law has shown sympathy toward us" (5:25 NRSV), for he has permitted the foods that were most appropriate and forbidden foods that were contrary to nature (5:26). Thus the author brings together the Jewish doctrine of creation, which determines the nature of things, with the demands of Torah.

### Conclusion: Ethics of 4 Maccabees

The author has offered a distinct ethical vision that brings together the Torah and the ideals of Greek ethics. Those who observe the law conform to the ideals of Greek ethics and to nature. The author recognizes the human capacity to be enslaved to the passions, and his vice lists illustrate the enslavement. In keeping with the issues involved in 4 Maccabees, the author focuses on the passion for forbidden foods, but also emphasizes the need for controlling the passion for sex. While recommending brotherly love among other values, the author asserts that even this is a passion to be controlled by reason.

## Ethics of the Wisdom of Solomon

Although the Wisdom of Solomon contains the elements of both an encomium and a protreptic speech,[22] this work by an unknown author who speaks in Solomon's name has a thorough ethical dimension, as the three imperatives introducing the book indicate. "Solomon" calls on those who judge the earth to love righteousness, "think of the Lord in goodness and seek him" (1:1 NRSV). The parallelism of the three imperatives indicates the close connection between one's relationship to God and ethical behavior. "Goodness" (agathotēs) is a divine quality (7:26; 12:22) that is associated with God's forbearance and mercy. "Singleness of heart" recalls David's claim in his prayer to God (1 Chron. 29:17) and indicates the significance of the integrity of the righteous person.[23] "Righteousness" (dikaiosynē; elsewhere translated "justice") is defined by the book in ethical terms.

After these imperatives and the rest of the extended introduction (1:1–15), the body of the book is divided into three major parts (1:16–6:11; 6:12–9:18; chs. 10–19). The appearance of dikaiosynē in 1:1, 15 forms an inclusio, framing the opening and introducing the major topic of the book (cf. 5:6, 18; 8:7; 9:3; 12:16; 14:7; 15:3). Thus three major themes will dominate the book. First, the author distinguishes between righteousness (dikaiosynē) and unrighteousness (adikia). In the challenge to the rulers of the earth to choose righteousness, the author has placed before them two radically opposite alternatives with no ground between righteousness (dikaiosynē) and ungodliness (asebeia; cf. adikia, 1:5; 10:3). Thus humanity is divided into two categories: the righteous (2:10, 12, 16, 18; 3:1, 10; 4:7, 16; 5:1, 15; 10:4–6, 10, 13, 20; 11:14; 12:9, 15, 19; 16:17, 23; 18:7, 20; 19:16–17) and the ungodly (asebeis, 1:9, 16; 4:3, 16; 5:14; 10:6, 20; 11:9; 12:9; 14:16, 30; 16:16, 18; 19:1).

A second theme introduced in 1:1–15 is the contrast between wisdom and folly, which is a corollary to the distinction between righteousness and unrighteousness. Wisdom comes only to the righteous and avoids the unrighteous (1:4). It will not enter into a treacherous soul or "dwell in a body enslaved to sin" (1:4 NRSV). Thus wisdom is a gift of God that enables the person to

---

22. The encomium is a speech of praise that can be directed to the deity, human beings, or topics worthy of praise. A protreptic speech is intended to win converts to a way of life.

23. Blischke, Die Begründung und die Durchsetzung, 392.

do righteous acts. The indicative of wisdom accompanies the demand to be righteous. This entry (*eiseleusetai*) and dwelling (*katoikēsei*) of wisdom can be compared to the coming of the "holy spirit of instruction" (1:5), which also flees from deceit (*dolon*) and perverted thoughts, just as wisdom flees from guile and sin. Wisdom and the holy spirit of wisdom converge in the rejection and uncovering of unrighteousness.[24] The spirit of the Lord that fills the world and "holds all things together" (1:7 NRSV) is thus the source of righteousness.[25]

In contrast to wisdom are perverse thoughts (*skolioi logismoi*, 1:3), which separate one from God, and foolish thoughts (*logismoi asynetoi*), which will be punished. The book consistently emphasizes that unrighteous behavior originates in human reasonings (*logismoi*) apart from wisdom (cf. *logizomai*, 2:1, 16, 21; 3:2, 10, 17; 5:4; 7:9; 8:17; 9:6; 14:20; 15:2, 12, 15; 17:13; *logismos*, 9:4; 11:15; 12:10; 17:12; 19:3). According to 1:1–15, this contrast is the basis for the author's ethical reflection. Wisdom is kind (*philanthrōpos*, 1:6) and will punish the blasphemer (1:6). Foolish thoughts are the origin of unrighteous speech (1:8), jealous ears (1:10), grumbling (1:10), and slander and lying (1:11). Thus the ethical dimension of righteousness consists of the contrast between philanthropic and anticommunal behavior, which are determined by the presence or absence of reason.

A third theme introduced in 1:1–15 is the contrast between the immortality of righteousness (1:15) and the mortality of unrighteousness. The unrighteous words will come to the Lord (1:9), and justice will punish those who are guilty (1:8). Those who are guilty of unrighteousness invite death (1:12–13). The author develops these themes in the first section, 1:16–6:11, giving a more detailed description of the ethical dimension of righteousness and unrighteousness. The imperative of 6:11, calling on the rulers of the earth to listen to the words of the fictive Solomon, forms an inclusio with the opening challenge to the rulers in 1:1. This imperative is the frame for the argument delineating the basis for this challenge as the author demonstrates the immortality of the righteous and the mortality of the unrighteous. The immortality of the righteous is evident in the words of the unrighteous in chapter 1. The ethical failures of the latter are rooted in their unsound reasoning (2:1), according to which they have made a covenant with death (1:16) and deny any hope for the future (2:1–5). Their perverse reasoning is a theme throughout this first section (cf. 2:21; 3:10; 4:12).

The author offers concrete examples of the results of their covenant with death and perverse reasoning in this section, contrasting the ethical values of the righteous and the unrighteous. In 2:6–20 the unrighteous speak for themselves, indicating that, because death is the inevitable end, they will spend their time in luxury, the pursuit of pleasure, and the satisfaction of the self. They

24. Weber, *Gesetz im hellenistischen Judentum*, 185.
25. Hübner, "Zur Ethik der Sapientia Salomonis," 169.

will take their fill of costly wine and perfumes (2:7) and of revelry (2:9). They will oppress the poor, the widow, and the aged (2:10). The sexual sins of the unrighteous receive special attention. The author contrasts foolish wives who have rejected wisdom with both the righteous woman and the barren woman (3:13). The children of the former are accursed, while the latter is blessed because she has not entered into a sinful union. Children of adulterers will not come to maturity, and the offspring of an unlawful union will perish (3:16) and be "witnesses of evil against their parents" (4:6 NRSV).

The righteous people are those Jews who are blameless (*amōmos*) in keeping the law (2:22). They are distinguished by their gentleness (*epieikeia*, 2:19) and forbearance (*anexikakia*), while the unrighteous are guilty of sins against the law (*hamartēmata nomou*) and instruction (*paideias*). The kings have not kept the law (6:4), which contains the purpose of God. Their might is their law (*nomos*). Thus the law defines the nature of righteousness.

Although the author indicates that the law is the norm for measuring righteousness, the virtues and vices are not entirely derived from the Torah. Neither the expensive wines (2:7) nor the revelry (2:9) are the concerns of the Torah. Oppression of the poor is a major concern of the legal tradition (cf. Deut. 15:1–11; 24:10–20). The author has adapted the sexual vices from the Torah, giving his primary concern to the sinful unions. The kindness and the forbearance of the righteous are also not derived from the Torah. Gentleness (*epieikeia*) is not mentioned in the legal tradition, but is a characteristic of God in Wisdom (12:18).

In 3:1–5:23 the author compares the eternal fate of the righteous and the unrighteous. Although the righteous are oppressed by the unrighteous in this life, they will ultimately prevail. Unlike the unrighteous, who have no hope (cf. *elpis, elpizō* in 2:22; 3:18), the righteous will receive a reward, for justice ensures their ultimate reward just as it ensures punishment for the unrighteous. The righteous are now being tested (3:5–6), but ultimately "they will rule nations" (3:8). Chapters 4 and 5 demonstrate that the "righteous will live forever" (cf. 5:15), while the unrighteous will perish.

In the second major division (6:12–9:18), "Solomon" commends wisdom to the rulers of the earth, indicating that the "love of her is the keeping of her laws" (6:18 NRSV). The persona of Solomon offers an idea of the author's anthropology and ethics. "Solomon" indicates his mortality, calling himself mortal (*thnētos*, 7:1), formed as flesh in his mother's womb, born of "the seed of a man and the pleasure of marriage" (7:1–6 NRSV). He prayed to the Lord, who gave *phronēsis* and a spirit of wisdom (7:7), which comes from God (7:25). This *phronēsis* is the basis for "Solomon's" ethical life. Chapter 9 records Solomon's prayer to the one who "[rules] the world in holiness and righteousness" (9:3 NRSV), the world in which Solomon confesses his weakness: "For I am your servant the son of a serving girl, a weak man and short lived, and who is ignorant of the judgments and laws" (9:5). Thus without the gift of wisdom Solomon is only a mortal and will fail as king. Without wisdom he is incapable of doing righteousness. With the gift he can know what is pleasing to God (*euareston*) and his commands. Thus with wisdom he can both know and do God's commands (cf. 4:10). God can love only the one in whom wisdom dwells. The result of righteousness is the acquisition of the virtues (8:7). The author has mentioned *phronēsis* already, but now lists the four cardinal virtues, which he does not develop elsewhere. He advocates through "the combination of Jewish wisdom tradition and Greek virtues a life of righteousness determined by wisdom."[26]

In the third section, chapters 10–19, the author places the contrast between righteousness and ungodliness within the context of Israel's history, with special emphasis on the exodus. According to chapter 10, wisdom has protected Israel by protecting the righteous—Noah, Abraham, Lot, and Jacob—from enemies throughout the biblical narrative. Throughout this section, Israel has continued to exist by God's righteous judgment. In 12:15, the only passage in Wisdom to describe God as righteous, the author shows that God rules the world with righteousness, condemning only those who are unrighteous. The judicial metaphor indicates that God judges all humankind. The unrighteous are punished through their own abominations (11:16; 12:23) and pursued by justice (*dikē*, 11:20), for they deserve the judgment of God (12:26). While God's righteousness means punishment for the ungodly, it means mercy for Israel. For the righteous, God loves "all things that exist" (11:24 NRSV) and "is merciful in all things" (11:23), overlooking their sins. God chastens the enemies, but judges Israel with gentleness and forbearance (12:18, *epieikeia kai pheidos*). "When we are judged, we may expect mercy" (12:22 NRSV).

The author does not describe the virtuous life of the righteous in detail, but the vices of the unrighteous he does. The righteous person, he says, like wisdom itself (7:23; cf. 1:6), is kind (*philanthrōpos*), having learned kindness from God's own kindness. To know God "is complete righteousness" (15:3 NRSV). The unrighteous, on the other hand, by their futile reasoning, are the source of all evil. Through their inability to reason, they did not know God (13:1; 14:22), but turned to idolatry, although the beauty of nature was sufficient to give them a knowledge of God (13:3–9). Thus the author locates the origin of unrighteousness in idolatry (cf. 13:1–14:31). The abominations of the unrighteous included sorcery and unholy rites, the slaughter of children, the "sacrificial feasting on human flesh and blood" (12:4–5 NRSV), and "frenzied revels with strange customs" (14:23 NRSV). Here one sees the progression from not knowing God to idolatry to moral breakdown. Idolatry is "the beginning of fornication" (14:12 NRSV) and the source of all of the evils.

The most detailed description of unrighteous acts appears in 14:22–27, a vice list framed by references to idolatry. This arrangement suggests that

---

26. Blischke, *Die Begründung und die Durchsetzung*, 398.

offenses against the first tablet result in the offenses against the second tablet of the Ten Commandments.[27] Having described sexual offenses earlier (3:13–16; 4:1–6), the author expands on this theme in 14:24–26, developing the earlier comment from 14:12. Sexual sins include the failure to keep marriages pure (14:24), adultery (14:24, 26), debauchery (*aselgeia*, 14:26), perverting of nature (*geneseōs enallagē*, 14:26), and disorder in marriage. In addition to the sexual vices, the author mentions vices that disrupt community life, including murder, theft, deceit, faithlessness, tumult, and perjury.

Consistent with the author's earlier argument that wisdom leads one to keep the commandments, the vices are based on the Torah and the Jewish interpretive tradition. The condemnation of adultery and homosexuality is based on the seventh commandment and the Torah's prohibition of homosexual acts. Debauchery (*aselgeia*) is commonly denounced in Jewish ethical instruction. The condemnation of unlawful unions may be indebted to Leviticus 18.[28] The antisocial vices are also indebted to the Torah and Jewish paraenetic tradition. References to theft and murder obviously appeal to the Decalogue. Deceit (*dolos*, cf. 1:5; 4:11) is mentioned in the Torah (Gen. 27:35; 34:13; Exod. 21:14; Lev. 19:15; Deut. 27:24) and Jewish tradition (*Ps.-Phoc.* 43; Josephus, *Ag. Ap.* 2.200, 216; *Pss. Sol.* 4:3, 23; 12:1; Tob. 14:9 LXX [‌א]).[29] Tumult (*tarachos*) belongs to the Wisdom literature (Sir. 40:5; Prov. 6:14; 26:21).[30] Perjury (*epiorkos*), the reference to which may reflect the author's interpretation of the command against false witness, is also common in Jewish literature (*Ps.-Phoc.* 16–17; *T. Ash.* 2.6; *Pss. Sol.* 8:10). Thus the offenses of the unrighteous are rooted in the Torah and Jewish paraenesis.

The list is indebted to the Septuagint. One observes a series of motifs that derive from a nonbiblical, Cynic-Stoic sphere. However, most of the offenses also parallel parts of the catechesis of Judaism that were based on the Torah. The Decalogue was one source of the paraenesis, but without reference to the cultic requirements of the Torah. Thus biblical content is poured into Hellenistic forms.[31]

## Ethics of the *Testaments of the Twelve Patriarchs*

Because the *Testaments of the Twelve Patriarchs* belong to the familiar genre of the last will and testament and look toward the last days,[32] scholarly

27. Hübner, "Zur Ethik der Sapientia Salomonis," 179.
28. A puzzling feature is the reference to the barren woman in 4:1–6.
29. Niebuhr, *Gesetz und Paränese*, 174.
30. Ibid., 215.
31. Ibid.
32. Because of Christian elements in the *Testaments of the Twelve Patriarchs*, interpreters dispute the extent to which this document can be used as evidence of Jewish thought or ethics. Because Christians derived ethical instruction from the Jewish tradition, one cannot separate

interest has focused on the apocalyptic expectation of the community that produced this literature. The ethical dimension has received less attention, but is a focal point of all of the *Testaments*. In each *Testament* the dying patriarch, after confessing his sins, urges his listeners to be faithful to the law. Indeed, the exhortation to keep "the whole law" or "all of the commandments" pervades the *Testaments*,[33] although references to the ritual requirements are rare. The author focuses on two primary themes: sexual morality and brotherly love. The patriarch Joseph plays a major role in the *Testaments*, as the patriarchs recall their sins against him and describe him as the model of obedience to the law.

In his treatment of sexual morality, the author of the *Testaments* speaks often of sexual immorality (*porneia*). The dying Reuben first confesses his sin, recalling his *porneia* (1:6) when he took his father's concubine (cf. Gen. 35:22; 49:4). He analyzes the origins of this evil deed (*to ponēron*, 1:8) and sin (*hamartia*, 1:10) in *Testament of Reuben* 2:1–3:7 within the framework of the origin of all sin. He describes the seven spirits of deceit, which are arrayed against all humankind (cf. *T. Gad* 6:2). He describes seven other spirits given to humankind (2:3). Although he lists life, sight, hearing, smell, speech, and taste as among the other spirits by which all human deeds are done (2:2), the focus of the list is on the "spirit of procreation and intercourse . . . with which come sins through fondness for pleasure" (2:8). This spirit "leads the young person like a blind man into a ditch and like an animal over a cliff" (2:9).

Reuben indicates that the spirits of deceit are commingled with the seven other spirits. For example, *porneia* (3:2) resides in the senses. He adds the spirit of insatiability, strife, flattery and trickery, arrogance, lying, and injustice (3:1–8) among the spirits that belong to the senses. These darken the mind from the truth (3:8). Reuben's discussion of the origins of sin becomes the basis for his instruction to his listeners as he focuses on *porneia*. His description of this sin is based on his analysis of the psychology of 2:1–3:7.[34] He warns, "Do not devote your attention to a woman's looks, nor live with a woman who is already married, nor become involved in affairs with women" (3:10). He warns similarly against giving attention to women's matters (*praxeis*) in 4:1. He returns to the incident with Bilhah, his father's handmaiden. Here the spirit of sight captivated him. His senses were captivated by her nakedness. From that point on, Jacob never touched Bilhah (3:15).

---

the Jewish from the Christian ethical instructions. The *Testaments* are probably based on an earlier Jewish text. Parallels with other Jewish paraeneses suggest that the *Testaments* reflect the common ethic of the Diaspora. See Niebuhr, *Gesetz und Paränese*, 83; Collins, *Between Athens and Jerusalem*, 156.

33. Niebuhr, "Tora ohne Tempel," 439. Cf. also Niebuhr, *Gesetz und Paränese*, 164–65, for texts.

34. Loader, "Sexuality in *The Testaments of the Twelve Patriarchs* and the New Testament," 299–300.

The author further advises his listener on sexuality in *Testament of Reuben* 4:1, instructing him not to devote attention to the beauty of women "nor occupy [his] mind with their activities," but to live in integrity of the heart "until the Lord gives [him] the mate whom he wills." He adds, "Do not sin, for the sin of *porneia* is the pitfall of life, separating man from God and leading on toward idolatry, because it is the deceiver of the mind and the perceptions, and leads youths down to hell before their time." Joseph is the model of one who purified his mind from all promiscuity. Despite the wiles of the Egyptian woman, Joseph remained pure (4:9–10).

In 5:1 the author shifts from a description of *porneia* to a warning against women: "Women are evil." He proceeds with a description of the evils of women, who employ stratagems and deal treacherously to entice young men (5:1–6). By decking themselves out, they hope to lead men astray (5:3). Thus he concludes, "Flee *porneia*. Order your wives and your daughters not to adorn their heads and their appearances so as to deceive men's sound minds" (5:5). He ends with the counsel, "So guard yourself against *porneia*" (6:1). Men are to avoid chance meetings with women "because in sexual promiscuity there is a place for neither understanding nor piety, and every passion dwells in its desire" (6:4).

The *Testament of Reuben* introduces consistent themes in inculcating a sexual ethic. First, the speaker emphasizes the battle with reason. Second, he emphasizes that women are dangerous, as they employ enchantments and stratagems to entice young men. Third, he emphasizes that young men are especially vulnerable. Fourth, he instructs against being captivated by the beauty of women. Finally, he indicates the appropriateness of sex within marriage.

The *Testament of Judah*, like the *Testament of Reuben*, recalls Judah's sexual offense in Genesis. Youthful impulses and strong drink first blinded Judah's reason (11:1), leading him to have intercourse with the woman from the evil Canaanites. Judah then recalls his encounter with Tamar, his daughter-in-law (cf. Gen. 38). Once more, Judah was drunk with wine and enticed by one who decked herself in bridal array (12:2). He was enticed by the beauty of the woman (12:3). A major theme is that wine led to Judah's sin (cf. ch. 16). This is the background for Judah's instruction to guard against promiscuity and lustful looks (chs. 17–18).

The same themes appear in the other *Testaments*. The dying Issachar says that he is one hundred years old. He looks back over his life and says, "I have not had intercourse with anyone but my wife, nor was I promiscuous with a lustful look" (7:2). He connects his chastity with his abstention from wine (7:3). The *Testament of Naphtali* speaks of those gentiles who have "changed the order" (3:3) and "departed from the order of nature" (3:5), an apparent reference to homosexuality. The patriarch concludes, "There is a time for intercourse with one's wife and a time for prayers" (8:8).

Other *Testaments* focus on the vices that undermine brotherly love and present Joseph as the virtuous one who acts in accordance with brotherly love. The *Testament of Simeon* follows the same structure as the *Testament of Reuben*, but the focus shifts from *porneia* to jealousy. The prince of error "blinded my mind so that I did not consider him as a brother" (2:7). Upon this remorse Simeon bases his counsel, "Beware of the spirit of deceit and envy" (3:1). "Envy dominates the whole of man's mind and does not permit him to eat or drink or to do anything good. Rather it keeps prodding him to destroy the one whom he envies" (3:3). That attitude makes the soul savage and corrupts the body. Just as Joseph is the model of chastity (*T. Reub.* 4:8–9), he is also the model of brotherly love: "He loved us as his own life; he extolled us more than he did his own sons, and he showered us with wealth, flocks, and produce" (4:6). Thus the author instructs, "And you, my children, each of you love his brothers with a good heart, and the spirit of envy will depart from you" (4:7). "If you divest yourselves of envy and every hardness of heart, my bones will flourish as a rose in Israel" (6:1).

Other testaments develop these themes. The *Testament of Levi* also mentions the sexual and social sins together, saying,

> You plunder the Lord's offerings; from his share you steal choice parts, contemptuously eating them with whores. You teach the Lord's commands out of greed for gain; married women you profane; you have intercourse with whores and adulteresses. You take gentile women for your wives and your sexual relations will become like Sodom and Gomorrah. (*T. Levi* 14:5–6)

The *Testament of Issachar*, which follows a similar format with autobiographical reflections from the patriarch, gives ethical instruction to his listeners. Issachar recalls the circumstances of his birth (chs. 1–2) and describes his own life in "rectitude of heart" (*euthytēti kardias*, 3:1) and integrity (*haplotēs*, 3:2, 6). Until he was married at the age of thirty-five, he had not experienced the "pleasure of a woman" (3:5). On the basis of his own example of integrity he instructs others to live in integrity of heart (*en haplotēti kardias*, 4:1). He describes the good person as one who does not desire gold, defraud his neighbor, or long for fancy foods or fine clothes (4:2). Nor will he look on feminine beauty (4:4). The good persons will have neither envy (*zēlos*) nor malice (*baskania*), but will live in integrity (*haplotēs*, 5:1). The good person will love the Lord and the neighbor and be compassionate toward poverty and sickness (5:2). In 7:1–7 Issachar recalls his own life, indicating that he has slept with no one but his wife and was never promiscuous. He neither drank wine nor was guilty of deceit (*dolos*) or lies. He lamented every oppressed human being and loved the Lord and every human being (7:6).

Unlike the others, Zebulun offers no confession, claiming that he did not share in the price for Joseph (3:1). In chapter 5, he summarizes the demands of the law, telling his listeners to do mercy (*eleos*), having compassion not only on human beings, but also on animals. He instructs listeners to have mercy (*eleos*) in their inner being (*splanchnoi*, 5:3). Zebulun reports on his own compassion in chapter 7, then instructs his listeners, "Without discrimination be compassionate and merciful to all" (*adiakritōs pantas splanchnizomenos eleate*, 7:2). After commanding his listeners to have compassion, he indicates that Joseph is the example of compassion. Then he concludes, "Love one another" (*agapate allēlous*, 8:5), and, "Do not reckon evil to the brother (*mē logizesthe hekastos kakian pros ton adelphon autou*)."

The *Testament of Dan* focuses on the dangers of jealousy (*zēlos*) and pretentiousness (*alazoneia*) in 1:8. He instructs his listeners to guard themselves from the spirit of falsehood and anger (*thymos*) and to love truth and patience (*agapēsēte alētheian kai makrothymian*). All of chapters 2 and 3 are about anger (*thymos*). The good person avoids anger, but speaks truth with the neighbor (5:2), lives at peace (5:3), and loves the Lord and the neighbor (5:3).

The *Testament of Gad* takes up similar themes, focusing on hatred. Gad confesses his own hatred for Joseph (2:1) and then instructs, "Do not be led away by hatred" (3:1). In chapters 4–5 he indicates the outcome of this vice. In contrast, he instructs, "Let each one love his neighbor," and, "love one another" (*agapate hekastos ton plēsion autou . . . agapēsate allēlous*, 6:2). In 6:3, he adds, "Love one another from the heart" (*agapēsate allēlous apo kardias*). It is the alternative to jealousy (7:3).

In the *Testament of Joseph* the two major concerns of the *Testaments* come together in the portrayal of Joseph, the one who struggled through a period of testing brought about by the hatred of his brothers (1:4) and the wiles of the evil woman. Chapters 3–9 describe her many stratagems, continuing the themes from the *Testament of Reuben* and *Testament of Judah*. After recalling his story, Joseph gives wise counsel in chapter 17. As the model of endurance, he instructs his descendants, "Love one another" (*agapate allēlous*) in patient endurance, to conceal one another's shortcomings (17:2), knowing that God is delighted by harmony among brothers and the intention of a kind heart that takes pleasure in goodness. He recalls his own love for his brothers, claiming, "Their pain was my pain," and, "every ailment was my sickness."

The *Testament of Benjamin* is an appropriate conclusion to the *Testaments of the Twelve Patriarchs*, for Benjamin brings the ethical concerns of the larger work together in his challenge to imitate Joseph, who embodies all of the virtues and none of the vices described by the other patriarchs. Benjamin describes Joseph throughout the work as a "good and pious man" (3:1), recalling, like the other patriarchs, Joseph's chastity, and that Joseph neither delighted in pleasures nor was led astray by visual excitement (6:3). That the patriarch is referring to sexual temptation is evident in the parallel in Issachar's claim, "I never committed fornication by the uplifting of my eyes" (*T. Iss.* 7:2; cf. Sir. 23:4). This portrayal of Joseph becomes the basis for the statement,

"He who has a pure mind in love does not look after a woman with a view to fornication" (*T. Benj.* 8:2).

The primary focus of the *Testament of Benjamin* is not on sexuality, but on brotherly love as the characteristic of the "good man." In 3:3 Benjamin exhorts his sons to fear God and love their neighbor. He continues, "And even though the spirits of Beliar ask for you to be delivered up to every evil of tribulation, yet shall no evil have dominion over you, even as it had no dominion over Joseph my brother." He says that humankind finds support by the love that he has for his neighbor. He adds that Joseph urged their father to pray for the brothers, that the Lord not hold them accountable for their sins. This becomes the basis for the challenge to follow "the good man" in chapter 4. Although Benjamin does not mention Joseph by name, he associates the virtues with Joseph. The "good man" is compassionate toward all (4:2). He responds to those who plot against him by doing good. He loves those who wrong him as his own life (4:3). He holds no envy or jealousy (4:4). He shows mercy to the impoverished and compassion to the ill (4:4). He loves the person with a good spirit as he loves his life (4:3). Such goodness causes evil men to repent and give to the oppressed the things that they covetously hold (5:1). In contrast, Cain is the exemplar of hatred of one's brother (7:5). Hence the patriarch encourages his sons to run from evil, corruption, and hatred of brothers (8:1).

### Conclusion: The Major Ethical Themes in Hellenistic Judaism

A common identity and ethos emerged among the Jews of the Diaspora that was essential for the continuing viability of these communities.[35] The writers urge their readers to appropriate the identity of ancient Israel as the people set apart from their contemporaries and called to demonstrate their election by a shared standard of conduct. The diverse witnesses agree that the law is the basis for the identity and ethos of the Jews, who live as minorities in the midst of an often-hostile culture. Rather than build an extensive case law, the writers summarized the law in order to meet the needs of the communities, often without explicit citations. The summaries include little of the ritual commandments of the Torah that served as boundary markers from others; only the Maccabean literature focuses on circumcision and food laws. The summaries frequently concentrate on love as the essence of the law.[36] Philo speaks of two main principles of the law: duty toward God in the form of piety (*eusebeia*) and holiness (*hosiotēs*), and duty toward humankind expressed in love for humankind (*philanthrōpia*) and justice (*dikaiosynē*).[37] The writers focus on issues of care for the poor, especially for members of these minority

---

35. Collins, *Between Athens and Jerusalem*, 137–67.
36. Schnelle, "Das Liebesgebot im Neuen Testament," 21.
37. *Spec. Laws* 2.63.

communities. While some writers advocate love for humanity (*philanthrōpia*),[38] Hellenistic Judaism was primarily concerned with love for others within the circle of the community and the avoidance of fraternal strife.

Summaries of the law also focus on sexual laws, consistently prohibiting sexual immorality (*porneia*) and homosexual practices, both of which characterize their neighbors in the view of the authors. Jewish heroes exemplify the capacity to control sexual passions. Paraeneses consistently warn against sexual vices.

Although the command to love the neighbor (Lev. 19:18) does not appear explicitly in the summaries of the law prior to Paul,[39] as part of the Holiness Code, Leviticus 19 plays an important role in the ethical thought of Hellenistic Judaism. Moreover, Leviticus 19:18 echoes frequently in this writing. In some instances the "neighbor" of Leviticus 19:18 is understood in a universalistic sense (cf. Sir. 13:15; *T. Iss.* 5:2; 7:6; *T. Zeb.* 5:1);[40] in most instances the neighbor is the fellow member of the covenant community (Tob. 4:13; *T. Reub.* 6:9; *T. Gad* 4:2; *T. Iss.* 5:2; 7:6; *T. Benj.* 3:3, 4).

The emphasis on sexual vices and care for the poor and disadvantaged is based primarily on a "canon-within-the canon" from the Pentateuch. Of special importance is the Holiness Code (Lev. 17–26), especially Leviticus 18–20, which contains both the sexual laws and the regulations for the care of disadvantaged people within the community. This list of laws repeats and elaborates on the rules of the Decalogue. Because the Holiness Code covered the spheres of family life, work, and relationships with others, it was useful for catechetical instruction in a variety of contexts.[41]

Although the writers agree that the law is the source of the ethical life, some are more open than others to the ethics of the philosophical tradition. Philo, 4 Maccabees, and the Wisdom of Solomon equate the four cardinal virtues with obedience to the law. Terms from Hellenistic ethics, including piety (*eusebeia*), goodness (*kalokagathia*), and love for humanity (*philanthrōpia*), appear in the ethical writings of Hellenistic Judaism. Philo, the Wisdom of Solomon, *Sentences of Pseudo-Phocylides*, and the *Testaments of the Twelve Patriarchs* associate the commands of the Torah with the Stoic concept of natural law. The Greek discussion of mastery over the passions is the topic of 4 Maccabees, which argues that the law is the means for attaining self-mastery.

---

38. In the New Testament *philanthrōpia* is used rarely: of God's "kindness" in the epiphany in the Christ event (Titus 3:4) and the barbarians who showed "kindness" to Paul (Acts 28:2). The adverb is used only in Acts 27:3 ("Julius treated Paul kindly" [NRSV]). *Philanthrōpia* was commonly used for sovereigns who showered their kindness to all humanity. Philo uses the word for God, who loves all humanity (*Virtues* 77, 188; *Abraham* 79, 137, 203). See Spicq, "Philanthrōpia," *TLNT* 3:442.

39. Wischmeyer, "Das Gebot der Nächstenliebe bei Paulus," 164.

40. Ibid., 162.

41. See Niebuhr, *Gesetz und Paränese*, 235–36.

Hellenistic Jewish writers rarely cite the Torah in giving moral instructions, but assume that all of the commands are derived from the Torah. While the ethical instructions of Hellenistic Judaism frequently intersect with the Greek ethical tradition, Jewish writers insist that the commandments derive from the will of God. Obedience to the commandments expresses their fundamental Jewish identity.

# 2

# Shaping an Identity

## *Moral Instruction and Community Formation*

Paul's preaching resulted in the formation of communities that transcended the traditional barriers between ancient peoples. While Paul acknowledges the division of humankind into such categories as "Greek and barbarian" (Rom. 1:14) and "Jew and Greek" (Rom. 1:16), he envisions communities in which those boundaries are removed. As his letters indicate, to survive, such an inclusive community must work hard at community formation, inculcating a common identity and moral norms. Converts came from diverse cultures, each with its own community ethos, and only through such a process, producing both identity and norms, would they survive as a community. Paul indicates that, while his communities are remarkably inclusive, their shared moral norms will separate them from their own past and from the world around them. Although the actual uniqueness of Paul's moral instruction is debatable, it is clear that he envisions communities that live "worthily of the gospel" (Phil. 1:27). To live "worthily" of God's call is to be "not conformed to this age" (Rom. 12:2).

Community formation involves more than shared moral norms, as the shape of Paul's letters indicates, for in them theological reflection commonly provides the foundation for the moral instruction. Paul's "ought" is thus based on the "is" of theological reflection. In the classic essay "The Problem of Ethics in

Paul,"[1] Rudolf Bultmann described the relationship between the "is" and the "ought" in terms of the indicative and the imperative, introducing the categories that have dominated the scholarship on Pauline ethics since Bultmann's time. For Bultmann, the indicative was God's redeeming act of justification in the Christ event, while the imperative, as the mode of existence of the justified, is both gift and the obedience of the recipient of God's gift.[2] While Bultmann correctly notes the intrinsic relationship between "is" and "ought" in Paul, he does not adequately indicate that Paul is establishing a group ethos for his communities, a collective identity as the basis for the "ought." Paul's indicative is not only God's act of justifying the individual, but also the foundation of the new group consciousness from which the "ought" emerges.

An alternative to the categories of indicative and imperative in conceptualizing the relationship between the "is" and the "ought," as the recent literature indicates, is the distinction between identity and ethos, which anthropologists have applied to many cultures. Our sense of "who we are"—our identity—is rooted in "the way things are."[3] According to Peter Berger and Thomas Luckmann, "Identity is ultimately legitimated by placing it within the context of a symbolic universe."[4] By constructing a "symbolic universe," communities are able to cohere and distinguish themselves from those who hold to alternative worldviews.[5] The symbolic universe includes the community's understanding of reality and is expressed in the myths and rituals that maintain this symbolic world. The community's behavior expresses its identity within the symbolic universe. Clifford Geertz surveys various religious cultures (Christian and non-Christian), distinguishing between worldview ("the assumed structure of reality") and ethos ("the approved style of life"). He concludes that the two are closely related: "The powerfully coercive 'ought' is felt to grow out of a comprehensive factual 'is.'"[6]

As Paul creates a community from diverse backgrounds, his task of establishing a common ethos begins with instilling a common identity for his readers within a new symbolic universe. Inasmuch as a shared narrative is central to a community's identity,[7] Paul consistently reminds people of the founding narrative that brought it together. At the center of this narrative is the Christ event—the descent, death, and resurrection of Christ (cf. 1 Cor. 15:1–4; 2 Cor. 5:14–15; Phil. 2:6–11), which determines the "new creation" in the epistemology of his readers (2 Cor. 5:17). This event is, however, the turning point in the larger narrative of Israel's story, which begins with Adam, the founder

1. Bultmann, "The Problem of Ethics in Paul" ("Das Problem der Ethik bei Paulus").
2. Ibid., 216.
3. See Horrell, "Particular Identity and Common Ethics," 199.
4. Berger and Luckmann, *The Social Construction of Reality*, 100.
5. Ibid., 107.
6. Geertz, *Interpretation of Cultures*, 126.
7. Horrell, *Solidarity and Difference*, 83–87.

of the old humanity, through whom sin entered the world (Rom. 5:12–21). The story continues in Abraham, through whom God promised to bless all nations (Gen. 12:1–3), including Paul's gentile recipients (Rom. 4:1–25; Gal. 3:6–29; 4:21–31). Paul's description of the Israelites as "our fathers" (1 Cor. 10:1) indicates that the gentiles' story, too, includes Moses's leadership of Israel from the giving of the tablets of stone (cf. 2 Cor. 3:1–6) to the wilderness wanderings (1 Cor. 10:1–13). Living at the turn of the ages, Paul is the minister of the new covenant (2 Cor. 3:6) promised by Jeremiah (31:31–34), the minister who announces good news to Israel (Isa. 52:7) and brings "light to the nations" (Isa. 49:6), bringing his gentile converts within Israel's story. While the same story is read in the synagogue, Paul's interpretation focuses on a particular thread: the universal significance of the story. In his interpretation, the promise to Abraham of a blessing for "all of the families of the earth" (Gen. 12:3) anticipates the inclusion of the gentiles (cf. Gal. 3:8), and the promise of "light to the nations" (Isa. 49:6) points to his ministry. Thus, to those who have "turned away from idols" and the accompanying symbolic world Paul offers an alternative symbolic world to establish their identity. They are converts to an Israel reconfigured around Christ.[8]

As gentile converts, they are not simply absorbed into Israel like the proselytes who entered Israel as converts and observed all of the commandments, including circumcision, the Sabbath, and food laws. Instead, they enter an Israel whose story has been redefined by the Christ event. They come into a community that erases the boundaries between Jew and Greek as both are "summoned by the gospel story to a sweeping reevaluation of their identities."[9]

Although Paul's letters consist of responses to concrete situations, they consistently presuppose an unfinished narrative of which the readers are a part. God has begun a good work. They live between the occasion when God began a good work at their conversion (Phil. 1:6) and the day of Christ (1 Cor. 1:8; 3:13; 5:5; 2 Cor. 1:14; Phil. 1:6, 10; 2:16; 1 Thess. 5:2, 4; cf. Rom. 2:5, 16; 13:12), when they will be ultimately transformed to the image of the Son (Rom. 8:23, 29; Phil. 3:20–21). In the meantime, the community waits for redemption. The time between the coming of Christ and the final day is the occasion for moral transformation.

The corporate narrative creates a collective memory, an essential aspect of a community's identity. The repetition of the community's story solidifies its common identity.[10] Rituals play a role in sustaining this narrative. In baptism and the Lord's Supper, Paul's communities reenact aspects of the founding narrative and reinforce the memory that shapes their place in the world and their identity.

8. Donaldson, *Paul and the Gentiles*, 236.
9. Hays, *Conversion of the Imagination*, 5.
10. Blischke, *Die Begründung und die Durchsetzung*, 17–18.

The corporate identity and ethos of the group requires its demarcation from other groups. This clear separation is especially important for those who live as a distinct minority within the larger society.[11] Paul demarcates these communities sharply from other communities that have alternative narratives. They are the insiders in contrast to "those outside" (*hoi exō*, 1 Cor. 5:12–13; 1 Thess. 4:12) or to "the rest" (*hoi loipoi*, 1 Thess. 4:13; 5:6). As the "children of light in the midst of a crooked and perverse generation" (Phil. 2:15; cf. 1 Thess. 5:5–8), they have their citizenship (*politeuma*) in heaven (Phil. 3:20). They are being saved (*sōzomenoi*, 1 Cor. 1:18; 2 Cor. 2:15) in contrast to those who are perishing (*apollymenoi*, 1 Cor. 1:18; 2 Cor. 2:15). They are "the believers" (1 Cor. 14:22; 1 Thess. 1:7; 2:10) in contrast to the "unbelievers" (1 Cor. 7:12; 10:27; 14:22–23). Like Diaspora Jews who live as minority communities with a sharply defined identity separating them from their environment, Paul's communities learn to think of themselves in terms of the group identity that separates them from others. Although scholars point out that their morality has points in common with the world around them, they present themselves as living differently from the "crooked and perverse generation" (Phil. 2:15 NRSV).

Paul reminds his communities in two ways of the radical separation that characterizes the community. First, he describes the radical separation of their present existence from their former identity. When they were "washed," "justified," and "sanctified" (1 Cor. 6:11), they "died to sin" (Rom. 6:2). Having been enslaved to entities that were not gods, they have turned to freedom in Christ (cf. Gal. 4:8–9).

Second, he recalls this separation from the surrounding communities and requires the strict maintenance of boundaries. While Paul acknowledges that his congregations will live among the unbelievers (1 Cor. 5:10; 10:27) and even be involved in mixed marriages (1 Cor. 7:12–16), he demands strict boundaries separating the believers from the unbelievers, assuming a clear distinction in the moral practices of each.

### Collective Identity and Separation in the Corinthian Correspondence

The challenge of maintaining collective identity, boundaries, and moral requirements of the community appears in the Corinthian correspondence, which indicates in great detail the problems of resocializing new converts into a new symbolic world. The major challenge in 1 Corinthians 5:1–11:1 is to maintain the boundaries between insiders and outsiders.[12] Paul addresses the

---

11. See Wolter, "Ethische Identität," 79–80.

12. Mitchell, *Paul and the Rhetoric of Reconciliation*, 225–26. This section treats sexual immorality (*porneia*) and idolatry, two topics frequently discussed among Jewish writers in their attempts to demarcate insiders (Jews) from outsiders (gentiles).

complicating factors in maintaining a distinctive identity and moral practice in the urban setting of Corinth. He has already catechized his new converts on the new moral practices regarding sexuality (cf. 1 Thess. 4:3–8) and reinforced this catechesis with a letter prior to 1 Corinthians (cf. 1 Cor. 5:9) encouraging converts not to associate with those who are sexually immoral (*pornoi*), in order to maintain strict boundaries. He responds to an apparent crisis involving sexuality and idolatry, two of the major themes of Jewish paraenesis. After offering a theological justification for the maintenance of boundaries, Paul says, "Flee fornication" (6:18), and, "flee idolatry" (10:14). Bruce Winter may be correct in suggesting that the congregation faced the dilemma in which the banquets attended by the men also included sexual promiscuity.[13] While Paul assumes considerable interaction between the church and the world, including invitations to banquets (10:27) and mixed marriages (7:12–16), he appeals to the new identity of his converts as the basis for his exhortations.

Paul first responds to a clear violation of his original catechetical instruction in 5:1–13 in the case of the man who is living with his father's wife. Having instructed the Corinthians in an earlier letter (1 Cor. 5:9) "not to mix with sexually immoral persons (*pornoi*)," he now writes with dismay that sexual immorality (*porneia*) exists in the church. Interpreters have noted that Paul directs his outrage at the community rather than the individuals involved (5:2, 6). The description of the man living with his father's wife and the recommendation of punishment for the man imply that the stepmother does not belong to the community, and their admitting her into their midst has violated Paul's previous instructions. Thus Paul objects both to the *porneia* within the community and to their failure to maintain boundaries.

Paul frames the issue in such a way that the identity of the community is the basis for its moral behavior. The sharp distinction between the collective "you" and the gentiles indicates the boundaries that Paul assumes. The plural "among you" (*en hymin*, 5:1) reflects the collective identity, indicating that the world is divided between the plural "you" and the gentiles. As in other contexts (cf. 1 Thess. 4:5), Paul speaks of gentiles as the "other" from whom the readers are separated. Although this community is predominantly composed of gentiles, the gentile has now become the "other" (cf. 12:2; 1 Thess. 4:5). Paul obviously envisions the community as Israel. As in Israel's experience, the sin of the individual pollutes the entire community.[14]

The community's identity as Israel becomes more evident in Paul's terminology. The offense is *porneia*, a word that was used primarily by Greek-speaking Jews to describe the offenses of the gentiles. Furthermore, Paul describes the offense in terms borrowed from Leviticus—"a man has his father's wife" (cf. Lev. 18:8; 20:11; Deut. 27:20)—rather than with the usual Greek term for

---

13. Winter, *After Paul Left Corinth*, 83–84.
14. Schrage, *Erste Brief an die Korinther*, 1:371.

stepmother (*mētryia*).[15] Thus Paul applies the terms of the Holiness Code to his community, identifying them with ancient Israel. Jewish literature recalled with horror the story of Reuben's liaison with his father's concubine (Gen. 35:22), indicating that this story was the reason for laws against a man lying with his father's wife (*Jub.* 33:1–17; cf. also *T. Reub.* 3:11–15).[16]

Paul indicates his community's identity also when he quotes the proverb "A little leaven leavens the whole lump" (5:6 ESV; cf. Gal. 5:9). In the two passages in which Paul cites the proverb, leaven is an image for impurity. One may recall also the references in the Synoptic Gospels to the "leaven" of the Pharisees and Sadducees (Matt. 16:6, 11–12) and of Herod (Mark 8:15). The leaven in both Galatians 5:6, 9 and Matthew 16:11–12 is the false teaching. The image recalls the place of leaven in the exodus, when the Israelites ate unleavened bread because of the haste with which they left Egypt (Exod. 12:15–20, 34, 39; 13:3–5), and in the annual feast of unleavened bread, when all leaven was purged from the house in order to make a fresh start. Because the old leaven was subject to impurity, it became a metaphor for an infection that could destroy the entire batch of bread. This metaphor is the background for Paul's description of the congregation as a "lump of dough" (*phyrama*) and as "unleavened" (*azymoi*) in 1 Corinthians 5:7. The identity of the community required that it throw out the old leaven in order to maintain its purity. In keeping with his previous letter (5:9), Paul insists that the community's moral conduct correspond to its identity. The final citation from Deuteronomy reflects this identity. In expelling the man, they conduct themselves according to their identity. They are not only the unleavened bread but also the people on the way in the wilderness who live according to their identity.[17] Paul concludes that the church should be a pure and holy community unmixed with the impurities of the world. The latter have no place among God's people.[18]

Interpreters have noted this issue as a case of Paul's agreement with popular morality, for he rightly indicates that gentile morality also prohibited this conduct.[19] However, Paul is not claiming agreement with gentile morality, but shaming the readers, indicating that their conduct has reached below the level of the gentiles. Paul does not want to compliment gentiles for the goodness of their morality, but to indicate the scandal of the community's behavior.[20]

---

15. LSJ 1131.

16. Horrell, "Particular Identity and Common Ethics," 206.

17. Hays, *Conversion of the Imagination*, 24.

18. Horrell, "Particular Identity and Common Ethics," 203.

19. Several texts from antiquity forbid marriage to a stepmother. Cicero indicates that the practice is rare—not unheard of, but not accepted: "Oh, to think of the woman's sin, unbelievable, unheard of in all experience save for this single instance" (Cicero, *Clu.* 5–6). Quoted in Horrell, "Particular Identity and Common Ethics," 205–6.

20. Schrage, *Erste Brief an die Korinther*, 1:370. Paschke ("Ambiguity in Paul's References to Greco-Roman Sexual Ethics") speaks incorrectly of the ambiguity of Paul's view of Greco-Roman ethics, contrasting 1 Cor. 5:1 with 1 Thess. 4:5. While he misses Paul's rhetorical point, he

Paul's threefold insistence that the community expel the man derives from Leviticus and Deuteronomy. While we may not be certain of the nature of the punishment in 1 Corinthians, we are certain of Paul's point. The holy community must maintain boundaries. It has assumed the identity of Israel in its separation from the nations; its identity determines its moral conduct. The emphasis on exclusion is indebted to the repeated insistence in Leviticus that no impurity will be tolerated among the holy people. The suggestion that they not behave like the gentiles is reminiscent of the command in Leviticus 18:3 introducing the sexual regulations: "You shall not do as they do in the land of Egypt . . . and you shall not do as they do in the land of Canaan" (NRSV). Paul's insistence on the purity of the entire community recalls the command, "None of you shall approach anyone near of kin to uncover nakedness" (Lev. 18:6 NRSV). His demand that the community expel the man resembles the repeated demands in Leviticus that the offenders be "cut off" from Israel (cf. Lev. 18:29; 19:8; 20:5). Consequently, Paul commands the Corinthians to "cleanse" the congregation from the impurity. The language of cleansing suggests his indebtedness to the purity and holiness traditions. Paul's command to cleanse the church from all evil corresponds to the command in Leviticus 18:29 to expel members of the community who commit the sexual offenses listed. Indeed, Qumran and other Jewish communities commonly expelled offenders to maintain the purity of the community.[21] Others were put to death.

Paul continues the appeal to the identity of the readers as the basis for morality in 6:1–11, where issues of lawsuits before pagan courts evoke further reflection. His language abounds in the binary view of the world. On one side, the community is composed of the saints (6:1–2), the *ekklēsia* (6:4), and the siblings (6:5–6, 8). The world is the unrighteous (6:1), those despised by the church (6:4), the unbelievers (6:6). This sharp distinction leads Paul to elaborate on the future status of the unrighteous (6:9), who will not inherit the kingdom of God. Under the heading of the unrighteous are the offenders mentioned in 6:9–10. David Horrell comments that Paul uses words for individuals rather than abstract types of sins (e.g., idolatry).[22] The community has left the world of the unrighteous. Washed, sanctified, and justified (6:11), they have a new identity that precludes the presence of these offenders.

### 1 Corinthians 6:12–8:11

Whereas in 1 Cor. 5:1–13 Paul expresses outrage over an actual situation of a community member's sexual immorality (*porneia*) with his stepmother,

---

provides numerous examples in ancient literature of both the existence of incestuous marriages among Greco-Roman elites and the abhorrence of the practice by others.

21. On traditions for expulsion at Qumran, see Hägerland, "Rituals of (Ex-)Communication and Identity," 43–60.

22. Horrell, "Particular Identity and Common Ethics," 203.

in 6:12–20 he confronts sexual immorality with a prostitute (*pornē*). In each instance the issue is both sexual immorality and the violation of boundaries. This latter passage may not reflect an actual situation, but may only be a potential concern. Since the prohibition of *porneia* was new to a wide segment of society, Paul now elaborates on potential issues or objections to his catechesis. "All things are lawful" (6:12; cf. 10:23) is probably the slogan of those who challenge Paul's original teaching. Similarly, "Food is for the stomach and stomach is for food" (6:13) is apparently a Corinthian slogan, which Paul corrects. The two slogans would offer justification for individual freedom and for equating the appetites for food and sex. Paul's response suggests that some Corinthians used the slogans to equate the stomach with the body. Those who employed these slogans would maintain that neither sex nor food involves the whole person and that both are private matters of no concern to others. The Corinthian slogans also reflected the individualism of Greek ethics.

Paul responds to both slogans. His response to the first claim, "But not all things are beneficial (*sympheron*)," gives a new meaning to the common argument from appropriateness.[23] As the subsequent argument indicates, "beneficial" has a corporate meaning; it is the equivalent to those things that "build up" the community (10:23; 12:7).[24] Sexual practices of individuals are not a private matter, but involve the life of the community of believers. He responds to the second claim by denying that the stomach is the equivalent to the body (6:13), for the latter involves the whole person and will ultimately be raised (6:14). Thus one cannot distinguish the person from the body.

Paul appeals to the collective identity of the members to demonstrate that sexual immorality is not a private matter, redefining the Corinthians' understanding of the body. In 6:15 he indicates the relationship between individual bodies (*sōmata*) and the body of Christ. Their bodies are "members" (*melē*). The reference to the "members" anticipates the extended description of the body of Christ with its "members" (12:14–26). Thus "member" does not have the modern English connotation of "card-carrier," but suggests that individuals find their identity only through their connection to the larger community, a connection which is as close as that of a limb to its body. As a result, the collective identity creates boundaries that Paul describes in 6:16–17 with echoes from Genesis. Being "joined" (6:16) with the prostitute is not an indifferent matter for the man, like consumption of food; it involves becoming "one body" with her in the relationship that Genesis describes as the union of the man and woman in "one flesh" (Gen. 2:24). Being a "member of Christ" in "one spirit" precludes being "one flesh" with the prostitute. The two are

---

23. *Sympheron* ("beneficial," "useful," "advantageous" [BDAG 960]) is a significant term in both Cynic-Stoic popular philosophy and ancient rhetoric. See Dio Chrysostom, *Or.* 14.16; 32.51; Epictetus, *Diatr.* 1.22.14; 1.28.5).

24. Schrage, *Erste Brief an die Korinther*, 2:19.

incompatible bodily relationships.[25] The alternative between being joined to Christ and to a harlot (6:16) continues the sharp distinction between insiders and outsiders. *Porneia* involves not only a sexual offense; it also presupposes a relationship between insiders and outsiders, violating the boundaries that Paul has established.

Paul concludes the argument with the final appeal to the communal identity by affirming, "Your body is a temple of the Holy Spirit" (6:19 NRSV), reiterating the earlier description of the church as God's temple (*naos*) and the dwelling place of the Holy Spirit (1 Cor. 3:16). In using the singular "body" in 6:19 rather than the plural "bodies" (cf. 6:15), Paul has brought together the collective and individual understandings of the body, indicating that they are not separable categories.[26] The concluding exhortation, "Glorify God in your body" (6:20), once again using the singular, reinforces the claim that the individual body is a part of Christ's body.

Paul's argument probably raised the questions that he answers in chapter 7. The Corinthians may have asked whether the logic of his argument implied a prohibition of all sexual activity. Paul answers that married couples ought to engage in regular sexual intercourse, assuming that both husband and wife are within the boundaries of the community (1 Cor. 7:2–6). The church may also have asked Paul about mixed marriages, in which the boundaries have been removed from the beginning (7:10–16). Paul does not follow the logic of his argument for separation from outsiders, but advises members not to separate from unbelieving spouses. Indeed, his assurance that the children of mixed marriages are holy (1 Cor. 7:14) assumes that the community is holy. Just as the unholiness of immoral people can infect the church (5:1–13), the holiness of the community can sanctify the children of mixed marriages. His permission to widows to remarry, but only "in the Lord" (7:39), indicates the importance of boundaries.

The issue of food offered to idols (8:1–11:1) is reminiscent of the numerous situations faced by Jewish communities of the Diaspora as they tried to determine how to maintain boundaries separating them from idolatry. The absence of an absolute prohibition of food offered to idols separates Paul from Jewish predecessors and other Christian traditions (cf. Acts 15:20; Rev. 2:14). Nevertheless, Paul concludes the argument with reasons for abstaining from all forms of idolatry (1 Cor. 10:14–11:1). Once more he appeals to the community's corporate identity, maintaining that believers face the alternative between *koinōnia* with the Lord and *koinōnia* with demons (10:16–21). As in the earlier case of sexual immorality, participation in the body of Christ creates a boundary that precludes participation with pagan deities. *Koinōnia* in the body and blood of Christ precludes *koinōnia* in pagan meals.

---

25. Horrell, *Solidarity and Difference*, 145.
26. Ibid. See the discussion in Nijay Gupta, "Which 'Body' Is a Temple," 518–36.

As the commands "Flee sexual immorality " (6:18) and "flee idolatry" (10:14) indicate, the community's identity is the basis for its behavior. The imperative is based on the community's shared symbolic world as the continuation of Israel and on its identity as a holy people. Paul challenges his readers to live in accordance with their collective identity.

By identifying the community as the temple, Paul establishes a separate identity, and he draws the sacrificial imagery associated with the ethical life from Israel's experience. The presence of the divine within the sanctuary required that the temple be kept pure. Only Jews could enter its inner portals, and only priests, in a state of purity, could minister in its precincts.[27] In 2 Corinthians 6:14–7:1 Paul elaborates the community's identity as the temple of God and challenges it to live out the implications of that identity. Although many interpreters have questioned the place of this passage at its current position, its basic outlook epitomizes Paul's understanding of the church. Here he establishes the identity of the people as the basis for his imperative.

### 2 Corinthians 6:14–7:1

On the basis of the purity of the temple, Paul issues another challenge to the community in 2 Corinthians 6:14–7:1. Although we need not concur with those interpreters who doubt that Paul wrote this unit, suggesting that it reflects more the theology of Qumran than of Paul, his demand for the expulsion of the offender in 1 Corinthians 5:1–13 does indicate that Paul shares with Qumran the concern for the purity of the community and the insistence on expelling those who undermine its solidarity as a holy community. In 2 Corinthians 6:14–7:1, he provides the theological foundation of his call for separation. His command "Do not be unequally yoked with unbelievers" (6:14) employs a metaphor from the legal tradition (Deut. 22:10) to indicate the radical separation between the holy community and the world. This demand is consistent with the community's identity as God's temple (6:16; cf. 1 Cor. 3:16; 6:19), the place of God's presence. Because the temple—more specifically, the sanctuary within the temple—was the place of God's dwelling, God's presence required keeping the sanctuary and its precincts pure.[28] Thus the temple was separated from impurity.

Paul develops the theme of holiness in the imperatives that follow his indication of their identity as the temple, connecting the divine promise of God's presence (6:16) to the imperative with *dio* in 6:17, indicating that the community must respond in accordance with this identity. The imperatives "Come out from among them and be separate, says the Lord" and "Do not touch anything unclean," drawn from the exilic prophets (Isa. 52:11; Ezek. 20:34, 41), are fundamental to Israel's identity as the elect and holy people.

27. Newton, *Concept of Purity at Qumran and in the Letters of Paul*, 79.
28. Ibid.

Paul cites passages once spoken to Israelites in exile, identifying the church's experience with that of ancient Israel. His final challenge in this section, "Let us cleanse ourselves from every impurity of the flesh and of the Spirit, completing holiness in the Lord" (7:1), indicates the expectation that, although God has called the people to holiness, they must implement this call in their own lives.

## The Identity of Israel and the Church

Paul shares with Aristotle and the Stoics a concern for behavior, but he speaks with a totally different vocabulary, which is nowhere more evident than in the terms with which he establishes the identity of his readers. Unlike ancient moralists, Paul is concerned not with the virtue or happiness of the individual,[29] but with the corporate identity of his communities as the basis for moral formation. Indeed, one may note the primary images that shape this moral identity.

Israel's narrative provided the means for Paul to establish the countercultural identity that enabled the community to cohere and differentiated its members from the world around them. Recalling Israel's identity as the *ekklēsia* of God, Paul regularly addresses them as the *ekklēsia* at a particular place,[30] connecting them with Israel's identity. In other instances he uses the singular *ekklēsia* to refer to the collective identity of all of the congregations (1 Cor. 15:9; Gal. 1:13). Paul inherited the term from the earliest Christ-believers. In the Septuagint it is a common rendering of the Hebrew *qāhāl*, the assembly of God's people. Early Christian usage also reflects the apocalyptic understanding of the eschatological people of God.[31]

### Election and Holiness

Paul's congregations found their identity in a complex of related terms drawn from Israel's self-understanding. Like the ancient Israelites, these communities are elect and holy. He consistently addresses the people as God's elect and called. He, like the ancient prophets, has been "called" (Rom. 1:1), and he consistently addresses his readers as "called" (Rom. 1:6–7; 8:28; 1 Thess. 2:12; 5:24). They were called to freedom (Gal. 5:13). He also mentions their "calling" (*klēsis*, Rom. 11:29; 1 Cor. 1:26; 7:20). Just as God called Isaac and Jacob (Rom. 9:7, 11–13), God has called those who were once "no people"— the gentiles—into Israel (9:25). This calling is indistinguishable from God's election of the people (cf. 9:11). Consequently, Paul speaks of the conversion

29. Judge, "St. Paul as a Radical Critic of Society," 103.
30. Paul speaks of the *ekklēsia* of God (1 Cor. 1:2; 11:16, 22; 2 Cor. 1:1) and the *ekklēsia* in God (1 Thess. 1:1). In most instances he employs the plural to describe congregations at specific places (1 Cor. 4:17; Gal. 1:2, 22; 1 Thess. 2:14). Occasionally *ekklēsia* refers to the assembly (1 Cor. 11:18; 14:4, 19, 23, 34).
31. The LXX also rendered *qāhāl* with *synagōgē*. See Roloff, "*Ekklēsia*."

of gentile communities as their election (1 Cor. 1:26–27; 1 Thess. 1:4–5), the occasion when God called them into the fellowship of the son (1 Cor. 1:9; 1 Thess. 2:12). God's election expresses his love for the people (Rom. 1:7; 11:28; 1 Thess. 1:4).

The terminology of God's calling, election, and love is rooted in Israel's identity. According to the classic election text, God chose Israel from all nations as an expression of divine love (Deut. 7:7–8; 14:2). Thus election and holiness are closely related. God called Israel to be a "holy nation" (Exod. 19:6) and chose Israel to be "a people holy to the Lord" (Deut. 7:6; 14:2). Israel shares in God's holiness (Lev. 19:2), and demonstrates holiness by keeping the commandments and walking in God's ways (Deut. 28:9). According to the Holiness Code (Lev. 17–26), the holy people keep God's commands.[32] This topic becomes a major theme in Hosea and 2 Isaiah. Hosea expresses the link between God's love and call, as indicated in the divine words, "When Israel was a child, I loved him, and out of Egypt I called my son" (11:1 NRSV). The exilic prophet anticipates a reaffirmation of God's election in the return from exile (Isa. 42:1; 43:10, 20–21; 45:4; 49:2–3; 54:9–10).

Election and holiness are inseparable in Paul's address to his readers. He addresses a largely gentile audience in Romans as "beloved of God, called to be holy ones" (1:7), using language borrowed from Israel's identity. He regularly addresses his letters to the "holy ones" (1 Cor. 1:2; 2 Cor. 1:1; Phil. 1:1; cf. Eph. 1:1; Col. 1:2). In other contexts, it is a favorite word for the community of believers (cf. Rom. 15:25–26; 16:2, 15; 2 Cor. 8:4; 9:1, 12; 13:12; Phil. 4:22).

Paul's use of verbal forms of *hag-* indicates the close connection between identity and ethics in the concept of holiness. Having addressed the Corinthians as "saints" (*hagioi*), he appeals to them to maintain a holy community by recalling their identity as people who have been "washed," "justified," and "sanctified" (1 Cor. 6:11). Sanctification is both a present reality that began in the past, as the perfect and aorist tenses indicate,[33] and a continuing reality among believers as it is expressed in the moral life (Rom. 6:19; 1 Thess. 4:3–4, 7). This fact determines Paul's perspective on the moral issues faced in 1 Corinthians 5–7, for he divides the world into the categories of the "holy ones" (6:1) and the "unrighteous" (*adikoi*, 6:1). Holy people, as in Leviticus, reject the practices of the nations. Indeed, the prayer that God "sanctify wholly" the community that Paul founded (1 Thess. 5:23; cf. 1 Thess. 3:13) suggests that holiness involves a process that extends from conversion until the end.

32. See Schrage, "Heiligung als Prozess bei Paulus," 206. Schrage notes correctly that Paul does not distinguish between the ritual and moral law. The Holiness Code includes regulations for the cult and festivals as well as laws for the treatment of others.

33. *Hēgiasmenois*, the perfect tense, appears in 1 Cor. 1:2, while the aorist (*hēgiasthēte*) is used in 1 Cor. 6:11.

Paul never uses the word to refer to an individual, but always uses it in a communal context.[34] As W. Schrage indicates, "The way of holiness is a common way in community with the saints."[35] As in Israel, the term suggests the corporate identity of the people of God, distinguishing it from the others who are neither holy nor elect.

The terminology of holiness, like the terms *ekklēsia* and *election*, identifies Paul's communities with ancient Israel. This focus extends to his description of the church as God's temple (1 Cor. 3:16; 6:19). As the place of God's presence,[36] the temple epitomized Israel's understanding of holiness, for the appropriate dwelling place for the holy God was a place removed from the unholiness of the world. The structure of the temple was arranged in such a way that the furniture, rituals, and attendants existed in a continuum from the profane areas outside the temple, to the sacred precinct, and finally to the inner sanctum, where God dwelt.[37]

Paul describes the church as the *naos* (1 Cor. 3:16; 2 Cor. 6:16) rather than with the more common word for temple, *hieron*. In the LXX, *naos* renders the words for the most sacred parts of the temple: the holy place (1 Kings 6:17; 2 Chron. 4:22; Ezek. 8:16; 41:1) and the porch, or vestibule (1 Chron. 28:11; 2 Chron. 8:12; 15:8; 29:7, 11). In Psalm 28:2 it refers to the holy of holies. Thus Paul chooses a name for the church that identifies it with the most sacred part of the temple. As the temple of the Spirit, the church assumes the role of the holy of holies, the dwelling place of God.[38] The pervasiveness of this terminology in all of Paul's letters suggests that the apostle shaped his communities with this group consciousness from the beginning. All of these terms establish the group consciousness of the people. To live "worthily of the gospel" is to place this identity into practice.

With this language Paul brings his gentile churches into Israel's story, establishing the identity that is the basis for moral conduct.[39] He undoubtedly recalls God's word to Israel in Deuteronomy (7:6; 14:2), "You are a people holy to the Lord. I have chosen you from all of the peoples of the earth." Paul knows the tradition, "You shall be a kingdom of priests and a holy people" (Exod. 19:6). Holiness was not an individual virtue, but the common identity of the people.[40]

Holiness was the foundation for Israel's moral conduct, for it was self-evident that Israel must demonstrate God's holiness in daily life. According

34. Schrage, "Heiligung als Prozess bei Paulus," 207.

35. Ibid.

36. Wolter, "Ethos und Identität in paulinischen Gemeinden," 434.

37. Meyers, "Temple," 6:360.

38. Newton, *Concept of Purity at Qumran and in the Letters of Paul*, 54.

39. Blischke, *Die Begründung und die Durchsetzung*, 388: "The ethic in Deuteronomy stands in a narrow connection with the self understanding of being alone God's elected covenant people, the first factor in establishing identity."

40. Schrage, "Heiligung als Prozess bei Paulus," 207–8.

to Deuteronomy 28:9, "The Lord lets you stand as the holy people if you keep the commandments." The command "You shall be holy as I am holy" (Lev. 19:2) introduces the requirements for life in the community, including the love command (Lev. 19:18) and the other commands on the daily life. The practice of holiness set Israel apart from non-Israelites, its way of life apart from theirs. Similarly, by designating his communities as saints (cf. 1 Cor. 6:1), Paul distinguishes them from the surrounding society.

One may observe Paul's appropriation of the language of purity in his numerous references to the "blameless" conduct that he desires from the people. When Paul prays that the Thessalonians will ultimately be blameless and encourages the Philippians to be blameless, he employs a term (*amemptos*) that is used in the LXX for Abraham (Gen. 17:1; Wis. 10:5), Moses (Wis. 18:21), and the holy people (Wis. 10:15). The term *amōmos* is linked with cultic practices. It appears extensively in Exodus, Leviticus, Numbers, and Ezekiel as a translation of the Hebrew *tam* and is applied to animals "without blemish" that are offered for sacrifice. It is used of David (Ps. 18:23–24; 2 Sam. 22:24–25): "I was blameless before God." Cf. Psalm 15:1–2: Who can ascend? He who walks blamelessly.[41] It is used in cultic context in Psalm 101:6.

### The New Family

Unlike the Jewish communities of the Diaspora, the churches established by Paul do not constitute an *ethnos*, a nation in the conventional sense, for they now live in communities that have transcended a primary source of identity in antiquity with the claim that there is no longer "Jew or Greek" (cf. Gal. 3:28). He identifies himself as a father (1 Cor. 4:14–21; 1 Thess. 2:11–12), mother (Gal. 4:19), and father of the bride (2 Cor. 11:1–4). He views the Christian fellowship as a group of siblings (*adelphoi*, literally "brothers").[42] *Adelph-* is used metaphorically 120 times in the seven undisputed letters; it appears no less than 5 times in Philemon.[43] Paul addresses the communities 64 times as *adelphoi*.[44] The frequency of this metaphor in Paul's letters is remarkable in comparison with its frequency in Greco-Roman literature and the Old Testament.[45] Paul employs the image to establish family solidarity among diverse people who have no natural solidarity and whose relationships with their natural families are strained or broken.

The imagery of the family established both a sense of belonging among those who had formerly been strangers and a sharp distinction between

41. Newton, *Concept of Purity at Qumran and in the Letters of Paul*, 84.
42. Aasgaard, "'Role Ethics' in Paul," 517.
43. Ibid., 516.
44. Ibid.
45. Ibid.

insiders and outsiders.[46] Like the terminology of election and holiness, the sibling image distinguishes members of the family from those who are "outside" (1 Thess. 4:9–12). Moreover, this metaphor has a central place in Paul's ecclesiology and his perception of Christian identity and ethics.[47] "What they are (i.e., siblings) has consequences for how they are (their ethical praxis)."[48] Thus Paul says little about issues of public life, but offers instructions for life within the family. Many of his prohibitions assume the familial context. A brother should not take a brother to court (1 Cor. 6:1–9), defraud him (1 Thess. 4:6), or cause him to stumble (Rom. 14:13; 1 Cor. 8:13). Siblings should not be guilty of strife, jealousy, envy, or quarreling (cf. Gal. 5:20).[49]

Paul's frequent appeals for love within the family also reflect an ideal of family life (see chapter 7). He appeals to the sibling relationship to resolve the dispute between Philemon and Onesimus (Philem. 16). Familial love demands that members take responsibility for the weaker brother (1 Cor. 8:11). Siblings must maintain the family honor, "walking appropriately among the outsiders" (1 Thess. 4:12). Paul's instructions are largely about the treatment of siblings, the avoidance of familiar sibling quarrels, and the appropriation of family responsibilities. Indeed, Paul's frequent use of "one another" reflects the family relationship and the solidarity of the community.[50] Paul encourages family members to

"love one another" (Rom. 13:8)

"be slaves to each other" (Gal. 5:13)

"be kind to one another in brotherly love" (Rom. 12:10)

"have high regard for one another" (Rom. 12:10)

"accept one another" (Rom. 15:7)

"pursue what serves for peace and reciprocal building up for one another" (Rom. 14:19)

"have the same mind for each other" (Rom. 15:5; cf. Phil. 2:2)

"comfort one another" (1 Thess. 4:18)

46. Aasgaard, 'My Beloved Brothers and Sisters!,' 307.
47. Schäfer, Gemeinde als "Bruderschaft," 25.
48. Ibid.
49. On these vices as common hindrances to family life, see Esler, "Family Imagery and Christian Identity in Gal 5:13 to 6:10," 134–38.
50. Schäfer, Gemeinde als "Bruderschaft," 25.

"encourage one another" (1 Thess. 5:11, *parakalein*; Rom. 15:14, *nouthetein*)

"care for one another" (1 Cor. 12:25)

"bear one another's burdens" (Gal. 6:2)

"eat with one another" (1 Cor. 11:33)

"greet one another with a holy kiss" (1 Cor. 16:20; 2 Cor. 13:12)

Paul also uses "one another" in negative formulations drawn from the sphere of family life

"do not judge one another" (Rom. 14:13)

"do not bite and devour one another" (Gal. 5:15)

"do not irritate one another" (Gal. 5:26)

"do not envy one another" (Gal. 5:26)

Reidar Aasgaard has demonstrated that Paul's instructions to Christian siblings have numerous parallels with the ancient understanding of the family. In providing a new identity and defining the responsibilities of members of the Christian household, Paul adapts understandings of the family from the surrounding culture. Most of the responsibilities listed above can be found in Plutarch's *On Brotherly Love* (*Frat. amor.*) and in other treatments of family life.[51] Paul also inherited a Jewish paraenetic tradition, which included major aspects of the identity and ethics of family life. Indeed, numerous parallels to the family ethic of Paul appear in the *Testaments of the Twelve Patriarchs*, as I have indicated in chapter 1. Here jealousy, strife, and anger undermine family life (cf. *T. Reub.* 3:3; *T. Dan* 5:2–3; *T. Gad* 2–4), as in Paul's instructions. The ideal for relationships is brotherly love (*philadelphia*) as exemplified by the seven brothers in 4 Maccabees (13:23–26). In the *Testaments of the Twelve Patriarchs*, Joseph is the model of love for his brothers (*T. Reub.* 4:8–9; *T. Benj.* 4:3–4). After looking back over a tale of brotherly strife, the patriarchs instruct their listeners, "Love one another" (*T. Zeb.* 8:5; *T. Gad* 6:2–3; *T. Jos.* 17:2). Thus Paul appropriated an ethic of the family that preceded him in Hellenistic Jewish writings.

The reciprocal pronoun "one another" (*allēlōn*) suggests two dimensions of communal identity that shape the moral conduct of the readers: readers are to respond to "one another" without a concern for differences in social

51. See Aasgaard, '*My Beloved Brothers and Sisters!*,' 93–106.

position, and they are to regard all fellow members as equal in status.[52] The term indicates the community's primary focus on the care of siblings in the new family rather than care for others outside the group.

Paul's images for his communities provide the background for his moral instruction as he regularly exhorts his communities to conduct themselves in accordance with their identity. They must accept their roles as the heir of ancient Israel and recognize the boundaries that distinguish them from the surrounding society. As an elect and holy people, they continue Israel's legacy of separating themselves from the practices of their neighbors, maintaining their status by keeping God's commandments. As a family, they separate themselves from others by demonstrating special concern for their siblings and avoiding activities that undermine family life.

### Insider Language, Ethos, and Identity

In addition to providing his communities with identities that enable their members to cohere and to distinguish themselves from outsiders, Paul also introduces a distinctive vocabulary for ethical discourse. A community needs such a vocabulary to maintain its identity, as George Lindbeck argues: "Human experience is shaped, molded, and in a sense constituted by cultural and linguistic forms,"[53] that is, by a symbolic world that includes the use of insider language by which communities define themselves. Paul's ethical discourse is notable both for its omission of the common language of ethical discourse from the Greek polis and its inclusion of the new vocabulary that he gives to his readers.

The language of Greek ethical discourse is rare in the Pauline literature. Paul speaks explicitly of virtue only once (Phil. 4:8) and never mentions the four cardinal virtues. Nor does he speak of the pursuit of the individual's *eudaimonia* (human flourishing), one of the principal themes of Greek ethics. The undisputed letters do not contain the common term *eusebeia* (piety). Nor do such aristocratic ideals as *kalokagathia* (nobility), *eleutheriotēs* (freedom of spirit), *megalophrosynē* (greatness of mind), *megalopsychia* (greatness of soul, magnanimity), and *megaloprepeia* (magnificence) appear in Paul's letters.[54]

### The Language of Request

While Paul omits the Greek terminology of moral discourse, he supplies an alternative insider language for the subject, which appears in the categories he employs in making requests. Although scholars commonly refer to his moral instructions as paraenesis, a term also commonly used for hortatory speech in

52. Wolter, "Ethische Identität," 86.
53. Lindbeck, *The Nature of Doctrine*, 34.
54. Zeller, "Konkrete Ethik im hellenistischen Kontext," 86. See LSJ for definitions of terms.

Greek rhetoric, Paul does not use this term.[55] Instead, he uses a variety of words,[56] including verbs denoting a request,[57] authoritative instruction,[58] and witnessing.[59]

The word most frequently associated with moral instruction is the verb *parakalein* and the related noun *paraklēsis*, with which he describes his original moral catechesis (1 Thess. 2:12) and introduces such instruction in his letters (Rom. 12:1; 1 Cor. 1:10; 4:16; 2 Cor. 2:8; Phil. 4:2; 1 Thess. 4:1, 10). The word is also used for the proclamation of the gospel (1 Thess. 2:3–4) and the invitation to receive it (2 Cor. 5:20; 6:1). It is the term for a request (2 Cor. 8:6; 9:5; Philem. 9), the encouragement of the disheartened (cf. 1 Cor. 4:13; 1 Thess. 3:2), and the comforting of the bereaved (1 Thess. 4:18; 5:11). Paul encourages Christians to display love to one another (2 Cor. 2:8), to earn their own living (2 Thess. 3:12; also 1 Thess. 4:10–11), to pray (Rom. 15:30; 1 Tim. 2:1), to be in agreement (1 Cor. 1:10; Phil. 4:2), to imitate their leaders (1 Cor. 4:16; Gal. 4:12), to respect them (1 Thess. 5:12; cf. Heb. 13:22), and to keep an eye on and admonish deviants (Rom. 16:17–18; 1 Thess. 5:14; cf. 1 Pet. 5:12).[60]

Although *parakalein* is the paraenetical term par excellence in the New Testament,[61] in many of his appeals Paul is less concerned with moral issues in a narrow sense than with Christian formation in general: the range in his use of *parakalein* and *paraklēsis* indicates that ethics cannot be demarcated from other aspects of Christian experience or theology. Paul's concern with Christian formation includes a comprehensive response to the gospel that incorporates ethical behavior with all of the responsibilities of life in the new family. This semantic range suggests that ethics is not a self-contained system, but is interwoven with both the Christian message and other aspects of Christian existence. Paul's preaching cannot be separated from the invitation to receive it and to live "worthily of the gospel." Nor can the encouragement for the fainthearted easily be separated from the exhortation to live out the implications of the gospel.[62]

That ethics is not a self-contained unit for Paul is also evident in the way that he interweaves traditional ethical topics with exhortations that are not common in ethical instruction. To instructions on marriage, brotherly love,

---

55. Stuhlmacher, *Paul's Letter to the Romans*, 214.

56. See Popkes, *Päranese und das Neue Testament*, 76.

57. *Deomai* ("I ask") is used both for prayers (Rom. 1:10; 1 Thess. 3:10) and for behavioral requests (2 Cor. 5:20; 10:2; Gal. 4:12). Paul also uses *erōtaō* ("ask") for behavioral requests (Phil. 4:3; 1 Thess. 4:1; 5:12; 2 Thess. 2:1–2).

58. *Parangellein* ("instruct," "direct," BDAG 760) is used in 1 Cor. 7:10; 11:17; 1 Thess. 4:11; 2 Thess. 3:4, 10, 12; cf. 1 Tim. 1:3, 4; 6:13; *parangelia* (instruction) is used in 1 Thess. 4:2; cf. 1 Tim. 1:5, 18. *Nouthetein* (admonish) is used in Rom. 15:14; 1 Cor. 4:14; Col. 1:28; 3:16; 1 Thess. 5:12, 14; cf. *nouthesia* in 1 Cor. 10:11; Eph. 6:4.

59. *Martureisthai* is used in 1 Thess. 2:12; *diamarturesthai* in 1 Thess. 4:6.

60. Aasgaard, *'My Beloved Brothers and Sisters!,'* 248.

61. Ibid.

62. Stuhlmacher, *Romans*, 215. See also Engberg-Pedersen, "Concept of Paraenesis," 69.

and work with the hands (1 Thess. 4:1–12), for example, Paul adds others for the bereaved: "Comfort one another with these words" (1 Thess. 4:18). In the concluding exhortations of 1 Thessalonians, he adds, "Rejoice always, pray constantly, give thanks in everything" (1 Thess. 5:16–18a). Paul places exhortations to rejoice (cf. Rom. 12:12; 2 Cor. 13:11; Phil. 2:28; 3:1; 4:4; 1 Thess. 5:16) and to pray (Rom. 12:12; 1 Thess. 5:17, 25; 2 Thess. 3:1) alongside instructions commonly included among ethical duties.

### "Walking" as Moral Conduct

Paul does not speak of ethics as such, but of how to walk, the primary term for ethical conduct. In his original catechesis, he encourages the converts to "walk worthily of God as the one who called [them] into God's kingdom and glory" (1 Thess. 2:12), and he writes to continue encouraging them to "walk and please God" (1 Thess. 4:1) and to "walk" appropriately in the presence of outsiders (4:12). In Romans, he urges readers to "walk in newness of life" (6:4) and to "walk according to the Spirit" (8:4; cf. Gal. 5:16). This image of walking continues in the disputed letters, Ephesians and Colossians, according to which the readers once "walked" in pursuit of the desires of the flesh (Eph. 2:12; 4:17; 5:15; Col. 3:5–7) with their new existence, which involves walking worthily of the calling (Eph. 4:1; Col. 1:10) and "in him" (2:6). In the paraenetic sections, he describes the nature of this walk in detail.

Paul's vocabulary indicates his indebtedness to Jewish instruction inasmuch as *peripatein* belongs to the Old-Testament (LXX) and Jewish vocabulary for moral instruction.[63] It has a theological/ethical significance in such phrases as "walking before Yahweh" (cf. Gen. 17:1; 24:40; 48:15) and "walking with God" (Gen. 5:22; 6:9). In the Deuteronomic writings, "walking in the ways of Yahweh" signifies the keeping of the commandments (Deut. 8:6; cf. 2 Kings 10:31; Ezek. 18:9, 17). It is a life under Torah, while the evil way is a life not under law.[64] Other passages speak of walking in a "good," "upright," "blameless," or "righteous" way (1 Kings 8:36; Isa. 57:2; Ps. 101:6; Prov. 8:20), in "integrity" (Ps. 84:11), in "faithfulness" or "truth" (Ps. 86:11), and in the law (Ezek. 18:17).[65] According to Ezekiel 11:19–20 and 36:26–27 Israel will again walk in the commands of God.

63. See Finsterbusch, *Die Thora als Lebensweisung für Heidenchristen*, 113. The Hebrew Bible employs a variety of words for *going* or *walking*. The predominant word is *llkt*. The LXX translates it primarily with *poreuomai* (947 times), less often with *peripatein* (24 times). "In early biblical times movement from one place to another distinguished the life of nomads. . . . It is astonishing that the Old Testament describes the life of the individual with the word family of walking or going and thus a profane meaning took on a religious color" (my translation). See also Seesemann, "*Pateō*," in *TDNT* 5:944; Carras, "Jewish Ethics and Gentile Converts: Remarks on 1 Thess 4,3–8," 306.

64. Finsterbusch, *Thora als Lebensweisung*, 113.

65. Banks, "'Walking' as a Metaphor of the Christian Life," 305–6.

### *"The Will of God" and "Pleasing to God"*

The goal of moral conduct for Paul is not the *eudaimonia* of the individual, but to do the will of God. He speaks of keeping the law and doing the will of God in synonymous terms (Rom. 2:17–18). He introduces his moral instructions in Romans 12 with the appeal to "discern the will of God" (Rom. 12:2). Similarly, the will of God heads the ethical instructions in 1 Thessalonians (4:3; cf. 5:18). References to the will of God as an ethical category appear frequently in the disputed letters, Ephesians (5:17; 6:6) and Colossians (1:9; 4:12). The phrase is also indebted to the Old Testament and Jewish tradition. The psalmist says, "I have come to do your will" (Ps. 40:8; cf. Ps. 143:10: "Teach us to do your will, O Lord"). Ezra calls on Israel to separate from non-Israelite wives and children (10:3) in order to act according to the law (10:3) and do the divine will (10:11). According to 4 Maccabees 18, to do the will of God is to keep Torah. The father of the seven martyrs had taught the law (18:10) and recounted Solomon's proverb, "There is a tree of life for those who do his will" (18:16; cf. *T. Naph.* 3:1–2). In the Sermon on the Mount, Jesus speaks of "the one who does the will of my father" (Matt. 7:21).[66]

The "will of God" is synonymous with doing what is "pleasing (*euareston*) to God" (Rom. 12:2; cf. Rom. 8:8; 2 Cor. 5:9; 1 Thess. 4:1) in Paul, as in Jewish literature.[67] The latter term is most often used of unblemished sacrifices, but is also often used for the keeping of the commandments. Paul appropriates the term to describe the conduct of his listeners, thus incorporating them into the vocabulary of Israel.

### Conclusion: Identity and Ethics

Paul shapes the moral consciousness of his gentile converts by instructing them with the vocabulary of ancient Israel. The corporate ethic of his communities is based on their identity as the elect and holy people who live out the consequences of their divine calling. Inasmuch as these communities, unlike the Israelites, are not united by physical kinship, Paul provides an identity of fictive kinship by which they assume the roles of families. These images indicate that the moral life cannot be lived in isolation, but only in the company of others who are called to be elect and holy members of the family. These images also draw boundaries between the in-group and the outsiders that the community expresses by adopting a code of conduct that distinguishes them from others. Insider language drawn from Israel's Scripture characterizes the moral discourse of this in-group. As in Israel, they respond to the holiness granted by God by being holy in their activities. They respond to their relationship as a family by behaving as family members.

---

66. Finsterbusch, *Thora als Lebensweisung*, 147–51.
67. Ibid., 150.

# 3

# From Catechesis to Correspondence

*Ethos and Ethics in 1 Thessalonians*

Paul's first letter to the Thessalonians is the third stage of his attempt at community formation in Thessalonica. In the first stage, the Thessalonians "received the word" (2:13) and "turned to God from idols to serve the living and true God" (1:9–10). This stage continued in Paul's appeal (*paraklēsis*, 2:3) and preaching (2:9) to the infant church. As he later recalls, he was like a father with his own children, "urging . . . and encouraging, and pleading" (*parakalountes kai paramythoumenoi kai martyromenoi*) with the converts to "walk worthily of God as the one who called [them] into God's kingdom and glory" (2:12). In the second stage, Paul sent his coworker Timothy to "strengthen and encourage" (*stērixai . . . kai parakalesai*) the new community in the context of persecution (3:2). Paul writes 1 Thessalonians in the third stage of his ministry, once more urging (cf. 4:1, *parakaloumen*) the community to continue walking in a way that pleases God (1 Thess. 4:1). At every stage of his ministry to the Thessalonians, Paul is engaged in *paraklēsis* with a concern for how his readers "walk" (*peripatein*, 2:12; 4:2, 12). Conversion not only involved a rejection of pagan deities in favor of Israel's God; it required a new existence that was "worthy" of (2:12) and pleasing (4:1) to the God who had called them. Thus Paul instructs the gentile converts of Thessalonica not to behave "like the Gentiles who do not know God" (4:5 NRSV).

The purpose of 1 Thessalonians, as Paul indicates in 4:1–2, is to "ask and urge" (*erōtōmen . . . kai parakaloumen*) the new converts to do "more and more" what they are already doing (4:1), recalling the instructions that he has already given (4:2). References throughout the epistle to what the community already knows (2:1, 9; 3:3; 4:2, 6, 9, 11; 5:1–2) suggest that 1 Thessalonians is largely composed of repetition of the earlier catechesis for new converts (cf. 2:12). Thus Paul's moral instructions are neither arbitrary nor ad hoc responses to crises, but a concrete and coherent vision of the life that is worthy of the gospel. Although we do not have a comprehensive record of Paul's catechesis, we may assume that the specific instructions of the last two chapters repeat at least a portion of what he has said previously. We may also assume that the instructions to the Thessalonians were consistent with moral instructions to the other churches. He describes what new converts in a pagan society need to know in order to survive as a community. Paul continues to assume the role of a father instructing his children on how to conduct themselves.

As the summary of Paul's ethical teaching, 1 Thessalonians is an appropriate place to begin examining that teaching, on which he will elaborate in subsequent letters. In the following chapters, we shall observe the extent to which the other letters demonstrate the coherence of Paul's moral instructions. The brevity of the letter prevents him from elaborating on his instruction. Whereas Paul offered few specific examples of the life that is "worthy" of God in his original catechesis, he gives specific examples of this instruction in chapters 4 and 5.

In the first three chapters of the epistle, Paul rehearses his past relationship with the readers (1:2–3:10), recalling their initial response and continued progress (1:5–10; 2:13–3:10) and reminding them of his example of blameless conduct (2:1–12). The epistle moves from a recitation of the community's moral progress (chs. 1–3) to instructions for future conduct (chs. 4–5). At the center of Paul's concern is the moral conduct of the community. The shape of the moral instruction becomes evident in Paul's relationship to the readers and the distinctive vocabulary that provides the framework for his moral teaching. As the one whom God used to convert the Thessalonians, Paul is like a father instructing his children in proper behavior (2:11–12) and a nursing mother taking care of her children (2:7). When he is absent from them, he is "orphaned" (2:17, *aporphanisthentes*) because he cannot see his "joy or crown of boasting" (2:19 NRSV). Thus his instructions for appropriate moral conduct reflect his parental concern for the converts.

Paul's recollection of his paternal instruction reflects his distinct vocabulary for moral conduct. He does not use the traditional vocabulary for ethics, but the terminology that reflects both his parental relationship to the community and his Jewish heritage. *Parakalein* and *peripatein* characterize Paul's ethical vocabulary in 1 Thessalonians (2:12; 4:1) and the later epistles. The range of meanings for *parakalein* (or *paraklēsis*) becomes evident in 1 Thessalonians (see also ch. 2, "The Language of Request").[1] It is the equivalent of preaching the gospel (2:3), encouraging in the midst of distress (3:2), giving moral instruction (4:1, 10; 5:14), and comforting (4:18; cf. 5:11). *Parakalein* and *paramytheisthai* (2:12) are semantically related and often appear together (cf. 1 Cor. 14:3; Phil. 2:1; 1 Thess. 5:14).[2] Paul avoids the more common Hellenistic term *parainein* and commonly chooses *parakalein* over direct commands because of his familial relationship to the readers (cf. Philem. 8, 10). The request formula probably has its background in Hellenistic-Greek family letters, although it also occurs in official letters.[3] Indeed, Paul's frequent inclusion of the vocative *adelphoi* with *parakalein* indicates the familial character of his request (cf. 4:1, 10; 1 Cor. 10:1; Rom. 12:1; cf. 1 Thess. 5:12, *erōtōmen*).[4] *Parakalein* reflects the familial context of Paul's instruction and his role as father (2:11–12; Philem. 8, 10).

As we saw in chapter 2 ("'Walking' as Moral Conduct"), Paul does not speak of ethics, but of how to walk. He recalls instructing the Thessalonians to "walk worthily" of the God who calls them (2:12), and he continues in the letter to challenge the readers to "walk and please God" (4:1) and to "walk decently" (*hina peripateite euschēmonōs*) before outsiders (4:12). Paul's vocabulary indicates his indebtedness to Jewish instruction, inasmuch as *peripatein* belongs to the Old Testament and Jewish vocabulary for moral instruction.[5]

## Identity and Community

The corporate nature of the moral life for Paul is evident in both the setting and the language of the letter. As chapters 1–3 indicate, the identity of the people is the foundation for the community's ethical life.[6] Paul writes to the *ekklēsia* (1:1) and requests that the letter be read in the assembly (5:27). The terminology places gentile converts firmly within the Old Testament narrative world, separating them from "the gentiles" (4:5). Not only do the readers share with ancient Israel the identity as *ekklēsia*, but they also share Israel's identity as the elect (1:4) and "beloved by God" (1:4). Just as God had called Israel (Hos. 11:1), God has now called these new converts (2:12; 4:7; 5:24). This language echoes the election tradition of Deuteronomy, according

---

1. BDAG 764–65 indicates the range of meanings: call to one's side, urge strongly, request, and comfort/cheer up.

2. Burke, *Family Matters: A Socio-Historical Study of Kinship Metaphors in 1 Thessalonians,* 144.

3. Aasgaard, "'Brotherly Advice': Christian Siblingship and New Testament Paraenesis," 247.

4. Ibid.

5. On *peripatein* as Paul's most frequent word for moral conduct, see chapter 2 ("The Language of Request").

6. Wolter, "Ethos und Identität," 431: "Ethos is a canon of habitualized actions which have validity in a group" (my translation).

to which God chose those whom he loved (Deut. 7:6–7). As in Deuteronomy, the identity of the people as God's chosen community separates them from the ethos and practices of the peoples around them (see ch. 2).

Paul reinforces the identity of the readers with the emphasis on holiness that pervades the epistle. Before he gives the specific commandments, he prays that God will "strengthen [their] hearts in holiness (*hagiōsynē*)" at the parousia of Jesus Christ (3:13), providing the transition to the moral instruction about the behavior that demonstrates holiness (4:3, 7). The closing benediction is Paul's prayer for God to "sanctify [them] wholly" (*hagiasai hymas holoteleis*) (5:23). Thus the community shares the identifying mark of Israel that distinguished them from the people around them.[7] As in the Holiness Code (see ch. 1), Paul places the moral commands under the rubric of holiness.

The expectation of the coming of God's wrath (1:10) and of the parousia of the Lord links the people with Israelite expectation (cf. 4:13–5:10). Paul describes their destiny "in strikingly Israelite terms."[8] They are the sons of light (5:5) who await the day of the Lord (5:1–2). In the meantime, they experience the affliction (*thlipsis*) that precedes the end (1:6; 3:3, 7). Their identity as the people of God requires that they wait in the midst of affliction, which Paul previously described as their destiny (3:3–4). Paul undoubtedly sees them as the eschatological people of God who undergo the afflictions that precede the end.[9]

The new identity requires an awareness that they are a part of the family of God.[10] In keeping with his self-description as the concerned father (2:12) and nursing mother (2:7), he speaks affectionately to his readers, addressing those who have no physical kinship ties repeatedly as *adelphoi* (1:4; 2:1, 9, 14, 17; 3:7; 4:1, 10, 13; 5:1, 4, 12, 14, 25), a term that is used more, proportionally, in 1 Thessalonians than in the other letters.[11]

The establishment of the in-group sharply distinguishes it and its conduct from other groups ("the rest," 1 Thess. 4:13; 5:6) and their conduct. Paul reminds the Thessalonians that they must "walk appropriately toward those who are outside" (4:13) and not behave "as the gentiles do" (4:5).

Paul's letters consistently refer to the identity of the people of God with the terms employed in 1 Thessalonians. He addresses them as the "saints" (*hagioi*), "those who are called to be saints" (Rom. 1:7; 1 Cor. 1:2), and those

---

7. Weima, "How You Must Walk to Please God: Holiness and Discipleship in 1 Thessalonians," 101.

8. Esler, "Keeping It in the Family: Culture, Kinship and Identity in 1 Thessalonians and Galatians," 166: "It is remarkable that Paul should have persuaded Gentiles to accept a strongly Israelite myth of the future."

9. On the Jewish expectation of eschatological affliction, see Kremer, "*Thlipsis*," *EDNT* 2:152.

10. De Villiers, "'A Life Worthy of God': Identity and Ethics in the Thessalonian Correspondence," 345.

11. Burke, *Family Matters*, 166.

who "are being sanctified in Christ" (1 Cor. 1:2). This term, which is rare in Hellenistic texts, is one of Paul's preferred terms for describing the identity of the members of his communities.[12] As in 1 Thessalonians 4:3, 7, the terminology of holiness plays an important role in paraenetic texts. The life of holiness (*hagiasmos*) is the alternative to the life controlled by the passions (1 Thess. 4:5; Rom. 6:18, 22). Those who have been "washed," "justified," and "sanctified" (1 Cor. 6:11) turn away from the sexual vices of their environment.

Paul also refers to his readers consistently in his letters as the "called" and the "elect," as in 1 Thessalonians (1:4; 2:12; 4:7). Indeed, his address to the Romans and Corinthians, "called to be saints" (*klētois hagiois*, Rom. 1:7; 1 Cor. 1:2), indicates the relationship between holiness and election in Paul's understanding of the church. He reminds his communities of their calling (Rom. 8:30; 9:12, 24; 1 Cor. 1:9; 7:15, 17, 21; Gal. 1:6; 5:13; cf. Eph. 1:11; 4:1, 4; Col. 1:12; 3:15; 2 Thess. 2:14) and election (Rom. 8:33; 11:5, 7; 16:13; 1 Cor. 1:27; cf. Eph. 1:4). This terminology indicates the place of Paul's churches within Israel's narrative world. Paul's usage reflects the influence of Deuteronomy, according to which God's choice of Israel requires Israel's separation from the practices of the world around them.[13] Just as God chose ancient Israel to be a holy people and called them to live a countercultural existence, God has called the gentile churches to holy living.[14]

## From Identity to Ethics in 1 Thessalonians

As in ancient Israel, the identity of the community is the presupposition for its conduct. The opening thanksgiving of 1 Thessalonians, like the thanksgiving in other letters, introduces the themes of the letter, providing the first indication of the concrete nature of the life that is pleasing to God. Paul expresses satisfaction that the readers already walk in a way that is pleasing to God, introducing the major themes of the letter in parallel genitive constructions, "remembering your work of faith and labor of love and steadfastness of hope" (*mnēmoneuontes hymōn tou ergou tēs pisteōs kai tou kopou tēs agapēs kai tēs hypomonēs tēs elpidos*). The possessive pronoun *hymōn* indicates that the terms are both distinguishable and related aspects of the basic stance of the Thessalonians' existence.[15] This triad forms an inclusio with 5:8, indicating the significance and interrelationship among these words. Paul lists two of the three words in 3:6 as he recalls Timothy's report of the Thessalonians' faith and love. The epistle refers to these words separately throughout the letter (see below). Thus while the parts of the triad are significant in Paul's ethical

---

12. Balz, "*Hagios ktl*," *EDNT* 1:17.
13. Blischke, *Die Begründung und die Durchsetzung*, 388.
14. Wolter, "Ethos und Identität," 432–34.
15. Söding, *Die Trias Glaube, Hoffnung, Liebe bei Paulus*, 31.

instruction, the triad takes on a special meaning when these words appear together. Paul expresses gratitude for the community's progress in faith, hope, and love in chapters 1–3 (1:3; cf. 1:8; 3:2, 6), prays for their progress in love (3:11–13), and encourages them in the same qualities in chapters 4–5.

### The Triad: Faith, Hope, and Love

This triad is significant in the Pauline correspondence. The classic formulation is the summary in 1 Corinthians 13:13 (elsewhere the order is faith-love-hope). One may assume that this triad belongs to Paul's original catechesis. In 1:3 and 5:8 it suggests the relationship among the three words. According to Thomas Söding, this triad is the foundation and summary of Christian existence.[16] Love presupposes faith (cf. 3:6; Philem. 5) and hope. The eschatological dimension of love is suggested by hope (*elpis*). It looks to the relationship to God (*pistis, elpis*) and relates to humankind.[17] It grows out of the eschatological expectation of the future of God.[18]

Although Greek sources refer to faith, hope, and love, these words have greater significance in Jewish literature,[19] where they have connotations that correspond to the Israelite tradition and appear in proximity to each other. At least two of the three appear together relatively frequently in the LXX.[20] According to Wisdom 3:9, "The faithful (*pistoi*) will abide with him in love (*agapē*)" (NRSV). Faith and hope are frequently linked in Sirach. According to Sirach 2:6 (NRSV), "Trust (*pisteuson*) in him, and he will help you; make your ways straight, and hope (*elpison*) in him." Conversely, "One who does not believe (*ou pisteuei*) will have no shelter" (Sir. 2:13). Love is sometimes listed alongside the other two terms, but is normally directed toward God (cf. Sir. 2:15–16).

### The Work of Faith

The "work of faith" is a major theme in 1 Thessalonians. Gentiles who have "turned to God from idols to serve the true and living God" (1:9) have been

16. Söding, *Das Liebesgebot bei Paulus*, 92.
17. Ibid., 93.
18. Ibid.
19. For texts, see Söding, *Liebesgebot bei Paulus*, 38; Söding, *Trias Glaube, Hoffnung, Liebe*, 51–55.
20. Cf. Ps. 78:22: "Because they had no faith (*episteusan*) in God and did not trust (*ēlpisan*) his saving power" (NRSV); Sir. 2:8–9: "You who fear the Lord, trust in him . . . ; you who fear the Lord, hope for good things." The relationship between faith and hope is especially evident in the Maccabean literature. The three young men "believed (*pisteusantes*) and were saved (*esōthēsan*)" (1 Macc. 2:59), while "all those who hope (*hoi elpizontes*) will not lose their strength" (1 Macc. 2:61). Cf. 4 Macc. 17:2, according to which the mother of the seven martyred sons "showed the courage of [her] faith," and 4 Macc. 17:4, which indicates that her courage came from "an enduring hope in God." The combination hope, expectation, and faith appears in 2 Bar. 51:7. See Söding, *Trias Glaube, Hoffnung, Liebe*, 53.

incorporated into Israel's narrative world and now exhibit "faith in God" (1:8, *pistis . . . pros ton theon*). In contrast to the most common usage in Galatians and Romans, *pistis* is frequently used in 1 Thessalonians without an object. In the second stage of Paul's relationship to the Thessalonians, he had sent Timothy back to strengthen and encourage on behalf of their *pistis* (3:2). The meaning of *pistis* becomes evident in the clause "so that no one be shaken by these persecutions" (3:3), about which Paul had warned in his catechesis. As the opposite of "shaken" (*sainein*),[21] *pistis* refers to the stability of the Thessalonians in the midst of persecution. Paul has this stability in mind when he recalls that Timothy had brought back good news about the Thessalonians' faith and love (3:6), leading him to be encouraged in the midst of his anguish through their *pistis*. Nevertheless, Paul still wants to return to this community to "complete what is lacking in [their] faith" (3:10).

Paul also uses the participial form as a term for Christians. Paul speaks of "those who believe" (*hoi pisteuontes*) in Macedonia (1:7), of his conduct among "those who believe" (2:10), and of the power of the word of God among "those who believe" (2:13). He also uses the verb in 4:14 to refer to convictions that belong to catechesis: "If we believe that Jesus died and rose." The work of faith (cf. Rom. 1:5) refers to activities, especially the steadfastness of those who have believed.

In describing the *pistis* of the Thessalonians, Paul employs the terminology of the descriptions of both God and Israel in the LXX. God is faithful (Deut. 32:4; Ps. 32:4 LXX; Ps. 145:13; *Pss. Sol.* 14:1; 17:10), and so are the major heroes of the Old Testament, including Abraham (Gen. 15:6), Moses (Num. 12:7; Sir. 45:4), Samuel (Sir. 46:15), the three young men in the flame (1 Macc. 2:59), and the Maccabean martyrs. In the Maccabean literature, *pistis* is demonstrated through courage (4 Macc. 17:2) in the midst of persecution. People saw the faithfulness of Simon (1 Macc. 14:35). The mother of the seven sons demonstrated her faith in God (*pros ton theon*, 4 Macc. 15:24; 16:22; cf. 1 Thess. 1:6). Thus the *pistis* of the Thessalonians in the midst of affliction recalls others who demonstrated stability and reliability under duress.

### The Labor of Love

In the Thessalonians' "labor of love," they exhibit the behavior that Paul inculcated when he taught them to "love one another" in his initial instruction (1 Thess. 4:9). Although he does not indicate an object in 1:3, the initial

---

21. The meaning of *sainein* is disputed. Some interpreters render it as "deceived." Cf. BDAG 910. Here the meaning is "move" or "shake," as early patristic usage suggests. Cf. Lang "*Sainō*," *TDNT* 7:55–56. The verb is the opposite of *stēkein en kyriō*, 1 Thess. 3:8. From the basic meaning "whisk" or "wave," it was used of dogs, "to wag" the tail, and metaphorically for the flatterer who tried to please others. Patristic writers interpreted the verb as "shake" or "be agitated." See Holtz, *Erste Brief an die Thessalonicher*, 127.

instruction (4:9–12) and the petition in 3:12 that they "abound in love to one another and to all" indicates that Paul is calling for a special bond uniting the community. While the love may extend beyond the community of faith (3:12), the community is the primary sphere for the "labor of love." This labor of love corresponds to the familial ethos that Paul has established. The Thessalonians' conversion has provoked hostility, which undoubtedly included alienation from their own primary families and the loss of the intimacy and care that the families provided. The "labor of love" included assuming the numerous roles that the family provided. The close link between the "work of faith" and "labor of love" suggests that Paul is calling for communal solidarity in the midst of suffering.

### The Steadfastness of Hope

Because converts "wait for the Son from heaven" (1:10), "steadfastness of hope" (*hypomonēs elpidos*) is a fundamental aspect of the life that is pleasing to God. The converts now form a counterculture, distinguishing themselves from "those who have no hope" (4:13). As participants in Israel's narrative world, the readers will put on the helmet of the hope of salvation (5:8).

Faith and hope are closely related in Paul, and both are associated with endurance (*hypomonē*). Abraham both "believed God" (Rom. 4:3; Gal. 3:6) and "hoped upon hope" (Rom. 4:18). Because those who belong to Christ have been "justified by faith" (Rom. 5:1), Paul challenges them to "boast in hope of the glory of God" (Rom. 5:2) in the midst of sufferings, knowing that the sufferings produce steadfastness (*hypomonē*). Paul instructs the Romans to rejoice in hope, being steadfast (*hypomenontes*) in sufferings (12:12). Through faith, Christians await the hope of righteousness (Gal. 5:5). The "steadfastness of hope" is, therefore, the capacity to remain firmly rooted in the midst of the tumults that tempt God's people to renounce their faith.

The focus on "the work of faith" and "steadfastness of hope" is firmly rooted in both Jewish wisdom literature and apocalyptic expectation. As Paul incorporates his readers into Israel's election tradition, he also incorporates the image of the faithful ones who believe in God and endure distress. The closest analogies to the love for insiders may be found in the Jewish paraenetic tradition of the *Testaments of the Twelve Patriarchs* (see ch. 1).

### The Will of God: Instructions for Holy Living

As a transition from reminiscencing about the moral impact of the Thessalonians' conversion to the living God (1:3; 3:2–6), Paul prays that God will cause the Thessalonians' love for each other and "for all" to multiply (1 Thess. 3:12) and to establish them "blameless in holiness" (3:13) before the parousia of the Lord. The prayer for God's continued work among the believers indicates that moral formation is a continuing process (cf. 2:13) in which God is at work. The prayer also introduces the themes of love and holiness that Paul will develop in the specific instructions that follow in chapters 4 and 5. This prayer indicates the divine agency in the transformation of the community.

In 4:1–2, Paul proceeds from divine agency to the human response, introducing the instructions that follow. The vocative *adelphoi* and the request "We ask you and we appeal to you" (*erōtōmen hymas kai parakaloumen*) continue the family setting as the context for the moral instruction (cf. 2:11–12). Consistent with the vocabulary of Jewish halakah, Paul adds, "Just as you learned (*parelabete*, literally "received") from us how you ought to walk and please God" (4:1). *Paralambanein*, the term for receiving a mental or spiritual heritage, corresponds to the Hebrew *qibēl*.[22] Paul employs the term for confessional (1 Cor. 15:3) and liturgical traditions (1 Cor. 11:23), using a term that was commonplace in Jewish paraenesis and often associated with the Decalogue.[23] In Jewish thought, the term is used for halakic traditions concerned with keeping the Torah.[24] This concern is reflected in Mark's explanation that the Pharisees have received many traditions "which they keep" (7:4).

Paul's roots in the Jewish tradition are also evident in the parallel expressions "to walk and please God" (*peripatein kai areskein theō*). The Old Testament and Jewish literature employed the image of walking for the keeping of the commands of Torah (see ch. 2, "'Walking' as Moral Conduct"). To please God is to keep the commandments of Torah. The legal injunctions of the Torah distinguish between sacrifices (Lev. 10:19; Mal. 3:4) that please and do not please (the Lord). The commandments of Torah are pleasing in God's sight (*areston*, Deut. 6:18; 12:25, 28; 13:18; 21:9). The offering of praise will please the Lord (Ps. 69:30–31), but rejoicing in the downfall of enemies will not be pleasing (Prov. 24:17–18). Both Isaiah and Sirach recall that Hezekiah did what was pleasing in God's sight (Isa. 38:3; Sir. 48:22). The paraenesis of Tobit 4 concludes with the father's instruction, "Do what is pleasing (*areston*)" to the Lord (4:21). Thus to "do what is pleasing" was commonly used for the keeping of the commandments of Torah.

In mentioning what the Thessalonians have "learned" with respect to "how to walk and please God," Paul recalls his earlier instruction when he took the paternal role of teaching the Thessalonians "how to walk" and describes his instructions for the Thessalonians using the language associated with keeping the Torah (2:12).

Paul introduces the first specific instruction (*parangelia*, 4:2) with the appositive construction "This is the will of God, your sanctification," equating God's will with sanctification. The combination of the two terms is reminiscent of the

---

22. BDAG 768.
23. Wegenast, *Das Verständnis der Tradition bei Paulus und in den Deuteropaulinen*, 116.
24. Kretzer, "*Paralambanō*," *EDNT* 3:30.

connection between God's will and sanctification in Jewish literature. God's will and sanctification are both frequently associated with keeping the Torah.[25] The juxtaposition of Paul's prayer that God may establish the community in holiness (*hagiōsynē*, 3:13) and the introduction to the paraenesis with *hagiasmos* (4:3) indicates that sanctification is both the work of God and the response of the community reminiscent of the command to Israel to "be holy" (Lev. 19:2). *Hagiōsynē* is a completed state, while *hagiasmos* is a process.[26] *Hagiasmos* in 4:3, 7 forms an inclusio. Similarly, fornication (*porneia*) (4:3) and uncleanness (*akatharsia*) (4:7) also form an inclusio[27] framing the discussion of sexual immorality, as Paul repeats his earlier catechesis (4:6). Corresponding to the ancient Holiness Code (Lev. 17–26), Paul extends the sphere of holiness from the cult to include aspects of daily life, including sexual relationships.[28] The content of the instruction is not, as Betz argued, the kerygma,[29] but the commands that follow, especially in 4:1–12. These commands are derived from the Torah. Like his predecessors in Diaspora Judaism, Paul gives a summary of the law.

### Sexual Matters (4:3–8)

"To abstain from sexual immorality" (*tou apechesthai . . . apo tēs porneias*) is a characteristic of holiness in Leviticus. *Apechesthai* conveys the idea of separation that is implicit in the term *hagiasmos*. The community's new identity as siblings (*adelphoi*) and as a holy community requires separation from their society and a strong distinction between insiders and outsiders (cf. 4:5, 12, 13). That *hagiasmos* is first defined with abstention from *porneia* indicates that the sexual practices of the new community separate them from the pagan society and their own previous existence. They now adopt the basic values associated with the new family.[30] *Hagiasmos* conforms to the

---

25. For the relationship between doing the will of God and keeping the Torah, cf. Ps. 40:8: "I have come to do your will." Cf. Ps. 143:10: "Teach me to do your will, O Lord." According to Ezra 10, Shecaniah calls on Israel to separate from non-Israelite wives and children (10:3) in order to act according to the law (10:3) and do the divine will (10:11). According to 4 Macc. 18, to do the will of God is to keep Torah. The father of the seven martyrs had taught the law (18:10) and recounted Solomon's proverb, "There is a tree of life for those who do his will" (18:16 NRSV; cf. Prov. 3:18). Cf. *T. Naph.* 3:1. In the Sermon on the Mount, Jesus speaks of the one who "does the will of my father" (Matt. 7:21). Paul speaks of keeping the law and doing the will of God in synonymous terms (Rom. 2:17–18). See Finsterbusch, *Thora als Lebensweisung*, 147–51.

26. Schrage, "Heiligung als Prozess bei Paulus," 203; R. Collins, "'This Is the Will of God: Your Sanctification' (1 Thess. 4:3)," 309.

27. *Porneia* and *akatharsia* frequently appear in Pauline paraenesis to describe sexual sins (2 Cor. 12:21; Gal. 5:19). *Akatharsia* is a synonym for *porneia* in Rom. 1:24; 6:19. Paul undoubtedly draws this combination from the ideas of purity expressed in the Holiness Code. See Dautzenberg, "Φεύγετε τὴν πορνείαν (1 Kor 6:18)," 289–90.

28. Schrage, "Heiligung als Prozess bei Paulus," 209.

29. Betz, "Foundations of Christian Ethics according to Romans 12:1–2," 58.

30. Meeks, *Moral World of the First Christians*, 13. Cf. Burke, *Family Matters*, 184.

Holiness Code, according to which a major aspect of holiness is to avoid forbidden sexual relationships (Lev. 18). Inasmuch as this instruction belongs to Paul's original catechesis (cf. 4:6), one may assume that Paul is repeating his customary moral exhortation for gentile converts rather than responding to a local crisis. The fact that 1 Thessalonians largely restates Paul's earlier ethical instructions also suggests that here Paul is repeating standard instructions. He encourages those who have "turned to God from idols" (1:9) to live within the Jewish sexual norms.

*Porneia* refers to "various kinds of unsanctioned sexual intercourse."[31] It includes prostitution, unchastity, and marriage to forbidden persons (cf. 1 Cor. 5:1). The command to abstain from *porneia* is basic to Jewish paraenesis and a characteristic of the holy life. *Porneia* is the LXX rendering for forbidden sexual relationships. The term is used for Tamar's sexual encounter with Judah (Gen. 38:24) and for the immoral practice of Jezebel (2 Kings 9:22). It is used metaphorically for Israel's infidelity in the prophetic literature. A significant part of the Holiness Code in Leviticus 17–26 is the demonstration that holiness involves separation from the sexual practices of others. Laws on forbidden relationships play an important role in the Holiness Code.

Prohibition of *porneia* is especially evident in the Wisdom literature and Jewish paraenesis. Sirach speaks of the woman who leaves her husband as one who "disobeyed the law of the Most High" and "through . . . fornication (*porneia*) has committed adultery" (23:23 NRSV). The unfaithfulness of a wife (*porneia gynaikos*) is characterized by haughty eyes (Sir. 26:9). According to Wisdom 14:12, "the idea of making idols is the beginning of *porneia*." In Jewish paraenesis, the prohibition of *porneia* has a central role. Tobit advises his son, "Beware . . . of every kind of fornication" (4:12 NRSV).

The command "to abstain from fornication" (*apechesthai apo tēs porneias*) is probably a commonplace in early Christian paraenesis. According to Acts 15:20, the apostolic council decreed that new converts "abstain from fornication." Jesus lists it as a vice in a conversation with the Pharisees (Mark 7:21). The author of Hebrews indicates that marriage is the appropriate status for believers, inasmuch as God will punish "the sexually immoral and adulterers" (*pornoi* and *moichoi*, 13:4). The author of 1 Peter instructs new converts to "abstain from fleshly lusts" (1 Pet. 2:11).

The prohibition of *porneia* appears in all of Paul's paraeneses. Although the term is not used in Romans (*akatharsia* is the preferred term, 1:24; 6:19), Paul describes the enslavement to the sexual passions as an example of the ungodliness and unrighteousness of idolaters (Rom. 1:18–32). Those who submit to God's righteousness in the new aeon put away the sexual vices (Rom. 6:1–23; 13:11–13). In the Corinthian letters, Paul assumes that the readers include those who were formerly *pornoi* (1 Cor. 6:9). In his previous letter

---

31. BDAG 854.

(1 Cor. 5:9), he instructed the readers not to mingle with sexually immoral people (*pornoi*). He instructs them at length on *porneia* in 1 Corinthians (6:12–20) because this vice has remained among community members (5:1). As he concludes 2 Corinthians, he expresses anxiety that *porneia* is still in their midst. At the beginning of the works of the flesh in Galatians 5:19 is *porneia*. The advice continues in the paraenesis of Ephesians and Colossians, as Paul instructs both communities to reject *porneia* along with other vices (Eph. 5:3; Col. 3:5).

Paul elaborates on the prohibition of *porneia* with an extended sentence in 1 Thessalonians 4:3–6 describing *porneia* in positive and negative clauses. The main clause, "This is the will of God, your sanctification," is followed by a series of subordinate clauses introduced by infinitives. "To abstain from fornication" defines *hagiasmos*, and the following clauses further define *porneia*. Parallel clauses in verses 4 and 6 give a positive and negative elaboration on *porneia*. "To know to take a vessel in holiness and honor" is further defined by "not in the passion of lust like the pagans who do not know God." The negative parallel in 4:6 is "not to transgress and take advantage of your brother in this matter," which has the subordinate clause "because the Lord is an avenger in all these things" (NRSV).[32] The inclusio in 4:3, 7 also suggests that all of 4:3–8 is an elaboration on *porneia*, for Paul summarizes that God has not called them to *akatharsia*, but to *hagiasmos*. The latter phrase forms an inclusio with *hagiasmos* and *porneia* in 4:3. *Akatharsia* (4:7) is commonly either a synonym for *porneia* or used in conjunction with it. Paul indicates the motivation in 4:7–8, relating the sexual instructions to their original calling (cf. 2:12). The added conclusion in 4:8 indicates that, because God is the one who has called the community, any rejection of the moral instructions is a rejection of God. Thus, although Paul does not cite Old Testament Scriptures, his instructions are clearly drawn from them.

Because Paul speaks in cryptic terms, the meaning of *porneia* in 1 Thessalonians 4:4–6 is scarcely clear to modern interpreters. In the two major dependent clauses he speaks with an ambiguity that has perplexed interpreters for centuries. Translators dispute the meaning of both *skeuos ktasthai* (4:4, literally "take a vessel") and *pleonektein . . . ton adelphon* (4:6, literally "defraud the brother"). This perplexity is evident in the modern translations. According to the NEB, NIV, and NRSV, Paul instructs each one to "control (NEB 'gain mastery over') his own (NRSV 'your own') body," while the RSV renders "that each of you know how to take a wife for himself." The central issue is the meaning of the metaphor *skeuos*, which literally means "vessel" or "instrument,"[33] but is commonly used as a metaphor for human beings in general (Acts 9:15; Rom. 9:21–22; 2 Tim. 2:20–21), the human body (2 Cor.

---

32. Burke says that v. 6 is resumptive (*Family Matters*, 182).
33. BDAG 927.

4:7), the penis,[34] or a wife (1 Pet. 3:7).[35] Those who interpret *skeuos* as anything other than "wife" render the verb *ktasthai* as "control." Although both "control the body" and "take a wife" as translations are both ancient, several reasons make the latter more compelling. In the first place, the common rendering of *ktasthai* is "acquire" or "get."[36] It is frequently used for financial gain (cf. Matt.10:9; Luke 18:12; 21:19; Acts 1:18; 22:28). Although the Pauline expression *skeuos ktasthai* is unknown in other texts, the similar expression "take a wife" (*ktasthai gynaika*) is attested (Sir. 36:29; Ruth 4:5).[37] Furthermore, *ktasthai* is frequently used in ancient Greek sources for the acquiring of a wife.[38] In the second place, numerous parallels suggest that *skeuos* is a common metaphor for a wife (cf. 1 Pet. 3:7). Third, Paul's elaboration in 1 Corinthians 7:2, in which he instructs each man to take a wife as the alternative to *porneia*, is probably a commentary on the earlier instruction in 1 Thessalonians 4:3. Thus Paul describes marriage as the alternative to *porneia*. This view of marriage is common in Jewish paraenesis.

Paul's instruction "not to transgress and take advantage of (*pleonektein*) the brother in this matter (*pragmati*)" is also unclear within the larger context of instructions on sexual morality. *Pleonektein* and the related terms *pleonektēs* and *pleonexia* are most frequently associated with financial exploitation and cheating (cf. 2 Cor. 7:2; 12:17–18). The root meaning, "to increase the number,"[39] concerns those who want more than is their due; thus it is a comprehensive term for greed or covetousness.[40] While the word most frequently has financial associations, it can be used as a generic term for "defraud" (cf. 2 Cor. 2:11). The parallel between "take a wife" and not "take advantage of the brother" raises the question: Has Paul introduced a second subject—greed—into the context?

To introduce two topics in one passage, as Paul does in 1 Thessalonians 4:3–7, would not be unusual in Jewish and Pauline paraenesis. In Jewish paraenesis, sexual sins and covetousness appear together frequently as the vices

---

34. Ibid. This view is held by Reese, *1 and 2 Thessalonians*, 44; Whitton, "A Neglected Meaning of *SKEUOS* in 1 Thessalonians 4.4," 142–43; Bruce, *1 & 2 Thessalonians*, 83–84. Elgvin argues, on the basis of a paraenetic text from Qumran, that "our text uses *skeuos* as a euphemism for the male organ, as is done twice in 1 Sam. 21:6," and that *skeuos* is a common image for the penis in both Greek and Jewish sources ("'To Master His Own Vessel'"). Smith adds supporting evidence for this view ("Another Look at 4Q416 2 ii.21, a Critical Parallel to First Thessalonians 4:4").

35. BDAG 928.

36. BDAG 572.

37. R. Collins, "'This Is the Will of God,'" 313.

38. Burke cites Xenophon, *Symp.* (2:10), in which Socrates responded to those who questioned his marriage to Xanthippe: "I have got her (*tautēn kektēmai*) well assured that if I can endure her, I will have no difficulty in my relations with the rest of humankind" (*Family Matters*, 188). He cites also the *Collectio Vindobonensis*, in which the sage Cleoboulos said, "Marry someone like yourself, for if you marry someone superior to yourself, you will obtain (*ktēsē*) a ruler and not a partner" (ibid.).

39. BDAG 824.

40. Ibid.

to be avoided. A survey of similar literature in both Paul and the Jewish tradition indicates that sexual morality and greed were often listed together, but as separate categories (1 Cor. 5:10; 6:9–10; cf. Mark 7:21–22; Rom. 1:27–29; Eph. 4:19; Col. 3:5). Paul's inclusion of lawsuits over financial matters within the larger framework of sexual morality (1 Cor. 6:1–20) may also suggest the close association of sexual and financial vices.[41] Both vices are commonplace in Pauline lists of vices (1 Cor. 5:10; 6:9–10; cf. Eph. 4:19; 5:3; Col. 3:5). Jewish paraenesis often connects them as well. In the *Testament of Judah* the patriarch instructs the children "not to love money or to gaze on the beauty of women" (17:1) and to guard themselves against *porneia* and the love of money (18:2). While the two vices are frequently treated separately, they are also treated together as summaries of two commands of the Decalogue.

Although the prohibition of sexual immorality and greed is commonplace in Pauline and Jewish paraenesis, the structure of 1 Thessalonians 4:3–7 suggests that Paul is addressing only one topic, elaborating on abstention from *porneia*: 4:3, 7 form an inclusio, and the expressions "take a wife" and not "take advantage of the brother" are parallel. Indeed, both phrases employ financial images in a sexual context to describe the relationship between the husband and the wife. The intimate relationships within the new family in the house church, where one brother might wrong another in sexual matters, presented a distinct temptation. Paul intends his advice to maintain the integrity of a new community. Thus *pleonektein* introduces not a new topic but a further elaboration on abstention from *porneia* and the "passion of lust." Those who avoid the "passion of lust" will not focus their lust on the wife of another. "Take advantage (*pleonektein*) of the brother" is parallel to "desire the wife (*epithymēseis tēn gynaika*) of the neighbor" in the Decalogue (Exod. 20:17). Thus Paul elaborates on the nature of *porneia* by paraphrasing two commandments of the Decalogue.

The difficulty of translating *skeuos ktasthai* in 4:4 has obscured the actual focus of Paul's instruction in 4:4–5, which is evident in the parallelism in the alternative between "in holiness and honor" (*en hagiasmō kai timē*) and "not in the passion of lust (*mē en pathei epithymias*) like the Gentiles who do not know God." The focus is on how to take a wife, echoing Jewish paraenesis, which speaks exclusively to men. Having provided the community with an identity as God's elect and holy people, Paul extends the sphere of holiness from the cult to matters of sexuality, distinguishing the holy people from the gentiles. "In holiness and honor" is the manner in which the husband relates to the wife, who is a member of the holy community. *Timē* suggests the honor given to one who, like oneself, belongs to the covenant community (cf. Rom. 12:10). The parallel expression in 1 Peter 3:7, according to which the role of the husband is to "pay honor to the woman as the weaker sex, since they too

41. Reinmuth, *Geist und Gesetz*, 18.

are also heirs of the gracious gift of life" (NRSV), suggests that the husband's honorable treatment of the wife is a theme of early Christian paraenesis. The identity of the people as family members and sanctified ones requires that they regard all, including wives, "with holiness and honor."

The meaning of "in holiness and honor" is further clarified by the parallel "not in the passion of lust like the gentiles who do not know God." Paul's reference to the "passion of lust" takes the conversation outside the halakic language based on the Holiness Code and into terminology that resonates with the conversations in the Greco-Roman world. Because the description of marriage without the "passion of lust" is elliptical—and disturbing to modern readers—interpreters have attempted to explain Paul's cryptic phrase by noting parallels in the Greco-Roman context, where the *pathē* (pl. of *pathos*), *epithymia*, and marriage are often discussed. Medical doctors spoke of the dangers of desires and recommended moderation in controlling them.[42] *Pathos* ("emotion" or "passion"; used elsewhere in Paul only in Rom. 1:26; Col. 3:5) is probably derived from the Stoics, who defined it as an irrational and unnatural movement of the soul.[43] Stoics considered *epithymia*, one of the *pathē*, a craving devoid of reason.[44] Thus Stoics strove to bring the desires for food and sex under control (see ch. 6, "Overcoming the Passions in Antiquity").

Ancient writers were particularly concerned about the dangers associated with sexual desire. According to Seneca, sexual desire is a lack of control, like slavery (*Ep.* 116.5).[45] The Stoics also believed that desire is a disease and that good health requires overcoming the passions (Seneca, *Ep.* 85.3–4; 116).[46] Consequently, the subject of whether to marry became a major theme. They warned against marrying because of a woman's beauty and thus becoming a slave of pleasure.[47] Within marriage, sexual intercourse was only for the sake of procreation.

These themes also appear in the literature of Hellenistic Judaism, where Jews in the Diaspora attempted to apply the demands of the Torah among the "gentiles who do not know God." Philo assumes that sexual intercourse is for the purpose of procreation. He speaks of those who are "pleasure-lovers when they mate with their wives, not to procreate children and perpetuate the race, but like pigs and goats in quest of the enjoyment which intercourse gives" (*Spec. Laws* 3.113). Similarly, he maintains that a man should not touch a woman during her menstruation, but should "respect the law of nature" (*Spec. Laws* 3.32), arguing that "it is just as if a husbandman should in intoxication

42. Martin, "Paul without Passion," 205.
43. Malherbe, *The Letters to the Thessalonians*, 229.
44. Vögtle, "Affekt," 162.
45. Cited in Martin, "Paul without Passion," 205.
46. Cited in Burke, *Family Matters*, 192.
47. *SVF* 3.254, 7; 256, 3–4; Musonius Rufus, frag. 13B; Hierocles, *On Duties* (Stobaeus, *Anthology* 4.22, 24; 4.506, 15; [Hense]). Cited in Malherbe, *Thessalonians*, 230.

or lunacy sow wheat and barley in ponds or mountain-streams instead of in the plains" (3.32). He also argues that one should not marry women whose sterility has already been proved with other husbands, for such people "copulate like pigs or goats" (3.36). However, while Philo follows the Stoic view that marriage is only for procreation, he speaks disapprovingly of those who "retain no conjugal affection for their wives," but "treat these gentlewomen as if they were harlots" (3.80).

Other Jewish writers of the Diaspora share Philo's views. Tobias prays on his wedding night, "I now am taking this kinswoman of mine, not because of lust (*porneia*), but with sincerity" (Tob. 8:7 NRSV). The Wisdom of Solomon describes the gentiles who do not keep their marriages pure (14:24) and engage in adultery and debauchery (14:24–26). Pseudo-Phocylides instructs young men:

> Do not outrage (your) wife by shameful ways of intercourse.
> Do not transgress with unlawful sex the limits set by nature
> . . . . . . . . . . . . . . . . . . . . . . . . . . . . . . . . . . . . . . . . . . . . . . . .
> Do not surrender wholly to unbridled sensuality toward (your) wife.
> For erōs is not a god, but a passion destructive of all
> Love your own wife, for what is sweeter and better than whenever a wife is
> kindly disposed toward (her) husband and a husband toward (his) wife. (189–96)

While Paul's advice belongs to the ancient conversation on the "passion of lust" within marriage, he neither shares the assumptions of the Stoics nor offers the specific advice associated with the Stoic view of marriage. He does not limit the purpose of sexual intercourse to procreation. Indeed, in his clarification of the instruction in 1 Corinthians 7:3–4, a commentary on the instructions in 1 Thessalonians 4:4, he speaks of a mutual obligation for regular sexual intercourse, reflecting the law's view of conjugal rights (1 Cor. 7:3–4; cf. Exod. 21:10). Nor does he give the extended instructions that Philo offers in prohibiting the passion of lust. Indeed, his instruction may echo Philo's condemnation of those who treat their wives as a harlot or *Sentences of Pseudo-Phocylides*'s commands against the sexual abuse of the wife.

Paul's primary concern is not to define the meaning of the "passion of lust," but to distinguish the behavior of new converts from "the gentiles who do not know God." Sharing the Jewish view of gentile morality, he portrays the gentiles as enslaved to passion (Rom. 1:24–25) as they dishonor their bodies in a variety of ways. Thus the "passion of lust" can refer to all sexual desires for the satisfaction of the self.[48] Such slavery would involve promiscuity and the abuse of one's wife. Although Paul gives no indication that he holds to modern romantic concepts of sexual passion in marriage (cf. 1 Cor. 7:1–7), he

---

48. Schlier, *Der Apostel und seine Gemeinde*, 66; Schrage, "Heiligung als Prozess bei Paulus," 212.

is less concerned with the "passionless sex" of the Stoics than with the control of the passions and the avoidance of gentile sexual morality.

In the conclusion in 4:7–8, which forms an inclusio with 4:3, Paul provides the foundation and motivation for the ethical instructions on sexuality, as *gar* indicates (4:7). The foundation for Paul's ethical instruction is the church's place within the story of Israel, for God's call (cf. 1:5; 2:12) is a summons to sanctification, which is evident in sexual practices that distinguish them from "the gentiles" (4:5). *Akatharsia* ("impurity," 4:7), which forms the inclusio with *porneia* (4:3), has a sexual connotation and is the alternative to holiness. The focus of the motivation is the work of God. Thus, while Paul cites no Scripture, he identifies the commands as God's. The comment that "one who rejects does not reject man but God" (4:8) corresponds to the introductory "this is the will of God" (4:3). According to 4:7–8, God worked in the past as he "called" (*ekalesen*) the community at their conversion, and he works in the present "giving [them] the Holy Spirit," who has been active in the community since its beginning (1:5). Thus God not only commands, but equips the community to obey the divine will through the Holy Spirit.

This foundation for ethics anticipates Paul's argument in the later epistles. He reminds the Corinthians that they were "washed," "justified," and "sanctified" in the Holy Spirit (1 Cor. 6:11), and he insists that the people abstain from *porneia* because the body is "the temple of the Holy Spirit" (1 Cor. 6:19). Indeed, the Holy Spirit is the source of power by which the people overcome enslavement to the passions (Rom. 8:1–11; Gal. 5:16–25).

In his claim that the Spirit gives them power to overcome the passions, Paul presupposes the exilic expectation of the time when God would pour out the Spirit. According to Ezekiel 11:19, when God provides a "new spirit" and a new heart at Israel's restoration, God's people will "keep [his] ordinances and obey them" (11:20 NRSV). God says, "I will put my spirit within you, and make you follow my statutes and be careful to observe my ordinances" (Ezek. 36:27 NRSV). This expectation parallels Jeremiah's prophecy of a new covenant in which Israel will keep the commandments (Jer. 31:31–34). Thus Paul places the new Thessalonian Christians within Israel's narrative world, according to which Paul will empower the people to keep the commandments. The specific commandment derives from Israel's Holiness Code (Lev. 18). This recalls Ezekiel 37:14 as well as 36:27 (see above; see also ch. 6).

### *Brotherly Love (4:9–12)*

With the introduction of *philadelphia* in 4:9–12, Paul turns to a second dimension of the holiness for which he has prayed (3:13). Inasmuch as both *porneia* and *philadelphia* were topics of Paul's original catechesis (4:2, 6, 9, 11), he is probably not responding to a crisis, but reinforcing his earlier teaching, challenging the readers to "increase and abound" (3:12; 4:2, 10) in the behavior that has distinguished them already. Indeed, Paul's thanksgiving for their "labor of love" (1:3) and Timothy's report of their "faith and love" (3:6) indicate the progress that the Thessalonians have already made. Thus he indicates that he has no need to write about the topic, for they have been "taught by God to love one another" (4:9 NRSV) and they are extending their love throughout Macedonia (4:10). The prayer for their increase in love (3:12), which anticipates the call for *philadelphia* in 4:9, indicates both the divine element and the continued process in the Thessalonians' moral formation as they prepare for the parousia of Christ (3:13).

Paul has also anticipated the encouragement to practice *philadelphia* in the consistent use of family language in the letter. Indeed, the counsel not to "wrong the brother" in sexual matters (4:6) provides a transition to Paul's advice on *philadelphia*. He elaborates on *philadelphia*, equating it with the instruction to "love one another" (*agapan allēlous*). Having prayed that God would cause their love "for one another" to increase and abound (3:12), he instructs the readers to love one another "more and more" (4:10).

In both 1 Thessalonians (1:3; 3:12) and other letters, *agapē* is an abbreviated form of *agapan allēlous* and the central category of Paul's ethics. Paul does not use the more common Greek word *philanthrōpia*, but employs the term that fits within the family setting, indicating regularly that the community exercises *agapē* toward each other. Every one of Paul's letters places *agapē* at the center of his ethics (Rom. 1–13; 14:15; 1 Cor. 8:1; 13; 16:14; 2 Cor. 2:8; 8:24; Gal. 5:6, 13, 22).

The call to "love one another" is known in the LXX only in 4 Maccabees 13:24 but is common in the *Testaments of the Twelve Patriarchs* (*T. Jos.* 17:2; *T. Zeb.*; *T. Sim.* 4:4). This instruction apparently belongs to Paul's catechesis in all of the churches, for he repeats this phrase (cf. Rom. 13:8) and variations of it throughout his letters (Rom. 12:10, *tē philadelphia eis allēlous*; cf. Gal. 5:13, *dia agapēs douleuete allēlous*). Indeed, Paul shares this focus with the paraenetic tradition of the early church (cf. John 13:34; 15:12, 17; 1 Pet. 1:22). In each instance, the object of love is the community, the new family.

Paul extends familial love beyond the local house church, including "all of the brothers in Macedonia" (4:10), suggesting that the family includes some whom the members have never met. Nevertheless, as Paul has indicated earlier (1:7–8), the new family extends to a wider circle of communities. The congregations probably extended hospitality and provide financial support to each other in times of crisis.

Paul's appeal to brotherly love is rooted in the interpretation of Leviticus 19:18, as he indicates in Romans 13:8–10 and Galatians 5:13–14. Like the author of the *Testaments of the Twelve Patriarchs*, Paul moves from the Levitical command to love the neighbor to the love within the family. Whereas Leviticus 19:18 and the subsequent tradition assumed that the object of love was the fellow Israelite, Paul indicates that the object is the member of the new family. He extends love toward "all the brothers in Macedonia."

Paul uses *philadelphia* in a metaphorical sense in one other instance (cf. Rom. 12:10) and shares this term with the early Christian paraenetic tradition (cf. Heb. 13:1; 1 Pet. 1:22; 3:8; 2 Pet. 1:7).[49] In contrast to *porneia* (4:3–8), *philadelphia* appears in the LXX only in 4 Maccabees (13:23, 26; 14:1; cf. *philadelphos* in 2 Macc. 15:14; 4 Macc. 13:21; 15:10), and it appears rarely in other Jewish literature (Josephus, *J. W.* 1.275, 485; Philo, *Embassy* 92). Although the word does not appear frequently in Greek literature, it has an important place in Greek life. Three cities in the ancient world were called *Philadelphia*, and the epithet *philadelphos* was used by Ptolemaic rulers.[50] Greek writers held *philadelphia* in high regard, employing the term for the solidarity and mutual care of siblings for each other.[51] In Greek literature *philadelphia* refers to the care of actual siblings for each other. While *philadelphia* was discussed by ethicists, Plutarch's work on *philadelphia* is the only completely extant text from antiquity on the subject.[52]

Although *philadelphia* does not appear in the LXX outside 4 Maccabees, both the writer of this document and that of the *Testaments of the Twelve Patriarchs* integrate this term from Hellenistic moral philosophy in describing a life in conformity to Torah. The seven brothers of 4 Maccabees are both faithful to Torah and exemplars of *philadelphia*. The author describes the roots of their brotherly love with a series of compounds formed with *syn*. They were nourished with the same mother's milk. Because of their brotherly affection, the seven young men demonstrated sympathy (*sympathesteron*) for one another (4 Macc. 13:23). Because they were educated in the same law, "they loved each other all the more" (13:24). The zeal for nobility that they held in common strengthened their "good will and concord" (13:25), leading them to encourage each other when confronted by torture (4 Macc. 14:1).[53]

The author of 4 Maccabees incorporates themes from Hellenistic moral philosophy into his understanding from Torah, taking over *philadelphia* as a topos from Hellenistic literature. His description of brotherly love shares themes with Plutarch's essay on the subject. For both the author of 4 Maccabees and Plutarch, *philadelphia* involves goodwill and concord (cf. *Frat. amor.* 478F). The former, with Plutarch (481B), recalls that brotherly love is rooted in common parentage and education.

In linking *porneia* with *philadelphia* in paraenesis, Paul follows the tradition of Hellenistic Judaism and its use of the Holiness Code in Leviticus. The

---

49. Cf. 1 John 2:10: "The one who loves his brother"; 1 John 3:15: "the one who hates his brother."

50. Aasgaard, *'My Beloved Brothers and Sisters!,'* 71.

51. Söding, *Liebesgebot bei Paulus*, 74.

52. Aasgaard, *'My Beloved Brothers and Sisters!,'* 93.

53. Klauck, *Alte Welt und neuer Glaube*, 94.

paraeneses in the *Testaments of the Twelve Patriarchs* focus on matters of sexuality and brotherly love particularly clearly, consistently presenting Joseph as the model of both chastity and brotherly love, and the older brothers as having violated either one or both of these commandments. Summaries of the law in Hellenistic Judaism also brought these two commandments together, following the pattern of Leviticus 18–19, which prohibits forbidden sexual activity and then commands love for the neighbor. Paul's instruction differs from these other writings, however, in its metaphorical use of *philadelphia* to designate the fictive kinship of his community.

In 4:9–12 Paul elaborates his conception of *philadelphia* so as to show the distinctive features it has in his paraenesis. First he introduces *philadelphia* and equates it with the command "to love one another" (*agapan allēlous*), which the Thessalonians have been "taught by God" and currently fulfill throughout Macedonia (4:10). The expression "taught by God" is parallel to the "will of God" in 4:3. Although the phrase probably derives from the prophetic tradition (Isa. 54:13; Jer. 31:33–34), Paul is likely alluding to the love command in Leviticus 19:18. He then encourages (*parakaloumen*, 4:10; cf. 4:1) them to continue to abound in love, adding specific instructions in 4:11–12. The parallel infinitives "to abound" (*perisseuein*) in love and "to make it your ambition" (*philotimeisthai*)[54] indicate that the following specific instructions describe aspects of love. The three infinitives "to live quietly" (*hēsychazein*), "to tend to your own affairs" (*prassein ta idia*), and "to work with your hands" (*ergazesthai tais chersin*) correspond to ethical values known in both Greek and Jewish literature.[55] However, the general heading of *philadelphia* and the combination of these infinitives indicate Paul's distance from the Stoic conversations about *hēsychia* and manual labor, for Paul is describing the essentials of community life. "To live quietly" (*hēsychazein*) is to refrain from activity that disrupts the peace and tranquility of community life.[56] Those who fail to live in *hēsychia* refuse to stay at home (cf. Prov. 7:11), but meddle in affairs that are not their own.[57] In 2 Thessalonians 3:11–12, Paul describes those who live in idleness (*ataktōs*) as people who refuse to work and insists that they work with *hēsychia*. When Paul was in Thessalonica, he was a model of this conduct (1 Thess. 2:9; cf. 1 Cor. 4:9), for he also worked with his hands and insisted that the new converts follow his example (1 Thess. 4:11).

Inasmuch as Paul's ethical instructions repeat his previous catechesis (4:11), one may not assume that he is confronted with a crisis over the refusal of some of the members to work, as in 2 Thessalonians 3:11–12.

---

54. *Philotimeisthai* refers not only to a special effort, but a zealous engagement in a task in which one places one's honor at risk (cf. Rom. 15:20; 2 Cor. 5:9). Söding, *Liebesgebot bei Paulus*, 85.

55. Söding, *Liebesgebot bei Paulus*, 85–86; Malherbe, "Hellenistic Moralists in the New Testament," 321.

56. BDAG 440.

57. Spicq, *"Hēsychazō," TLNT* 2:181.

The intimacy of community life and the practice of brotherly love probably led to an outpouring of generosity within the community, creating a temptation for some to be "disorderly" (*ataktoi*, 5:14). Having instilled in his new converts a corporate consciousness as a family, Paul indicates that the practice of familial love requires members not to burden the family, but to contribute to its well-being.

Although manual labor is a common theme in Greco-Roman philosophy, Paul's instructions have a firm place in Jewish literature. The Decalogue mandates, "Six days you shall labor" (Exod. 20:9). The Wisdom literature frequently reminds the people of the dangers of idleness and the importance of working with the hands (Prov. 6:6–11; 24:30–34; 28:19; Sir. 7:15).[58] In the *Testament of Issachar*, the patriarch instructs his children not to meddle in the neighbor's affairs, but to "love the Lord and your neighbor," to be compassionate, and to "bend your back in farming" (5:1–3). The author of the *Sentences of Pseudo-Phocylides* places the instructions on manual labor alongside instructions for marriage and family life (153–74). Thus Paul follows established Jewish paraenetic traditions in placing manual labor alongside the love of neighbor and the instructions for family life.

The command to work appears elsewhere in Pauline paraenesis only in Ephesians 4:28 and 2 Thessalonians 3:11–12. Paul may have a special reason for repeating his instructions on manual labor in 1 Thessalonians, as the motivation in 4:12 suggests. By their conversion the Thessalonians (1:9–10) have provoked hostility from the larger society (1:6; 2:14) and been prompted to create an alternative family of those who care for each other and adopt moral conduct that distinguishes them from "the gentiles who do not know God" (4:5), whom Paul also describes as "outsiders" (4:12). Inasmuch as outsiders commonly criticize the morality of Christians, one may assume that the Thessalonians faced the same problem as they lived "in the eyes of outsiders" (*pros tous exō*).[59] Here Paul insists that *philadelphia*, expressed by living quietly and working with the hands, will correspond to values that the outsiders will approve.

### Expressions of Love (4:13–5:25)

That Paul gives few specific examples of *philadelphia* suggests that he has already acquainted the readers with the specific conduct that expresses their love for one another. In subsequent letters, Paul will appeal to the demand for love in situations of conflict and give more concrete examples of familial love (Rom. 12:1–15:13; 1 Cor. 5:1–14:40). He probably has in mind all the duties normally associated with the extended family in antiquity. Christians

58. See Van der Horst, *Sentences of Pseudo-Phocylides*, 216.

59. Malherbe, *Thessalonians*, 251. Cf. Best: "in the judgment of the outsiders" (*The 1st and 2nd Epistles to the Thessalonians*, 170).

care for the sick, receive strangers into their homes, provide financial support, and comfort those who are bereaved.

Although the exhortations to the community in 4:13–5:25 offer examples of the practice of familial love, the list is not exhaustive, for it appears in expanded form in Romans 12:1–15:13. Indeed, inasmuch as most of the exhortations in 1 Thessalonians 5:12–25 appear also in Romans 12 and 1 Peter 3:8–12, one may assume that Paul is drawing on a common stock of Jewish paraenetic traditions, some of which also appear in the gospel tradition. Thus he is probably not responding to specific circumstances, but repeating the catechesis that he gave to the Thessalonians at their conversion.

In 4:13–5:25, Paul describes both reciprocal responsibilities among the members and obligations toward specific groups within the church family that are necessary for building up the community. He first expands on "steadfastness of hope" (1:3) as the characteristic of Christian existence (4:13–5:11), placing it within the context of the mandate "Encourage one another" (*parakaleite allēlous*, 4:18; 5:11) and "build one another up" (*oikodomeisthe eis ton hena*, 5:11) in view of the Lord's return. The community thus takes on the role of pastoral care, expressing their love to one another by mutual encouragement. Paul's community ethic reflects the familial context of the church.

Paul's community-centered ethic is evident in the barrage of paraenetic instructions in 5:12–22. Because family life necessitates the role of leaders, members of the community should "know" (*eidenai*) and "recognize" (*hēgeisthai*) those who are laboring (*kopiōntes*), leading (*proistamenous*), and admonishing (*nouthetountas*). Indeed, brotherly love extends to the leaders who have emerged, for Paul encourages the readers to regard them "in love" (*en agapē*) because of their work (cf. 1 Cor. 16:16).

The imperative "Be at peace among yourselves" (*eirēneuete en heautois*) further delineates the concrete expression of love, for to live in love is to avoid the wrangling and strife that undermines community life and to acknowledge those who lead. This challenge to "be at peace" is a standard feature of early Christian paraenesis. Paul elaborates on the meaning of *agapē* in Romans, indicating that the kingdom is "righteousness and peace and joy in the Holy Spirit" (14:17), concluding with the exhortation, "Let us pursue the things for peace and the things for building one another up" (14:19). The fact that "God is not a God of disorder but of peace" (1 Cor. 14:33 NRSV) determines the orderliness of the assembly (1 Cor. 14:17). Similarly, he lists joy and peace after *agapē* in describing the fruit of the Spirit (Gal. 5:22).

The imperative "Be at peace" echoes two wisdom sayings of the gospel tradition, Matthew 5:9a (*makarioi hoi eirēnopoioi*) and Mark 9:50 (*eirēneuete en allēlois*). The phrase *diōkō eirēnēn*, which Paul shares with the author of Hebrews (12:14), was apparently an idiom in Jewish-Christian circles, perhaps derived from Psalm 34:14 (NRSV), "Seek peace, and pursue it." The Wisdom literature places high priority on the peaceable life, contrasting it with the anticommunal activities of those who gossip (Sir. 28:13) or sow discord (Sir. 28:9). Thus Paul appeals to an established paraenetic tradition to encourage his readers to make peace by recognizing the legitimate work of leaders rather than undermining their work through factious behavior.

According to 5:14–15, brotherly love involves not only communal recognition of those who lead, but the sharing of their responsibilities through care for those who are in special need within the community and the proper behavior toward outsiders. Although community members recognize those who admonish, they themselves admonish the disorderly (*ataktoi*). *Nouthetein* ("admonish") is constructive criticism that commonly belongs to the setting of the family, where either the father "admonishes" (cf. 1 Cor. 4:14) or siblings admonish each other (cf. Rom. 15:14; Col. 1:28; 3:16; 2 Thess. 3:15).[60] This fraternal correction is an expression of the love command, as Leviticus 19:17–18 indicates.[61] The disorderly undermine the peace established by the leaders of the church, sow discord, and free themselves from the discipline of community life. Thus they disturb the peace of the community.[62]

The parallel imperatives "comfort the fainthearted" and "bear with the weak" are also expressions of brotherly love, as Paul turns from the insubordinate to the marginalized within the community. The "fainthearted" are probably those who are discouraged (cf. Sir. 7:10) by the pressures from a hostile society. The parallelism between "fainthearted" and "weak" suggests that the latter are weak in faith. Paul employs *asthenēs* in a variety of ways, always indicating that the strong should have special deference for the weak because of love. To "comfort" (*paramytheisthe*) is to continue the pastoral work initiated by Paul himself (1 Thess. 2:12). To comfort and bear with the fainthearted and weak is to ensure that they remain within the community.

Although Paul's moral instruction focuses primarily on familial love, he extends this communal care to the wider society, indicating that communal care is not limited to those who are within the family. Just as Paul has prayed that God increase the community's love "for one another and for all" (3:12 NRSV), he encourages the community to "be patient toward all" (*makrothymeite pros pantas*), making the transition to the command to "pursue the good to one another and to all" (5:15). Familial love, therefore, extends to the wider society.

*Makrothymia* has a special place in Jewish moral instruction. It is the distinguishing attribute of God (Num. 14:18; Ps. 86:15; 145:8; *Odes* 12:7; Rom. 2:4), who is slow to anger in response to Israel's offenses. Jewish Wisdom

60. See Spicq, "*Nouthesia*," *TLNT* 2:550–51.
61. Söding, *Liebesgebot bei Paulus*, 78. See also Prov. 25:9–10; 27:5–6; 28:23; Deut. 25:1.
62. *Atak-* appears only here and in 2 Thess. 3:6, 11. Although translators commonly translate it as "idle," it has the meaning of "not remaining in his/her/its place, out of order, undisciplined." It could be used for those who live unshackled by moral norms (Diodorus Siculus 1.8.1), or it could refer to rebels, the disobedient, insurgents, or troublemakers. See Spicq, "*Atakteō*," *TLNT* 1:225–26.

literature praised individuals who were "slow to anger" (Prov. 14:29; 15:18; 16:32), indicating that the hot tempered stir up strife. In listing his own personal qualities, Paul speaks of his own patience (2 Cor. 6:6) and includes it in his ethical instruction (Gal. 5:22; cf. Eph. 4:2; 2 Tim. 3:10; 4:2). Indeed, one of the characteristics of *agapē* is that it "is patient" (*makrothymei*, 1 Cor. 13:4). Thus patience with others is one dimension of the love that binds the new family together.

The emphasis on patience "with all" marks the transition to those who do evil to the believers (1 Thess. 5:15). Although the command "Do not render evil for evil" may refer to circumstances in Thessalonica, parallels to the admonition are present in both Hellenistic and Jewish literature,[63] and are derived from the Old Testament and Jewish paraenesis, which became the common stock of early Christian paraenesis. An almost identical injunction appears in *Joseph and Aseneth* 28:4: "Do not return evil for evil to any person." This passage may be based on Proverbs 17:13: "Whoever returns evil for good, evil shall not be removed from his house." Paul gives an almost identical instruction in Romans 12:17. Inasmuch as similar injunctions appear in the Synoptic tradition (Matt. 5:43–48) and 1 Peter (2:18–25; 3:8–9), one may conclude that Paul drew on the common stock of early Christian paraenesis, which was derived from the Wisdom literature.

### Conclusion: The Template for Paul's Moral Instructions

As the restatement of Paul's catechesis for new converts, 1 Thessalonians contains the basic template for Paul's moral instructions. While he expands and interprets these instructions in later epistles (cf. 1 Cor. 5:9–10), his focus on sexual morality and love among siblings remains the consistent feature of his moral teaching. The believers who accept these instructions will become a cohesive community, for this conduct will distinguish insiders from outsiders. Paul's work of community formation was preceded by the Jewish writers of the Diaspora, who interpreted the Torah for their circumstances, emphasizing sexual morality and communal responsibility. Although Paul's communities do not share the ethnic identity of Diaspora communities, they come from a variety of backgrounds into a common identity and a common ethic. The community's moral behavior is the expression of its identity within Israel's narrative world.

---

63. For Hellenistic parallels, see Söding, *Liebesgebot bei Paulus*, 81; Wilson, *Love without Pretense*, 187.

# 4

# Pauline Catechesis and the Lists of Vices and Virtues

Paul undoubtedly reiterated only a small portion of his original catechesis in 1 Thessalonians. One may assume that his catechesis included both confessional (cf. 1 Thess. 4:14) and ethical traditions (1 Thess. 4:1–5:22).[1] His comments in other letters reminding the readers of moral instruction that they have already received indicate that to that original teaching he added moral instruction in the form of lists. He introduces the vice list in 1 Corinthians 6:9 with the question, "Do you not know that the unrighteous will not inherit the kingdom of God?" The question suggests that the Corinthians are familiar with the vices that Paul mentions. Following the vice list in Galatians 5:19–21, he adds, "just as I told you previously that those who do these things will not inherit the kingdom of God." The reference to the community's familiarity with the list of vices suggests that they played an important role in catechesis. The appearance of similar vice lists elsewhere (Rom. 1:18–32; 1 Cor. 5:10; 2 Cor. 12:20–21) indicates that Paul continued to use them. Inasmuch as he provided no thorough case law regulating conduct, he probably used the vice lists to sum up his moral expectations for gentiles incorporated into the communities. The brevity of the lists indicates that they were only illustrations of the vices to be avoided and the virtues to be adopted.[2] Since the lists in Paul overlap but are not uniform, one may conclude that he draws on a larger pool of vices and virtues and adapts them for his audience. As we will note, the themes in the lists reflect a consistent view of the specific aspects of the Christian existence.

1. See Dunn, *Unity and Diversity in the New Testament*, 66–69.
2. Malherbe, *Moral Exhortation*, 138.

Although vice lists dominate Paul's catechesis, in some instances he also lists contrasting attributes that are appropriate for members of the community of believers (Gal. 5:22–23; Phil. 4:8) and indicates that he also embodies those attributes (2 Cor. 6:6). Twice in the undisputed letters (Gal. 5:22–23; Phil. 2:1–4) he places the list of positive attributes alongside a vice list, contrasting two modes of life and urging his readers to choose the correct path. The contrasting lists become a significant feature in Colossians and Ephesians in which the readers are urged to "put off," or "put to death," the vices (cf. Eph. 4:25; Col. 3:8) and "put on" (Eph. 4:24; Col. 3:12) the positive attributes. Paul indicates that these lists distinguish the communities from their larger society and their previous existence. This contrast between two modes of existence has analogies in both Greek literature and the Old Testament.

## Paul's Lists in the Greco-Roman Context

Scholars have observed that the form of the ethical list is rare in the Old Testament and a common feature in Greco-Roman ethical instruction.[3] Lists appear in rhetorical and astrological texts as well as epitaphs and inscriptions,[4] and they play an important role in philosophical discussion.[5] In exhortations to the moral life, philosophers used the lists of vices and virtues to distinguish between the healthy and diseased soul.[6]

The most prominent list in antiquity was the catalog of cardinal virtues attributed to Plato, which shaped the consciousness of a major portion of Greek ethical thought. In several dialogues (*Phaedr.* 69c; *Resp.* 427d–e; *Leg.* 631c; 963a), Plato lists wisdom (*sophia* or *phronēsis*), courage (*andreia*), self-control (*sōphrosynē*), and justice (*dikaiosynē*) as the four cardinal virtues (*aretai*).[7] For ancient writers each of the cardinal virtues was a form of knowledge, as is indicated by the common introduction of each of the virtues as *epistēmē*.[8] The four cardinal virtues later played an important role among the Stoics, who also divided them into subcategories.[9] Aristotle abandoned the fourfold form, adding other virtues to the list.[10]

---

3. Berger, *Formen und Gattungen im Neuen Testament*, 209.
4. See Zeller, "Konkrete Ethik," 84–85.
5. Ibid.
6. Malherbe, *Moral Exhortation*, 138.
7. See discussions in Ranieri, "Virtue," 15:458–59.
8. Cf. Stobaeus, *Ecl.* 2.59.4; *SVF* 3:262.
9. See Weber, *Das Gesetz im hellenistischen Judentum*. Stoic texts in Diogenes Laertius, *Vit.* 7.92.126 and in *SVF* 1.199–204; 3.255–94; 1.406 = Diogenes Laertius, *Vit.* 7.92; *SVF* 1.200 = Plutarch, *Stoic. rep.* 7; *SVF* 3.262, 264–66. See also Pohlenz, *Die Stoa*, for Chrysippus; and Wibbing, *Die Tugend- und Lasterkataloge im Neuen Testament*, 16.
10. Weber, *Das Gesetz im hellenistischen Judentum*, 349.

Greeks also named four cardinal vices (*kakiai*): folly (*aphrosynē*), intemperance (*akolasia*), injustice (*adikia*), and cowardice (*deilia*).[11] The cardinal vices were sometimes placed alongside the cardinal virtues (Stobaeus, *Ecl.* 2.59). Just as each of the cardinal virtues was a form of knowledge, the vices were regarded as a form of ignorance (*agnoia*). Alongside the tradition of the cardinal vices was the list of emotions delineated by Zeno: desire (*epithymia*), fear (*phobos*), grief (*lypē*), and pleasure (*hēdonē*). These were also subdivided into further categories.[12]

The Greek ethical tradition, as reflected in the cardinal virtues and vices, was primarily concerned with the well-being of the individual.[13] Philosophy provided the knowledge and skills by which one could attain *eudaimonia*. The individual could reach this goal only by overcoming those irrational forces that prevented one from acquiring the cardinal virtues, the path to human flourishing.

Hellenistic Jewish writers appropriated and adapted the list of four cardinal virtues.[14] The list appears once in Wisdom of Solomon (8:7) and many times in 4 Maccabees (1:1–6, 16–18; 5:23). Josephus indicates that the Torah incorporates the four cardinal virtues: "For he (Moses) did not make religion a department of virtue, but the entire complement of the virtues—I mean justice, temperance, fortitude and mutual harmony . . . departments of religion." Philo is an especially important witness to the Jewish incorporation of the cardinal virtues. In some instances he mentions them all: prudence (*phronēsis*), moderation (*sōphrosynē*), courage (*andreia*), and justice (*dikaiosynē*) (*Alleg. Interp.* 1.63; *Moses* 2.185; *QG* 1.12; *QE* 2.112); in other instances he replaces one or more of these. Philo claims that each of the Ten Commandments "separately and all in common drill and inculcate *phronēsis* and *dikaiosynē* and *theosebeia* (godliness) and the rest of the company of virtues" (*Spec. Laws* 4.134). He describes *eusebeia* and *hosiotēs* as "the queen of the virtues," placing them alongside *phronēsis* and *sōphrosynē*.[15] Philo claims that the commandments "drill and inculcate . . . the whole company of [Greek] virtues." Thus, like the authors of 4 Maccabees and Wisdom, Philo maintains that the life in obedience to the Torah will result in the practice of the cardinal virtues.

Hellenistic Jewish writers not only employed the Greek cardinal virtues, but also included expanded lists of vices and virtues. The Wisdom of Solomon not only indicates that wisdom is the source of the cardinal virtues (see above), but also describes the vices that result from ignorance. After describing the killing of children and the frenzied revels of the ignorant (14:23), the author adds, "They no longer keep either their lives or their marriages pure, but they either

---

11. Stobaeus, *Ecl.* 2.59, 40; *SVF* 3.63; see Fitzgerald, "Virtue/Vice Lists," 6:857.
12. Wibbing, *Tugend- und Lasterkataloge*, 17.
13. Ibid., 18.
14. See Fitzgerald, "Virtue/Vice Lists," 6:857.
15. Cohen, "The Greek Virtues and the Mosaic Laws in Philo," 10.

treacherously kill one another, or grieve one another by adultery, and all is a raging riot of blood and murder, theft and deceit, corruption, faithlessness, tumult, perjury, . . . defiling of souls, sexual perversion (*geneseōs enallagē*), disorder in marriages, adultery (*moicheia*), and debauchery (*aselgeia*)" (14:24–26 NRSV). Fourth Maccabees describes the malevolent tendency associated with pleasure, distinguishing between the tendencies of the body and soul (1:26–27). Those of the soul include boastfulness (*alazoneia*), covetousness (*philargyria*), thirst for honor (*philodoxia*), rivalry (*philoneikia*), and malice (*baskania*); in the body, indiscriminate eating (*pantophagia*), gluttony (*laimargia*), and "solitary gormandizing" (*monophagia*).

Vice lists play an important role in the *Testaments of the Twelve Patriarchs*. In the *Testament of Reuben*, the patriarch lists the "spirits of error" (3:1) as promiscuity, insatiability in the stomach, strife, flattery, trickery, arrogance, lying, rivalry, and injustice (3:2–7). The *Testament of Judah* describes the four evil spirits as desire, heated passion, debauchery, and sordid greed (16:1). In the *Testament of Issachar*, the dying patriarch proclaims his innocence, declaring that he neither had intercourse with anyone but his wife nor gave lustful looks. He did not drink wine, nor lie. He lamented the oppression of the poor, and he did not eat alone (7:2–5). According to the *Testament of Gad*, hatred "teaches slander, conflict, violence, and all manner of greed" (5:1). The *Testament of Asher* describes someone who "steals, deals unjustly, robs, and cheats" (2:5).

The common themes of the vice lists include sexual vices, greed, and murder, which the authors may derive from the Torah. The other common themes include offenses that disrupt community life—slander, strife, selfish ambition—as well as injustice against the poor. While the cardinal virtues and vices play a role in some passages (Wisdom of Solomon, 4 Maccabees), they have little significance in others (*Testaments of the Twelve Patriarchs*). The lists appear regularly as elaborations of the demands of Torah.

### Themes in the Pauline Lists

Because lists of vices and virtues appear in both the Pauline letters and the Greek philosophical tradition, numerous interpreters have suggested that Paul's lists are derived from popular philosophy and reflect the conventional morality of the Greco-Roman lists. Hans Dieter Betz, having analyzed Paul's most extensive list (Gal. 5:19–25), concludes that "the catalogues sum up the conventional morality of the time."[16] He adds that "Christianity was interested in that morality to the extent that Christian existence should not be 'against the conventions' (cf. Gal. 5:23b)." The primary function of the lists was "to make clear that Christian ethical life should roughly conform to the moral conventions of the time."[17]

16. Betz, *Galatians*, 282.
17. Ibid.

Paul employs the term *aretē* only once (Phil. 4:8) and never mentions any of the Greek cardinal virtues in the undisputed letters.[18] Eulogistic terms reflecting popular morality are largely missing in the Pauline writings. Compounds with *eu-* and *phil-*, which were common in popular morality (*eukosmia, eunomia, eutaxia, philodoxia, philokalia*), are absent altogether. Similarly, Paul does not mention aristocratic and humanistic ideals such as *kalokagathia, eleutheriotēs, megalophrosynē, megalopsychia,* and *megaloprepeia.*[19] Nor does he have the categories of merit, notably those that speak of courage (*andreia, andragathia, philoponia*).[20] Thus while the form of the Pauline lists is reminiscent of Hellenistic lists, the former do not contain the central categories of the latter. In some instances, Paul balances vice and virtue lists (i.e., Gal. 5:19–25; Phil. 2:1–4), while in other lists he mentions only vices (Rom. 1:18–32; 1 Cor. 5:9–10; 6:9–11; 2 Cor. 12:20–21). The lists appear in contexts in which Paul differentiates the new behavior of gentile Christians from their previous behavior and from that of the society around them. Indeed, as table 4.1 indicates, vice lists predominate in Paul's letters.

### Table 4.1. Pauline Virtues and Vices

| | Rom. | 1 Cor. | 2 Cor. | Gal. | Eph. | Phil. | Col. | 1 Thess. | Past. Ep. |
|---|---|---|---|---|---|---|---|---|---|
| **Sexual Sins** | | | | | | | | | |
| sexual immorality, fornication *porneia* | | 6:9 | 12:21 | 5:19 | 5:3, 5 | | 3:5 | | |
| licentiousness *aselgeia* | 13:13 | | 12:21 | 5:19 | 4:19 | | | | |
| uncleanness *akatharsia* | 1:24 | | 12:21 | 5:19 | 5:3, 5 | | 3:5 | 4:3, 8 | |
| sexual excess *koitē* | 13:13 | | | | | | | | |
| effeminate *malakos* | | 6:9 | | | | | | | |
| one who has sexual intercourse with someone of one's own sex *arsenokoitēs* | 1:27 | 6:9 | | | | | | | |

18. Echoes of the cardinal virtues appear in Acts and Titus. According to the Acts account of Paul's speech before Felix, Paul discussed "justice, self-control, and the coming judgment" (Acts 24:25 NRSV). According to Titus 2:12, God's revelation teaches the believer to live "soberly and justly and godly in this present world."

19. Zeller, "Konkrete Ethik," 86.

20. See Horsley, *New Documents Illustrating Early Christianity,* 2:105–6.

| | Rom. | 1 Cor. | 2 Cor. | Gal. | Eph. | Phil. | Col. | 1 Thess. | Past. Ep. |
|---|---|---|---|---|---|---|---|---|---|
| **Antisocial Offenses/Offenders** | | | | | | | | | |
| strife, discord, contention *eris* | 1:29; 13:13 | 1:11; 3:3 | 12:20 | 5:20 | | 1:15 | | | |
| jealousy, envy *zēlos* | 13:13 | 3:3 | 12:20 | 5:20 | | | | | |
| thief, to steal *kleptēs, kleptein* | 2:21; 13:9 | 6:10 | | | 4:28 | | | | |
| a greedy person, greed *pleonektēs* | 1:29 | 5:10; 6:10 | 9:5 | | 4:19; 5:3, 5 | | | | |
| greediness, insatiableness, avarice, covetousness *pleonexia* | | 5:10; 6:10 | | | | | 3:5 | 2:5 | |
| be drunk; drunkard; drunkenness *methyein, methysos, methē* | 13:13 | 5:11; 6:10; 11:21 | | 5:21 | 5:18 | | | 5:7 | |
| reviler, abusive person *loidoros* | | 5:11; 6:10 | | | | | | | |
| anger, wrath, rage, indignation *thymos* | | | 12:20 | 5:20 | 4:31 | | 3:8 | | |
| strife, contentiousness; selfishness, selfish ambition *eritheia* | 2:8 | | 12:20 | 5:20 | | 1:17; 2:3 | | | |
| evil speech, slander, defamation, detraction; slanderous *katalalia, katalalos* | 1:30 | | 12:20 | | | | | | |
| (secret) gossip, tale-bearing; rumor-monger, tale-bearer *psithyrismos, psithyristēs* | 1:29 | | 12:20 | | | | | | |
| swelled-headedness, pride, conceit *physiōsis* | | | 12:20 | | | | | | |
| disorder, unruliness *akatastasia* | | 14:33 | 12:20 | | | | | | |
| enmity *echthra* | | | | 5:20 | | | | | |

| | Rom. | 1 Cor. | 2 Cor. | Gal. | Eph. | Phil. | Col. | 1 Thess. | Past. Ep. |
|---|---|---|---|---|---|---|---|---|---|
| sorcery, magic *pharmakeia* | | | | 5:20 | | | | | |
| dissension *dichostasia* | 16:17 | 3:3 | | 5:20 | | | | | |
| faction *hairesis* | | 11:19 | | 5:20 | | | | | |
| injustice *adikia* | 1:18, 29; 6:13 | | | | | | | | |
| evil *ponēria* | 1:29 | 5:8 | | | | | | | |
| wickedness *kakia* | 1:29 | 5:8 | | | 4:31 | | 3:8 | | Titus 3:3 |
| envy *phthonos, phthoneō* | 1:29 | | | 5:21, 26 | | | | | |
| murder *phonos* | 1:29 | | | | | | | | |
| deceit *dolos* | 1:29 | | | | | | | | |
| meanness *kakoētheia* | 1:29 | | | | | | | | |
| God-haters *theostygēs* | 1:30 | | | | | | | | |
| insolent *hybristēs* | 1:30 | | | | | | | | |
| arrogant *hyperēphanoi* | 1:30 | | | | | | | | 2 Tim. 3:2 |
| boastful *alazones* | 1:30 | | | | | | | | |
| inventors of evil *epheuretai kakōn* | 1:30 | | | | | | | | |
| disobedient to parents *goneusin apeitheis* | 1:30 | | | | | | | | 2 Tim. 3:2 |
| foolish *asynetoi* | 1:31 | | | | | | | | |
| faithless *asynthetoi* | 1:31 | | | | | | | | |
| heartless *astorgoi* | 1:31 | | | | | | | | 2 Tim. 3:3 |
| merciless *aneleēmones* | 1:31 | | | | | | | | |

Although Paul's lists vary, common themes emerge. In the two lists in which Paul depicts alternative types of behavior (Gal. 5:19–23; Phil. 2:1–4), he contrasts self-centered conduct with care for others. In the vice lists, Paul routinely lists sexual offenses before the other vices, which concern individual self-seeking and "the failure in the appropriate other-directedness, resulting in communal breakdown and quarreling."[21]

### Sexual Offenses

Sexual offenses (or offenders) appear in all of the vice lists in the Pauline literature, but do not appear in Hellenistic vice catalogs.[22] The triad *porneia*, *akatharsia*, and *aselgeia* appears in two instances (2 Cor. 12:21; Gal. 5:19), while two of the terms appear together elsewhere (*porneia* and *akatharsia* in 1 Thess. 4:3, 8; Col. 3:5; Eph. 5:3, 5; *aselgeia* with the related word *koitai* in Rom. 13:13). The terms also appear separately on numerous occasions. *Porneia* is the most frequently listed among the vices mentioned by Paul[23] and commonly appears first (cf. 1 Cor. 5:10–11; 6:9; Gal. 5:19; Eph. 5:3, 5; Col. 3:5). That *akatharsia* (literally "uncleanness" or "impurity") has a sexual dimension is evident in the paraeneses (Rom. 1:24; 6:19; Eph. 4:19; 1 Thess. 4:3, 7). Similarly, *aselgeia* (Rom. 13:13; 2 Cor. 12:21; Gal. 5:19; Eph. 4:19), which was used in classical sources to describe wanton or outrageous behavior,[24] has a specific sexual connotation in Paul. The related words *koitai* (sexual impurities, Rom. 13:13)[25] and *moichoi* (adulterers, 1 Cor. 6:9) also appear in the vice lists. In 1 Corinthians 6:9 Paul adds *malakoi* and *arsenokoitai* among the sexual offenders (see below). Like Hellenistic Jewish writers (cf. Wis. 14:12), Paul associates these offenses with idolatry (Rom. 1:18–32; 1 Cor. 6:9; Gal. 5:20) and the previous existence of his readers (1 Cor. 6:11; 10:6–7). Thus he urges his readers to put these vices away (Rom. 13:12–13; 1 Thess. 4:3), knowing that those who practice these offenses "will not inherit the kingdom of God" (1 Cor. 6:10; Gal. 5:21).

While *porneia* means "unlawful sexual intercourse,"[26] in the New Testament it is often ambiguous, as is reflected in the translations. The NRSV, for example, renders the word as both "sexual immorality" (1 Cor. 5:1; 7:2; 2 Cor. 12:21) and "fornication" (1 Cor. 6:18; Gal. 5:19; 1 Thess. 4:3). In Greek literature, it is used for prostitution.[27] In the LXX, *porneia* is used for prostitution (cf.

21. Engberg-Pedersen, "Paul, Virtues, and Vices," 621.
22. Vögtle, *Tugend- und Lasterkataloge*, 26; Wibbing, *Tugend- und Lasterkataloge*, 99.
23. According to R. Collins, "Of the 110 vices in the New Testament catalogues, *porneia* is the only one mentioned in a majority of texts. It is cited in twelve of the twenty-two lists: Matt. 15:19; Mark 7:21; 1 Cor. 5:10, 11; 6:9; 2 Cor. 12:21; Gal. 5:19; Eph. 5:3, 5; Col. 3:5; 1 Tim. 1:10; Rev. 9:21; 21:8; 22:15" (*Sexual Ethics and the New Testament*, 80). Cf. also Heb. 12:16; 13:4.
24. LSJ 255.
25. Collins, *Sexual Ethics and the New Testament*, 83.
26. BDAG 854.
27. LSJ 1450.

Gen. 38:21, 24; Deut. 23:18; Joel 3:3), adultery (Sir. 23:23; 26:9), and Israel's unfaithfulness (Jer. 2:20; 3:9; Ezek. 16 passim). As I have shown in chapter 3, Paul employs the term for sexual relationships outside of marriage.

The extended discussion in 1 Corinthians 5:1–11:1 provides Paul's most comprehensive elaboration on the sexual offenses mentioned in 1 Corinthians 6:9. This unit treats the topics of sexual immorality (5:1–7:40) and idolatry (8:1–11:1), two topics that were commonly linked in Jewish paraenesis. Paul is probably answering questions (cf. 1 Cor. 7:1) and elaborating on earlier catechesis.[28]

This discussion provides an insight into both the meaning and the function of Paul's lists in 1 Corinthians 5:9–10 and 6:9–10, Paul's most extensive list of sexual offenses. Because of the problems among the Corinthians, Paul expands on his original catechesis to address issues in the Corinthian church. Paul initiates the discussion by responding to the report in that church that there is a kind of *porneia* that would be unacceptable even among the gentiles (5:1). Inasmuch as Jewish paraenesis commonly associates the gentiles with *porneia*, Paul's charge is especially harsh. As in 1 Thessalonians 4:4–5, by identifying the gentiles as the other, Paul implies that he identifies this gentile congregation with Israel. He indicates the nature of the *porneia* by saying that "a man has his father's wife," an echo of the Levitical code (Lev. 18:8). Thus in this instance he identifies *porneia* with incest. His prescription also assumes the identity of the community at Corinth with Israel. He urges the readers, like Israel at Passover, to "cleanse out the old leaven" (5:7) and to "expel the evil from [their] midst" (5:13; cf. Deut. 17:7). He reminds the readers that he has urged the Corinthians in his previous letter "not to mix with *pornoi*" (5:9). His instructions are shaped by Israel's identity as a holy people who avoid the idolatry (Lev. 19:4) and the practices of their neighbors (Lev. 18:2–3). These practices include a variety of sexual offenses (Lev. 18).

The same distinction between insiders and outsiders governs Paul's further discussion of the two issues mentioned in 1 Corinthians 6, issues involving the community's separation from outsiders. In his comments on lawsuits before pagan courts (1 Cor. 6:1–11), Paul identifies Christians as *hagioi* and *adelphoi*, whom he distinguishes from the *adikoi* (6:1). As in the Levitical code, the *hagioi* maintain separation from the practices of their neighbors. Having distinguished between the saints (*hagioi*) and the unrighteous (*adikoi*) in 6:1–8, Paul reinforces his appeal for separation with the list of offenses characteristic of the *adikoi* in 6:9–10. In this reminder of previous catechesis in which he had instructed them of the offenses that preclude entrance into the kingdom of God, he indicates that they once practiced these offenses (6:11). He concludes, "You were washed, you were sanctified, you were justified," pointing to the singular event of their conversion, which separated them from

---

28. Yarbrough, *Not Like the Gentiles*, 89–93.

the practices of the *adikoi*. The list identifies offenses that were apparently common in Corinthian society and practices that the *hagioi* have put away. Indeed, in saying that "[they] were washed, . . . sanctified, . . . justified," Paul indicates that their status as holy people precludes their continuing in the sexual behavior of Corinthian society. Thus, as in Leviticus, the holy people separate from the sexual practices of their neighbors.

*Hagioi* maintain their separation, not only from pagan courts (6:1–11), but also from the sexual practices of their neighbors. The community avoids the common acceptance of prostitution, rejecting the pagan understanding of the body and sexuality (6:12–15). Using the identical words of the *Testament of Reuben* (5:5), Paul says, "flee fornication" (6:18). Thus in this instance *porneia* means prostitution. Paul's counsel is consistent with the Levitical prohibition of prostitution.

The questions raised in 1 Corinthians 7 suggest that Paul's catechesis on sexuality raised further questions about sexuality within marriage. While recommending that men follow his example of singleness (7:1, 7) rather than "touch a woman" (7:1), Paul concedes that those who do not have this gift should marry "because of *porneia*." That is, marriage is the alternative to *porneia* (7:2) and lack of self-control (7:5). The view that marriage is the alternative to *porneia* expands on earlier instructions (1 Thess. 4:3). In the extended discussion, therefore, *porneia* is a term for incest (1 Cor. 5:1–11), prostitution (6:12–20), and other sexual activities outside of marriage. Inasmuch as marriage is the alternative to *porneia* and the lack of self-control (1 Cor. 7:2, 5), *porneia* is the term for all sex outside of marriage.[29] Thus in 1 Corinthians 6:9, as elsewhere, *porneia* is an inclusive term at the beginning of the list.

Paul also employs related terms in his ethical lists. In the list in 1 Corinthians 6:9, he includes adulterers (*moichoi*), and in the list in Romans 13:13 he mentions debauchery (*koitē*). The root word *moich-*, referring to the violation of the seventh commandment (Exod. 20:14; Deut. 5:18), is used both literally (Lev. 20:10; Jer. 7:9; Prov. 6:32; Mal. 3:5; Jer. 13:27; 23:14; Ezek. 23:45; Prov. 30:20; Job 24:15; Wis. 14:26) and metaphorically (Ezek. 23:43; Hos. 4:2) in the LXX for one who breaks the marriage vows. *Koitē*, literally "bed," is a metaphor in the Old Testament for sexual intercourse (Lev. 19:20; Judg. 2:12), especially unlawful sexual intercourse (Lev. 18:23; 20:13; Num. 5:13, 20; 31:18, 35; Judg. 21:11; Wis. 3:13, 16). The author of Hebrews instructs readers to keep "the bed undefiled" (*hē koitē amiantos*), equating those who defile the bed with fornicators and adulterers (Heb. 13:4).

Although *akatharsia* refers to any impurity,[30] Pauline usage of it is indebted to the Levitical distinction between clean and unclean. In contrast to Levitical usage, however, with one exception (1 Thess. 2:3), Paul associates *akatharsia*

29. Jensen, "Does *Porneia* Mean Fornication?," 182.
30. BDAG 34.

exclusively with sexual matters (cf. Rom. 1:24; 6:19; 2 Cor. 12:21; Gal. 5:19; 1 Thess. 4:7). Whereas impurity in Leviticus applied to bodily discharges (Lev. 7:20; 15:3, 24; 18:19; Ezek. 36:17), sexual intercourse with the woman during her menstrual period (Lev. 15:24), incest (Lev. 20:21), and other sources of uncleanness (cf. Lev. 7:20; 15:3; 20:25), Paul employs the term as a synonym for *porneia* (cf. 1 Thess. 4:3, 7). Thus Paul derives *akatharsia* from the Holiness Code. While he does not inculcate all the purity rules, he derives the association of impurity and sexual offenses from it.

*Aselgeia*, meaning literally "lack of self-restraint,"[31] is a comprehensive term for evil and perversion.[32] While it can refer to outrageous behavior in general within the triad that includes *porneia* and *akatharsia*, the term suggests sexual debauchery. Paul's including it in the triad of sexual offenses reflects its use in Wisdom 14:26, where it is listed with adultery. The term also appears in vice lists in the *Testaments of the Twelve Patriarchs*. While *porneia* specifies the offense and *akatharsia* places it within the context of the Holiness Code, *aselgeia* refers to the total lack of self-restraint in sexual matters.[33]

In 1 Corinthians 6:9, Paul adds to the list of offenders *malakoi* and *arsenokoitai*, which appear in neither Hellenistic nor Jewish texts prior to Paul. The latter is used elsewhere in the New Testament only in 1 Timothy 1:10. The absence of these words elsewhere presents a problem for translators. Inasmuch as these terms appear in a catalog of sexual offenders, one may assume that Paul includes these words for those who commit certain sexual sins. *Malakoi*, which literally means "soft men,"[34] is translated as "male prostitutes" (NIV, NRSV) or "effeminate" (KJV, ASV), and *arsenokoitai* is rendered as "sodomites" (NRSV), "homosexual offenders" (NIV), and "abusers of themselves with men" (KJV, ASV). The RSV lumps the two words together, rendering them as "sexual perverts." Most interpreters envision these as complementary words that refer to sexual offenders not already mentioned in the list.

While most interpreters agree that *malakoi* refers to effeminate men who made their bodies soft and prettied themselves up, they do not agree on the precise meaning of the word. Several scholars maintain that *malakoi* were male prostitutes who took the passive role in homosexual intercourse.[35] Dale Martin disputes the categorization of the *malakoi* as male prostitutes and insists that the word means "effeminate" with no indication of their sexual activity.[36] Contrary to Martin, Plutarch uses the term for those who are "mounted like cattle" (*Amat.* 751). Philo of Alexandria offers the best clue as to the use of the term, especially among Diaspora Jews. In his exposition of the Levitical

---

31. BDAG 141.
32. Goldstein, "*Aselgeia*," *EDNT* 1:169.
33. R. Collins, *Sexual Ethics*, 97.
34. BDAG 613.
35. Cf. Elliott, "No Kingdom for Softies?," 27.
36. Martin, "*Arsenokoitēs* and *Malakos*," 124–28.

laws, he identifies the homosexual relationships prohibited by the Levitical code with pederasty (*paiderastein*), indicating that those who do such things are worthy of death (cf. Lev. 20:13). He clearly distinguishes between the active and passive partners (*Spec. Laws* 3.37), describing the lengths to which the latter went to assume a female role. They "braid and adorn the hair of their heads," and "they scrub and paint their faces with cosmetics and pigments and the like," using perfumes to enhance their seductiveness. Philo says that these "hybrids of man and woman" (*androgynoi*) emasculate themselves in order to take the feminine role. He describes their conduct as "licentiousness and effeminacy" (*akrasia kai malakia, Spec. Laws* 3.40). He speaks elsewhere of those who emasculate themselves in taking on the role of the woman (*Abraham* 136). Thus Philo identifies the *malakos* with the passive partner in a homosexual relationship, identifying the practices prohibited in Leviticus with those with which he is familiar in Alexandria. He does not associate the word with prostitution. Paul probably inherited the term from Hellenistic Jewish writers who connected Levitical prohibitions with the homosexual practices known to them.[37]

Since *arsenokoitēs* is not attested prior to Paul, the word is also a challenge to translators. The literal meaning is "bedding down with a man."[38] The term is probably derived from the phrases *meta arsenos ou koimēthēse koitēn gynaikos* ("lie with a man as with a woman," Lev. 18:22 RSV) and *hos an koimēthē meta arsenos koitēn gynaikos* ("whoever lies with a man as with a woman," Lev. 20:13 NRSV). This term probably depends on the usage in Hellenistic Judaism (cf. *arsenokoitein, Sib. Or.* 2:73). The word continued to be used in 1 Timothy (1:10) and the literature of the apostolic fathers (Pol. *Phil.* 5:3).

Paul's elaboration in Romans 1 gives further evidence of his indebtedness to the paraenetic instructions of Hellenistic Judaism. As in the vice lists in the earlier letters (1 Cor. 6:9–10; Gal. 5:19–21), he proceeds from sexual vices (Rom. 1:24–27) to antisocial offenses (Rom. 1:29–31), referring to both female (1:26) and male (1:27) homosexual practices, describing these practices as "contrary to nature" (*para physin*, 1:26). The condemnation of the flaming passion in which "men do shameless acts with men" (1:27) is reminiscent of the Levitical prohibition of a man lying "with a man as with a woman" (Lev. 18:22; 20:13). Paul is not only dependent on Leviticus, but on the Jewish interpretative tradition on Leviticus. The condemnation of females "who exchanged (*metēllaxan*) the natural use into what is contrary to nature" recalls the indictment in Wisdom of those who were guilty of "interchange of sex roles" (*geneseōs enallagē*, 14:26).[39] The description of this conduct as "contrary to

37. D. Wright, "Homosexuals or Prostitutes? The Meaning of *Arsenokoitai*," 136.
38. R. Collins, *Sexual Ethics*, 89.
39. Translation by David Winston, in *The Wisdom of Solomon: A New Translation and Commentary*, 280. See also *T. Naph.* 3:4; Philo, *Cher.* 92.

nature" also indicates Paul's dependence on the Jewish paraenetic tradition, according to which homosexual acts were a violation of the natural order.[40] Thus the inclusion of same-sex relationships at the beginning of the list, like the inclusion of sexual immorality in other lists, reflects Paul's dependence on the Jewish interpretations of Leviticus.

The list of sexual offenses suggests that Paul derives the specific vices from the Holiness Code in Leviticus 17–26. He envisions the church as a holy community separated from the society around them, as does Leviticus. Paul's instructions on sexuality reflect his Jewish heritage, according to which the Holiness Code defines obedience to the law in a pagan environment. Paraeneses in Jewish literature focused on separating the sexual practices of the Jewish community from those of the idolaters. They repeatedly instructed communities to abstain from *porneia* and homosexual relationships. Just as the Holiness Code was important in Hellenistic Jewish paraenesis, it shaped Paul's sexual paraenesis, for Paul placed the paraenetic instructions on sexuality under the rubric of holiness in 1 Corinthians.

### Offenses against the Community

While one finds consistency in Paul's lists of sexual offenses, the lists of vices vary considerably, as the chart indicates. The lists of anticommunal offenses also vary. Because Paul apparently draws from a large pool, his vice lists do not overlap significantly. Indeed, a majority of the terms appear in only one list. Selfish ambition (*eritheia*) appears in four instances (2 Cor. 12:20; Gal. 5:20; Phil. 1:17; 2:3). Strife (*eris*), jealousy (*zēlos*), drunkenness (*methē*), anger (*thymos*), and envy (*phthonos*) appear three times in the lists in the undisputed Pauline letters. Paul speaks also of whisperers (*psithyrismoi*) twice (Rom. 1:30; 2 Cor. 12:20). Numerous other vices, including disorder (*akatastasia*, 2 Cor. 12:20), dissension (*dichostasia*, Gal. 5:20), and those who insult (*loidoroi*) appear once. Inasmuch as Paul suggests that he is repeating previous catechesis, one may assume that his lists were part of that instruction (Gal. 5:21) and are only marginally related to the issues in the churches he addresses. One may assume that the local situation has not determined Paul's paraenesis in most instances.

Most of these offenses also appear in Greek descriptions of unseemly behavior, especially in descriptions of the impediments to civic concord. According to Plutarch, "A government which has not had to bear with envy (*phthonon*) or jealous rivalry (*zēlon*) or contention (*philoneikian*)—emotions most productive of enmity (*echthras*)—has not hitherto existed" (*Mor.* 86). *Eris* was personified as the goddess of discord who incites war, the opposite of concord (*homonoia*).[41] The term was used in Greek literature for political

---

40. See ch. 1 for references.
41. LSJ 689; Mitchell, *Paul and the Rhetoric of Reconciliation*, 81.

strife and frequently appears with lists of synonyms.[42] *Zēlos* was the root of civil strife and the cause of war (Lysias *Epitaphius* 48.2).[43] It also was linked to *staseis, echthra*, and *philoneikia*.[44] Except for two references in Aristotle, selfish ambition (*eritheia*) is unknown in the LXX and in the Greek language prior to Paul,[45] but is commonplace in Pauline ethical instruction (cf. 2 Cor. 12:20; Phil. 1:17; 2:3; cf. James 3:14).

Inasmuch as the anticommunal vices (drunkenness, revelry, theft, greed, and murder) are disruptive to all human communities, the fact that Paul shares them with Hellenistic writers is not surprising.[46] Greek sources denounce greed and envy as the greatest vices. Menander says, "Greed is a very great evil for humans; for those who wish to have their neighbors' goods often fail and are vanquished." Plutarch links this vice with debauchery, soft living, luxury (*Ag. Cleom.* 3.1; 10.5), and injustice (*Ti. C. Gracch.* 9.3; 20.8). He denounces spiteful envy as the source of political rivals (*Lyc.* 3.6). Insults (*loidoriai*) were also the source of discord, according to Greek sources,[47] which also condemn dissension (*dichostasia*; cf. Gal. 5:20) and disorder (*akatastasia*, 2 Cor. 12:20). Both are equivalent to *stasis*, a common vice in Hellenistic texts.[48]

The inclusion of sorcery (*pharmakeia*) alongside idolatry (Gal. 5:20) suggests that the former is one form of the latter. Thus it is not included in Hellenistic lists, but is rooted in the Torah and Jewish paraenesis. Those who worship other gods practice sorcery (Exod. 7:11, 22; 9:11; Dan. 5:8), which the Torah forbids (Deut. 18:10). It is linked with debauchery (2 Kings 9:22; Nah. 3:4). Accordingly, in Wisdom's contrast between the righteous and the ungodly, sorcery is the practice of the ungodly (Wis. 12:4; 18:13).

The vices listed by Paul also have antecedents in the literature of Hellenistic Judaism. As I demonstrated in chapter 1, summaries of the law and vice lists are common in Hellenistic Jewish texts. These summaries focused on sexual offenses, care for the weak and oppressed, and the self-serving behavior that undermined community relationships. Although the Hellenistic Jewish authors often listed offenses that are not specifically mentioned in the Torah, they presented the vices and virtues as interpretations of the demands of the

42. LSJ 689 cites Sophocles, *Oed. col.* 1234, as containing *phonoi, stasis, eris, machai*; cf. Aristophanes, *Thesm.* 788, which contains *erides, neikē, stasis . . . polemos. Eris* is commonly linked with *stasis* (Dio Chrysostom, *Or.* 39.8); *echthra* (Dio Chrysostom, *Or.* 38.43; *Or.* 39.8; *Or.* 48.6; *Or.* 49.9. Texts in Mitchell, *Paul and the Rhetoric of Reconciliation*, 79–81.

43. Welborn, *Politics and Rhetoric in the Corinthian Epistles*, 4.

44. Mitchell, *Paul and the Rhetoric of Reconciliation*, 81.

45. Spicq, "*Erethizō*," *TLNT* 2.69–72; Welborn, *Politics and Rhetoric in the Corinthian Epistles*, 3–7. The word is used seven times in the New Testament, including the two appearances in the Pauline vice lists. The word is used in Aristotle (*Pol.* 1302b, 4; 1303a, 4) for self-seeking pursuit of political office. See BDAG 392.

46. Wibbing, *Tugend- und Lasterkataloge*, 99.

47. Spicq, "*Loidoreō*," *TLNT* 2:408.

48. See the discussion in Welborn, *Politics and Rhetoric in the Corinthian Epistles*, 3–7.

Torah. While the writers drew heavily from the Holiness Code of Leviticus 17–26, they gave little attention to the ritual commands of the law, choosing to present a morality that was intelligible in the Diaspora environment.

Interpreters have recognized that Paul's assessment of the moral consequences of idolatry in Romans 1 is indebted to the Wisdom of Solomon or a common Hellenistic Jewish tradition. Like those earlier writers, he often associated idolatry and sexual offenses in his ethical instruction. Moreover, he follows the same basic structure as the summaries of the law in Hellenistic Judaism, proceeding regularly from sexual offenses to anticommunal vices. As I demonstrated in chapter 1, boastfulness, greed, envy, strife, and selfish ambition were major themes in the Wisdom literature. The *Testaments of the Twelve Patriarchs* repeatedly warn against these vices (cf. *T. Reub.* 3:1–8; *T. Sim.* 3:1–3; *T. Iss.* 4:1–4; 5:1; *T. Dan* 1:8; *T. Gad* 3:1; 7:3; *T. Benj.* 7:5; 8:1) as well as sexual offenses. Like Hellenistic Jewish moral instructors, Paul sees the offenses as the result of the absence of love.

## Positive Attributes

Paul mentions significantly fewer positive attributes than vices. Like both Hellenistic and Jewish writers, he contrasts positive attributes with the vices that he instructs his readers to abandon. Troels Engberg-Pedersen has correctly noted that Paul's attributes are other-directed in a way that is analogous to Hellenistic ethical traditions.[49] Table 4.2 indicates the major themes in the Pauline lists. One may observe the importance of love and other values that build the community.

Several items in the list in Galatians 5:22–23 are highly regarded in the Hellenistic ethical tradition. For example, Hellenistic writers praise those who possess kindness (*chrēstotēs*), gentleness (*praytēs*), and self-control (*enkrateia*). Kindness (*chrēstotēs*) is the attribute of princes and kings who demonstrate their nobility through their philanthropy and justice.[50] It was an expression of love. These occurrences are so common and so diverse that it is impossible to discern the specific nuance in each use of *chrēstotēs*; it can mean goodness, kindness, willingness to be of service, honesty, nobility, loyalty, and probity.[51] Gentleness (*praytēs*) was a calm and soothing disposition in contrast to savagery (Plato, *Symp.* 197d). It implies moderation (Aristotle, *Eth. nic.* 4.3.1125b), which permits reconciliation. The term was identified with leniency toward offenders[52] and was common in epithets for rulers. Self-control (*enkrateia*),

49. Engberg-Pedersen, "Paul, Virtues, and Vices," 621.

50. Cf. Spicq, "*Chrēsteuomai*," *TLNT* 3:511–16.

51. Spicq, "*Chrēsteuomai*," *TLNT* 3:513. Christian *agapē* was so stunning that, according to Tertullian, Christians were called *chrestiani*, "made up of mildness or kindness," rather than *christiani*.

52. See texts in Spicq, "*Praypatheia*," *TLNT* 3:160–61.

Table 4.2. Positive Attributes

| Virtues | Rom. | 1 Cor. | 2 Cor. | Gal. | Eph. | Phil. | Col. | 1 Thess. | Past. Ep. |
|---|---|---|---|---|---|---|---|---|---|
| love *agapē* | 12:9; 13:10; 14:15 | 4:21; 8:1; 13:1–4, 8, 13; 14:1; 16:14 | 2:8; 6:6; 8:7–8, 24 | 5:6, 13, 22 | 1:15; 4:2, 15–16; 5:2 | 1:9, 16; 2:1–2 | 1:4, 8; 2:2; 3:14 | 1:3; 3:6, 12; 5:8, 13 | 1 Tim. 1:5, 14; 2:15; 4:12; 6:11; 2 Tim. 1:7, 13; 2:22; 3:10; Titus 2:2 |
| joy *chara* | 14:17; 15:13 | | 2:3; 8:2 | 5:22 | | 2:29 | | 1:6 | |
| peace *eirēnē* | 3:17; 5:1; 14:17, 19; 15:13 | 7:15; 14:33; 16:11 | 13:11 | 5:22; 6:16 | 2:14–15, 17; 4:3; 6:15, 23 | 4:7, 9 | 3:15 | | 2 Tim. 2:22 |
| patience *makrothymia* | 2:4 | | 6:6 | 5:22 | 4:2 | | 1:11; 3:12 | | 1 Tim. 1:16; 2 Tim. 3:10; 4:2 |
| kindness *chrēstotēs* | 2:4; 11:22 | | 6:6 | 5:22 | | | 3:12 | | Titus 3:4 |
| goodness *agathōsynē* | 15:14 | | | 5:22 | 5:9 | | | | |
| faith *pistis* | 1:5, 8, 17; 3:28, 30; 4:5, 9, 12–14, 16, 19–20; 10:17; 11:20; 12:3, 6; 14:22–23; 16:26 | 2:5; 12:9; 13:2, 13; 15:14; 16:13 | 5:7; 8:7 | 3:7–25; 5:5–6, 22 | 1:15; 3:12 | 1:27; 3:9 | | 1:3; 3:2, 5–7, 10; 5:8 | 1 Tim. 1:19; 2:7, 15; 3:9; 4:6, 12; 5:16; 6:11; 2 Tim. 3:10; Titus 2:10; 3:15 |
| gentleness *praytēs* | | 4:21 | 10:1 | 5:23; 6:1 | 4:2 | 3:12 | | | |
| self-control *enkrateia* | | | | 5:22 | | | | | |

| Virtues | Rom. | 1 Cor. | 2 Cor. | Gal. | Eph. | Phil. | Col. | 1 Thess. | Past. Ep. |
|---|---|---|---|---|---|---|---|---|---|
| like-minded *to auto phronein* | 12:16; 15:5 | | | | | 2:2; 4:2 | | | |
| one-spirit *sympsychos* | | | | | | 2:2 | | | |
| one-purpose *to hen phronountes* | | | | | | 2:2 | | | |
| humility *tapeinophrosynē* | | | | | | 2:3 | 3:12 | | |
| true *alēthēs* | | | | | | 4:8 | | | |
| noble *semnos* | | | | | | 4:8 | | | 1 Tim. 3:4, 8; Titus 2:2, 7 |
| right, just *dikaios* | | | | | | 4:8 | | | |
| pure *hagnos* | | | | | | 4:8 | | | |
| lovely *prosphilēs* | | | | | | 4:8 | | | |
| admirable *euphēmos* | | | | | | 4:8 | | | |
| excellence *aretē* | | | | | | 4:8 | | | |
| praiseworthiness *epainos* | | | | | | 4:8 | | | |

mentioned nowhere else by Paul, was also an important Greek virtue. Aristotle devotes a major section of *Nicomachean Ethics* to this virtue, explaining that it is the intermediate state between the unrestrained pleasures of the body and the failure to take proper pleasure in matters of the body (*Eth. nic.* 7.9.5). According to Aristotle (*Eth. nic.* 7.1.1145b), the opposite of the self-controlled man (*enkratēs*) is the one who is without restraint (*ho akratēs*). *Enkrateia* is equivalent to *sōphrosynē*, one of the cardinal virtues, for "the temperate man (*ho sōphrōn*), as well as the self-restrained, is so constituted as never to be led by the pleasures of the body to act against principle" (*Eth. nic.* 7.9.6).

While kindness (*chrēstotēs*), gentleness (*praytēs*), and self-control (*enkrateia*) have an important place in the Greek ethical tradition, they also have a place in the paraenetic traditions of the Old Testament and Hellenistic Judaism. In the LXX *chrēstotēs* is a defining characteristic of God (Pss. 20:3; 24:7; 30:19; 36:3; 52:3; 64:11 LXX). Forms of the word are used for human uprightness and piety (Pss. 13:1, 3; 5:24; 36:3 LXX) and the generosity of a ruler (Esther 8:12c LXX).[53] Philo (*Sacrifices* 27) employs the word in an ethical list with gentleness (*praytēs*) and self-control (*enkrateia*).[54] Gentleness/humility (*praytēs*) also has an important place in the LXX to describe the ideal of piety and humility toward God and others. Both Moses and David exemplify this ideal (Num. 12:3; Ps. 131 LXX). The psalms regularly present the ideal of those who are meek before God (Pss. 25:9; 34:2; 37:11; 76:10; 147:6; 150:4). The Wisdom literature also presents *praytēs* as the ideal of the pious person (Sir. 1:27; 3:17–18; 4:8; 10:14, 28; 36:28; 45:4), on two occasions placing it alongside faith (Sir. 1:27; 45:4; cf. Gal. 5:22–23). Paul shares the high evaluation of this term with early Christian paraenesis (cf. Matt. 5:5; Eph. 4:2; Col. 3:12; 2 Tim. 2:25; Titus 3:2; James 1:21; 3:13; 1 Pet. 3:16), identifying himself with the "meekness and gentleness of Christ" (2 Cor. 10:1 NRSV; cf. 1 Cor. 4:21).

Self-control (*enkrateia*) appears in the LXX only in the Wisdom literature, where it is a gift of God (Wis. 8:21 LXX). It refers to the readiness to accept torture (4 Macc. 5:34). In the *Testaments of the Twelve Patriarchs*, it is used for Rachel's choice of continence over sexual intercourse (*T. Iss.* 2:1). According to the *Epistle to Aristeas*, the virtuous disposition, acquired through the law, restrains the search for pleasure and commands the people to respect justice and self-control (278).

Paul's use of a form of *enkrateia* in 1 Corinthians 7:9 indicates his place within Jewish paraenetic traditions. His advice, "Do not separate from one another except by agreement for a season" (7:5), corresponds to the advice in the *Testament of Naphtali* 8:8, where the patriarch concludes, "There is a time

---

53. Zmijewski, "*Chrēstotēs*," *EDNT* 3:475.

54. Philo's list of virtues includes these among 34 qualities possessed by those who follow virtue. He lists 147 vices of those who follow pleasure (*Sacrifices* 32).

for intercourse with one's wife and a time for prayers" (see ch. 1). Moreover, his concession that one who does not have self-control may marry (7:9) corresponds to Jewish paraenesis.

Paul's placement of these Greek virtues within the larger list indicates the nature of his appropriation of these categories and his roots in a larger tradition of moral reflection. Two items from the familiar Pauline triad, faith and love, appear in this list, with love at the head. These terms, as I have shown in chapter 3, are rooted in the Old Testament and Hellenistic Jewish moral tradition. *Agapē*, echoing the call to "love one another" (Gal. 5:14), provides the orientation for understanding the other attributes. "Joy and peace" (or peace and joy) are a common word pair in Paul (cf. Rom. 14:17; 15:13), and both are used separately in Pauline instruction. Paul speaks of joy as a dimension of Christian experience (2 Cor. 1:24; 2:3; 7:4, 13; 8:2; Phil. 1:4, 25; 1 Thess. 1:6; 3:9; Philem. 7) and instructs his communities to rejoice (Phil. 3:1; 4:4; 1 Thess. 5:16). The term has no analogue in the Greek ethical tradition.[55] Peace is the opposite of the vices mentioned by Paul, the absence of the behavior of the dogs that rip each other apart (Gal. 5:15). The words recall Paul's instructions, "Let us pursue the things that make for peace" (Rom. 14:19), and, "be at peace" (2 Cor. 13:11). Peace also recalls numerous passages in the Old Testament and Jewish tradition.

Patience (*makrothymia*), kindness (*chrēstotēs*), and goodness (*agathōsynē*) also focus on relationships within a community and elaborate on the meaning of love. *Makrothymia*, the capacity to bear up under provocation,[56] is commonplace in the Old Testament to describe God and faithful people but is not a virtue in Greek literature (see the discussion in ch. 3). It is common to Pauline paraenesis (2 Cor. 6:6; 1 Thess. 5:14; cf. Eph. 4:2; Col. 3:12). Indeed, Paul indicates that it is an expression of love (1 Cor. 13:4). While kindness (*chrēstotēs*) has a firm place in the Greek tradition,[57] it is also firmly rooted in the LXX. Goodness (*agathōsynē*), a term that Paul uses to characterize his communities (Rom. 15:14), is unknown in secular Greek and in the papyri but attested frequently in the LXX.[58] In the context with kindness and patience, it probably connotes generosity or good deeds toward others.[59] The fruit of the Spirit is an expression of the love command. While some dimensions of the fruit of the Spirit have corollaries in Greek life, all are rooted in the LXX. Just as Paul lists vices that disrupt community life, he depicts attributes that express love and are necessary for life in the community. These

---

55. Spicq, "*Chara*," *TLNT* 3:498.
56. BDAG 612.
57. See Vögtle, *Tugend- und Lasterkataloge*, 78–81. *Chrēstotēs* is one of the qualities of a good general, according to Onasander (*Strategeticus*). Libanius (fourth century AD) associates the quality with the good physician (*Progymnasmata* 7).
58. Spicq, "*Agathopoieō*," *TLNT* 1:3–4.
59. BDAG 4.

qualities are consistent with the ethos of family that he inculcates in his communities.

In Philippians 2:1–4 and Galatians 5:19–23 he indicates the contrasting behaviors, while in 2 Corinthians 6:6 he describes his own attributes. He does not speak of virtues, but of the "fruit of the Spirit" (Gal. 5:22) and the behavior that will make his joy complete (Phil. 2:2). In all three lists, he indicates the importance of *agapē* (2 Cor. 6:6; Gal. 5:22; Phil. 2:1). Indeed, *agapē* heads the list in Galatians 5:22–23, the most comprehensive of Paul's catalogs of virtues. As I demonstrate in chapter 7, *agapē* belongs to the ethical tradition of Hellenistic Judaism. "Joy and peace" are a familiar pair in Pauline paraenesis.

In Philippians 2:3, Paul contrasts the vices selfish ambition (*eritheia*) and conceit (*kenodoxia*) with humility (*tapeinophrosynē*), a term that has an important place in early Christian paraenesis. The contrast with *eritheia* and *kenodoxia* indicates that the phrase "counting others better than yourselves" (2:3) is the opposite behavior.[60] Paul provides a christological foundation for his exhortation, recalling that the preexistent Christ did not display the anticommunal trait of self-seeking or vainglory, but "humbled himself" (*etapeinōsen heauton*, 2:8). Only by choosing concern for others over self-assertion can community members maintain their unity.

Humility (*tapeinophrosynē*) takes on a significant role in early Christian paraenesis. In the ethical lists of Ephesians and Colossians, it appears alongside meekness and patience (Eph. 4:2; Col. 3:12), and in Colossians it appears alongside kindness. According to Paul's own self-description in his speech to the Ephesian elders in Acts 20:19, he conducted himself with *tapeinophrosynē* during his time there. The author of 1 Peter encourages members of the community to extend *tapeinophrosynē* to each other (1 Pet. 5:5).

Although forms of *tapein-* appear rarely in Hellenistic texts in a positive sense as the opposite of insolence (*hybris*), willfulness (*authadeia*), and arrogance (*hyperēphania*),[61] the words normally have a derogatory sense to denote "service, weakness, obsequious groveling, or on the other hand mean-spiritedness (e.g., Epictetus, *Diatr.* 3.24)."[62] In secular Greek, it is used for a person who is base, ignoble, and of low birth or someone who works at a low occupation.[63] Thus it could be used for the demeanor of a slave. According to Aristotle (*Eth. nic.* 4.3.1125a, 2), the *tapeinoi* are flatterers who grovel before others, hoping to gain an advantage.

Paul's use of *tapeinophrosynē* reflects a clash of values with those of Greco-Roman culture, as his debate with the Corinthians suggests. In their eyes, he is

60. Grundmann, "*Tapeinos*," *TDNT* 8:21.
61. Spicq, "*Tapeinos*," *TLNT* 3:370. See also Rehrl, *Das Problem der Demut*, 26–28.
62. Bockmuehl, *Jewish Law in Gentile Churches*, 138. Dihle, "Ethik," 681; see Grundmann, "*Tapeinos*," *TDNT* 8:1–27.
63. Spicq cites *P.Oxy.* 74, verso 2: "nothing humble or ignoble or despised" ("*Tapeinos*," *TLNT* 3:369).

*tapeinos* (2 Cor. 10:1) insofar as he does servile work (2 Cor. 11:7) and lacks the boldness to speak openly to his readers. The value that Paul places on *tapeinophrosynē* is rooted in his Christology, for he responds to the charge that he is *tapeinos* by appealing to the "meekness and gentleness of Christ" (2 Cor. 10:1 NRSV). When he encourages his readers to adopt *tapeinophrosynē* as a way of life, he offers the christological motivation that the preexistent Christ "humbled himself" (Phil. 2:8) at the incarnation.

Paul's evaluation of *tapeinophrosynē* is also rooted in the Old Testament (LXX), which uses forms of *tapein-* frequently. *Tapeinos* can mean both the lowly estate of those who are afflicted and the disposition of those who humble themselves before God.[64] The word is used to contrast the haughty with the one who is humble (cf. Prov. 15:33; 18:12). In most instances the word is used for humility before God and for the humble circumstances of many people. They are the humble in contrast to the powerful (Matt. 18:4; 23:12), the arrogant (James 4:6), and the rich (James 5:1). They are the poor, the unfortunate sufferers, and the "little people" whom God blesses. All of these qualities continue in the New Testament's portrayal of the humble.[65] While Paul's positive appreciation of *tapeinophrosynē* reflects continuity with the Old Testament, his focus on humility, not only before God but also before others within a community, distinguishes his use of the word from that found in the Old Testament.

## Philippians 4:8

The list of attributes in Philippians 4:8 is distinctive among Paul's paraeneses, not only because "virtue" (*aretē*) appears only here, but also because the six attributes that characterize virtue have few parallels elsewhere in the undisputed letters of Paul. Concluding a letter that has focused on the development of the proper frame of mind (*phronēsis*), Paul challenges the readers, "Think on (*logizesthe*) these things": "Whatever is true (*alēthē*), whatever is honorable (*semna*), whatever is just (*dikaia*), whatever is pure (*hagna*), whatever is lovely (*prosphilē*), whatever is commendable (*euphēma*)." Because of the distinctive vocabulary,[66] Dibelius observes that this statement is drawn from Greek popular morality.[67] Although Paul does not name the cardinal virtues, the list in 4:8 would have resonated with the popular values of the Greek polis because of its correspondence to the popular ethic of the period. *Euphēmos* (NRSV "commendable") does not appear in the LXX, but does have a role in Greek

---

64. Grundmann, "*Tapeinos*," *TDNT* 8:6.

65. Spicq, "*Tapeinos*," *TLNT* 3:370. Cf. Luke 1:52, 68; 2 Cor. 7:6; 12:21.

66. The adjective "true" (*alēthēs*) appears in 2 Cor. 6:6. "Honorable" (*semnos*) appears elsewhere only in the Pastoral Epistles (see ch. 8). *Aretē* appears elsewhere only in 2 Pet. 1:5.

67. Dibelius, *An die Thessalonicher I–II und die Philipper*, 95.

philosophy (cf. Marcus Aurelius 6.18). While the entire list does not appear elsewhere in Greek sources, the terms appear in a variety of combinations. Vögtle observes that the "Stone of Miletopolis" contains the words *aretē*, *dikaia*, and *euphēma*.[68] *Dikaia* ("just") is the only one of the four cardinal virtues mentioned here. *Semnos* ("honorable") and *hagna* ("pure") are also known in Hellenistic texts (Epictetus, *Diatr.* 1.16, 13; 3.20, 15). Greek philosophy was dominated by the search for what is "true" (*alēthēs*).[69]

Although these attributes were common in Greek popular philosophy, they are also firmly rooted in the literature of the Old Testament and Hellenistic Judaism, where concern for things that are true, just, and pure is pervasive. *Semnos* ("honorable, respectable, noble, pure") appears in Proverbs (8:6; 15:26) and the Maccabean literature.[70] Philo uses forms of the word 139 times. *Prosphilē* ("lovely") appears in Sirach 4:7; 20:13. Thus while the list in Philippians 4:8 would resonate with a Greek audience, the language was also familiar to those who were schooled in the LXX. While the language is distinctive in Philippians 4:8, some of the terms appear elsewhere. In 2 Corinthians 6:6–8, Paul characterizes himself as one who lives "in purity" (*en hagnotēti*), as "deceived but true," and as "in bad report" (*dia dysphēmias*) and good report (*euphēmias*). Three of these terms correspond to the list in Philippians.

### Conclusion: Pauline Lists within the Context of Diaspora Judaism

Although Paul did not give a comprehensive code of conduct, the lists of vices and virtues provided concrete examples of appropriate behavior for his converts. Several of the examples were commonplace for all cultures, including both the Greco-Roman and Jewish traditions. The prohibition of strife, quarreling, theft, murder, drunkenness, and other vices is a basic value for human communities. Paul's list goes beyond the commonplace values, however. One may note both his omission of virtues that were highly prized in antiquity and the inclusion of elements not found in ancient lists of vices and virtues.

The omission of the Greek cardinal virtues is noteworthy. Unlike some of the Hellenistic Jewish predecessors, Paul never listed the four cardinal virtues. Among the four, he alludes to two (*dikaios/dikaiosynē* in Phil. 4:8; *sōphronein*

---

68. Vögtle, *Tugend- und Lasterkataloge*, 90–92, 180–82; Zeller, "Konkrete Ethik," 84.

69. Cf. Plutarch, *Is. Os.* 351E: "The effort to arrive at the Truth, and especially, the truth about the gods, is a longing for the divine. For the search for truth requires for its study and investigation the consideration of sacred subjects, and it is a work more hallowed than any form of holy living or temple service" (LCL). See also Diogenes Laertius, *Vit.* 9:10. Marcus Aurelius 6.21.2 says, "I seek the truth." See Spicq, "*Alētheia*," *TLNT* 1.66–67, for additional texts.

70. In 4 Macc. 7:15, the author praises the aged Eleazar as one who was "a man of blessed age and venerable (*semnēs*) gray hair" (NRSV). In 17:5 the author praises the mother of the seven martyred sons: "The moon in heaven, with the stars, does not stand so august (*semnē*) as you" (NRSV; cf. 4 Macc. 5:36).

[*sōphrosynē*] in Rom. 12:3). The elaboration of the latter as communal existence does not fit the standard definition of *sōphrosynē*. Moreover, he did not include some of the major virtues, including *philanthrōpia*, which had an important place in antiquity and Hellenistic Judaism. The Greek emphasis on the human flourishing (*eudaimonia*) of the individual has no place in Paul's moral instruction.

In addition to the commonplace vices and virtues, Paul includes those that are rooted in the traditions of the Old Testament and Hellenistic Judaism. His warnings against the sexual vices are indebted to the Levitical laws (Lev. 18; 20) and the interpretative traditions that commonly included sexual offenses in the summaries of the law. The positive attributes also reflect dependence on the Jewish paraenetic tradition. Although love has a place in Paul's moral instruction that is unparalleled in Greek and Jewish literature, Paul's instructions are based on the love command of Leviticus 19:18. The emphasis on patience and humility also reflects the positive evaluation of these virtues in the Old Testament. Undoubtedly, the Christ event shapes Paul's understanding of these attributes.

Paul shaped the vices and virtues for the sake of a community that had come together without shared traditions and moral values. In contrast to Greco-Roman lists, the specific vices and virtues in Paul's letters are not intended for life in the polis or the individual's place in the cosmos. Nor do Paul's vices and virtues focus on individual self-improvement. Unlike Hellenistic Jewish writers, he does not depict an ethic for an ancient people with ancestral ties. His vices and virtues focus on relationships of community members with each other. Vices are primarily anticommunal, while positive attributes are those that involve others within the house church. This communal dimension is a distinctive element in Paul's moral instruction.

Although the form of the vice and virtue lists in Paul resembles aspects of Greco-Roman moral instruction, little in the actual content of Paul's lists is indebted to the Greco-Roman moralists. The parallels that he shares with them were commonplace items shared by Diaspora Jewish writers. Indeed, Paul reflects the influence of the Greco-Roman moralists less than do his predecessors in the Diaspora. He is indebted to the Holiness Code, the summaries of the law, and the Jewish paraenetic tradition. Undoubtedly, the humiliation and self-denying love of Jesus provided Paul's deeper insights into the nature of love, the dominant feature in Paul's lists.

# 5

# Paul, the Law, and Moral Instruction

Paul's claim that "circumcision is nothing and uncircumcision is nothing, but keeping the commandments of God is everything" (1 Cor. 7:19) epitomizes both his moral instruction and the conundrum that confronts the interpreter who attempts to understand the coherence of his moral teaching. The aphoristic ring and the repetition of the phrase "Circumcision is nothing and uncircumcision is nothing" (cf. Gal. 5:6; 6:15) suggest that Paul coined a slogan summarizing his instructions on the law. Inasmuch as circumcision is the primary issue in Paul's confrontation with those who insist that gentile converts obey the law, he uses the word as metonymy for the law itself (cf. Gal. 6:12–13). However, for his brief instructions to new communities, he derives a limited number of commandments from the Torah, omitting (as I maintained in chapter 4) the laws that are the badges of membership: circumcision, Sabbath, and the food laws. Thus he affirms in Galatians and Romans that the believers are not under law but under grace (Gal. 3:10–12; Rom. 6:14), but insists that they keep commandments that are derived from the law.

In view of Paul's negative assessment of the law, the statement that "keeping the commandments is everything" presents the challenge of determining what "keeping the commandments" means. Is Paul referring to the words of Jesus? Or is he referring, as U. Schnelle maintains, to the general commandments that one discerns from nature and popular morality?[1] A third possibility is that, while "circumcision is nothing and uncircumcision is nothing," Paul

1. Schnelle, *Apostle Paul*, 232.

111

instructs his communities to keep some commandments of the Torah while not insisting on those that set Jews apart from the gentile world. In chapter 3, I argued that the instructions (*parangeliai*) of Paul's earliest catechesis (1 Thess. 4:2) were the standard topics of Jewish moral teaching based on the Torah. In this chapter, I will examine Paul's subsequent correspondence, observing the continuity between the earliest catechesis and the commandments he provides in the midst of the controversies that he faced. We may resolve this conundrum presented by 1 Corinthians 7:19 by examining not only Paul's negative statements about the law, but also (a) his positive comments about the usefulness of the law for instruction and (b) his actual appeals to the law as a warrant for the behavior of his converts.

## Freedom from the Law in Paul

As the apostle to the gentiles, Paul broke with established traditions by admitting new converts without requiring circumcision, a sign of the covenant, command of the Torah, and badge of membership among the people of God. His catechesis makes no mention of the other badges of membership that have become critically important in the second temple period, the Sabbath and food laws. Thus Paul makes no reference to these badges of membership in 1 Thessalonians, and his only reference in 1 Corinthians is the claim that "neither circumcision nor uncircumcision is anything" (1 Cor. 7:19). When other teachers challenge Paul's practice in Galatia, he articulates a position about the role of the law among gentile converts, insisting once more that "neither circumcision nor uncircumcision is anything" (Gal. 6:15) and that the "truth of the gospel" requires table fellowship between Jewish and gentile Christians (2:11–14) without regard for the distinction between clean and unclean foods.

In responding to the challenge of his practice of admitting gentiles to full fellowship in the people of God, Paul adamantly denies that the law saves. When he denies the saving significance of the law, he usually describes its role in relationship to God's righteousness (*dikaiosynē*) or God's role as the one who justifies (*dikaiōn*) the sinner. Paul announces the major issue in the thesis statement (*propositio*) of Galatians, maintaining that one "is not justified (*ou dikaioutai*) by works of the law" (Gal. 2:16), adding, "If righteousness (*dikaiosynē*) were from the law, Christ died in vain" (Gal. 2:21). He later claims that those who rely on "works of the law are under a curse" (3:10 NRSV), presumably because they do not do all of the requirements of the law. Thus "no one is justified (*dikaioutai*) by the law" (3:11). Consequently, he maintains to those who "wish to be under the law" (4:21) that such an existence is a return to slavery (4:21–31).

In Galatians Paul speaks interchangeably of the "works of the law" (2:16; 3:2, 10) and the law (2:19; 3:11; 4:21; 5:18), expressing sharp antitheses. He himself "died to the law" in order to "live to God" (2:19). He contrasts works of the law with faith (or the "hearing of faith," 3:2) as paths of salvation (Gal. 2:16; 3:10–11). He maintains that those who are led by the Spirit are not under law (Gal. 5:18). The law was only a disciplinarian until the coming of faith and of Christ (3:24). Thus Paul speaks in the antitheses of law-Christ, law-Spirit, and works of the law versus faith. The law belongs to the old age (3:19–25), while Christ is the seed promised to Abraham (3:16; cf. Gen. 13:15; 17:8) and the one who inaugurates the new era (4:4). Because Christians are the adult children (3:24; 4:1–7), they are no longer under the disciplinarian (5:25). To relapse into the law is to fall from grace (5:4).

In Romans, Paul repeats and elaborates the denial that the law saves, again discussing the law and works of the law in connection with the theme of *dikaiosynē* and speaking in sharp dichotomies about the way to salvation. One is justified by faith and not by works of the law (3:28). We are not under law, but under grace (6:14). Like widows and widowers, believers are no longer bound to the law regarding their former spouse; they are free from the law in order to belong to another (7:4). When people dispute the validity of food laws, Paul declares that the food laws are of no consequence (Rom. 14:14).

Paul comments negatively about the law, however, only in debates about terms of admission for the gentiles. When he speaks of laws that are inconsequential, he illustrates only with references to circumcision and food laws. He does not require the three boundary markers of the Torah that have become the badges of Jewish identity. Thus Paul is not making sweeping statements about the place of the law as a source of ethical reflection, but is focusing on the place of the gentiles within the family of God.

### The Law as Warrant in Paul's Churches

As I observed in chapter 2, Paul establishes an identity for his gentile converts, according to which they have adopted Israel's self-understanding as the "elect" and "saints" who no longer behave "like the gentiles." As Richard Hays has observed,[2] Scripture plays a role in establishing an identity for the communities. They are Abraham's children (Gal. 3:6–29), the culmination of the promise to the patriarch. As the elect and the holy people, Paul's communities live out the destiny of Israel. Indeed, "keeping the commandments" (1 Cor. 7:19) was a common phrase equated with observance of the ordinances of the law. One cannot easily separate the role of Scripture in establishing the identity of the readers from Scripture's role in formulating the behavioral norms for Paul's communities. Thus if the world of the Torah provided the churches with an identity, it also provided their ethos as they placed themselves within Israel's story (cf. ch. 3).

2. Hays, "The Role of Scripture in Paul's Ethics," 33–34.

As interpreters have shown, in some instances Paul instructs his churches in morals without reference to the Torah. In Philippians, for example, his warrant for the behavior of readers is the story of Christ, which forms the identity and the ethos of Paul, his coworkers, and the community. Similarly, in Philemon, he appeals to the familial relationship in Christ to call for a decision. However, in the other letters, Scripture plays an important role in determining the specific conduct of believers. Indeed, at critical points in his argument, Paul declares that the law should guide the behavior of his readers. For example, in his discussion of his right to receive payment for his ministry, he cites Deuteronomy 25:4: "Does the law not say . . . , 'Do not muzzle the ox while it treads the corn'?" (1 Cor. 9:8–9). He adds, "Does God care about oxen? Was it not written for us? The scripture was indeed written for our sake" (1 Cor. 9:10). After recalling the story of the exodus and wilderness wanderings of "our fathers" and their subsequent punishment (1 Cor. 10:1–5), he adds, "These things happened as examples (*typoi*) for us" (10:6 NRSV). The negative examples become the basis for the moral appeals not to repeat the sins of idolatry and sexual immorality (10:7). He cites the narrative of Exodus 32:6 LXX ("The people sat down to eat and rose up to play"), interpreting the passage as a reference to sexual immorality. He concludes that the story was "written down for our instruction" (*nouthesia*, 10:11).

In the conflict between the weak and the strong in Romans 14:1–15:13, Paul concludes the section by appealing to both sides not to please themselves, citing the example of the Christ, who "did not please himself" (Rom. 15:3 NRSV), supporting this claim by citing Psalm 68:10 LXX ("The abuse of the abusers has fallen on me"). He adds, "Whatever was written in former times was written for our instruction" (*didaskalia*, Rom. 15:4). His positive comments occur in the midst of arguments in which he attempts to shape the moral conduct of his readers. *Nouthesia* (1 Cor. 10:11) refers to general instruction, warning, and behavioral correction (cf. Acts 20:31; 1 Cor. 4:14; Eph. 6:4; 1 Thess. 5:12; 2 Thess. 3:15; Titus 3:10).[3] *Didaskalia* refers to both doctrinal and behavioral instruction (cf. 1 Tim. 1:10; 2 Tim. 4:3; Titus 1:9; 2:1). Thus, contrary to a long tradition of interpreters of Paul's ethics,[4] Scripture plays a decisive role in forming the moral insights of new converts. These explicit comments indicate Paul teaches his congregations to read Scripture with the lenses of Christology (Rom. 15:3) and eschatology (1 Cor. 9:10; 10:11), demonstrating its role as example and moral guide.

---

3. Spicq, "*Nouthesia*," *TLNT* 2:548.

4. Cf. Harnack, "The Old Testament in the Pauline Letters and in the Pauline Churches," 33: "The apostle has not given the Old Testament simply as the book of edification to the churches and the Gentiles; he has not fed them out of Scripture from the beginning, nor later on." See also the introduction for the similar arguments of Lindemann and Schnelle.

## The Use of Scripture in Theological and Ethical Discourse

The role of Scripture in shaping the consciousness of believers becomes evident in the wider context of Paul's appeals to Scripture as the warrant for his argument. While he does not appeal to specific Scriptural texts in 1 Thessalonians, Philippians, and Philemon, he places the readers within Israel's symbolic world, and he derives the norms of 1 Thessalonians from the Jewish moral tradition. In the other undisputed letters, he appeals to Scripture. In the Corinthian correspondence, Galatians, and Romans he assumes that his audience will find his arguments from Scripture persuasive. While he assumes the narrative world of Scripture in all his letters, in these he appeals to Scripture to instruct on specific behavior.

### The Corinthian Correspondence

One may observe the function of Scripture in the Corinthian correspondence as Paul moves to shape the identity and ethics of his pagan converts. This identity becomes apparent when Paul calls the readers people who, like the ancient Israelites, are "being sanctified" (1 Cor. 1:2; cf. Lev. 19:2) and "called" by God (1:9; cf. 1:26). Scripture is a guiding norm in both letters. When Paul faces the problem of boasting about human leaders and wisdom in 1 Corinthians (3:21; cf. 4:7), he lays the foundation for the entire book with the reminder that "the word of the cross is foolish to those who are perishing" (1:18) and that he originally founded the church by preaching "Christ crucified" (1:23; 2:2).

He supports his argument for God's reversal of human wisdom with appeals to Scripture, interpreting the situation at Corinth through the lenses of the prophetic and wisdom traditions of the Old Testament. In 1:19–31 prophetic statements provide the frame for interpreting the preaching of the cross in 1:21–25.[5] The rejection of the preaching of the cross by those who celebrate wisdom in Corinth corresponds to the situation recorded in Isaiah 29:14, according to which God says, "I will destroy the wisdom of the wise, and the discernment of the discerning ones I will nullify." The rhetorical questions that follow ("Where is the wise man? Where is the scribe? Where is the debater of this age?" [1:20 RSV]) echo Isaiah 19:12 and 33:18. The Scripture provides the warrant for the command, "Let the one who boasts, boast in the Lord" (1 Cor. 1:31 NRSV). This imperative, a citation of Jeremiah 9:23–24, is the conclusion to 1:26–31, providing the lens for interpreting the situation at Corinth. According to Gail O'Day, "Jeremiah's critique of wisdom, power, and wealth as false sources of identity that violate the covenant are re-imaged by Paul as a critique of wisdom, power, and wealth that impede God's saving acts in Jesus Christ."[6] The words of Isaiah and Jeremiah to the

---

5. Brown, *The Cross and Human Transformation*, 81.
6. O'Day, "Jeremiah 9:22 and 1 Corinthians 1:26–31: A Study in Intertextuality," 259.

boastful and "wise" people are now addressed to the boastful and "wise" people of Corinth.[7]

The entire argument of 1:18–4:21, addressed to those in Corinth who celebrate their own wisdom, is a reflection on Old Testament passages that declare that God is beyond human wisdom,[8] which he will ultimately destroy. Paul employs the words of Scripture to ask, "Who has known the mind of the Lord so as to instruct him?" (1 Cor. 2:16 NRSV; Isa. 40:13 LXX; cf. Jer. 23:18; Wis. 9:13). He interprets the current situation with the words "The one who catches the wise in their deceit" (1 Cor. 3:19; cf. Job 5:12) and "the Lord knows the thoughts of the wise, that they are futile" (Ps. 93:11 LXX). He concludes with the imperative, which echoes the earlier citation of Jeremiah 9:23–24 (1 Cor. 1:31), "Let no one boast among human leaders" (3:21 NRSV). Thus the Old Testament is a resource for understanding the folly of the cross and determining the behavioral norms for the church at Corinth.

While Paul rarely cites the law directly in discussing problems over sexuality and idolatry in 5:1–11:1, he echoes Scripture often and follows established biblical and halakic traditions, as Peter Tomson and Brian Rosner have shown.[9] Having prohibited sexual immorality (porneia) in his original catechesis and subsequent correspondence (1 Cor. 5:9), he must respond to the violation of his instructions (5:1–13), elaborate further on the topic (6:12–20), and answer questions about marriage and the avoidance of porneia (ch. 7). First he responds to incest in the congregation, identifying it with the phrase "a man has his father's wife." The offense of taking one's father's wife is well known in the Torah (cf. Lev. 18:8; 20:11; Deut. 22:30; 27:20). The directive that the man should be removed (arthē) from the congregation (5:2) and the final imperative, "Remove the evil one from your midst" (5:13), form an inclusio indicating Paul's demand, which is also parallel to the instruction "to deliver such a person to Satan" (5:5) and "clean out the old yeast" (5:7). The command "Remove the evil one from your midst" (5:13) is a citation of Deuteronomy 17:7, according to which the holy people should purge all evildoers from the congregation. Indeed, according to Deuteronomy 22:22 (NRSV), the law requires that the community "purge the evil from Israel" when a man takes his father's wife. Not only does he cite Scripture, but as his command to "clean out the old leaven" indicates (5:7), Paul presupposes an identity of the congregation as the holy covenant people as the basis for the morality of separation from the practices of the "gentiles" (5:1).[10]

The appeal to Scripture also shapes the argument throughout Paul's attempt to maintain the separation of the Corinthian believers from fornication and

---

7. Hays, Conversion of the Imagination, 17.

8. Wagner, "Not beyond the Things Which Are Written," 283–85.

9. Rosner, Paul, Scripture, and Ethics, 97–150.

10. See also the discussion of the Corinthians' identity in ch. 2. See also Rosner, Paul, Scripture, and Ethics, 68–80.

idolatry in 5:1–11:1. Although he does not cite Scripture in discussing lawsuits in 6:1–11, the separation between the holy people and the unrighteous shapes the argument (see ch. 2). In the discussion of prostitution in 6:12–20, Paul elaborates on his original catechesis, responding to the Corinthians' own claim about the body and sexuality. He argues against prostitution at four levels, maintaining that (a) the eschatological destiny of the body precludes the believer's intercourse with prostitutes (6:14); (b) union with Christ and union with a prostitute are mutually exclusive (6:15); (c) the body is the temple of the Holy Spirit (6:19); and (d) the believer has been "bought with a price" (6:20). While Paul appeals to a variety of warrants to prohibit sexual immorality, the Old Testament and Jewish paraenetic tradition play a significant role. In 6:16, he appeals to the creation story (Gen. 2:24) to establish that the sexual union involves becoming "one flesh," thus precluding the believer's union with a prostitute. He follows this Scriptural warrant with the imperative, "Flee fornication," which is identical to the demand in *Testament of Reuben* 5:5. In the latter passage, the words "flee fornication" appear as the conclusion to the story of Joseph's refusal of the sexual advances of Potiphar's wife. Paul is apparently citing either the *Testaments of the Twelve Patriarchs* or a common Jewish paraenetic tradition.

Although Paul's advice on marriage and singleness in 1 Corinthians 7 sounds antithetical to the Jewish evaluation of marriage and has analogies to philosophical discussions of marriage,[11] the appeal to the Old Testament and Jewish paraenetic traditions is evident. The discussion is an extension of Paul's prohibition of *porneia* in 1 Corinthians 5–6 and an answer to questions raised by Paul's earlier catechesis. The Corinthians may easily have concluded that the prohibition of *porneia* extended to all sexual relationships. The argument that one must choose between cleaving to the prostitute and cleaving to the Lord (6:16–17) probably raised questions about all sexual relationships, including marriage.

Inasmuch as Paul consistently maintains a preference for singleness throughout chapter 7 (7:7–8, 26, 40), one need not conclude that the phrase "It is good for a man not to touch a woman" (7:1) was a Corinthian slogan. Paul prefers singleness for those who have the gift (7:7) because of the "present distress" (7:26), but offers a firm place for sexual relationships within marriage among the community of saints. His claim that marriage is the alternative to sexual immorality (cf. 7:2, 5) is firmly rooted in the Jewish paraenetic tradition and a part of his catechesis for new converts (cf. 1 Thess. 4:3–8). The idea of conjugal duty (7:3) is consistent with Torah (cf. Exod. 21:10). That one may refrain from sexual relationships for a time of prayer is well known in the halakic traditions.[12]

---

11. Deming, *Paul on Marriage and Celibacy*, 50–106.
12. Cf. *T. Naph.*: "There is a time for intercourse with one's wife, and a time for self-control (*enkrateia*) for prayer" (8:8). See also ch. 1.

In discussing divorce, Paul appeals to the words of Jesus (7:10–12), which were an interpretation of the Torah (Deut. 24:14). Paul's argument provides the background for understanding the comment in 7:19 that what matters is "keeping the commandments." The commandments include instructions from Torah and the words of Jesus, which were based on Torah interpretation. Paul offers behavioral norms based on Scripture and the words of Jesus.

In the treatment of idolatry in 8:1–11:1, Paul faces questions of both community cohesion and idolatry. He introduces the subject of food offered to idols by discussing the importance of love and then defines love in communal terms. One who violates the command to love places a stumbling block (*proskomma*) before the weak (8:9) and causes the brother to fall (*skandalizei*, 8:13). This image of the stone that causes another to fall is probably indebted to the prohibition of placing a stumbling block in the path of the blind person (Lev. 19:14), which belongs in the same context as the love command (Lev. 19:18).

In 14:34, he cites "the law" as warrant for the command for the silence of the women in the assembly without indicating what law he has in mind.[13] Since no Scripture contains those words, one must assume that he is citing a common interpretation of Scripture (cf. Gen. 3:16). While we cannot identify the Scripture under consideration, the fact that Paul cites the law suggests that he assumes its persuasive effect among the Corinthians.

One observes a similar appeal to Scripture in 2 Corinthians. As a defense of Paul's qualifications as a minister, this letter focuses on Paul's conduct in the past rather than on the ethical conduct of the readers. The paraeneses are limited to 12:20–21 (see ch. 4), which reflects a surprising turn in the argument of an epistle that has not focused on the moral conduct of the listeners. Nevertheless, Paul's goal for the Corinthians is that they be his "boast" at the day of Christ (2 Cor. 1:14), and that he may present the church as a pure virgin at the end (11:1–2). Paul can reach this goal only when the Corinthians have been reconciled to God and to the apostle (2 Cor. 5:18–6:2).

Paul defends his ministry by placing himself and his readers within Israel's story. He identifies his ministry with the new covenant of Jeremiah, declaring that he is a minister of the new covenant (2 Cor. 3:6), which has been written on "fleshy hearts" (2 Cor. 3:3). Inasmuch as the new covenant is associated with the restoration of Israel and a new exodus to Israel's homeland,[14] Paul places his defense within Israel's story. As the minister of the new covenant, he

---

13. Because of the instability of 1 Corinthians 14:34–35 within the textual tradition (i.e., these verses appear after 1 Cor. 14:40 in a few manuscripts) and its apparent interruption of the topic of tongues and prophecy, many interpreters treat the passage as an interpolation. Since the passage appears in all extant manuscripts and after 14:33 in the major witnesses, I see no compelling reason to treat it as an interpolation. See the evaluation of the evidence in Niccum, "The Voice of the Manuscripts on the Silence of Women," 242–55.

14. Webb, *Returning Home*, 87.

is the prophet who leads the people back from exile to a restored relationship to God.[15] He identifies his own role as that of the servant of Isaiah 49:1–6 as he appeals to his readers not to "receive the grace of God in vain" (2 Cor. 6:1).[16] He envisions the church as the recipient of God's offer of a new creation (2 Cor. 5:17), which results in reconciliation (2 Cor. 5:18–19).

After defending his ministry (1:15–5:21) and appealing to the Corinthians to respond (6:1–2), Paul makes the extended appeal to them in the combination of indicative and imperative in 2 Corinthians 6:14–7:1. In chapter 2 I discussed this unit in reflections on the identity of the congregation. This unit is also important for its hermeneutic of Scripture in Paul's rare use of a catena of Scriptures cited with little or no comment (cf. Rom. 3:10–18). In 6:14 the imperative, "Do not be unequally yoked with unbelievers," a challenge to separate from the opposition in order to be reconciled to God, recalls the Levitical command prohibiting the yoking of farm animals from different species (Deut. 22:10). Paul reassures the readers with the promise, "I will dwell among them and walk among them, I will be their God and they will be my people," citing Leviticus 26:12. He reiterates the call for separation in the imperative, "Come out from among them, and be separate, says the Lord, and touch no unclean thing" (6:17), echoing Isaiah 52:11. This imperative is followed by the promise, "I will be your father and you will be my sons and daughters" (6:18), an interpretation of 2 Samuel 7:14. Paul places his readers within the narrative of the Israelites in exile, challenging them to "come out from among them." Under the eschatological reading of Scripture, the ancient imperatives now address the church.

Similarly, in the message on the collection, Paul draws the analogy between the Corinthians and the Israelites in the wilderness, recalling the narrative of the gathering of manna (Exod. 16:18) as a warrant for the principle of equality that he inculcates in the Corinthians (2 Cor. 8:15). The narrative provides a precedent for the church. By placing the church within Israel's narrative, he can reassure them of the positive results of their generosity, citing Psalm 119:9 LXX (112:9): "He scatters abroad, he gives to the poor, / His righteousness abides forever" (2 Cor. 9:9). Thus Paul appeals to both the narratives and the legal traditions to provide the identity and shape the behavior of the Corinthians.

### Romans

Romans offers an especially important window into Paul's task of moral formation. Writing to a community that he neither founded nor visited previously, Paul speaks with extraordinary thoroughness, recognizing that

---

15. Thompson, "Reading the Letters as Narrative," 93.
16. Ibid. Like the servant of Isaiah 40–55, he brings a covenant (cf. Isa. 42:6–7) of light (49:6) to those who are blind (43:8; 60:1–2).

this community did not have the benefit of his normal catechesis. Although scholars debate whether Paul is addressing a specific Roman problem or answering criticisms of the theological claims of the earlier letters, Paul undoubtedly "did not allow his immediate situation to govern completely what he had to say,"[17] but elaborated and clarified what he had said in earlier letters.

The moral concerns of Romans are not an addendum to the theological argument, for the symmetry between the first major section (1:18–3:20) and the concluding argument (12:1–15:13) indicates Paul's concern for moral transformation. In 1:18–3:20 he portrays the moral decadence of idolaters and those who have the law, both of whom know the will of God but are disobedient. In 12:1–15:13 Paul describes a new humanity composed of both Jews and gentiles who do the will of God (12:2). The law is the criterion for determining righteousness in 1:18–3:20.[18] We shall see below the role of the law in determining the conduct of the multiethnic community described in 12:1–15:13.

In Romans, he appeals to Scripture both to interpret the situation and to appeal to his readers for appropriate behavior. After insisting that his gospel is "witnessed by the Scriptures" (3:21; cf. 1:2), he argues his case for including gentiles on the basis of Scripture in chapters 1–4 and 9–11, clarifying his message in chapters 5–8. In Romans 12:1–15:13, Paul summons the readers to a life "not conformed to this world" (12:1), to the unrighteous way of life described in 1:18–3:20. After instructing the readers to "discern what the will of God is, the good, the acceptable, and the perfect" (12:2), he instructs them specifically on the transformed existence. Inasmuch as Scripture continues to play a significant role in 12:1–15:13, one may conclude that Scripture plays a major role in ethical discernment. Paul follows the wisdom tradition in assuming that people can interpret a specific course of action within the boundaries of the will of God.[19]

Walter T. Wilson has shown that in chapter 12 the formal characteristics of the moral advice are indebted to the Wisdom tradition. The structure, which consists of a programmatic statement (12:1–2), descriptive statement (12:3–8), and prescriptive section (12:9–21),[20] is common in the Wisdom literature.[21] A similar pattern is present in Romans 13:1–7. The extended paraenetic unit in Romans 12:1–15:13 not only exhibits the common form of moral instruction, but also continually appeals to Scripture, as table 5.1 indicates.[22]

17. Keck, "What Makes Romans Tick?," 329.
18. Although Paul speaks only of those idolaters who know the "righteous judgment of God" (1:32), the offenses he describes are defined by the law.
19. See Wilson, *Love without Pretense*, 138. Cf. Prov. 1:1–7; 2:1–15; Sir. 39:1–11.
20. Wilson, *Love without Pretense*, 132.
21. See the texts in ibid., 95–125.
22. This graphic is adapted from Hübner, *Corpus Paulinum*, 190–210.

## Table 5.1. Old Testament Background of Romans 12–15

| Romans 12–15 | LXX |
| --- | --- |
| 12:1 Therefore, I beseech you, brothers, by the mercies of God (*tōn oiktirmōn tou theou*), to present your bodies as a living sacrifice, holy and pleasing to God, (this is) your spiritual act of worship. | Ps. 24(25):6 Remember your acts of compassion (*tōn oiktirmōn sou*), O Lord. Dan. 2:18 . . . and they sought mercies (*oiktirmous*) from God (*tou theou*). Exod. 34:6 And the Lord passed by before his face, and he called, "The Lord, the Lord God (*kyrios kyrios ho theos*), compassionate (*oiktirmōn*) and merciful, patient and very compassionate and true." |
| 12:9 Love (*hē agapē*) must be sincere. Abhor evil (*to ponēron*); cling to that which is good (*kollōmenoi tō agathō*). | Amos 5:15 We have hated evil (*ponēra*) and loved (*ēgapēkamen*) good (*ta kala*). Ps. 36(37):27 Turn from evil and do good (*ekklinon apo kakou kai poiēson agathon*). Ps. 96(97):10 The ones who love (*agapōntes*) the Lord hate evil (*miseite ponēron*). Prov. 3:7 . . . but fear God and turn away from everything evil (*ekkline apo pantos kakou*). |
| 12:14 Bless (*eulogeite*) those who persecute you; bless (*eulogeite*), and do not curse (*katarasthe*). | Ps. 108(109):28 They will curse (*katarasontai*), but you will bless (*eulogēseis*). |
| 12:15 Rejoice with (*meta*) those who rejoice, weep (*klaiein*) with those who weep (*meta klaiontōn*) (NRSV). | Sir. 7:34 Do not fail to be with those who weep (*klaiontōn*), and mourn with those who mourn (*meta penthountōn penthēson*). |
| 12:16 Be of the same mind (*phronountes*) with one another; do not set your mind (*phronountes*) on high things, but associate with the low ones. Do not be wise (*mē ginesthe phronimoi*) by your own estimation (*par heautois*). | Prov. 3:5 Trust in God with all your heart, and on (*epi de*) your own wisdom do not be encouraged (*sophia mē epairou*). Prov. 3:7 Do not be (*mē isthi*) clever in your own estimation (*phronimos para seautō*), but fear God and turn away from everything evil. Isa. 5:21 Woe to the ones wise in their own estimation (*hoi synetoi en heautois*) and knowledgeable in themselves. Jer. 51:35(45:5) And you will seek (*zētēseis*) for yourself great things (*seautō megala*). Do not seek them (*mē zētēsēs*). |
| 12:17 Do not repay anyone evil for evil. But take care (*pronooumenoi*) to do good before (*kala enōpion*) all people (*anthrōpōn*). | Prov. 3:4 And consider (*pronoou*) what is good before (*kala enōpion*) the Lord and people (*anthrōpōn*). |
| 12:19 Beloved, do not avenge yourself, but allow space for the wrath (of God), for it is written: "Vengeance is mine (*emoi ekdikēsis*), I will repay (*egō antapodōsō*), says the Lord (*kyrios*)." | Deut. 32:35 In the day of vengeance (*ekdikēseōs*), I will repay (*antapodōsō*), in a time when their foot slips, because near is the day of their destruction and things prepared for you are at hand. Lev. 19:18 And your own hand shall not avenge (*ekdikatai*), and you shall not be angry at the sons of your people. . . . |

| Romans 12–15 | LXX |
|---|---|
| | Nah. 1:2 God is jealous and the Lord is avenging (*theos zēlōtēs kai ekdikōn kyrios*), the Lord avenging (*ekdikōn kyrios*) with wrath (*meta thymou*), the Lord avenging himself on (*ekdikōn kyrios*) his adversaries, and removing his enemies.<br><br>Prov. 24:29 Do not say, "In the manner in which he treated me, I shall treat him; and I shall repay him as he wronged (*ēdikēsen*) me." |
| 12:20 But if your enemy is hungry (*ean peina ho echthros sou*), feed him (*psōmize auton*); if he is thirsty (*ean dipsa*), give him drink (*potize auton*); for by doing this you will heap coals of fire on his head (*touto gar poiōn anthrakas pyros sōreuseis epi tēn kephalēn autou*). | Prov. 25:21–22 If your enemy is hungry (*ean peina ho echthros sou*), nourish him (*trephe auton*); if he is thirsty (*ean dipsa*), give him drink (*potize auton*). For by doing this you will heap coals of fire on his head (*touto gar poiōn anthrakas pyros sōreuseis epi tēn kephalēn autou*), and the Lord will reward (*kyrios antapodōsei*) you with good things.<br><br>4 Bas.(2 Kings) 6:21–22 And the king of Israel said, when he saw them, "Shall by striking, I strike them, father?" And he said, "You shall not strike; if you did not strike them with your sword and your bow, would you strike them? Serve up food and water before them, and let them eat and drink, and let them go to their master." |
| 13:1 Let every person be subject to the governing authorities, for there is no authority except from God. The authorities that exist were established by God. | Prov. 8:15 Through me kings rule, and rulers prescribe justice/righteousness.<br><br>Prov. 8:16 Through me great men are magnified, and through me tyrants rule the earth.<br><br>Wis. 6:1–3 Hear therefore, you kings, and understand; learn, you judges of the ends of the earth. Give ear, you who preside over the multitudes, and boast over nations, because your dominion was given you from the Lord, and your dominance from the Most High. He will examine your deeds and inquire into your counsels.<br><br>Sir. 10:4 In the hand of the Lord is the authority/governance of the earth.<br><br>Sir. 17:17 For each nation he appointed a leader, and the Lord's portion is Israel.<br><br>Dan. 2:21 And he changes seasons and times; he ordains kings and deposes, giving wisdom to the wise, and intelligence to the ones knowing understanding.<br><br>Dan. 2:37 You, O King, are king of kings to whom the God of heaven has given a kingdom—strong, fortified, and honorable.<br><br>Dan. 5:21 . . . until he knew that the Most High God is sovereign over the kingdom of men and he gives it to whomever it seems good. |
| 13:9 For the commandments, "You shall not commit adultery (*ou moicheuseis*), | Deut. 5:18 You shall not commit adultery (*ou moicheuseis*). | Exod. 20:14 You shall not commit adultery (*ou moicheuseis*). |

| Romans 12–15 | LXX | |
|---|---|---|
| You shall not murder (*ou phoneuseis*), | Deut. 5:17 You shall not murder (*ou phoneuseis*). | Exod. 20:13 You shall not murder (*ou phoneuseis*). |
| You shall not steal (*ou klepseis*), | Deut. 5:19 You shall not steal (*ou klepseis*). | Exod. 20:15 You shall not steal (*ou klepseis*). |
| Do not covet (*ouk epithymēseis*)," | Deut. 5:21 You shall not covet (*ouk epithymēseis*) your neighbor's (*plēsion*) wife; you shall not covet (*ouk epithymēseis*) your neighbor's (*tou plēsion sou*) house or his field. | Exod. 20:17 You shall not covet (*ouk epithymēseis*) your neighbor's (*plēsion*) wife; you shall not covet (*ouk epithymēseis*) your neighbor's (*tou plēsion sou*) house or his field. |
| . . . and any other commandment, are summed in this word, "Love your neighbor as yourself (*agapēseis ton plēsion sou hōs seauton*)." | Deut. 5:20 You shall not testify falsely against your neighbor (*plēsion*) with a false testimony.<br><br>Wis. 6:18 (19) . . . and love (*agapē*) is keeping her laws (*nomōn*).<br><br>Lev. 19:18 And you shall love your neighbor as yourself (*agapēseis ton plēsion sou hōs seauton*). | Exod. 20:16 You shall not testify falsely against your neighbor (*plēsion*) with a false testimony. |
| 13:10 Love (*agapē*) does not do wrong to a neighbor (*plēsion*); therefore, love (*agapē*) is the fulfillment of the law (*nomou*). | Lev. 19:18 you shall love your neighbor as yourself. | |
| 14:8 For if we live, we live to the Lord (*tō kyriō zōmen*), and if we die (*apothnēskōmen*), we die to the Lord. Therefore, if we live (*zōmen*) or if we die (*apothnēskōmen*), we are the Lord's (*tou kyriou esmen*). | 4 Macc. 7:19 . . . since they believe they do not die (*apothnēskousin*) to God (*theō*), even as our patriarchs Abraham and Isaac and Jacob, but live (*zōsin*) to God (*theō*).<br><br>4 Macc. 16:25 And this they knew also: that those who die (*apothnēskontes*) for the sake of God (*tō theō*), live (*zōsin*) to God (*tō theō*), just as Abraham and Isaac and Jacob and all the patriarchs. | |
| 14:11 For it is written, "As I live, says the Lord (*zō egō legei kyrios*), every knee shall bow to me (*hoti emoi kampsei pan gony*), and (*kai*) every tongue (*pasa glōssa*) shall confess (*exomologēsetai*) to God (*tō theō*)." | Isa. 49:18 As I live, says the Lord (*zō egō legei kyrios*).<br><br>Isa. 45:23 For every knee shall bow to me (*hoti emoi kampsei pan gony*), and every tongue confess (*kai exomologēsetai pasa glōssa*) to God (*tō theō*). | |
| 14:13 never to put a stumbling block (*proskomma*) or hindrance in the way of another (NRSV). | Lev. 19:14 You shall not revile the deaf or put a stumbling block before the blind (NRSV). | |
| 14:19 Therefore, let us pursue (*diōkōmen*) that which promotes peace (*eirēnēs*) and the building up of one another. | Ps. 33:15(34:14) Turn away from evil, and do good. Seek peace (*eirēnēn*), and pursue it (*diōxon autēn*). | |

| Romans 12–15 | LXX |
|---|---|
| 15:1 We who are strong ought to bear with the infirmities of the weak, and not please ourselves. | |
| 15:3 For Christ did not please himself, but just as it is written, "The insults of those who insulted you fell upon me (*hoi oneidismoi tōn oneidizontōn se epepesan ep' eme*)." | Ps. 68:10(69:9) . . . and the insults of those who insulted you fell upon me (*hoi oneidismoi tōn oneidizontōn se epepesan ep' eme*). |
| 15:4 For whatever was written in former times was written for instruction, in order that through endurance and through the encouragement (*paraklēseōs*) of the scriptures (*tōn graphōn*) we might have (*echōmen*) hope. | 1 Macc. 12:9 We too, then, not being in need of these things and taking comfort (*paraklēsin*) in the holy books (*echontes ta biblia ta hagia*) in our hands . . . |
| 15:9 Just as it is written, "On account of this I will praise you among the nations and sing hymns to your name (*dia touto exomologēsomai soi en ethnesin kai tō onomati sou psalō*)." | Ps. 17:50(18:49) On account of this I will praise you among the nations (*dia touto exomologēsomai soi en ethnesin*), O Lord, and sing hymns to your name (*kai tō onomati sou psalō*). |
| 15:10 Rejoice, gentiles (*ethnē*), with his people. | Deut. 32:43 Rejoice, O nations, with his people. |
| 15:11 And again, "Praise (*aineite*) the Lord (*ton kyrion*), all you nations (*panta ta ethnē*), applaud him all you peoples (*epainesatōsan auton pantes hoi laoi*)." | Ps. 116(117):1 Praise (*aineite*) the Lord (*ton kyrion*), all you nations (*panta ta ethnē*), applaud him all you peoples (*epainesate auton pantes hoi laoi*). |
| 15:12 And again Isaiah says, "The root of Jesse will come (*estai hē riza tou Iessai*), one who will rise up to rule the nations (*kai ho anistamenos archein ethnōn*), in him the nations shall hope (*ep' autō ethnē elpiousin*)." | Isa. 11:10 And it shall be (*estai*) in that day, the root of Jesse will come, one who will rise up to rule the nations, in him the nations shall hope (*hē riza tou Iessai kai ho anistamenos archein ethnōn ep' autō ethnē elpiousin*). |

Paul speaks with the language of the LXX, appealing to all parts of it, especially the psalms and the Wisdom literature. The words of Proverbs continue to provide a behavioral norm for his congregation (Prov. 25:21–22; Rom. 12:19–21). The Decalogue and the love command from Leviticus 19:18 play an important role in guiding the community (Rom. 13:8–10). As in 1 Corinthians, Paul appeals to the Levitical prohibition against placing a stone in the path of a blind person when he instructs the "strong" not to place a stumbling block in the path of the weak (14:13). He supports the imperative to the church to "welcome one another" with appeals to Scripture, which, he claims, was "written for our instruction."

Like his contemporaries in Second Temple Judaism, Paul appeals to the interpreted Scripture to provide guidance for his communities. He finds precedent in the narratives (1 Cor. 10:1–11; 2 Cor. 8:15) and guidance from the legal sections (cf. 1 Cor. 9:9), prophets, psalms, and Wisdom literature. In several instances he refers to his hermeneutical method in applying Scripture to his own situation. In 1 Corinthians 9:9–10, for example, he argues that the instructions for oxen are "written for us," and he elaborates on this principle in 10:1–11. All the events described were "for our instruction," upon whom the end of the ages has come. As the eschatological community, the church still looks to the Torah as its own story. As the heir of Israel, the church continues to turn to Torah as a warrant for behavior.

Paul is more explicit in his use of Scripture in Romans 14:1–15:13. He places his ministry within the narrative of Israel, indicating that the gentile mission is the realization of the prophetic hope for the inclusion of the nations (15:7–13). At the conclusion of the argument prescribing communal ethics, Paul urges the readers, "We the strong ought to bear the burdens of the weak and not please ourselves" (15:1), adding the imperative, "Let each one please his neighbor for the good for edification" (15:2). The reference to the "neighbor" suggests that Paul's instruction is a paraphrase of the love command, "You shall love your neighbor as yourself" (Lev. 19:18), which he has cited previously (Rom. 13:9). The warrant for the command is christological: "For Christ did not please himself" (15:3). Paul supports the christological reading with the citation, "The abuse of the abusers has fallen on me" (15:3), an echo of Psalm 69:9 (68:10 LXX). Thus the psalm tells the story of Jesus. The christological reading of the psalm blends with the appeal to the story of Jesus.

This warrant is followed by Paul's hermeneutic in 15:4. Whereas he said in 1 Corinthians that Scripture is written for our instruction (*nouthesia*, 1 Cor. 10:11), here it is written for our teaching (*didaskalia*). "Our teaching" (NRSV "instruction") refers not only to the role of Scripture's story, but also to Scripture's role in shaping the behavior of the community. Scripture has an important place in the discernment of the will of God (cf. 12:2). Texts that guided the lives of agrarian peoples remain normative for the church. Paul interprets texts through christological and eschatological lenses, but he appeals to them nevertheless. While he regards some laws as of no consequence (1 Cor. 7:19; Rom. 14), the interpreted Torah remains a warrant for behavior. Paul filters his appeal to the Scriptures through his understanding of the Christ event and the eschatological moment, combining both with his appeal to Scripture.

## The Nature of the Law in Paul

In the two epistles in which Paul argues that believers are not under law, he encourages his listeners, "Love your neighbor as yourself," citing Leviticus

19:18 as a norm for behavior. Since Paul has insisted that believers are not under the law, this citation in Galatians 5:14 and Romans 13:9 comes as a surprise to the reader. While believers are "not under law" (Gal. 5:18), the love command remains obligatory and is the fulfillment of the law (5:14; cf. 6:2). Although love is central to Paul's ethic in all of the letters, only in these two passages does Paul cite Leviticus 19:18.

### The Law in Galatians 5–6

In Galatians 5:13–14, Paul introduces the paraenetic section, instructing the readers to maintain their freedom by serving each other through love (5:13) rather than biting and devouring one another (5:15). Paul provides the warrant in 5:14, saying that "the whole law is fulfilled in a single commandment, in this, 'you shall love your neighbor as yourself'" (5:14 NRSV; Lev. 19:18). In the following paraenetic section, he offers other statements about the law. In 5:23 he concludes the list of the fruit of the Spirit with, "Against such as these there is no law." In 6:2 (RSV) he says, "Bear one another's burdens, and so fulfill the law of Christ." These passages raise questions about the place of the law in Paul's ethics; that is, what is the "law of Christ"? How is it related to "the whole law" (5:14)? What does Paul mean by the puzzling statement, "Against such as these there is no law"?

The parallels in 5:14 and 6:2 suggest that Paul associates "the whole law" with "the law of Christ." "Love your neighbor as yourself" (Gal. 5:14) is parallel to "Bear one another's burdens" (6:2). Paul uses the passive voice, "the whole law is fulfilled," in 5:14 while he uses the active, "you will fulfill (*anaplērōsete*) the law," in 6:2. These parallels suggest a relationship between the "whole law" and "the law of Christ." Hence the law has a place in Paul's ethics, even if it does not include the regulations on circumcision, Sabbath, food laws, and festivals.

The question is, what law does Paul have in mind? In two passages as well as in Roman 13:8, Paul uses forms of *plēroun* with *nomos*; the word also appears in Romans 8:4. In his use of *plēroun* with the law, Paul always speaks in positive terms, whereas he uses other verbs to speak in negative terms (cf. Gal. 5:3, "keep the law," *ton nomon poiēsai*). Thus believers fulfill the law that does not include the Jewish boundary markers. Inasmuch as the references to the fulfillment of the law frame the paraenetic section in 5:13–6:2, one may conclude that the specific "works of the flesh" (5:16–21) and "fruit of the Spirit" (5:22–23) offer examples of the negative and positive qualities elaborating on the love command. The law "is fulfilled" (5:14) and believers "fulfill the law of Christ" (6:2) when they shun the vices listed and exhibit the positive qualities of the "fruit of the Spirit." Paul has reinterpreted the love command of Leviticus 19:18 to focus on the community as a family. Just as Hellenistic Jewish writers summarized the law without mentioning the Jewish boundary markers (see ch. 1), Paul has redefined the law in view of the Christ event. Unlike Hellenistic Jewish writers, he does not identify the law with the Greek cardinal virtues, but adopts a list of vices and virtues that are consistent with Diaspora instruction and early Christian catechesis.[23]

The statement that concludes the fruit of the Spirit in 5:23, "Against such as these there is no law," has perplexed interpreters. The parallel to the statements in 5:14 and 6:2 suggest that the statement is an elaboration on the idea of fulfilling the law; that is, Paul is indicating that the vice and virtue lists are coherent with the law. As John Barclay has suggested, "No law (certainly not the Mosaic law) could be cited against these qualities."[24] Paul obviously leaves out circumcision and food laws, an omission that no Jewish writer would make. The "law of Christ" (6:2) is the law as interpreted through the Christ event with a focus on the love command. As the context indicates, it is not the words of Jesus but the law interpreted in light of Jesus that is normative.[25]

### The Law in Romans 13:8–10

Paul's last reference to the law in Romans also comes as a surprise to the reader, inasmuch as Paul speaks positively of fulfilling the law (13:8, 10) after insisting consistently throughout the argument that believers are neither under law (6:14) nor capable of doing the good. Romans 13:8–10 is a pivotal point in the concluding ethical section in 12:1–15:13. After urging believers to discern the will of God and the good and the perfect (12:2), Paul describes the transformed existence as a communal life (12:3–15:13). The command to love without hypocrisy within the familial context (12:9–10) and the call for readers to love one another (13:8) form an inclusio of a major unit of the ethical section. In an additional inclusio in 13:8–10, Paul says that the one who loves the other has "fulfilled the law" (13:8) and that "love is the fulfillment of the law" (13:10). Paul anticipated this statement earlier in the argument with the claim that "the just requirement of the law [is] fulfilled in us who walk not according to the flesh, but according to the Spirit" (8:4 NRSV). Thus, as in Galatians, Paul claims that believers who are not under the law "fulfill the law."

Paul illustrates his claim that believers fulfill the law with references to four of the commands of the Decalogue, all taken from the second tablet. These four—and any other commandment—are summed up (*anakephalaiountai*) in the love command, "You shall love your neighbor as yourself." As in Galatians, the love of neighbor involves others within the community. In Romans, the neighbor includes those who belong to different ethnic groups.

23. Barclay, *Obeying the Truth*, 124.
24. Ibid.
25. Lohse, "Das Gesetz Christi," 387–89.

The four commandments from the Decalogue are incorporated into the love command. One who practices the love command will not violate the second tablet. Thus, while Paul will go on to say, contrary to the Torah, that "nothing is common of itself" (14:14), he speaks of the Torah in positive terms. Indeed, by framing the instructions in 12:9–13:10 with the love command, he gives concrete instructions for loving conduct within the community.

In Romans 14:1–15:13, Paul illustrates the case. Consistent with chapters 1–4, he continues to maintain that "nothing is common." Nevertheless, he insists that believers walk according to love (14:15). His final summary, calling on believers to please the neighbor (15:2), echoes the directive of Leviticus 19:18 to love one's neighbor. The love command remains in force. The practice of the love command fulfills the law. As in Galatians, Paul envisions a community that fulfills the Torah, but does not separate Jew from gentile. The instructions of 12:1–15:13 are not comprehensive, but illustrative of the life of fulfilling the law as Paul has redefined it.

### The Law of God and the Law of Nature: Romans 1:18–32 (1 Cor. 11:2–16)

Paul appeals to the law, as I noted earlier (see above, "The Law as Warrant in Paul's Churches"), to establish community norms for the role of women in the public assembly (1 Cor. 14:34). These instructions conclude the major section on corporate worship (11:2–14:40) and form an inclusio with 11:2–16, which addresses concerns about the attire of men and women at Corinth. Although Paul does not indicate specifically what evoked these instructions, one may assume that he is continuing to answer questions that have emerged in the Corinthian church. Contrary to many interpreters, one need not assume that Paul is responding to a crisis initiated by women who exercised new freedom as a response to Paul's claim that "there is no male and female" (cf. Gal. 3:28).[26] Inasmuch as this community was composed of people from a variety of cultural backgrounds, questions about decency in clothing and the public role of women were probably inevitable. The reference to the practice of the churches (11:16; 14:33) indicates that Paul's catechesis included norms for dress and conduct in the assemblies.

Although Paul's initial praise of the Corinthians for keeping the traditions is a *captatio benevolentiae*[27] introducing the conversation, the introduction of the discussion of the Lord's Supper in the following unit ("I do not praise you," 11:17) suggests that Paul is not responding to a crisis as with the case of the Lord's Supper (11:17–34). Paul's introduction of the community's traditions

---

26. Cf. Scroggs, "Paul and the Eschatological Woman," 291–93; Meeks, "The Image of the Androgyne," 165–208.

27. *Captatio benevolentiae* is a rhetorical device at the beginning of a speech that seeks the good will of the listener.

was probably a response to the questions raised by the community.[28] Previous references to sexual matters in 5:1–13 and 6:12–7:40 suggest that unresolved issues on such matters in both private and community life undermine the harmony of the church.[29] Paul's previous catechesis constitutes the "traditions" that he has delivered. Thus, here as earlier (1 Cor. 6:9–10), Paul lays the foundation for the argument with an appeal to the earlier instruction.

The tradition consists of the ontological hierarchy in 11:3, expanding on earlier versions of the hierarchy to include the relationship between men and women (cf. 3:23; 8:6). Anticipating the argument about head coverings, Paul employs the term *kephalē* to describe the hierarchy of being. His commentary in 11:7–9 indicates that the hierarchy is derived from the creation story. Because the man is in the image of God (Gen. 1:27) and created prior to the woman (11:9), he is *kephalē* over the woman. The order of creation is the warrant for the commands in 11:6–7. The woman should be covered (11:6), but the man "ought not to cover his head" because he was made in the image of God (11:7). Creation and ontology are the basis for behavioral norms; "is" is the basis for the "ought."

Paul elaborates on the foundation of his argument in 11:13–14, appealing to what is "fitting" (*prepon*) and to nature (*physis*) as the basis for his claim that a woman should wear a head covering while praying (11:13) because long hair is her glory (11:15), while it is a dishonor for a man to wear long hair (11:14). Paul undoubtedly employs a common Stoic argument as the basis for moral conduct. Stoics commonly appealed to nature as the basis for ethical judgment,[30] including norms for beards and long hair as well as sexual relationships.[31]

Scholars have found Paul's transition from the argument from creation to the Stoic argument from nature puzzling, if not contradictory. Hellenistic Jewish writers, however, maintained that the laws of the Torah were consistent with the laws of nature. Philo demonstrated the assumption of the convergence of the Torah with the laws of nature in his allegorical treatment of the Pentateuchal narratives.[32] "The world is in harmony with the law, and the law with the world, and . . . the world" (*Creation* 3). He also presents many individual laws as laws of nature (*Rewards* 108; *Spec. Laws* 2.129–30; 3.112; *Decalogue*

28. The content of the tradition has been debated. Ellis suggests that 11:3–16 and 14:34–36 are variations on the domestic code that Paul handed on to his churches ("Traditions in 1 Corinthians," 492). Tomson argues that the traditions are the common halakic norms of the synagogue (*Paul and the Jewish Law*, 132–33).

29. Thompson, "Creation, Shame and Nature in 1 Cor 11:2–16," 244.

30. Diogenes Laertius, *Vit.* 7.87. "Zeno was the first . . . to designate as the end 'life in agreement with nature,' which is the same as the virtuous life."

31. Cf. the argument of Epictetus (*Diatr.* 1.16.9–14) on the wearing of a beard: "Wherefore, we ought to preserve the signs which God has given; we ought not to throw them away; we ought not, as far as in us lies, to confuse the sexes which have been distinguished in this fashion."

32. See Najman, "The Law of Nature and the Authority of Mosaic Law," 55–73; Horsley, "The Law of Nature in Philo and Cicero."

132; *Sobriety* 25).[33] The common view in Hellenistic Judaism that the specific regulations in the Torah are rooted in the law of nature is the background for Paul's appeal both to the creation story and to nature as the basis for the regulations on head covering. Thus Paul's argument from nature presupposes that nature agrees with the Torah.

Paul's specific statement that the woman who prays and prophesies "with an uncovered head (*akataklyptō tē kephalē*) disgraces her head" (11:5) insofar as it "is one and the same thing as being shaved" (*tē exyrēmenē*) is probably based on the midrashic reading of Old Testament texts, according to which the woman's shaved head is the symbol of shame (cf. Deut. 21:12; 2 Sam. 10:4; 1 Chron. 19:4; Isa. 7:20). Paul's equation of the uncovered head with the shaved head in 11:5b is probably based on Numbers 5:18 (LXX), according to which the priest will "uncover the head" (*apokalypsei tēn kephalēn*) of the woman suspected of adultery.[34] Thus Paul stands in continuity with Hellenistic Jewish writers in maintaining a convergence between the Torah and the law of nature.

Paul's argument in Romans 1 also appeals to creation (1:19–23) as he describes behavior that is "contrary to nature" (*para physin*, 1:26). This passage appears within the larger context of 1:18–3:20, which depicts the wrath of God (1:18) that is revealed against "all impiety (*asebeia*) and unrighteousness (*adikia*) of those who hold the truth in unrighteousness (*adikia*)." As the inclusio of 1:18, 32 indicates, Paul focuses on those who conduct themselves contrary to their knowledge of the divine will; he speaks of those who "hold the truth in unrighteousness" (1:18) and know "the just requirements of God" (1:32). Some know God's will as it is revealed in nature (1:19–23) but fail to conform to it, while others know God's will as it is revealed in the law (2:1–29) and do not do it. As a result, both gentiles and Jews are under the power of sin (3:9). Thus all humanity knows God's will, but falls short of it (cf. 3:23). Paul presents this pessimistic depiction of humanity's corrupt mind (1:28; cf. 1:21) in 1:18–3:20 as a prelude to his challenge to the community to be "transformed" by the renewing of their minds (12:2). The concluding depiction of the community that does God's will (12:1–15:13) envisions the reversal within the believing community of the pessimistic description in 1:18–32.

Although Paul does not specifically refer to gentiles in Romans 1:18–32, his argument conforms to the traditional depiction of gentiles in Hellenistic Jewish sources. Interpreters have observed the close connection between Paul's argument and the polemic against idolatry in Wisdom 12–14. Indeed, Romans 1:19–23 follows the argument from natural revelation and the criticism of idolatry as the source of human immorality that is found in Wisdom 13:1–14:21 and other texts of the period.[35] Just as Wisdom 14:12 declares that

---

33. Koester, "*Physis*," *TDNT* 9:269.

34. Thompson, "Creation, Shame and Nature in 1 Cor 11:2–16," 250.

35. The seer in *2 Baruch* accuses the unrighteous ones of ignoring the evidence of God's will revealed in creation (*2 Bar.* 54:17–18; cf. 48:9) and falling into inexcusable sin. According

idolatry is the beginning of sexual immorality (*porneia*), Paul maintains that, as a result of idolatry, "God gave them up to the desires (*epithymiai*) of their hearts" (1:24) and that "God gave them up to the passions of dishonor" (*pathē atimias*, 1:26). As in other moral instructions, Paul lists the sexual offenses (1:24–27) and then continues with antisocial vices (1:29–31; cf. 1 Cor. 6:9–11; Gal. 5:19–21). Paul assumes that the violation of the first commandment of the Decalogue (1:23) results in the rampant violation of commandments prohibiting offenses against other human beings.[36]

As in his earlier catechesis, Paul assumes that the "passion of lust" is the characteristic offense of the gentiles (cf. 1 Thess. 4:5), which believers may overcome (Rom. 6:12; Gal. 5:16). This characterization of gentiles was commonplace in the literature of Hellenistic Judaism. Paul describes the effects of the "passion of lust" under the heading of "uncleanness" (*akatharsia*, 1:24), placing the moral requirements within the Levitical categories of clean and unclean, as he does in the other letters (cf. Rom. 6:19; 2 Cor. 12:21; Gal. 5:19; Eph. 4:19; 1 Thess. 2:3; 4:7). In contrast to the earlier letters, however, Paul does not illustrate the effects of *epithymia* with a reference to *porneia* (cf. 1 Cor. 5:10–11; 6:9; Gal. 5:19). Instead, he offers a vivid illustration in parallel expressions concerning women and men: "Women exchanged the natural use" (*tēn physikēn chrēsin*) for behavior that was "contrary to nature" (*para physin*), and men likewise left the "natural use" (*tēn physikēn chrēsin*) of women as "they burned in their impulses for one another, men doing shameless things with men" (1:27). One cannot be sure why he draws the parallel between the deeds of men and women. Paul focuses on these vices rather than on *porneia*, as he does elsewhere. Having made the argument from nature, he makes it his primary concern to vividly describe behavior that is unnatural.

Paul's terminology suggests that what is natural is the relationship between a man and a woman. "Natural" (*kata physin*) and "unnatural" (*para physin*) were common ways to distinguish between heterosexual and homosexual intercourse.[37] Plato records the comment of one who says that "when male unites with female for procreation, the pleasure experienced is held to be due to nature" (*kata physin*). On the other hand, it is "contrary to nature [*para physin*] when male mates with male or female with female" (*Leg.* 636c). In speaking out against prostitution, Dio Chrysostom says that brothel keepers have no respect for Aphrodite, "whose name stands for the normal [*kata physin*] intercourse between a man and a woman" (*Or.* 7.135). Plutarch (*Amat.* 751) indicates that "to consort with males" is "weakness and effeminacy [*malakia*

---

to *Sib. Or.* 3:8–15, sinners have not followed the straight path of the Creator. Idolatry results in the violation of God's will (3:35–45) and vices that destroy human society. These include both sexual and antisocial vices.

36. Reinmuth, *Geist und Gesetz*, 47.

37. See Hays, "Relations Natural and Unnatural," 192.

*kai thēlytēti*] on the part of those who, contrary to nature [*para physin*], allow themselves to be 'mounted like cattle.'"[38]

In maintaining a convergence between the law of nature and the Torah, Hellenistic Jewish authors applied the Stoic concept of living according to nature, distinguishing between natural and unnatural sexual acts. Philo speaks of the "use prescribed by nature" (*kata physin chrēsis*) of the seven natural capacities of the human: sexual potency, speech, and the five senses (*Names* 111–12). Hence he insists that the laws governing sexual distinctions are founded on the laws of nature and that violations of these laws are offenses against nature. In his discussion of sexual laws in *Special Laws* 3, he interprets the statutes of Moses as the dictates of nature. According to Philo, the men of Sodom "threw off from their necks the law of nature" and applied themselves to "forbidden forms of intercourse." He adds, "Not only in their mad lust for women did they violate the marriages of their neighbors, but also men mounted males without respect for the sex nature which the active partner shares with the passive" (*Abraham* 135).[39] Philo condemns the men who submit to the "disease of effemination," obscuring their masculinity by wearing women's clothes, braiding their hair in women's style, putting on perfumes, attempting to "transform the male nature into the female." These people debase "the sterling coin of nature" (*Spec. Laws* 3.38). In the *Testament of Naphtali*, the patriarch describes the order of nature, encouraging the listeners to conduct themselves in accordance with nature rather than "become like Sodom which departed from the order of nature" (3:4). Josephus interprets Jewish marriage laws, indicating that the law "recognizes no sexual connections, except the natural [*kata physin*] union of man and wife, and that only for procreation" (*Ag. Ap.* 2.199). He adds that the law prohibits same-sex relations, alluding to prohibition of these relationships in Leviticus (20:13). The author of *Sentences of Pseudo-Phocylides* advises parents, "If a child is a boy, do not let locks grow on his head. Braid not his crown nor make cross-knots on the top of his head. Long hair is not fit for men, but for voluptuous women." He adds, "Transgress not for unlawful sex the natural limits of sexuality."[40]

The view, shared by Greek and Jewish literature, that homosexual acts are "contrary to nature" (*para physin*) indicates that the unnatural acts of men and women in Romans 1:26–27 are the homosexual practices commonly condemned in Jewish literature. Like the writer of the *Letter of Aristeas*, who claims that "the majority of other men defile themselves in their relationships" (152), procuring males and defiling mothers and daughters, Paul distinguishes his own community (cf. Rom. 6:12–20; 12:1–15:13) from those who engage in unnatural acts. Although Paul does not mention the law, he is dependent on

38. A paraphrase of Plato, *Phaedr.* 250e; cf. *Leg.* 636c.
39. Thompson, "Creation, Shame and Nature in 1 Cor 11:2–16," 255.
40. Van der Horst, *Sentences of Pseudo-Phocylides*, 190.

the Jewish interpretative traditions based on Leviticus, assuming that the law of nature converges with the written law. Although the law does not mention female homosexuality, the interpretative tradition expands the statutes to include females. Like his Jewish contemporaries, he appeals to the Holiness Code (Lev. 17–26) for the behavioral norms of his community.

As I demonstrated in chapter 1, ancient summaries of the law consistently affirmed marriage and condemned the sexual practices prohibited in Leviticus 18–20. Summaries of the sexual laws were commonly adapted for the Diaspora situation. Just as Paul relies on the traditions of Wisdom 13–14 to articulate a morality based on natural law (Rom. 1:19–23), he demonstrates his dependence on this tradition in his reference to homosexual acts (cf. Wis. 14:25–26), a common theme in summaries of the law.[41] His describing of prohibited sexual practices under the heading of "uncleanness" both here (1:24) and in his other moral instructions (cf. 1 Thess. 4:3, 7) indicates that he articulates his ethics within the framework of the Holiness Code.

Consistent with the portrayals of human depravity in Wisdom 14:22–31, Paul does not isolate the sexual offenses from those that undermine social order. As in his other moral instructions (cf. 1 Cor. 6:9–11; Gal. 5:19–22), he places sexual offenses alongside antisocial vices (Rom. 1:29–31). This linkage is a regular feature of Jewish summaries of the law, which commonly warn against both sexual vices and such offenses as greed, strife, envy, and slander. Thus Paul does not focus only on homosexual practice, but includes it among other vices that demonstrate the unrighteousness of those who know the "just requirements of God" (1:32) but fail to practice them.

### Conclusion: Keeping the Commandments under the Law of Christ

Paul's declaration that "circumcision is nothing and uncircumcision is nothing, but keeping the commandments is everything" appropriately summarizes the place of the law in his moral instruction. Although he does not insist that gentiles keep the commandments that served as boundary markers for Jews, he does rely on the law, especially as his predecessors in the Diaspora had interpreted it, when composing his moral instructions. The statutes of the law determine Paul's views of good and evil. He assumes that all humanity is subject to the law's demands.[42] Like Diaspora Jews, Paul turned to the Holiness Code for guidance. He appropriated the love command (Lev. 19:18), which originally concerned care for other Israelites, and applied it to multiethnic communities. Paul also interpreted the laws regulating sexual activity in Leviticus 18 and 20 for his communities. He followed his predecessors in presupposing that the law of nature was consistent with the written law.

41. Sterling, "Universalizing the Particular," 70, 76.
42. Reinmuth, *Geist und Gesetz*, 47.

Like his predecessors, Paul does not apply the entire Torah to his communities, but appeals only to a limited range of passages. He challenges his communities to "keep the commandments" as they were interpreted within the community under his guidance. Under the "law of Christ" (Gal. 6:2), the community interpreted the commandments through the lenses of the Christ event, which gave special insight to them as they fulfilled the love command (Lev. 19:18). In his appeal to nature as a warrant for human behavior, Paul follows the Jewish paraenetic tradition, which equated the Torah with the law of nature. Thus his appeal to nature is inseparable from his appeal to the law.

# 6

# Paul, the Passions, and the Law

When Paul instructed his communities on appropriate conduct, a long tradition of moral instruction preceded him in both the philosophical and biblical traditions. Indeed, both traditions offered a path to human improvement through fulfilling moral obligations. For the philosophical tradition, the highest human good was *eudaimonia*, which Martha Nussbaum renders as "human flourishing."[1] Philosophers were the physicians of the soul, and their ethical instruction was the therapy for those who wished to reach this goal.[2] Only those who performed "the good" could attain *eudaimonia*. For the biblical tradition, the goal is "life," and the path to life is variously described as the keeping of the commandments of the Torah (cf. Deut. 8:6; 30:16; Ezek. 18:9, 17), the pursuit of wisdom (cf. Prov. 4:5; 5:1; 7:4; 8:1), or doing the will of God (Pss. 40:8; 143:10; Ezra 10:11).[3]

Paul's attempt at community formation and his exhortation to live worthily of the gospel presuppose, like these traditions, a human goal that his readers may reach by adhering to his moral instructions. Paul describes the goal for believers variously. He prays that they will be "blameless at the day of Christ" (Phil. 1:10) and "blameless in sanctification" (1 Thess. 3:13) at the final day. He is the father of the bride who ensures the purity of his daughter until the wedding, the mother of the unborn child that is being "formed" (Gal. 4:19),

1. Nussbaum, *The Therapy of Desire*, 15.
2. See ibid., 13–47.
3. See the introduction.

and the father who urges his children to conduct themselves appropriately
(1 Thess. 2:11–12). His moral instructions are a means toward that goal.

## Overcoming the Passions in Antiquity

Both the philosophical and biblical traditions struggle with the fact that many,
perhaps most, people do not reach the goal because of obstacles. Paul suggests
that those who have the law do not keep it (Rom. 2:17–24; Gal. 3:10–14), and
he offers a means to overcome the obstacles (cf. Rom. 8:1–11; Gal. 5:13–6:10).
His instruction may be illuminated from both the Greco-Roman and the Jewish contexts.

### The Greco-Roman Context

The philosophic tradition of therapy often sought to remove obstacles to
human *eudaimonia*, of which the most important was failure to control the
passions (*pathēmata*). In individual treatises, ancient writers divided these
passions into subcategories such as anger,[4] sexual desire, hunger, envy, thirst,
and love. In many instances, love drives the human to sexual excess or to
homicidal rage, as in the classic case of Euripides's Medea, who did not do
the good that she knew. Driven by anger over being betrayed by Jason, she
exacts revenge by killing her children.

> I know indeed what evil I intend to do,
> But stronger than all my afterthoughts is my fury,
> Fury that brings upon mortals the greatest evils.[5]

Ovid's Medea expresses the same view, describing her emotional state:

> I should be more myself if I could,
> but some strange power holds me against my will;
> Desire persuades me one way, reason another;
> I see the better and approve it,
> but I follow the worse.[6]

Plato assumed that ordinary diseased people do not have the leisure for
reflection that will result in human flourishing.[7] He recognized the destructive

---

4. For the numerous treatments of anger, see Fitzgerald, "The Passions and Moral Progress,"
11.

5. Warner, *Medea* 1078–80. See the translation by David Kovacs (LCL): "I know well what
pain I am about to undergo, but my wrath overbears my calculation, wrath that brings mortal
men their greatest hurt."

6. Ovid, *Metamorphoses* 7.18–21.

7. Nussbaum, *Therapy of Desire*, 33.

role of the passions. In the *Phaedrus*, he described the soul as having three parts, two being like steeds and the third a charioteer. The two steeds are of opposite character; one is wantonness, the other temperance. The task of the charioteer is to control the destructive side. Similarly, the individual is confronted with the power of desire. The *Phaedrus* focuses especially on the passion of love: "When irrational desire, pursuing the enjoyment of beauty, has gained the mastery over judgment that prompts to right conduct, and has acquired from other desires, akin to it, fresh strength to strain toward bodily beauty, that very strength provides it with its name—it is the strong passion called love" (486c). Socrates examines the power of the passion of *erōs* in the *Protagoras*. He describes the common view of most people that "it is not the knowledge that a man possesses which governs him, but something else—now passion, now pleasure, now pain, sometimes love, and frequently fear" (352b). He adds, "They maintain that there are many who recognize the best but are unwilling to act on it" because they are "overcome by pleasure or pain or some other of the things I mentioned just now" (352d–e).

The philosophical tradition provided an answer to the dilemma expressed by Medea. Plato's Socrates maintains that "no one ever does wrong knowingly." He insists that humans can do the good, and that the path to the good is education. In the *Phaedrus*, the soul can see beyond this world and recognize eternal norms and the standards for ethical virtues. It "sees justice itself, it sees moderation, it sees knowledge—not the knowledge that changes and varies with the various objects that now we call beings, but the genuine knowledge seated in that which really is" (247d). The good is "out there." Those who grasp it can live by it.[8]

Although Aristotle differs from Plato in his understanding of ethics, he agrees that (a) humans can do the good if (b) they are appropriately educated. *Eudaimonia* is available for those who work in order that they and their actions should be of a certain sort (*Eth. eud.* 1215a). Aristotle argued that the task is to ensure that the passions are educated and brought into harmony with a correct view of human existence.[9] Because one may desire the wrong things, education involves teaching the other not to long for the wrong food or drink or for the wrong amount (*Eth. nic.* 3.11.1119b). By a process of moral education, one may teach a child to make the right distinctions and to long for the right objects. The object of a well-educated appetite is "the good" (*kalon*, 111b16). Because the passions are connected to false beliefs, the task of philosophy is to arrive at the truth, for correct beliefs provide the foundation for controlling the passions. Aristotle insists that people can suppress the passions in order to achieve self-control. By an intelligent process of education, the person learns to educate the appetite and not to long

8. Ibid., 17.
9. Ibid., 96.

for excess in food and drink and the other appetites (*Eth. nic.* 3.10.1118b; 3.11.1119b15; 3.11.1119b).[10]

In the *Nicomachean Ethics*, Aristotle addresses the conflicts that prevent people from doing the good, attributing their weakness to unrestraint (*akrasia*), the opposite of self-restraint (*enkrateia*, *Eth. nic.* 7.1.1145b; 7.7.1150b). While pleasures are appropriate for human existence, the unrestrained person pursues bodily pleasures in excess (*Eth. nic.* 7.8.1151b; 7.14.1154a). The unrestrained person "is convinced that he ought to do one thing and nevertheless does another thing" (*Eth. nic.* 7.2.11). This individual is swayed by the desires (*epithymiai*) of the body (*Eth. nic.* 7.8.4). A fundamental problem for unrestrained persons is the character of their knowledge. They may claim to have knowledge, but they are like those who can repeat propositions of geometry without knowing their meaning. They are like actors who say the right words though the actual knowledge has not penetrated to the tissues of their minds (*Eth. nic.* 7.3.8). Those who practice self-restraint have evil desires (*phaulas epithymia*s, *Eth. nic.* 7.9.6), but are able to stand firm against the impulses of the passions (*Eth. nic.* 7.8.5; 7.9.2), because they are guided by knowledge of the truth.

Similarly, the Stoics recognized the destructive power of the passions as obstacles to the ethical life. The early Stoics identified four classes of passions (*pathē*): appetite or desire (*epithymia*) and pleasure (*hēdonē*) assent to the good, while the latter two, fear (*phobos*) and grief (*lypē*), assent to negative emotions.[11] Passions, according to the Stoics, are the result of false beliefs, not the stirrings of our animal nature.[12] They are based on beliefs about what is "good and bad, worthwhile and worthless, helpful and noxious."[13] Consequently, in contrast to Aristotle, the goal of the Stoics was the extirpation rather than the moderation of the passions.[14] The passions can be cured only by the employment of reason. The philosopher plays the role of curing the diseased soul by modifying the false beliefs that underlie the passions, teaching what things in life are worth pursuing.[15]

While the philosophical schools differed in fundamental ways, they shared the concern to overcome the passions and to lead others on a path to virtue. Since false beliefs were the major impediment to the virtuous life, they insisted that appropriate education provided the means to virtue. Even though various passions stood in the way of the virtuous life, the philosophical schools agreed

10. Ibid., 82.
11. Krentz, "Πάθη and Απάθεια in Early Roman Empire Stoics," 124; Vögtle, "Affekt," 1:162; Aune, "Mastery of the Passions," 126.
12. Diogenes Laertius, *Vit.* 7.111; Nussbaum, *Therapy of Desire*, 367.
13. Nussbaum, *Therapy of Desire*, 370.
14. Ibid., 389.
15. Cicero, *Tusc.* 4.26=SVF 3:427; Seneca, *Ep.* 75.11=SVF 3:428. See Nussbaum, *Therapy of Desire*, 377.

that the virtuous life was possible for those who accepted the cure that they offered.

### The Jewish Context

In the biblical tradition Israel responds to God's gracious gift by keeping the commandments, which are designed to cover all aspects of community life. God will bless Israel when the people keep the commandments (Deut. 6:3) and punish them when they disobey. Because of disobedience, Israel goes into exile, and it returns from exile only when God acts to cover Israel's sins.[16] According to Deuteronomy, when the Israelites return from exile, they will again observe all of the commandments (Deut. 30:8), for the commandments are not beyond their capability. "This commandment that I am commanding you today is not too hard for you, nor is it too far away" (Deut. 30:11 NRSV). God sets before Israel the choice of good and evil, challenging the people to choose life. Only through instruction in God's commands will Israel make the right choices. Parents teach God's statutes to the children (Deut. 6:7). Indeed, teachers play an important role in the life of Israel.

Although Jewish literature acknowledged the temptations that undermine obedience, no one suggested that humans cannot keep God's laws. Rabbinic literature often speaks of the power of the "evil inclination" (*yezer hara*) opposing the Torah, an inclination implanted in all people.[17] However, nothing prevents the people from obeying God, for their task is to subdue the evil inclination.[18] "Everyone has the inborn propensity, but not hereditary compulsion, to disobedience. It is fully conceivable to the very end of life to be obedient to the law."[19] Josephus describes Jewish laws in *Against Apion*, indicating that good laws that are beyond the capacity to fulfill them would be of no use and emphasizing the Jewish success in keeping the laws (*Ag. Ap.* 2.220–24). While Jewish literature sometimes attributed evil to demonic forces, no one suggested human enslavement to destructive forces or claimed that humans could not do the good. Indeed, the law was the means for overcoming evil desires.[20]

The Jewish literature of the Hellenistic Age describes "desire" (*epithymia*) as the source of human disobedience (cf. Philo, *Spec. Laws* 4.80, 84). This topic is covered in considerable detail in 4 Maccabees, a homily of the first century, which retells the story of the martyrdom of the seven brothers for the sake of the law (see ch. 1). The author announces the thesis in 1:1: "Devout reason

---

16. See N. T. Wright, *The New Testament and the People of God*, 272–79. Wright correctly observes that the writers are concerned with Israel's corporate sin rather than the sins of individuals.

17. Avemarie, "The Tension between God's Command and Israel's Obedience," 58.

18. Ibid., 65.

19. Laato, *Paul and Judaism*, 73.

20. Avemarie, "Tension between God's Command and Israel's Obedience," 65.

(*ho eusebēs logismos*) is sovereign over the passions" (*pathōn*). This thesis is the refrain throughout the book as the author illustrates the principle in the narration about the martyrs (cf. 1:4, 7, 13, 19, 30, 33, 35; 2:4, 9, 15, 24; 3:17; 6:31; 16:2). While the author lists passions of both the mind and the body that inhibit virtue (see ch. 1), he focuses primarily on desire for forbidden foods, the major point of conflict for the Maccabean martyrs and probably for the original readers as well, because for Diaspora Jews the food laws constituted one of the major boundary markers of identity that prevented assimilation to the larger populace.[21] He also illustrates the thesis statement with a discussion of sexual desire, recalling that Joseph, "who was young and in the prime for intercourse," and subject to the "frenzied urge of sexual desire" (2:3–4 NRSV), was able to control the passions. This account reminds the readers of another topic in which Jews demarcated themselves from their surroundings.

Fourth Maccabees aims to demonstrate the possibility of faithful observance of the law, which the author illustrates with the story of the martyrs, maintaining that under no circumstances is the transgression of the law unavoidable.[22] The author acknowledges the enslaving power of the passions (3:2), indicating that they cannot be completely eradicated (3:4), but insists that reason will provide the means to control them (3:1). Because the law is an expression of reason,[23] the law is the means by which one overcomes the passions. In recalling the story of Joseph, for example, the author cites the tenth commandment, "You shall not covet (*ouk epithymēseis*) your neighbor's wife" (2:5), and then abbreviates the phrase to a general prohibition of desire (*mē epithymein*, 2:6), concluding that the commandment is evidence that one can control the passions. Although the desires have been implanted by God or nature, those who keep the law can overcome the passions. Similarly, the aged Eleazar responds to the tyrant's demand that he yield to the desire for forbidden foods, arguing that the demands of the law are not irrational, but that the commandment "teaches us self-control, so that we master all pleasures and desires, and it also trains us in courage, so that we endure any suffering willingly" (4 Macc. 5:21 NRSV). Indeed, all other commandments presuppose both a desire and the possibility to restrain it.[24] For example, Moses commands that interest-free loans be given to the poor (Lev. 25:35–38; cf. Exod. 22:25), that debts should be cancelled every seventh year (Deut. 15:1–11), and that the remnants of the harvest be given to the poor (Lev. 19:9–10; 23:22; Deut. 24:19–22). Those who turn to the law are able to overcome the natural temptations to withhold aid to the needy and are able to observe those commandments (4 Macc. 2:8–9).[25]

---

21. Gemünden, "Der Affeckt der *Epithumia* und der *Nomos*," 67.

22. Watson, "Constructing an Antithesis," 109.

23. See Niebuhr, *Gesetz und Paränese*, 219. *Logismos* is used in 2:4, 6, 7, 13, 15, 29; *nomos* appears in 2:5, 6, 8, 9, 10, 13.

24. Watson, "Constructing an Antithesis," 112.

25. Ibid., 113.

Thus the author acknowledges the power of *epithymia*, but insists that those who keep the law can overcome the passions and obtain eternal life.

Philo of Alexandria also described the law as the means for overcoming the greatest of human problems, the destructive power of desire (*epithymia*). Desire is "a treacherous enemy and source of all evils" (*Virtues* 100),[26] and he is very concerned about this issue in retelling the stories of the patriarchs. Abraham overcame the passion of family ties (*Abraham* 70). Jacob overcomes the passions through rigorous training (*askēsis*).[27] Aaron controls the passions through reason and virtuous conduct (*Alleg. Interp.* 3.128–29). Moses is the ultimate example of the victory over the passions, for he not only controls them but fully expels them (cf. *Alleg. Interp.* 3.129). Philo also describes his own mastery of the passions (*Alleg. Interp.* 3.156).

No one questioned the possibility that humans could do the good. Both the biblical and philosophical traditions maintain that humans can reach the goal of human existence if they submit to the proper therapy for the destructive passions. In the philosophical tradition, the passions are not only blind emotional forces, but are associated with false beliefs. Therefore, the task of the philosopher is to teach the truth, for correct beliefs are the foundation for ethical living. We can grasp the transcendent good and then live by it. Since the human problem is ignorance of the good, the task of the philosopher is to inform others. Similarly, in the Jewish tradition, one overcomes the destructive passions through obedience to the law.

## Overcoming the Passions in Pauline Literature

Paul's catechesis for new converts reflects his understanding that his communities can do the good. He urges his readers to "walk worthily of the gospel" (Phil. 1:27), and he gives specific directives on matters of sexuality and responsibility within the community, assuming that his readers can do the good and be lights "in the midst of a crooked and perverse generation" (Phil. 2:15 NRSV). While Paul makes demands on his readers in all of the letters, reminding them of their identity as a holy people (cf. 1 Thess. 4:3, 8), he is aware of the challenges facing them, for he agrees with Aristotle (see above) that lack of self-control (*akrasia*) persistently undermines the moral life. In his original catechesis, he urged the readers to avoid "the passion of lust" (*pathos epithymias*, 1 Thess. 4:5), which he and the Jewish tradition identified with gentiles. After expanding on the original instruction prohibiting *porneia* (1 Thess. 4:3) in 1 Corinthians 6:12–20, he addresses the problem of lack of self-control in 1 Corinthians 7:1–7, maintaining that marriage is the alternative to *porneia*. Not only does he recommend marriage; he commends regular sexual intercourse between

26. Stowers, *A Rereading of Romans*, 59.
27. *Alleg. Interp.* 2.89; 3.18, 190–91. See Aune, "Mastery of the Passions," 150.

husbands and wives because of the dangers of *akrasia*. On this concern he also bases his recommendation that the unmarried and widows who do not have self-control (*ouk enkrateuontai*) marry, inasmuch as "it is better to marry than to burn" (7:9 KJV). This image of burning was commonly employed in Greco-Roman and Jewish literature for sexual desire.[28] Near the end of the section on idolatry and sexuality, he concludes the discussion of ancient Israel's failure, indicating that the story was an example so that the believers would not be "desirous of evil things" (10:6). As the context indicates, Paul identifies the desires with sexual impulses (10:8) that are associated with idolatry. Thus Paul regards the lack of self-control (*akrasia*) as a source of continuing temptation in his communities. In keeping with the problems at Corinth, he identifies desire specifically with sexual impulses.

Dale Martin has argued that the alternative between burning up and marriage indicates that Paul has no place for passion in the marital relationship, for Paul speaks of sexual desire only in negative terms.[29] According to Martin, Paul proposes a sexual relationship without passion.[30] However, Paul's brief comments are addressed to a specific situation in which his concern is that desire will result in *porneia*. His insistence on marriage and regular sexual intercourse does not suggest that he commends the expulsion of desires, but that the desires should be channeled into the marriage relationship between spouses within the body of Christ. Inasmuch as his task is not to offer a guide to marital satisfaction, he makes no positive comments about sexual desire in marriage. Thus the insistence on sexual experience among those who do not have the gift of celibacy indicates that the sexual relationship in marriage prevents the misuse of the desires.

### The Desires in Galatians

In the ethical section of Galatians (5:13–6:10), Paul places the moral instructions within the framework of the control of desire (*epithymia*), as the introduction and conclusion of the lists of vices and virtues indicate (5:16–17, 24). Inasmuch as the Jewish tradition represented by Philo and 4 Maccabees claimed that the law was the means for controlling the desires, Paul is probably replying to opponents who have insisted that gentile converts should turn to the law in order to overcome the desires. In 5:16–25, Paul addresses the obstacles facing the community's capacity to do the good and the means to overcome them, indicating both at the beginning (5:16) and the end (5:25) the

---

28. Cf. BDAG 899. Cf. Sir. 23:16: "One who commits fornication (*porneia*) with his near of kin will never cease until the fire burns him up" (NRSV); Rom. 1:27: "Men . . . burned in their desire for one another." *Erōs* is commonly described as a fire. For Greco-Roman texts, see Martin, *The Corinthian Body*, 212–13.

29. Martin, *Corinthian Body*, 212–13.

30. Martin, "Paul without Passion," 205.

problems associated with desire that face the community. In 5:16 he mentions the "desire of the flesh" (*epithymia sarkos*), and in 5:24 he mentions "the flesh with its passions and desires" (*tēn sarka syn tois pathēmasin kai tais epithymiais*). Like his contemporaries, Paul points to "passions" and "desires" as the obstacles to the ethical life, using the terms interchangeably rather than in the technical Stoic sense (see above). Paul argues elsewhere that the "passion of desire" characterizes the gentiles (1 Thess. 4:5; cf. Rom. 1:26) and the mode of existence of his community before they entered the new aeon (Rom. 7:5). The "desires of the flesh" result in the "works of the flesh" (5:19), which Paul enumerates in the vice list (5:19–21). Thus Paul joins other ancient writers in attributing evil deeds to the power of desire.

While Paul assumes that those who belong to the old aeon, including those who want to return to it, are enslaved to the power of desire, his imperatives indicate that the community has been rescued from evil powers and now has the potential to choose an alternative power. Accompanying this rescue is the gift of the Spirit (3:2; 4:4–6), which empowers the community to keep the moral demands. Thus Paul does not speak of virtue when he lists the attributes of believers, but the "fruit of the Spirit" (Gal. 5:22). This view corresponds to comments elsewhere about the divine agency at work in believers (cf. Phil. 2:12–13). Believers must nevertheless "walk in the Spirit" (5:16), be "led by the Spirit" (5:18), and crucify the flesh with its desires (5:24). The role of the Spirit in the moral life and the insistence that the community live by the Spirit continue a theme from the earliest catechesis (cf. 1 Thess. 4:8). Only those who have the Spirit are capable of overcoming the passions. When they yield to the divine empowerment, they "do the good to all, especially those of the household of faith" (Gal. 6:10).

The imperatives (5:16, 25–26) indicate the continuing challenges that believers face in overcoming the desires. Paul explains these challenges in 5:17, indicating that "the flesh rises up against the Spirit and the Spirit against the flesh,[31] for these things are opposed to each other." The opposition between flesh and Spirit is not to be understood as an anthropological or ontological statement, for flesh and Spirit are the powers of the old and new aeons.[32] Flesh is the locus of natural human desire (5:16). It refers to the natural human condition apart from the empowering work of God's Spirit.[33] Thus believers live between the times. The powers of the new age have become a reality, but believers continue to experience the physical limitations of the flesh. Paul challenges them to choose the reality of the new age.

The warfare between flesh and Spirit prevents one from doing what one wants to do (5:17). That is, Paul addresses the old problem of the human

31. Cf. BDAG 372: *Epithymei kata tinos* means "rise up in protest" or "desire against." Cf. NRSV: "What the flesh desires is opposed to the Spirit."
32. Thompson, *Pastoral Ministry according to Paul*, 75–81.
33. Weder, "Die Normativität der Freiheit," 140.

capacity to do the good and the conflict between willing and doing that philosophers had discussed. In this warfare, believers fall prey to the vices described in 5:15, 19–21. If controlled by the "desire of the flesh," they will "bite and devour each other" (5:15) and be engaged in the sexual and social vices that disrupt community life (5:19–21). Even though the flesh and the Spirit continue to struggle (5:17), believers can choose to do the good. Although the desires continue to threaten because of the vulnerability of the flesh, he envisions a community that is not subject to the desire of the flesh.

### The Desires in Romans

In Romans, Paul elaborates on the instructions in Galatians, treating the relationship between willing and doing (7:7–25) comprehensively and concluding the book with the ethical instruction to "discern the will of God, the good, the well pleasing and the perfect" (12:2), along with the ethical obligations that follow (12:3–15:13). As the prior argument demonstrates, this exhortation presupposes a community that has overcome the desires (*epithymiai*) that hinder the moral life. This capacity to do the will of God distinguishes them from the rest of humanity, which is under the power of sin (3:9), and from their former existence, when "the passions of sins" (*pathēmata tōn hamartiōn*) worked in their bodies (7:5). As in the other letters, Paul envisions a community that is capable of doing the good if the readers follow his instructions.

The dismal portrayal of humankind in Romans 1:18–3:20 contrasts sharply with the moral community that Paul envisions in Romans 12:1–15:13. After the epistolary introduction (1:1–15) and thesis statement (1:16–17), he describes the "impiety and unrighteousness" of humankind in 1:18–3:20, indicting both idolaters (1:18–32) and those who have the law (2:1–29) and concluding the section with a bleak assessment of humankind: "There is no one righteous" (3:10), and, "By works of the law no one will be justified" (3:20).

Interpreters have observed an apparent inconsistency in the argument of 1:18–3:20. On the one hand, this section argues that neither idolaters nor those who have the law do the good, although they have adequate knowledge to do so. On the other hand, in contrast to a major theme of the letter (cf. 3:20), Paul says, "It is not the hearers of the law who are justified in God's sight, but the doers of the law will be justified" (2:13). He even elaborates with the suggestion that gentiles who do not have the law "do the things of the law" (2:14). Observing this inconsistency, scholars have resolved the anomaly of 2:13–14 in a variety of ways. Some suggest that the passage does not reflect Paul's thinking. E. P. Sanders said that the entire section of 1:18–2:29 reflects widely held views in the Judaism of the Diaspora and that chapter 2 in particular does not fit Paul's message in Romans. "It is slashing and exaggerated, as many sermons are, but its own natural point is to have its hearers become better Jews on strictly non-Christian Jewish terms, not to lead them to becoming true descendants of Abraham by faith in Christ."[34] Some have suggested that Paul is speaking in hypothetical terms, while others argue that the reference to gentiles who "have the law written on their hearts" (2:15; cf. 2:26–27) describes gentile Christians.[35] One can unravel this apparent contradiction only by recognizing the role of the desires (*epithymiai*) in 1:18–3:20 and in the entire argument. I shall return to the problem of the righteous gentile below.

The tone of the argument in 1:18–3:20 reinforces the anomaly of Paul's apparent inconsistency in 2:13–14. The larger section portrays human corruption in dismal terms, as suggested by the refrain "They are without excuse" (1:20; 2:1), which states the condition of all humanity—both those who do not have the law (1:18–32) and those who do (2:1–29). In both instances, Paul focuses on the fact that humankind does not do the good that it knows (1:32; 2:26). Some know the will of God as revealed in nature (1:19–21; cf. 2:14), while others know God through the law (2:18). The former know the righteous judgment of God, but live in unrighteousness (cf. 1:32), while the latter know the will of God revealed in the law, but dishonor God through their transgressions (2:23). Thus, unlike Socrates, Paul does not maintain that "no one does wrong knowingly." Neither the philosophers nor the writers of the biblical tradition would agree with Paul that "there is no one righteous."

Paul does not indicate explicitly why those who know the law do not keep it until later in the argument (7:7–25), but explains why those who know God through nature fail to use the knowledge that they have. In 1:18–32, he depicts "those who hold the truth in unrighteousness" as those who, because of their idolatry, have "become vain in their reasoning" (1:21). As a result of their distorted understanding, God "handed them over" to the desires (*epithymiai*, 1:24), to the passions (*pathē*, 1:26), and to a "debased mind" (*adokimon noun*, 1:28). His threefold use of *paredōken* ("handed them over") suggests that he envisions the passions as an overwhelming power.[36] His examples of *epithymia* indicate that he associates the passions specifically with sexual offenses, which he illustrates with references to homosexual practices of men and women (1:26–27), following the tradition of Jewish writers of the Diaspora of naming homosexual practice as a particularly outrageous sin (Cf. *Sib. Or.* 3:599–600; 5.386–93; Wis. 14:26; *T. Naph.* 3:5; *Ps.-Phoc.* 195).[37] The description of men who "burned in their desire" (*exekauthēsan en tē orexei autōn*) also suggests

---

34. Sanders, *Paul, the Law, and the Jewish People*, 129.

35. Hahn, *Theologie des Neuen Testaments*, 237.

36. Gathercole, "Sin in God's Economy," 164.

37. See the discussion in ch. 1. Laws against homosexual activity appear in the summaries of the Torah. Diaspora Jews also maintained that homosexual activity was contrary to nature (Wis. 14:26; *Ps.-Phoc.* 190; *2 En.* 10:4). This background in Jewish paraenesis indicates why Paul chooses homosexual acts as the primary illustration of enslavement to the passions. His place in the Jewish paraenetic tradition also indicates that Paul's concern is not only with passion in general, for the illustration drawn from homosexual acts is the common way of referring to especially egregious offenses in the Jewish tradition.

the power of *epithymia* to control people and make them incapable of doing the will of God. Thus he agrees with the philosophical tradition that the challenge of ethical living is to overcome the desires.

The problem of overcoming the passions is the topic of chapters 6–8. After describing sin as an invading power in 5:12–21, Paul clarifies the relationship between human capability to do the good and God's power, describing how believers overcome *epithymia* in order to do the good. Using images drawn from slavery (6:18–23) and marriage (7:1–4), Paul describes the believers' change of ruling powers, speaking of the transition from the past (6:20; 7:5) to the present (7:6). In describing the past, when they were "slaves to impurity and lawlessness" (6:19) and "slaves of sin" (6:20), Paul equates the past existence of his readers with that of those whom he described in 1:18–32. Thus, before their break with the past, they were enslaved to their desires. Having died to that form of enslavement, they are now the slaves of righteousness.

Having described the believers' liberation from the "passions of sins" (7:5–6), Paul continues in Romans 7:7–8:11 to reflect on the conflict between willing and doing created by the passions. Responding to the interlocutor's question "Is the law sin?" (7:7), he speaks now in the first person singular. Paul is not speaking autobiographically, however, but is using the literary device of speech-in-character.[38] He speaks first in the past tense, saying, "I would not have known desire (*epithymia*, NRSV 'what it is to covet') if the law had not said, 'You shall not desire' (*ouk epithymēseis*, NRSV 'You shall not covet')." The abbreviation of the words of the tenth commandment ("You shall not desire your neighbor's house; you shall not desire your neighbor's wife," Exod. 20:17) recalls the similar abbreviation in 4 Maccabees (2:5–6). The translation of the Hebrew with *epithymia* allowed Jews such as Philo and the author of 4 Maccabees to claim that the law agreed with the Greek view of desire as the source of evil impulses.[39] Like the author of 4 Maccabees, Paul abbreviates the tenth commandment in order to focus the attention on *epithymia*, which he equates with the passions (*pathēmata*, cf. 7:5). He agrees with his contemporaries that *epithymia* is a human problem. The transition from "desire" (*epithymia*) to "sin" (*hamartia*) in 7:8 indicates that Paul agrees with his contemporaries that "desire" is the source of sin. He also agrees with other ancient writers on the attractive power of what is forbidden.[40]

Because of the command, sin "worked every sort of desire (*epithymia*)" in the fictive speaker (7:8). Thus the speaker, like those described in chapters 1–3, knows the will of God, but is subject to the power of desire (cf. 1:19–23). Thus one who has the law confronts the power of desire just as the idolaters do

---

38. Stowers, *Rereading of Romans*, 269–72.
39. Ibid., 278.
40. Gemünden, "Der Affeckt," 70.

(1:24). The story in 7:7–11 echoes not only the Exodus account of the giving of the law (Exod. 20), but the story of Adam and Eve as well.[41] The claim, "I was once alive apart from the law" until the coming of the commandment, can refer both to Adam and to Israel's experience. The memory that "sin deceived me and through it [i.e., through the commandment] killed me" (7:11) echoes the Genesis story (cf. Gen. 3:13) and summarizes Paul's interpretation of Israel's story. This claim suggests the reasons for the earlier statement that "no one is righteous" (3:10). Not only are the gentiles slaves of passion; those who serve the law "in the letter" and not "in the Spirit" (cf. 2:25–29) live by the flesh, and so they cannot please God (cf. 8:11). Whereas the author of 4 Maccabees maintained that the law is the means by which one controls the desires, Paul indicates that the law evoked the power of the desires.

Paul further analyzes the human capacity for the moral life in 7:14–25, moving from the past to the present tense. Having associated sinful desire with the law in 7:7–11, he now assures readers that the law is not the problem, but is "just and good and holy" (7:12), preserving an appreciation of the law by driving a wedge between it and the person who is enslaved to sin (the "I"). The entire section elaborates the opening words, "We know that the law is spiritual (*pneumatikos*), but I am of the flesh (*sarkinos*), sold under sin" (7:14). Paul has introduced the dichotomy of Spirit and flesh earlier (2:28–29; 7:5–6; cf. Gal. 3:3; 5:16–25), indicating that those who know the law and serve "in the flesh" rather than "in the Spirit" do not keep God's commandments. Indeed, he has shown that the "weakness of the flesh" (cf. 6:19) characterizes all of his listeners, but that the enslavement to the flesh belongs to their past (6:19; 7:5). That the person of the flesh is "sold under sin" also recalls Paul's verdict on all humanity earlier in the argument (3:9, 20, 23). As Paul has indicated earlier, the enslavement to the desires has characterized both Jews and gentiles, both of whom suffer from the "weakness of the flesh."

The inclusio of 7:14, 23–25 frames the bleak assessment of the human situation. The "I" of 7:14 is the "inner man" (7:22) who agrees with the law and serves with the mind (*nous*, 7:23, 25). "Sold under sin" continues the image of slavery that has dominated Paul's argument (1:24; 6:16–23), as Paul uses a verb (*pepramenos*) commonly used for the selling of a slave.[42] Developing the metaphor at the end of the section, he describes warfare (cf. Gal. 5:17) between the "law in [his] members" and the "law in [his] mind," resulting in his becoming a prisoner of war (7:23)[43] to sin.

Paul describes the nature of this slavery in 7:15 and the refrain that follows. "I do not know what I am achieving" (*katergazomai*) anticipates the subsequent statements, "It is not I who do it (*katergazomai*), but sin living in me"

41. Gathercole, "Sin in God's Economy," 160.
42. BDAG 815.
43. See BDAG 31.

(7:17, 20), indicating that the fictive person cannot do the good (7:18) while living in the flesh (cf. 2:25–29). The synonyms for *katergazomai* in 7:14–25 indicate the incapacity for the individual to do the good (*poiein*, 7:15, 19, 21; *prassein*, 7:15, 19). Paul explains why humans do not do the good with the refrain about willing and doing.

I do not do what I want to do, but I do what I hate (7:15).

If I do what I do not want to do, I agree that the law is good (7:16).

To want to do is at hand for me, but to do the good is not (7:18).

For I do not do the good I want, but the evil I hate is what I do (7:19).

But if I do what I do not want, it is not I that do it but sin living in me (7:20).

I agree with the law in my inner person, but I see another law in my members (7:22–23).

Paul summarizes this pessimistic view later: "Those who are in the flesh cannot please God" (8:8 NRSV).

This contrast between willing and doing, first introduced in Galatians 5:17, is a fundamental feature of Paul's ethics and an echo of the philosophical conversations about the capacity to do the good. Indeed, Paul's contrast echoes the ancient story of Medea, which was a major theme among ancient philosophers (see above). He offers a pessimistic anthropology describing humankind without the capacity to do the good. Paul shares with Plato and Aristotle the emphasis on the weakness of the will. However, unlike the philosophers, Paul does not suggest that the problem can be overcome with proper education. His anthropology sets him apart from both the Jewish and Socratic traditions. He envisions an enslavement of the person to sin and to the passions. In Romans he places Jew and gentile on the same level under the power of sin. He portrays a warfare between the flesh and the Spirit (Gal. 5:17) in which the person is caught between the two powers. The result is the person who cannot do the good because of the *epithymia*.

Having earlier described the idolater as a slave of *epithymia* (1:18–32), Paul now places words resembling those of Medea into the mouth of the mysterious "I," who says, "I do not do what I want, but I do the very thing I hate" (7:15, 19). The reason that the "I" cannot do the good, according to 7:7–11, is the power of *epithymia*, which came through the commandment and produced "every desire" (7:8). Thus both gentiles (1:18–32) and Jews (7:7–25) are under the power of desire, and all humanity is "under sin" (3:9). Paul appears to stand alone in the Jewish tradition in suggesting that no one is able to do the good or to keep the law. He focuses on the law as a religion of doing, but indicates that no one is righteous, no one does the good.

### Overcoming the Passions in Romans

In announcing at the beginning of Romans that "the gospel is the power of God for salvation" (Rom. 1:16), Paul suggests that his message is capable of overcoming the other powers that prohibit human transformation. As the subsequent argument indicates, the gospel enables one to overcome the power of desire and of sin. Paul envisions a moral community in which the time has passed when the "passions of sins worked in our members to produce death" (7:5). His exhortations indicate that his task is to shape a community that has overcome the enslaving passions. Indeed, he urges his readers, "Do not let sin reign in your mortal bodies to obey its desires" (*epithymiai*, 6:12). He also introduces the paradox according to which he assures his readers of divine empowerment while instructing them to conduct themselves in an appropriate way. It is God "who works in you both to will and to do God's good favor" (Phil. 2:13); it is God's word (1 Thess. 2:13) and the Holy Spirit that God has given to the community (1 Thess. 4:8) that are active among the believers. Whereas in the earlier correspondence Paul encourages his converts not to live "in the passion of lust, like the gentiles who do not know God" (1 Thess. 4:5), only in Galatians and Romans, where he defends the gentile mission, does he develop the anthropological concerns about overcoming the passions. In both letters he instructs his readers in how to develop a group ethos, describing a community with boundaries separating it from its surroundings while rejecting the customary boundaries—circumcision, Sabbath, and food laws—that separated Jews from gentiles. He assumes that the gentiles live in the "passion of lust," while believers are now capable of overcoming the passions and obeying God's commands.

With the imagery of baptism, Paul elaborates on the radical change in the moral life and the change of powers. Just as the death and resurrection of Jesus are once for all (6:10–11), believers have died to the old enslaving power (6:10–11) at baptism in order to "walk in newness of life" (6:4). The subjunctive statement indicates a new moral possibility, suggesting that believers in the new aeon can actually overcome the old power. Consistent with Jewish moral terminology, Paul speaks of the new existence with the imagery of walking (cf. chs. 2 and 3). The new moral possibility is also evident in the metaphor of marriage in 7:1–4, as Paul again draws the conclusion from the change of status with the subjunctive statement. Believers have died to the law "in order to bear fruit to God" (7:4). Paul employs the image of bearing fruit elsewhere for the moral life (cf. Gal. 5:22; Phil. 1:11; cf. Matt. 3:10; 7:16). Whereas believers once "bore fruit for which they are ashamed" (6:21), they now bear fruit that leads to sanctification (6:22; 7:4).

This distinction between those who overcome the passions by yielding to God's Spirit (cf. 7:5–6) and those who are enslaved to the flesh solves the apparent contradiction in 1:18–3:20 created by the reference to the righteous gentiles in 2:12–26. Unlike those who are overwhelmed by the passions and unable to keep the law, the righteous gentiles keep the law because it is written on their hearts (2:15). Paul contrasts them sharply with the interlocutor, who knows the will of God and does not keep it (cf. 2:18). Combining both the Old Testament and Stoic terms for moral cognition (2:18),[44] Paul identifies his interlocutor as one who knows the will of God. Unlike those whom Paul later encourages to "test the will of God and the good" (Rom. 12:2), his interlocutor does not do what the law demands (2:17–24), as the rhetorical questions indicate. Thus he contrasts those who have the law with those who do not, indicating that only the latter do the will of God.

Paul explains the distinction between gentiles who obey the law (2:12–13) and the Jews who fail to keep it (2:17) in 2:25–29 in the contrast between circumcision and uncircumcision. Because circumcision was an essential feature of the law and the issue Paul confronts in defending the admission of gentiles, he introduces the topic for the first time in 2:25, equating it with the law. In 2:26 he elaborates on the righteous gentiles, suggesting that they keep "the just requirement of the law" and that their uncircumcision will be reckoned as circumcision. The language echoes Deuteronomy 30, which attributes Israel's exile to sin and states the conditions for a new relationship to God at the end of the exile. In the new situation God will circumcise the heart of the Israelites in order that they may keep the commandments (Deut. 30:6). These comments anticipate Paul's reflections on the community in 8:1–11. There the righteous gentile is not only a hypothetical case, but a reality in the church (see below on 8:1–11). Paul claims elsewhere, "We are the circumcision, those who serve in the Spirit of God . . . and not boasting in the flesh" (Phil. 3:3). Indeed, he is the minister of the new covenant "written on hearts." Thus Paul's claim that gentiles may be circumcised in heart anticipates the argument in Romans; that is, he envisions a community that overcomes the passions described in 1:18–32.

While divine agency is evident in the coming of the new power, human agency is evident as Paul draws the consequences of the new existence: "Do not let sin reign in your mortal bodies to obey its desires" (6:12). Thus, unlike the old humanity that God has "handed over to the desires" as the people "dishonored their bodies" (1:24), those who participate in the death of Jesus are now able to turn away from the old ruling power and present their bodies to God. The new ruling power is God's righteousness (6:16, 18–19), and believers are enslaved both to righteousness and to God (6:22).

---

44. "Will of God" is the common term in the OT for God's law. To "approve the better things" is a common Stoic phrase.

2:13). Unlike his contemporaries, Paul does not indicate that humankind can do the will of God, but only that the "just requirement of the law" may be fulfilled in the community of believers empowered by the Spirit.

The divine agency does not preclude human choice, as the exhortations indicate. In Galatians, Paul encouraged his readers to "walk by the Spirit," promising that they will not submit to the desire of the flesh (Gal. 5:16). In Romans 8:4–13, as in Galatians 5:16–25, Paul places before his readers the choice between "the mind of the flesh" and the "mind of the Spirit" (8:5–6), concluding that they are debtors to "live according to the Spirit" (8:12). Similarly, the imperative in 6:12, "Do not let sin reign in your mortal bodies," indicates that the readers stand before the choice between two modes of existence. Thus the description of the conflicted person who is controlled by the desires (7:7–25) not only portrays the existence of the readers prior to their baptism (6:1–11), but also points to a continuing possibility for those who do not submit to the empowering Spirit.

The statement that the "law is fulfilled" by those who walk "according to the Spirit" (8:4) suggests that this law is identical to the "law of the Spirit" that has liberated believers (8:1). This claim develops enigmatic statements made earlier in the letter. Paul has affirmed the possibility that gentiles "do the things of the law" because they have the "law written on their hearts" (2:15). Against his interlocutor, he has argued, "If the uncircumcised keep the just requirement of the law, will not their uncircumcision be reckoned as circumcision?" (2:26); that is, Paul envisions a community of people who keep the law without being circumcised. Moreover, "the Jew in secret" serves in the newness of the Spirit and not in the oldness of the letter (2:29). In 8:4, Paul claims that this possibility is now a reality. The contrast between service in the letter and in the Spirit corresponds to the distinction between "the law of the Spirit" and the "law of sin and death" (8:2).

Paul's answer to the human dilemma of overcoming the passions and doing the good is indebted to his reading of Deuteronomy and the exilic prophets, according to which Israel's sin resulted in exile and Israel's return from exile will be characterized by a renewed covenant in which Israel will keep God's commandments. According to Deuteronomy, the Lord will circumcise the heart of the Israelites and their descendants (30:6), and Israel will again obey the Lord's commandments (30:8). When Israel turns to the Lord with "all [its] heart and all [its] soul" (30:6), it will observe God's "just requirements" (*ta dikaiōmata*, 30:16). Those commands are not hard to keep, for they are in Israel's mouth and heart to observe (Deut. 30:11–14). Paul's description of those who walk in the Spirit and in whom the just requirements of the law are fulfilled echoes the promise in Deuteronomy.

The image of the return from exile is also vividly portrayed in Jeremiah's visions. According to Deuteronomy 30:10, God will bless those who "observe the just requirements of God" (cf. Deut. 30:16). These commands are not hard to keep because they are "in your mouth and in your heart" (30:14).[45] The prophet challenges Israel, "Circumcise the foreskin of your hearts" (Jer. 4:4), and offers the indictment, "All Israel is uncircumcised in heart" (Jer. 9:26). Paul identifies his own interlocutor in terms that Deuteronomy and Jeremiah applied to disobedient Israel. Their circumcision does not benefit because it does not involve the heart. He elaborates on the status of disobedient Israel in 9:1–11:25, indicating that they have not followed the true righteousness. Following the narrative of Deuteronomy and Jeremiah, he envisions a community that keeps the just requirement of the law, composed of those who are "circumcised in the heart" (2:29). Jeremiah's prophecy included not only an indictment of Israel's disobedience; it also included the eschatological hope for a new covenant that will be written "on the hearts" (Jer. 31:33).

One may observe also the promises of Jeremiah and Ezekiel, which reflect hope for Israel's postexilic situation. According to Jeremiah 31[LXX 38]:31–34, God will make a new covenant that is unlike the covenant that Israel did not keep (31[38]:31–32). The new covenant will be on their hearts (31[38]:33). Similarly, Ezekiel anticipates the postexilic situation when God will sprinkle clean water on Israel and cleanse it from its uncleannesses (Ezek. 36:25). God will give a new heart and new spirit (Ezek. 36:26) to Israel. As a result, God will make Israel follow the commandments (*dikaiōmata*, Ezek. 36:27) and ordinances. The renewed people of God will be empowered to keep God's requirements through the Spirit.

Paul envisions himself as a minister of the new covenant announced by Jeremiah and Ezekiel (cf. 2 Cor. 3:1–18) and describes his message as the word that is near (Rom. 10:8), announced by Deuteronomy (30:14). Thus he envisions a renewed people of God composed of Jews and gentiles who overcome the passions and keep God's commandment through the power of the Spirit announced by Ezekiel. The gentiles who have the law written on their hearts (Rom. 2:15) are thus gentile Christians. Just as the faith of Abraham "was reckoned" as righteousness while Abraham was uncircumcised (Rom. 4:9–12), the uncircumcised gentiles are reckoned as circumcised (Rom. 2:26). Thus Paul resolves the dilemma of the righteous gentile mentioned earlier (2:14–15, 25–29), describing a community of uncircumcised gentiles who keep the "just requirement of the law" without circumcision.

Paul elaborates in 8:5–8 on the new possibility that the "just requirement of the law may be fulfilled in us who walk not according to the flesh, but according to the Spirit" (8:4), describing a general principle about the "mind of the flesh" and the "mind of the Spirit," before returning to address his readers directly in 8:9–13. *Phronēma* ("mind"), which is used in the New Testament only in Romans 8 (vv. 6, 7, 27), derives from the verb *phronein* (8:5, "to set one's

45. Cf. Paul's use of this passage in Rom. 10.

mind on").[46] The word is used in the LXX to describe alternative dispositions, sides between which one chooses.[47] Similarly, Paul uses the verb to describe alternatives on which one may set one's mind. One may either set one's mind on the higher calling he has described (*touto phroneite*) or "think otherwise" (*heterōs phroneite*, Phil. 3:15). He contrasts those who "set their mind on earthly things" (*hoi ta epigeia phronountes*) with those whose citizenship is in heaven (Phil. 3:19–20).

What Paul means by keeping the law is evident in Romans 12:1–15:13, in which he explicitly denies that the gentile community observes special days or the food laws, just as he has insisted that gentile believers are justified without circumcision. However, his frequent appeals to the law suggest that gentiles keep the law without the boundary markers demarcating gentiles from Jews. While he does not mention the role of the Spirit in 12:1–15:13, he presupposes the power of the Spirit that he described earlier in the argument (7:6; 8:1–13). This community is the renewed people of God. Whereas both Jews and gentiles outside of Christ were controlled by the passions and failed to do the good that they knew (1:18–3:20; 7:5–16), the Spirit has empowered the new community to do the good (12:2), making the exilic promises a reality.

### Conclusion: Overcoming the Passions through the Spirit

Paul's claim that "no one is righteous" (Rom. 3:10), as I have argued in this chapter, is without parallel in antiquity. The philosophical tradition offered a path to the good, and the Jewish tradition looked to the Torah. The Greeks assumed that with knowledge the individual would learn to do the good, and Jewish writers assumed that the laws were not too difficult to keep.[48] While both Greek and Jewish writers recognized that many people did not live up to the ideal, they nevertheless believed in the human possibility of doing the good. Paul's distinctive anthropological pessimism is probably the logical conclusion of his soteriology.[49] Recognizing that the answer is the righteousness of God revealed in Christ, Paul concluded that the question was the human enslavement to sin, with which he associates the passions. While Paul looks at humanity's capacity for the good with extraordinary pessimism, he looks to the potential of his communities with optimism. Unlike the author of

46. Bertram, "*Phrēn*," *TDNT* 9:232; BDAG 1065.

47. Cf. 1 Macc. 10:20: "You are to take our side (*phronein ta hēmōn*) and keep friendship with us" (NRSV). Cf. 2 Macc. 14:26.

48. See Laato, *Paul and Judaism*, 73; Westerholm, "Paul's Anthropological 'Pessimism' in Its Jewish Context," 71–98.

49. Westerholm correctly indicates that "the radical nature of humanity's sinfulness can only have been underlined by the drastic nature of the divine remedy." He adds, "It would also seem to follow . . . that a Judaism for which Jesus is not the Christ does not have the same reasons for thinking humanity incapable of doing good" ("Paul's Anthropological 'Pessimism,'" 96).

4 Maccabees, he does not claim that the law is the means for overcoming the destructive passions. He envisions his gentile communities as the community of the new covenant anticipated by Jeremiah (cf. Deut. 30). Through the power of the Spirit, which God pours out on the returning exiles, the communities are able to fulfill the just requirement of the law (Rom. 8:4).

# 7

# Putting Love into Practice

The central category in Paul's moral instruction is love, an emphasis that he shares with other New Testament writers, especially John.[1] Of the four Greek words for love, Paul employs forms of *agap-* almost exclusively. He uses the verb *agapan* to declare that God (or Christ) loves (Rom. 8:37; 9:13, 25; 2 Cor. 5:14; 9:7; Gal. 2:20; cf. Eph. 1:6; 2:4; 5:2; 2 Thess. 2:16), to say that the people love God in return (Rom. 8:28; 1 Cor. 2:9), to indicate that he himself loves the community (2 Cor. 11:11; 12:15), and to encourage his communities to love one another (Rom. 13:8; Gal. 5:14; 1 Thess. 4:9). The instruction to "love one another" was a basic part of Paul's catechesis (1 Thess. 4:9). At the beginning of his letters, he gives thanks for the growth in love among his communities (1 Thess. 1:3; Philem. 5), and he prays that love will continue to increase among them (Phil. 1:9; 1 Thess. 3:12). By placing love first in the list of the fruit of the Spirit (Gal. 5:22), he suggests that the remaining terms in the list fall under this category. He also appeals to love as the motivation for his requests (Philem. 5, 9). He manifests his own love for his communities by his care for them (1 Cor. 4:21; 2 Cor. 2:4), and he lists his own "sincere love" as one of the qualities in his existence (2 Cor. 6:6). Thus

1. See Söding, "Das Wortfeld der Liebe," 284. With 320 occurrences, *agapaō* (143), *agapē* (116), and *agapētos* (61) compose one of the predominant word stems in the New Testament. It occurs most frequently in Paul (137 in the undisputed letters and 22 in Ephesians) and the Johannine literature (106, including 44 in the Gospel of John and 52 in 1 John). The synoptic tradition also contains the double commandment of love of God and love of neighbor (Mark 12:28–34; Matt. 22:35–40; Luke 10:25–28) and love of enemies (Matt. 5:43–48 par. Luke 6:27–36).

love for others within the community is undoubtedly the dominant ethical category in the letters of Paul. The dominance of the term corresponds to the community's identity as a family, for Paul assumes that the new communities will replace many of the functions of the ancient family (see ch. 2).

## Agapē in Context

The prominence of *agapē* in Paul sets him apart from both ancient moralists and the Old Testament. The Greeks employed four words of love, of which *agapē* was the least common. Although the words for love were almost synonymous, each had a specific nuance, connoting a specific aspect of love. Of the four words, *storgē*, used in the New Testament only in compounds (*astorgos*, Rom. 1:31; *philostorgos*, Rom. 12:10), is the simplest to demarcate. In Greek literature it is used primarily for the affection for members of the family, but can be extended to the circle of friends or political associations.[2] A second term, *erōs*, which is never used in the New Testament, was the topic of considerable reflection. The term was used primarily for passionate, overpowering desire. It was most often used for sexual desire, but could also refer to the desire for fame or wealth. It became a theme for philosophical reflection, especially in the work of Plato and later in neoplatonism. It came to be used for the joy in beauty, the desire for knowledge, and ultimately the desire for unity with the divine.[3] The third word, *philia*, was originally used for the solidarity among members of the family, comrades in arms, allies, and friends. Aristotle devoted books 8 and 9 of *Nicomachean Ethics* to philosophical reflection on *philia*, defined as reciprocal kindness (*eunoia*), which determines the relationship between two friends. One can speak of true friendship only where the other is loved, not for one's own sake, but for the sake of the good (*Eth. nic.* 8.3–10). Plutarch, Cicero, and others in the Hellenistic age whose works have been preserved attest to the Greek reflection on friendship.[4]

Of the four words for love in Hellenistic literature, *agapē* (verb *agapaō*) is the least significant. The noun first occurs in the LXX (cf. 2 Sam. 13:15; Song 2:4; 8:7; Jer. 2:2). The verb can refer to the reception of a guest, political loyalty, personal sympathy and friendship, the gratitude to a benefactor, and the friendly affection for a patron, and for the erotic, the marital, and family love. The Stoics, however, included *agapēsis* in philosophical reflection. It is a

2. Söding, "Wortfeld," 288. It is used for the reciprocal love of parents and children (Plato, *Leg.* 754; Aristotle, *Eth. nic.* 8.11.1161b), especially of parents for children (Xenophon, *Oec.* 7.24; Sophocles, *Oed. tyr.* 1023; *Oed. col.* 1529) or children for parents (Euripides, *El.* 1102), the love for the wife (Herodotus, *Hist.* 7.69; Aeschylus, *Sept.* 512; Sophocles, *Trach.* 486.577; *Aj.* 212) and for the husband (Theocritus, *Id.* 17.130), as well as siblings for each other (Euripides, *Iph. aul.* 502).

3. Söding, "Wortfeld," 299.

4. Ibid., 291.

virtue in Stoic popular philosophy, appearing in a list with *eunoia* (goodwill), *eumeneia* (kindness), and *aspasmos* (affection). For Chrysippus, it is the term for the permanent striving for the good.[5]

Greeks also employed other words to describe obligations to others. Justice (*dikaiosynē*), one of the four cardinal virtues, commonly encompassed all of the obligations to humankind and society.[6] Indeed, a common theme in Greek ethics was the human obligation of reverence for the gods and justice toward others. Justice often stood alongside *philanthrōpia* as the proper conduct toward humankind.[7]

The LXX precedes Paul in its preference for *agap-*. Although forms of *erōs*, *philia*, and *storgē* appear there,[8] the LXX most frequently employs *agap-* to translate the Hebrew *ahab*, which extends to every sphere of life.[9] It is used for God's love for Israel, a major theme in the election tradition of Deuteronomy. God chose Israel because God loved Israel (Deut. 4:37), not because of strength or numbers (Deut. 7:7–8). Similarly, the prophets use *agap-* for Yahweh's love for Israel. According to Hosea, Yahweh recalls concerning earlier days, "I led them with cords of human kindness, in the bonds of my love (*en desmois agapēseōs mou*)" (11:4). God looks forward to the future: "I will love them freely" (14:4 NRSV). According to Jeremiah, Yahweh declares, "I have loved you with eternal love" (Jer. 31:3). In return, Israel loves God. A major theme of Deuteronomy is the command to love God (Deut. 6:5; 10:12; 11:1, 13, 22; 13:3; 19:9; 30:6, 16, 20).[10]

The verb is used for human relationships. It refers to the love between a man and a woman, such as Jacob's love for Rachel (Gen. 29:18, 20, 30, 32), the love of Samson for Delilah (Judg. 16:4, 15), and Elkanah's love for the barren Hannah (1 Sam. 1:5). It is used for the erotic love of Amnon for Tamar (2 Sam. 13:1, 15), and it appears frequently in the Song of Solomon for erotic love (2:4, 5, 7; 3:5, 10; 5:8; 7:6; 8:4, 6, 7). The same word can be used for the friendship between men, as indicated in the fact that Jonathan loved David as his own life (1 Sam. 18:1, 3; 20:17). David sings about his fallen friend that his love was "more wonderful than that of women" (2 Sam. 1:26 NIV).[11]

It also refers to the love between parents and children, in-laws, and even slaves and masters. In the first instance of a form of *agap-*, God says to Abraham,

5. Chrysippus, *Fragmenta moralia*, frags. 292, 431.

6. K. Berger, *Die Gesetzesauslegung Jesu*, 144–45.

7. See the numerous texts in ibid., 144–49.

8. *Stergein* is used in Sir. 27:17 for the love for friends; *storgē* is used in 3 Macc. 5:32 for the relationship between those who have a common education. In 4 Macc. 14:13, 14, 17, it is used for the love for parents. *Erōs* is used in Prov. 7:18 and 30:16 for sexual love. *Philia/philein/philos* is used frequently. See Söding, "Wortfeld," 299.

9. Although *agapē* is used most frequently, no sharp distinction can be made among the four words for love, which overlap in meaning. See Barr, "Words for Love in Biblical Greek," 9–11.

10. Seebass, "Liebe II," 130.

11. See Söding, "Wortfeld," 304.

"Take your son, whom you love" (Gen. 22:2) to sacrifice. According to Proverbs, "Whom the father loves, he chastens" (Prov. 13:24). Isaac loved Esau, Rebecca loved Jacob (Gen. 25:28), and Israel loved Joseph (Gen. 37:3–4) and Benjamin (Gen. 44:20). Similarly, Ruth loved her mother-in-law (Ruth 4:15). In some instances, the slave loves his master so much that he prefers not to go free when the opportunity comes (Exod. 21:5).[12]

Although the proper treatment of others outside the immediate family is a major theme in the Old Testament, the demand to love the neighbor (or stranger) appears only in three instances (Lev. 19:18, 34; Deut. 10:19). Similarly, while the law has multiple statutes governing the proper treatment of others, the command to love the other appears only in Leviticus 19. Thus when Paul cites the command, "You shall love your neighbor as yourself" (Rom. 13:9; Gal. 5:14), he turns to this passage as the warrant for love in his own communities. Leviticus 19:18, the primary passage cited by New Testament writers (cf. Matt. 5:43; 19:19; 22:39; Luke 10:27; Rom. 13:9; Gal. 5:14; James 2:8), appears within the Holiness Code (Lev. 17–26) at the conclusion of a series of commandments on the appropriate conduct toward the neighbor (19:13, 16, 17) or brother (19:17) within the covenant community. The meaning of love becomes evident when one recognizes that the term summarizes the prohibitions in 19:9–18 in positive terms. Love is not an emotional response, but the responsibility for others. It is expressed in concern for the poor who must glean what others have left behind (19:9–10), for the laborer who works in the field (19:13), and for the deaf and blind (19:14). It is incompatible with stealing, false witness, swearing falsely (19:11–12), fraud, partiality in judgment (19:15), slander (19:16), and revenge (19:18a). Thus love is metonymy for the many obligations toward the neighbor, who is a fellow Israelite. In 19:34 (cf. Deut. 19:10), love extends beyond the fellow Israelite to the alien. Thus all of the protections given to the poor among the Israelites also extend to the alien, though the identity of the alien is not certain.[13]

In the literature of Hellenistic Judaism, as we have seen, brotherly love becomes a major topic in the *Testaments of the Twelve Patriarchs* and 4 Maccabees. In both texts, brotherly love is the love of actual siblings for each other. While the love command in Leviticus 19:18 is rarely cited in Jewish literature, the focal point of piety is nevertheless the care for others. In some instances, the love command is understood as care for others within the Jewish community, while in other instances it is used in a universalistic sense.[14] A major theme in all of the paraenetic literature is love toward humankind. The *Letter of Aristeas*, for example, describes the Jewish values of goodwill (*philanthrōpia*, 225) and love (*agapē*, 229) toward all people. Philo summarizes the Decalogue

12. See Seebass, "Liebe II," 130.
13. Söding, *Liebesgebot bei Paulus*, 49.
14. Wischmeyer, "Das Gebot der Nächstenliebe bei Paulus," 163.

under the categories of reverence for God and love (*philanthrōpia*) toward humankind (*Spec. Laws* 2.61–63).

While Paul's writings focus on love, most references give no concrete indication of the meaning of love in actual practice. This lack of concreteness has raised questions about the meaning of love in Pauline ethics, leading to a variety of interpretations. Augustine's dictum "Love God, and do as you please" is a common interpretation.[15] According to this view, "Because one knows what one expects of the other, one knows what one needs to do and needs no other instruction. In the encounter with the other, one who loves knows how love comes to realization. One's conscience determines the course of action."[16]

While Paul customarily speaks only in general terms of love, in two instances he gives concrete instructions for the practice of love in actual circumstances. Just as he needs to elaborate on his catechesis on sexual matters, he also needs to apply his instructions for love when the situation demands it. In Romans 12:1–15:13, Paul elaborates on the nature of love in general terms. In 1 Corinthians he follows his explanation on sexual matters with instructions on love.

## Love in 1 Corinthians 8–14

In 1 Corinthians 8–14, Paul responds to two issues confronting the church with an elaboration on the meaning of love. This section is a response to Corinthian divisions (cf. 1 Cor. 1:10–12; 11:17–34) that were undoubtedly exacerbated by the cultural and socioeconomic differences within the community. The strife (1:11; 3:3), jealousy (3:3), and arrogance (4:18) that have undermined community life have clearly appeared in the self-seeking behavior to which Paul responds. In this section he introduces the image of the church as a building under construction, anticipating his subsequent appeals to participate in the construction of a cohesive community (cf. 8:1; 14:1–5).

### 1 Corinthians 8–11

In response to the Corinthian arrogance (cf. 5:2) and insistence on individual rights (cf. 6:12; 10:23) that have ruptured the community, Paul attempts to rebuild a unified community that transcends the normal divisions among humankind. He lays the foundation in 1 Corinthians 1–4, interpreting his original preaching and insisting that the message of the cross undermines all human pretension (cf. 1 Cor. 3:18–23; 4:6–12). He applies this foundation to matters of sexuality, again interpreting his original catechesis (1 Cor. 5–7; cf. 1 Thess. 4:3–8) and insisting that the edification of the community takes precedence over individual rights (6:12; cf. 10:23). Similarly, he addresses conflicts involving

15. See Schrage, "Zur formalethischen," 171.
16. Ibid.

idolatry (8:1–11:1) and public worship (11:2–34), which were also rooted in the anticommunal tendency that Paul addressed at the beginning of the book.

In addressing the subject of idolatry (8:1–11:1), Paul elaborates on his original preaching, which called for the believers to "turn to God from idols" (cf. 1 Thess. 1:9), addressing an issue calling for clarification. It is not coincidental that Paul proceeds from sexual vices (chs. 5–7) to issues involving idolatry (8:1–11:1), for these were the primary issues faced by the Jews in the Diaspora and in Paul's original catechesis.[17] The Corinthians faced a dilemma common among the Jews of the Diaspora and much discussed by rabbis. How does one turn from idols when one knows that the gods do not exist? How rigorously does one maintain distance from idolatry, which is interwoven in daily life in numerous ways? Jewish tradition prohibited eating meat offered to idols and entering an idol's temple.[18] The author of *The Sentences of Pseudo-Phocylides* instructs, "Do not eat blood; abstain from food sacrificed to idols." While Jews did participate in the guilds of Alexandria, they did not join in the guild dinners in pagan temples.[19] These questions affected Corinthians who considered whether to buy meat in the marketplace, eat meat that had been offered to idols, or accept invitations for meals at the temple of the idols. Those who insisted on their knowledge (8:1) concluded that their knowledge gave them the right (*exousia*, 8:9) to participate in activities associated with idolatry.

Paul begins his response in 8:1 with a thesis statement that will guide the discussion in the two units, 8:1–11:1 and 11:2–14:40. As in other instances (cf. 6:12; 10:23), he introduces a slogan of the Corinthians before offering a correction. In this instance, the Corinthians claim, "We know that we all have knowledge" (8:1), a topic central to the issues in Corinth (cf. 1:5; 8:7, 10; 12:8; 13:2, 8; 14:6). Based on their claim to have knowledge, they say, "We know that there is no idol and no God but one" (8:4), a conviction that Paul undoubtedly has passed on to new converts. As with matters of sexuality, the Corinthians conclude that "all things are lawful" (*panta exestin*, 6:12; 10:23). Hence they have the right (*exousia*) to eat meat offered to idols (8:9) without consideration of the sensibilities of others. They represent a moral view that was individualistic and anticommunal, reflecting common Greco-Roman values.[20]

Paul's response, "Knowledge puffs up, but love builds up" (8:1), implies a critique of Corinthian behavior, recalling Paul's earlier complaints that the Corinthians are "puffed up" (4:18; 5:2). He suggests that those who claim to possess knowledge are destroying the solidarity of the community with their arrogance. The statement that "loves builds up" recalls Paul's extended ecclesiological metaphor of the building (3:10–17), suggesting that the Corinthians

17. Lips, "Heiligkeit und Liebe," 174–77.
18. Winter, "Theological and Ethical Responses to Religious Pluralism," 215–18.
19. Ibid.
20. See the discussion in Söding, *Liebesgebot bei Paulus*, 104.

have a responsibility for building the church and that love is indispensable for that task. Paul will elaborate on the relationship between love (*agapē*) and the building (*oikodomē*) in 12:1–14:40.

After stating the common ground that he shares with the Corinthians in 8:1–6, Paul elaborates on the meaning of love in 8:7–13, demonstrating both the effects of the absence of love within the community and the destruction that the contrary behavior results in for others. In mentioning "some" who do not have the knowledge (8:7), Paul turns to communal responsibility, referring three times to the "brother" (8:11, 12, 13). Such exercise of this knowledge would destroy rather than build. Using imagery drawn from the Old Testament prohibition of placing a rock in the path of a blind man (Lev. 19:14), Paul describes the consequences. The conscience of the one who lacks the knowledge and thus associates idol meat with deities "is defiled" (8:7). Speaking ironically, Paul says that this "weaker brother" will be "built up" (*oikodomēthēsetai*) to eat food offered to idols and, as a result, be "destroyed" (8:11) rather than ultimately "built up." The result of such self-serving behavior is the opposite of that of the exercise of love, which builds up.

Paul's definition of love has two dimensions. In the first place, he employs the language of the family. The identity of the community as a family shapes Paul's ethic and his view of responsibility for others (see ch. 3). He shares the common view that members of the family ensure the well-being of parents, children, and siblings. In response to the Corinthians who have exhibited the strife and jealousy that have no place in the family, Paul challenges the readers to take responsibility for members of the family. Three times he describes this brother as "weak." Thus he assumes the familial responsibility of caring for family solidarity by caring for the weak within the family.

Paul's understanding of love is rooted in the ancient understanding of family life. Plutarch's essay *On Brotherly Love* describes the responsibility within the family to take care of those who are weak. The love that Paul commends is a familial love, as his references to the brother indicate. The one who is destroyed is "a brother for whom Christ died" (8:11; cf. Rom. 14:5). One does not scandalize or sin against a brother (8:11–13). Paul applies what ancient people said about family to the fictive kinship of the church. Paul does not speak of *philanthrōpia*, but of love for a brother. The "neighbor" of Leviticus 19:18 has become for Paul the equivalent of the sibling.

Paul's focus on love as the central category for morality places him alone in the ancient world. Love was not the central category for the ancient moralists. The neighbor in the Levitical command is the fellow Israelite and the stranger in Israel's midst (Lev. 19:18, 34). Whereas the Levitical command extended to the neighbor, that is, the fellow Israelite, Jewish paraenetic tradition described the brotherly love within families. While Jewish paraenesis preceded Paul in applying the Greek ideal of brotherly love in paraenetic contexts (see ch. 1), he has applied this ideal to the fictive kinship of the community. Like those from both contexts who spoke of familial love, Paul focuses on love within the family rather than on humankind in general. Paul has applied this to the fictive family of the congregation at Corinth.

The second dimension shaping Paul's understanding of love is the memory of the cross. Not only is the other a sibling; this is one "for whom Christ died" (8:11). Paul illustrates the destructive results of individualistic behavior in 8:10–11 with the example of the one who is "destroyed" by those who insist on their individual right to eat food offered to idols. As the reference to the "brother for whom Christ died" indicates, Paul defines love in sacrificial terms, as the denial of one's own rights and the concern for the weaker sibling. Thus, having laid the foundation of the argument with a reminder of his original preaching of the cross (chs. 1–4), Paul appeals to the cross to demonstrate the meaning of love.

Having given an example of unloving conduct, Paul develops the theme of love further, offering his personal example in 1 Corinthians 9. This autobiographical section digresses from the topic of food offered to idols, to which Paul returns in 10:23–11:1. Comparing himself to the Corinthians who insist on their own right (*exousia*, 8:9), Paul insists on his own right (*exousia*, 9:4–6, 12, 18), but indicates that he has chosen not to use his "right" in the gospel (9:18), but to be a slave to all (9:19) in his desire to "save the many" (9:19). Indeed, he has accommodated to all people in order that he might save them. In renouncing his rights in order to save others rather than cause their destruction, he has exemplified the love that Jesus enacted at the cross. His conduct is the model for the Corinthians. He concludes the argument, challenging the readers to follow his example: "Be blameless to the Jews and Greeks and to the church of God, just as I do not seek my own benefit" (10:32–33). "Be my imitators as I am of Christ" (11:1). The crucified one has defined the meaning of love.

Paul's concluding exhortation in 10:32 forms an inclusio with 8:1, for Paul is calling for loving behavior, having defined what love is. The call for imitation in 10:33–11:1 indicates that Paul has exemplified loving behavior. Love means not seeking one's own (10:24). It is maintained within the family as members enact the sacrificial love of Christ. Thus, while Paul's description of loving behavior is indebted to ancient views of family responsibility, it is also shaped by the memory of the cross.

### 1 Corinthians 12–14

In 12:1 Paul introduces the topic of spiritual gifts (*pneumatika*), which extends to 14:40. Inasmuch as the argument runs smoothly if the extended unit on love is omitted (ch. 13), some interpreters have suggested that the section on love is an interpolation, for *agapē* appears in chapters 12 and 14 only in 14:1 as Paul resumes the topic of *pneumatika*.[21] An analysis of the complete unit reveals, however, that Paul has carefully structured the argument in an a-b-a pattern as he resumes the topic of love, which he introduced in 8:1. As in 8:1–11:1, he employs a digression in the middle of the argument. He lays the foundation in chapter 12, describing the ideal of harmony within the community without indicating the problem he is addressing. Only in chapter 14 does the reader discern that this harmony is being undermined by self-seeking behavior in the public worship. The Corinthians are apparently claiming to be seeking "the more excellent way" (12:31), competing in the exercise of the *pneumatika*. Paul's most extended statement on love, in 1 Corinthians 13, is not an interruption in the argument but is, like chapter 9, a purposeful digression. The references to tongues, prophecy, and knowledge in 13:1–3 indicate that the extended description of love is an implied polemic directed at the Corinthian individualists.

Chapter 13 is divided into three parts. In 13:1–3, Paul addresses the problem of competition in Corinth, indicating that the absence of love renders all of the gifts meaningless. Thus *agapē* is not one gift among many, but the indispensable reality in the exercise of all gifts. In 13:4–7, he describes concretely the behavior that love produces, echoing other lists of "virtues" in his instruction (cf. Gal. 5:19–25). After two positive statements, he lists the negative aspects of love. That "love is patient, love is kind" (13:4) is reminiscent of Paul's description of his own demeanor "in patience, in kindness, in the Holy Spirit, in sincere love" (2 Cor. 6:6) and his inclusion of patience and kindness in the fruit of the Spirit (Gal. 5:22; cf. 1 Thess. 5:14). Both patience and kindness are divine qualities that will build community in Corinth. Patience (*makrothymia*) is the willingness to bear with the failures of the other and the readiness to forgive (see ch. 4). Kindness is the care for the poor, the sick, and others in need.[22]

In the negative descriptions of love, Paul continues to address the Corinthian situation. That "love is not jealous" (*ou zēloi*, 1 Cor. 13:4) implies a critique of Corinthian behavior (cf. 3:3) in their zeal for *pneumatika* (12:31; 14:1, 39), recalling a common feature of Paul's stock of vices (2 Cor. 12:20; Gal. 5:20). The claim that "love is not boastful" (*ou perpereuetai*) and "is not puffed up" (*ou physioutai*) implies further critique. Although *perpereuomai* appears in the New Testament only in this passage, it recalls the Corinthian boasting that Paul criticizes in the first four chapters (cf. 1:29, 31; 3:21; 4:7; 5:6), and it is probably synonymous here with "puffed up," a reference to the Corinthian arrogance that Paul has addressed earlier in the letter (1 Cor. 4:18; 5:2).

In the remaining negative statements, Paul continues to describe the negative qualities of love. The phrase "does not behave disgracefully" (*ouk aschēmonei*) appears elsewhere to describe sexual offenses (Rom. 1:27; 1 Cor. 7:35–37), and

21. See the discussion in Söding, *Liebesgebot bei Paulus*, 124.

22. See the discussion in ch. 4 ("Positive Attributes"). Kindness (*chrēstotēs*) is connected with *agapē* also in 2 Cor. 6:6. It is an attribute of God (Rom. 2:4; 11:22). See the discussion in Söding, *Liebesgebot bei Paulus*, 135. See also Spicq, "*Chrēsteuomai*," *TLNT* 3:511–16.

may allude to the Corinthians' questions about sexuality, but in this context is a reference to antisocial behavior that undermines the community. The love that "does not seek its own" (13:5) is at the heart of Paul's advice in 1 Corinthians (10:24, 32–33) and a reminder of Jesus's ultimate demonstration of self-denying love. That love "is not provoked" (*ou paroxynetai*) and "does not take account of evil" (*ou logizetai to kakon*) reminds those who create factions that their behavior, which is rooted in self-seeking, is the opposite of the love Jesus manifested at the cross.

In the conclusion of the section in 13:4–7, "Love bears all things, . . . hopes all things, endures all things," Paul makes the transition to the third section, in which he indicates that love is the better way because it is eternal, in contrast to the gifts that have been the cause of Corinthian competition. The triad of faith, hope, and love probably belongs to Paul's earliest catechesis (cf. 1 Thess. 1:2–3), suggesting their essential inseparability in the life of the church. However, because only love endures eternally, it—not the gifts that created community rivalries—is "the greatest of these." Thus it is a priority in the community and the foundation for its solidarity.

This digression on love prepares the way for Paul's response to the Corinthian situation when they come together (14:26) in the assembly. Having established earlier that "love builds up" (*agapē oikodomei*), Paul now demonstrates the significance of *agapē* in the assembly in chapter 14, encouraging the Corinthians to pursue the gifts that do not build up the individual (14:4) "in order that the church receive edification" (14:5). Indeed, Paul addresses the apparent chaos and self-seeking of the Corinthians with a consistent use of forms of *oikodomē* (14:1–5, 12, 26) and synonyms (14:6, 19) as the criterion for the assembly. In this way, he indicates that "love builds up" the whole community.

### Romans 12:1–15:13

The argument of Romans culminates in the ethical instructions in 12:1–15:13, which demonstrate the implications of Paul's doctrine of the righteousness of God as it creates a community that is for both Jew and Greek. In this section, which is characterized by an extended series of imperatives, Paul portrays an existence in sharp contrast to the human unrighteousness that he described in the initial argument in 1:18–3:20. Whereas human unrighteousness is evident in the sexual and antisocial vices in 1:18–3:20, life under the righteousness of God is distinguished by communal responsibility for others. Having described those who dishonored their bodies in 1:24, Paul challenges the readers to present their bodies "a living sacrifice to God" (12:1). In the description of human unrighteousness, Paul had described those who worshiped and served (*esebasthēsan kai elatreusan*) the creature rather than the Creator and now encourages the readers to be engaged in "reasonable worship" (*logikē latreia*).

Having described those who had a "reprobate mind" (*nous*, 1:28), he challenges the readers to a renewed mind (*nous*).

The description of the transformed existence in 12:1–15:13 apparently serves a dual purpose. First, as the culmination of Paul's argument, it addresses the Roman situation, elaborating on Paul's earlier claim that "the just requirement of the law [is] fulfilled in us, who walk not according to the flesh but according to the Spirit" (8:4 NRSV).[23] Having declared that believers are not under law, Paul now indicates the nature of Christian conduct in the absence of the traditional understanding of the law. Unlike the boundary markers of the Torah, which separated Jew from gentile, Paul's moral vision can be lived by Jews and Greeks in common fellowship. Thus the initial instruction after the introduction in 12:1–2, "not to think more highly of yourself than you ought to think" (12:3), both resumes the earlier argument of the book (cf. 11:18, 20, 25) and establishes a major theme of the exhortation, as the inclusio with 12:16 indicates. Indeed, within the context of Romans, this instruction is a challenge to ethnic groups to live in harmony with each other.

Second, while Paul's moral instructions in 12:1–15:13 are the culmination of the argument of Romans, they also summarize arguments Paul has made elsewhere. As in other sections of Romans, he applies his previous arguments to fit new situations, and he says more than he has to say in addressing the Roman situation. As table 7.1 indicates, much of Romans 12:1–15:13 recapitulates moral instruction from earlier letters or the common property of early Christian paraenesis.

**Table 7.1. Pauline Literature and Early Christian Paraenesis**

| Romans 12:1–15:13 | Earlier Pauline Paraenesis |
|---|---|
| 12:1–2 Discern the will of God. | 1 Thess. 4:3 This is the will of God. |
| 12:1 well-pleasing (to God) | 2 Cor. 5:9 We make every effort to be well-pleasing to [God].<br>Eph. 5:10 discerning what is well-pleasing to the Lord |
| 12:3 just as we have many members in one body | 1 Cor. 12:12 (NRSV) just as the body is one and has many members |
| 12:10 brotherly love | 1 Thess. 4:9 brotherly love |
| 12:10 outdoing one another in showing honor | Phil. 2:3 counting others better than yourselves |
| 12:11 not lacking in showing zeal | 2 Cor. 8:7–8 as you abound in zeal |
| 12:11 alive in the Spirit | Rom. 8:13 (NRSV) If by the Spirit you put to death the deeds of the body, you shall live.<br>1 Thess. 5:19 (NRSV) Do not quench the Spirit. |
| 12:11 serving the Lord | 1 Thess. 1:9–10 to serve the true and living God |

23. See ch. 6.

| Romans 12:1–15:13 | Earlier Pauline Paraenesis |
|---|---|
| 12:12 Rejoicing in hope | Rom. 5:2 We boast in hope of the glory of the Lord.<br>1 Thess. 1:3 your steadfastness of hope<br>Phil. 3:1; 4:4 Rejoice in the Lord.<br>1 Thess. 5:16 Rejoice always. |
| 12:12 endurance in tribulation | Rom. 5:3 We boast in our tribulation.<br>1 Thess. 1:3 endurance of hope |
| 12:12 continuing in prayer | 1 Thess. 5:17 Pray constantly. |
| 12:13 Contribute to the needs of the saints. | Gal. 6:6 Let those who are taught share with those who teach. |
| 12:13 Pursue hospitality. | 1 Tim. 3:2 A bishop must be . . . hospitable.<br>Heb. 13:2 Practice hospitality.<br>1 Pet. 4:9 Practice hospitality. |
| 12:14 Bless those who persecute you. | 1 Cor. 4:12 When persecuted, we bless. |
| 12:15 Rejoice with those who rejoice. | |
| 12:16 Have the same mind among one another, not being proud. | Phil. 2:2 Be of the same mind; 4:2 I encourage Euodia and . . . Syntyche to be of the same mind. |
| 12:16b Associate with the humble, do not be wise among yourselves. | 1 Pet. 3:8d Have a humble mind. |
| 12:17 Do not return evil for evil. | 1 Thess. 5:15 Do not return evil for evil. |
| 12:17 Noble in the sight of all | Gal. 6:10 Do good to all.<br>1 Thess. 5:15 Pursue the good to one another and to all. |
| 12:18 Be at peace with all people. | 1 Thess. 5:13b Be at peace among yourselves. |
| 13:1–7 Be submissive to the authorities. | 1 Tim. 2:1–2 supplications . . . for kings and all who are in high positions<br>Titus 3:1 To be subject to rulers . . .<br>1 Pet. 2:13–17 Accept the authority of every human institution. |
| 13:8–10 Love one another. . . . The law is fulfilled in one word, "Love your neighbor as yourself." | Gal. 5:14 The law is fulfilled in one word, "You shall love your neighbor as yourself." |
| 14:1–15:13 [the strong and the weak]<br>14:1 Accept the weak in faith.<br>14:13 stumbling block to the brother | 1 Cor. 8:1–11:1 [the strong and the weak]<br>8:7 Their conscience, being weak<br>8:9 Stumbling block to the weak |

For example, in the first description of the will of God in 12:3–8, the opening imperative, "Do not think of yourselves more highly than you ought to think" (12:3), corresponds to "have the same mind" (Phil. 2:2; cf. 12:16; 15:5; NRSV "live in harmony"). Thus Paul develops the same theme that he had earlier developed in Philippians when he urged his readers to "mind one thing" (2:2) rather than live in self-centeredness and strife (2:3). The "will of God, the good, the well pleasing and the perfect" (12:2), therefore, is a corporate existence, as the imagery of the body (12:3–8) indicates. The significance of 12:1–15:13 is that it is probably the most thorough example of Paul's moral instruction to his communities.

Interpreters have suggested that both this passage and other moral sections of Paul fall under the definition that Dibelius gave to paraenesis: loosely connected ethical directives.[24] While the asyndetic style (note the absence of conjunctions) may suggest a lack of coherence, 12:1–15:13 has a thematic unity that one may discover in Paul's use of interlocking inclusios framing the discussion. The programmatic statement in 12:1–2 forms an inclusio with 13:11–13, indicating the eschatological and countercultural nature of Paul's moral instruction. The eschatological dimension is evident in the claim that believers should not be conformed "to this age" (12:2), knowing "the time, that the hour has come for you to awaken from sleep" (13:11). The countercultural dimension of Christian existence is evident in the instruction not "to be conformed to this world" (12:2) and in the challenge to "put off" (13:12) the old existence and "put on the Lord Jesus and make no provision for the flesh" (13:14). One may observe also the outer frame marked by the instruction "not to think of [oneself] more highly than [one] ought to think" (12:3) and the imperative, "Have the same mind-set toward one another; do not be haughty" (12:16), which Paul reiterates in 15:5. Similarly, the command to love forms an inclusio in 12:9 and 13:8–14. The thematic unity, therefore, is the corporate nature of Christian morality, which believers express by caring for one another.

### Romans 12:1–16: Life within the Community

After the general statement calling for a transformed existence in 12:1–2, Paul describes the new existence. The function of 12:3–8 is to provide the necessary foundation for the instruction in 12:9–15:13. The description of the unity and diversity within the body establishes the corporate nature of Christian morality before Paul explores the implications of the love command in the life of the community in 12:9–15:13.[25] Although love appears only once (14:15) in 14:1–15:13, this entire section elaborates on the love of neighbor mentioned in 12:9–13:10.[26]

24. Dibelius, *From Tradition to Gospel*, 239.
25. Peng, *Hate the Evil, Hold Fast to the Good*, 195.
26. See Dunn, *Romans*, 2:797; Peng, *Hate the Evil*, 192.

In Romans 12:1–2, Paul introduces the extended treatment of moral conduct with, "I appeal to you therefore, brothers," his customary language for introducing moral instruction (cf. Phil. 4:2; 1 Thess. 4:1; 5:12). The identification of the readers as siblings (*adelphoi*) places the moral instruction within the context of the family, an image that Paul maintains throughout his moral instructions in 12:1–15:13 (cf. 12:10–12; 14:10–13, 15; cf. *agapētoi* in 12:19) as he establishes the identity of the readers. The "mercies of God" are tantamount to the love of God (cf. 5:5–8) and the righteousness of God, the major themes of chapters 1–11. The content of Paul's appeals is stated in the two parallel clauses in 12:1b–2, both of which define moral conduct as a response to God. In 12:1b, Paul instructs the readers to present their bodies as a living sacrifice "pleasing to God" (*euareston tō theō*), while in 12:2 he challenges readers to "discern the will of God, the pleasing (*euareston*) and the perfect."

Paul draws his parallel expressions for moral conduct from the language of Jewish moral discourse. What is "pleasing to God" is the common way to describe conduct that conforms to the law (Exod. 21:8; Pss. 55:14 LXX; 114:9 LXX; Wis. 4:10; 9:10; 17:1). The "acceptable" (*euareston*), used twice in 12:1–2, is a common phrase in the Old Testament and Jewish literature for sacrifices and behavior that are acceptable to God (Wis. 4:10; Philo, *Spec. Laws* 1.201; *Virtues* 67; *T. Dan.* 1:3; cf. 14:18; 2 Cor. 5:9). Consequently, Paul says later in the argument that the one who serves Christ is "pleasing to God" (14:18). Indeed, Paul describes his own ambition to be "pleasing to God" (2 Cor. 5:9), and he describes the work of others in similar terms (Phil. 4:8; cf. Eph. 5:10). This is "the will of God," a term common in Jewish moral teaching. The "good" (*agathos*), a term widely used in ethical instruction in both Hellenistic and Jewish texts, is the leitmotif of the entire section (12:9; 13:3–4; 15:2) and a common term in Paul for moral instruction (cf. Gal. 6:10; 1 Thess. 5:15; Philem. 14). The "will of God" is a common way to describe the life in conformity to the Torah (see ch. 2, "'The Will of God' and 'Pleasing to God'").

Contrary to many interpreters, to "discern" (*dokimazein*) the will of God is not to discover the right course of action in every situation, but to understand God's will within the instructions that follow in 12:3–15:13. Paul envisions a community that is the opposite of those whom he has described earlier as "those who did not see fit (*edokimasen*) to have a knowledge of God" (Rom. 1:28) and the one who "[knows] the will of God and [approves] (*dokimazeis*) the better things" (2:18) but does not keep God's law. Paul envisions a countercultural community that discerns God's will and fulfills the "just requirement of the law" (cf. 8:4; 13:8–10).

The programmatic statement in 12:1–2 both resumes the argument of chapters 1–11 and introduces what is to follow. To present their bodies as a living sacrifice to God is to overcome past behavior, to be a contrast to those who "dishonor their bodies" (1:24), and to recognize that the body of sin has been destroyed (6:6) and that sin will no longer reign in the body (6:12; cf. 8:10–13).

To speak of this life in the body as a "living sacrifice" echoes the sacrificial language Paul frequently uses to describe the ethical life. The rational worship of the new aeon occurs in everyday life through the deeds of the body. The call to spiritual formation—to be "not conformed to this world, but . . . transformed by the renewing of [the] mind" (12:2)—introduces an extended description of the moral life that is obedient to this call. The heading offers multiple words to introduce the specific moral conduct, which Paul describes as "rational worship."

Interpreters have observed the Stoic overtones of Paul's language, noting that "rational worship" (12:1), "think with sober judgment," and the imagery of the body (12:3–8) were used in Stoic discussions of ethics.[27] However, Paul's description of the rational worship and sober judgment has a distinctive quality that grows out of his prior argument and reflects his own understanding of the identity of the community as a body (12:3–8) and family (12:9–14:15).[28] The body is not, as in Stoic ethics, the body politic, but the local house church, just as the family is the multiethnic community created by God's saving act. The family imagery is evident in Paul's consistent references to brotherly love (12:10), brother (14:10, 15, 21), and the orientation toward "one another" (12:5, 10, 16; 14:13, 19; 15:5, 7). The congruence of the images of the body and family is suggested by the ancient comparison of the family with a body.[29]

The identity of the community as a body is the basis for the ethical instructions in 12:3–8. Consistent with the reference to the *nous* in 12:2, words for cognition, using forms of *phron-*, indicate that ways of thinking determine moral conduct. Paul challenges the community members not to "think more highly of themselves than they ought to think" (*mē hyperphronein par' ho dei phronein*), but to think (*phronein*) about what is reasonable (*sōphronizein*). Although *sōphronizein* is widely used in philosophical discussions to describe modesty and self-restraint—the mean between license and insensibility—and is one of the four cardinal virtues,[30] in this context the sober judgment involves recognizing one's place as only one of many parts of the body of Christ. Although this instruction is drawn from Paul's words in 1 Corinthians 12, it has a special significance for the argument of Romans. The transformed existence is a corporate response to the mercies of God. Those who are transformed live within a community that crosses ethnic and social lines, denying the egoism that Paul described in 1:18–3:20.

Inasmuch as Paul commonly contrasts self-centeredness to loving action (cf. 1 Cor. 12–14; Phil. 2:1–4; Gal. 5:13–26), the transition from describing the corporate existence within the body to discussing love at length in 12:9–13:10

27. See Thorsteinsson, "Paul and Roman Stoicism," 147. See also Engberg-Pedersen, "Paul's Stoicizing Politics in Romans 12–13," 163–72; Esler, "Paul and Stoicism," 106–24.

28. Contra Schnelle, "Liebesgebot im Neuen Testament," 29.

29. See the discussion by Sandnes, *A New Family*, 119–30.

30. Peng, *Hate the Evil*, 126; see also Zeller, "Konkrete Ethik," 89.

is not unusual. Having established that one should think of oneself within the context of the body, Paul now elaborates on communal responsibility, offering extended moral instruction under the heading, "Let love be unhypocritical" (12:9). Sincere love extends to the community (12:9–13, 15–16; 13:8–10) and to the surrounding world (12:15, 17–21; 13:1–7), and is the basis for resolving conflicts within the church (14:1–15:13).

As the parallel in 13:8–10 indicates, Paul's reflection on *agapē* is an interpretation of Leviticus 19:18 (cf. Gal. 5:14). Undoubtedly, his understanding is rooted not only in the Levitical command, but also in the demonstration of God's sacrificial love (Rom. 5:8; 8:31–35). The command, "Abhor the evil, hold on to the good" (12:9), which employs language derived from the Old Testament (cf. Amos 5:15; Pss. 37:27; 97:10), also serves as a heading for the entire section, as the inclusio with 12:21 indicates. Paul places love as the central category in distinguishing between good and evil. Drawing on common distinctions in the Old Testament (see ch. 5), he also reiterates what he has said in the moral instructions of previous letters.

Paul elaborates on the good in 12:10–13, 15–16 and describes the evil to be avoided in 12:17–21. He describes the good in familial terms, drawing on the moral instructions from earlier letters as he stacks up *phil-* words in verses 10–13. Whereas the unredeemed existence manifests itself as "without natural affection" (*astorgos*, 1:31), he urges readers to be devoted to one another in brotherly love (*tē philadelphia eis allēlous philostorgoi*, 12:10), practicing the care for one another in the fictive family that was not even practiced in natural families. Here Paul elaborates on his customary catechesis associated with *philadelphia* (cf. 1 Thess. 4:9), using the term that had been appropriated in Hellenistic Judaism from Greek reflections on brotherly love. For Paul, however, *philadelphia* is the characteristic of the metaphorical family. He intensifies the expression with the word *philostorgoi*, rendered by Bauer as "loving dearly,"[31] a term used for the love of parents for children (cf. 4 Macc. 15:13; *Jos. Asen.* 7:252). Esteeming one another with honor echoes Paul's correspondence in other letters (cf. Phil. 2:3). As the repetition of "one another" (*allēlous*) indicates, "outdoing each other in showing honor to each other" suggests the familial context of the practice of love. This also belongs to Paul's customary paraenesis (cf. Phil. 2:3).

In 12:11–12, Paul describes the united stance of the community, again drawing on the moral instruction of earlier letters and the preceding argument in Romans. "Rejoicing in hope, patient in tribulation" echoes the early argument in 5:2. It also echoes Paul's instructions from other letters. Paul expresses gratitude for the Thessalonians' "steadfastness of hope" (1 Thess. 1:3; cf. 5:8) and frequently calls on his readers to rejoice in the context of adversity (cf.

31. BDAG 1059.

Rom. 5:2–3; Phil. 3:1; 4:4). "Continuing in prayer" also recalls Paul's earlier instruction (cf. 1 Thess. 5:17).

In the instructions, "Contribute to the needs of the saints" (*tais chreiais tōn hagiōn koinōnountes*) and "practice hospitality" (*philoxenia*) (Rom. 12:13), Paul envisions the practice of love to both the local community and the believers in other places. The saints are identical to other participants in the body of Christ. This recalls the acts of mercy and generosity within the body of Christ (12:8). It may also include the contribution for the saints that unites the churches (cf. 15:25–26). Hospitality, mentioned first here, becomes a standard part of early Christian paraenesis, as it was also directed toward fellow believers (cf. 1 Tim. 3:2; Heb. 13:2; 1 Pet. 4:9). Therefore, love extends not only to the local family, but to the extended family of believers.

The instruction in 12:15–16 appropriately concludes the first section, for the multiple uses of *phron-* form an inclusio with the parallel in 12:3, indicating that moral conduct is rooted in the new mind-set of those who live in the new age. "One another" (*allēlous*) resumes the usage from 12:10. The challenge to "have the same mind-set" (*to auto phronein*, 12:16) is common in Paul's attempts at community formation (cf. 2 Cor. 13:11; Phil. 2:2; 4:2; Rom. 15:5). The contrasting behavior, "Do not be haughty, but associate with the lowly" (*mē ta hypsēla phronei alla tois tapeinois synapagomenoi*, 12:16 NRSV), recalls 11:20, "Do not be proud but stand in awe" (*mē hypsēla phronei alla phobou*), and the instruction in 12:3 "not to think of [oneself] more highly than [one] ought to think, but to think with sober judgment" (NRSV). The concluding line, "Do not be wise among yourselves," derived from Proverbs 3:7, focuses on life within the multiethnic community of Rome.

### Romans 12:17–13:7: Relations with Outsiders

Although Paul has suggested a concern for those outside the church in earlier moral instructions (cf. 1 Thess. 4:12; 5:15), among the undisputed letters it is only in Romans 12:17–13:7 that he elaborates on the relationship between the saints and outsiders. His counsel on avoiding pagan courts (1 Cor. 6:1) suggests the sharp distinction between the saints and the others. His move from a concern for the saints in Romans 12:13 to the larger society is indicated in his twofold focus on "all humankind" (12:17–18). He challenges readers not to "return evil for evil, but to take thought for the good before all men" and to "be at peace with all men." This advice belongs to early Christian moral instruction and is rooted in Jewish literature. "Do not return evil for evil" is a restatement of Paul's common catechetical advice (cf. 1 Thess. 5:15) and an echo of Proverbs 17:13. This saying echoes numerous injunctions against violence, vengeance, and anger (cf. Prov. 3:29–31; 12:16; 14:29; 15:1).[32] Similarly, the concern to pursue

---

32. See ch. 6; Wilson, *Love without Pretense*, 188. See also Keesmaat, "If Your Enemy Is Hungry," 148.

the good for one another and for all echoes Paul's earlier instruction (1 Thess. 5:15) and is probably a part of Paul's catechesis. According to Proverbs 3:4, the one who is faithful and loyal "will find favor and good repute in the sight of God and of people" (NRSV). The expression "be at peace with all" is also common early Christian moral instruction (cf. Heb. 12:14; 1 Pet. 3:11) and derived from the Psalms (34:14). Paul anticipated the advice in 12:14, which belongs to early Jewish paraenesis and the Jesus tradition, and he incorporated it as a description of his own conduct (cf. 1 Cor. 4:12–13).

The injunction not to take revenge (12:19), a virtual rewording of 17a, echoes Leviticus 19:18, expressing a theme common in the Wisdom literature (cf. Sir. 28:1; *Ps.-Phoc.* 77). Paul supports the injunction with a paraphrase of Deuteronomy 32:35 before concluding the section with a full quotation of Proverbs 25:21–22. He chooses not to cite the final line of the traditional gnomic saying.[33] These injunctions indicate that Paul does not limit love to the community of faith, but assumes that the church extends love to outsiders.

In 13:1–7, Paul continues the series of injunctions but now departs from the asyndetic style to offer a careful argument to support the imperative, "Let every soul be subject to the ruling authorities" (13:1). Although the community's relationship to the governing powers is a common theme in the New Testament (cf. Mark 12:13–17; 1 Tim. 2:1–2; Titus 3:1; 1 Pet. 2:13–17), only here does Paul address the believers' relationship to governing authorities in detail. Indeed, as I have noted above, Paul rarely speaks of relationships with outsiders in his moral instruction, but focuses primarily on the relationships of believers to each other.

The change of style may suggest that Paul has adapted a topic from early Christian moral instruction. Contrary to the view of some interpreters, however, Romans 13 is neither an interpolation in Paul's argument nor an interruption in his moral instruction. The numerous verbal links between 12:17–21 and 13:1–7 indicate that the latter applies the principles enunciated in the former. As the community submits to the governing authorities, it will both enhance the good to all men and contribute to "peace with all" (cf. 12:17–18). The choice between doing good and doing evil (13:3–4) continues the theme of chapter 12 (cf. 12:10, 21). Believers do not avenge themselves (12:19), but acknowledge the role of the governing authorities as instruments of God's wrath and punishment (13:4–5). Thus to submit to the governing authorities is one way of responding even to those who persecute (12:14) or do evil.

Inasmuch as Paul has not mentioned the relationship to governing authorities in earlier letters, interpreters have speculated as to whether a specific Roman situation has evoked a response. As with all of the instructions in 12:1–15:13, Paul offers few clues about his knowledge of the Roman situation.

33. Keesmaat, "If Your Enemy Is Hungry," 146.

Nevertheless, all of his communities have a tenuous relationship to the society and governing authorities. Indeed, the Neronian persecution of Christians a decade after Paul wrote Romans indicates the tenuous relationship between Christians and others. The claim that Jesus is Lord placed the communities on a collision course with Roman authorities. Thus Paul may be drawing on common paraenetic instructions that he gave to communities that had largely withdrawn from civic life and evoked the hostility of their communities.

Paul's integration of the topic into the moral instructions for the Roman church is evident in the connecting links not only to 12:17–21 but also to the larger unit. Appropriate conduct toward the ruling powers is an example of worship in everyday life (12:2) and an expression of the love command. The placement of this injunction between two expressions of the love command (12:9; 13:8–10) suggests that Paul envisions a community that expresses its love for the larger society by its recognition of the role of governing authorities. Those who bless those who persecute them (12:14) will also submit to the government.

Paul states the injunction four times (13:1, 5, 6, 7), offering reasons for this conduct in 13:1b–4, 5b, 6b. "Every soul" (13:1), the equivalent of "everyone of you" (12:3), is an address to the entire community, continuing Paul's focus on the community's cohesiveness. Paul elaborates on the twofold use of "be submissive" (*hypotassesthai*, 13:1, 5) with the injunctions, "Pay taxes" (13:6), and, "pay your debts to all" (13:7). Both the restatement in verses 6 and 7 and the description of the contrary behavior in 13:2 clarify the nature of submission and the options open to the listeners: to submit to (*hypotassesthai*) or resist (*antitassesthai*) what has been ordained (*tetagmenai*) by God. A form of resistance would be to withdraw from paying taxes and other obligations. The repeated use of forms of *tassō* indicates Paul's interest in the order of society, which God has ordained. In order to be at peace with all, believers do the good by acknowledging God's orderly arrangement. They do not "think more highly of themselves than they ought to think," and they live in peace with others and with all.

The relationship to governing authorities is a topic of Greco-Roman moralists,[34] the Old Testament, and Jewish tradition. Paul's moral reasoning fits well within the Old Testament and Jewish tradition, especially the Wisdom tradition. According to Proverbs 8:15 (NRSV), Wisdom says, "By me kings reign, and rulers decree what is just; by me rulers rule, and nobles, all who govern rightly." The author of Proverbs says, "My child, fear the Lord and the king, and do not disobey either of them" (Prov. 24:21 NRSV). The prophets portray rulers as the instruments of God (cf. Isa. 10:5–6; 41:2–4, 25; 45:1; Jer. 21:5–7). Similarly, Josephus says that God is the one who presides over the exercise of worldly power (*J.W.* 2.142, 390).[35] In Diaspora Judaism,

---

34. See Malherbe, *Moral Exhortation*, 149–50.
35. Byrne, *Romans*, 390.

communities faced issues analogous to the situation of the Roman church. A frequent theme of Daniel is that God "deposes kings and sets up kings" (2:21 NRSV; cf. 2:37–39; 4:17, 25–26; 5:18–20).

Paul does not address the multiple issues that have been raised in two thousand years of reflection on Romans 13. He offers no general theology of the state. He does not address the situations described in the Maccabean literature or Revelation in which the ruling authorities threaten the existence of the believing community. Nor does he envision a time when Christians will hold the sword and claim to be instruments of God's wrath. Like the other moral instructions in Romans 12:1–15:13, the injunctions here are general and echo general themes from the Jewish moral tradition. They are addressed to house churches that now must choose between resistance, including the withholding of taxes, and submission to the order God has provided.

Although Paul does not address the issues that will arise when Christians later hold the instruments of power and the potential for civic engagement, one can ascertain ways to appropriate Paul's message. First, the Christian practice of love of neighbor includes the larger society and the recognition of its institutions. Second, belief in God as the one who places rulers in power limits the deification of a political ideology or form of government. Third, one must have respect for the offices of leaders. Nevertheless, loyalty to country or political party is limited by loyalty to God.

### Romans 13:8–14: Fulfilling the Law in the New Age

With the injunction, "Owe no one anything, but love one another" (13:8), Paul makes the transition from the community's relationship to outsiders to the members' care for one another. To owe no one is the equivalent of the injunction, "Pay your debts" (13:7). Whereas Paul instructs the community to fulfill obligations and to be at peace with all in the larger society, he instructs them to "love one another," resuming the exhortation that began with the initial mention of *agapē* in 12:9. This command repeats Paul's basic catechesis (cf. 1 Thess. 4:9), which presupposes the familial identity associated with *philadelphia*. Indeed, the repetition of "one another" (*allēlous*) recalls the usage in 12:10, 16, indicating that Paul has given examples of love for one another earlier (12:10–13).

As with the injunction on submission to the authorities, Paul offers reasons for the injunction in 13:8 with two *gar* clauses (13:8b, 9), enveloping his argument with the inclusio in 13:8b and 13:10. In the initial justification for the injunction, he says, "The one who loves the other has fulfilled the law." As the final specific reference to the law in Romans, the conclusion of the argument that marks the inclusio with 12:9–10 is a remarkable statement in an epistle that repeatedly speaks in negative terms of one's capacity to submit to the law. Early in the argument Paul described all humanity under the power of sin, maintaining that some know the righteous commandment of God but do not obey it (1:32), while others know God's will and "approve the better things" because they have been instructed in the law (2:18). Paul now speaks of the community of believers, who, in contrast to the old humanity, "discern the will of God" (12:2) and fulfill the law. Unlike those who can neither submit themselves to the law (8:7) nor please God (8:8), the one who loves the other fulfills the law. In contrast to those who insist on circumcision and the observance of special days, only the community of believers fulfills the law. As Paul indicated earlier, "the just requirement of the law [is] fulfilled in us who walk not according to the flesh, but according to the Spirit" (8:4). To meet the obligations laid down in 12:1–15:13 is to fulfill the law.

The second *gar* clause (13:9) reinforces Paul's claim that those who love fulfill the law. He clarifies the meaning of *nomos* with the listing of four prohibitions from the Decalogue as examples of the commandments of the law and "any other commandment," indicating that they are summed up in the one saying, "You shall love your neighbor as yourself," adding, "Love does no evil to the neighbor." The term "sum up" (*anakephalaiōsasthai*) is a mathematical metaphor, suggesting that the love command is the summation of the other commandments. He mentions only the commandments of the second tablet of the Decalogue, all of which concern relationships with others. He does not say that the love command has replaced the other commandments, but that commandments dealing with relationships with others find their essence in the love command.

Paul's use of Leviticus 19:18 earlier, in Galatians 5:14, indicates that he is drawing on earlier moral instruction based on Leviticus 19:18. Whereas the neighbor in Leviticus is the fellow Israelite, Paul expands the term's significance to fellow believers within the house church.

### Romans 14:1–15:13: A Concrete Example of the Practice of Love

Having described aspects of loving behavior in chapters 12 and 13, Paul now focuses on the specific challenges of maintaining the corporate identity that he described in 12:3–8 and developed in 12:9–13:10. The church has not only a diversity of gifts, but also a diversity of opinions (14:1). These differences are probably rooted in the basic challenge of uniting Jews and gentiles in one community. Although Paul does not identify those who hold different opinions as Jews and gentiles, their differences suggest that the house churches in Rome are separated along ethnic lines, although the avoidance of ethnic categories in describing the differences of opinion may suggest some overlap. Some gentiles may have held to Jewish laws and some Jews may have expressed freedom from the laws. Nevertheless, the points of contention—the eating of meat (14:2, 21), the judging of one day better than the other (14:5)—are reminiscent of the fundamental problems associated with the ritual aspects of the law that Paul has faced earlier (cf. Gal. 2:11–14).

While the quarrels over opinions may be reminiscent of the regulations of the Torah that separated Jews and gentiles, Paul's description of the issues does not correspond precisely to questions of Torah observance. Neither vegetarianism (14:2) nor the drinking of wine (14:21) is an issue of the observance of Torah. Thus Paul has probably generalized the questions, avoiding the designations of Jew and gentile so as to make the discussion applicable to a variety of situations. The similarities to and differences from the related argument in 1 Corinthians 8:1–11:1 indicate that Paul has generalized an argument that he has made previously, as he did in 12:3–8 (cf. 1 Cor. 12–13).

The inclusio in 14:1 ("Receive the one who is weak in faith, not for quarrels about opinions") and 15:7 ("Receive one another") provides the frame and the focus for the argument, indicating the challenges the community faces in implementing the injunctions in chapters 12–13. To "receive" (*proslamba-nein*) is to "receive in(to) one's home or circle of acquaintances (cf. Acts 28:2; Philem. 17)."[36] The injunction is consistent with the earlier instructions to recognize one's identity within the body of Christ (12:3–7), "pursue hospitality" (12:13), and not think more highly of oneself than one ought to think, but "accommodate to the lowly" (12:16). The injunction, "Receive one another" (*proslambanesthe allēlous*, 15:7), continues the focus on "one another" from chapters 12–13 (12:10, 16; 13:8), suggesting that Paul is describing one dimension of love for one another (13:8). Thus brotherly love extends to those who hold different opinions and come from a different cultural background. This is likely the culmination of Paul's insistence on the righteousness of God for all.

Paul supports this injunction in 14:1–15:13. Chapter 14 is marked by the inclusio formed by "the weak in faith" (14:1) and the concern for those whose conduct is not "of faith" (14:22–23). One may also note periodic injunctions (14:1, 13; 15:1, 7) accompanied by arguments. Although 14:13 (cf. 14:6–12) indicates reciprocal responsibilities, the primary focus is the concern of the strong for the weak, as the introductory statement (14:1) indicates. Paul summarizes the argument in 15:1–13, giving a twofold christological argument (15:1–6, 7–13) aimed at the strong.

One may assume that the categories of weak and strong are designations from the strong. Paul has employed these categories earlier (cf. 1 Cor. 8:7; 9:22), and he has mentioned the weaker parts of the body (1 Cor. 12:22). Consistent with the entire argument of Romans concerning the law, Paul agrees with the strong that one may "eat everything" (14:2) and that one need not recognize special days (14:5), adding that "nothing is unclean in itself" (14:14). These statements indicate the insignificance of the ritual parts of the law. Nevertheless, the diversity of the body described in 12:3–8 extends to the diversity of opinions over these issues. Paul elaborates on the love command in three stages of the argument, each marked by an injunction (14:1, 13; 15:1).

36. BDAG 883.

Paul first addresses the strong (14:1), but speaks to both strong and weak in 14:2–12, calling for reciprocal responsibilities. He distinguishes the two points of view in 14:2, 5 and frames the discussion with the injunction, "Let the person who eats not despise the one who does not eat, and let the person not eating not judge the one who eats" (14:3), and, "Who are you to judge your brother? And who are you to despise your brother?" (14:10). Such behavior toward siblings is a violation of the command for brotherly love (12:10). Paul offers a theological argument for the injunction. In the first place, he argues from God's saving action in the past: "God received him" (14:3). He elaborates, "For unto this Christ died and lived" (14:9). The appeal to God's action recalls the earlier statement that "while we were yet weak, . . . [Christ] died for the ungodly" (5:6), and the elaboration, "God commends his love to us, in that while we were yet sinners, Christ died for us" (5:8). Thus God's love toward the weak defines the human response toward those who are "weak in faith."

As Paul has demonstrated throughout the argument of Romans, the love of God toward the ungodly, demonstrated in the death of Jesus, places everyone on the same level as servants before the same master (*kyrios*, 14:4, 6, 8, 9) and siblings within the same family (14:10). Paul reiterates the earlier claim that "no one lives to himself and dies to himself" (14:7; cf. 2 Cor. 5:15), but if we live, we live to the Lord (14:8). This submission to the Lord creates the solidarity of a community across ethnic lines. Thus the Christ event indicates the implications of the love command for communal solidarity.

Just as Paul addressed the strong in 14:1 and gave instructions focusing on the responsibilities of both weak and strong in 14:2–12, in 14:13 he speaks of reciprocal responsibilities (14:13a) before giving instructions specifically for the strong in 14:13b–23. "Let us not judge one another" (14:13a) summarizes the preceding section. The repetition of "one another" (*allēlous*) connects the passage with the same word in verse 13, indicating that judging one another is incompatible with loving one another. The injunction "not to place an obstacle (*proskomma*) or temptation (*skandalon*) in the way of a brother" elaborates on the injunctions to receive the brother as Paul reiterates the advice he gave to the Corinthians in another setting (1 Cor. 8:9–13). As in the earlier argument, Paul indicates the insignificance of food (14:17; cf. 1 Cor. 8:8).

Paul's imagery of the stumbling block and *skandalon* is derived from Leviticus 19, which has played a consistent role in his moral instruction. The Levitical statement, "You shall not revile the deaf or put a stumbling block before the blind" (Lev. 19:14 NRSV), provides the imagery for Paul's counsel. Paul's metaphorical use applies, however, to a larger context. The stumbling block will cause grief and destroy the brother (14:15, 20). Inasmuch as we will all appear before the judgment seat of God, we assume responsibility for the eschatological salvation of the other. Therefore, the task of the strong is not to destroy, but to pursue things that "build up one another."

Paul established the relationship between *agapē* and *oikodomē* ("building up") in 1 Corinthians 8:1 and 1 Corinthians 14. Here in Romans 14:15, in the only explicit use of *agapē* in 14:1–15:13, he indicates that love assumes responsibility for the ultimate salvation of those who are weak in faith. As in 14:8, the death of Jesus defines the nature of love, for the weaker brother is one "for whom Christ died." One practices familial love to ensure the solidarity between weaker and stronger members of the family.

Paul reaches the climax of the argument in chapter 15, identifying himself with the strong and urging those who are strong "to bear the burdens of the weak, and not please ourselves" (15:1). As an appropriate conclusion to the entire section, he appeals to the imitation of Christ, who "did not please himself" (15:3), but "became a servant" (15:8; cf. 2 Cor. 8:9; Phil. 2:6–11). Jesus's sacrificial love at the cross defines the relationship of members to one another in a new family in which Jews and Greeks "glorify God with one voice" (15:6) and love each other.

### Conclusion: Love as the Care for the Family

Most interpreters have recognized the central place of love in Paul's ethic. This emphasis sets Paul apart from ancient moralists. While Paul derives the term *agapē* from the Septuagint and the word *philadelphia* from the Jewish paraenetic tradition, the new experience in Christ brings new dimensions to the concept. First, the love of God (Rom. 5:7–8) and the sacrificial death of Christ determine Paul's understanding of love, which he adopts as his own way of life and inculcates among his converts. Second, Paul faces the unique challenge of bringing people from a variety of cultures into one community by providing a new identity as a family. Love involves assuming the roles of the family as the social safety net and the care of family members for one another. Indeed, the care for the family transcends the individual's ambitions.

Within the environment of the house church in the midst of an often hostile society, Paul neither develops a public ethic of love nor adopts the Greek ideal of *philanthrōpia*. However, his concern for the public good (cf. Gal. 6:10; Rom. 12:17–13:10) set in motion the impulses that would result in the church's subsequent involvement with the needs of the larger society. This extension of the love command to the wider society could come only when the churches had grown and acquired the necessary resources.

As the central focus of Paul's ethic, love does not negate other imperatives in his moral instructions. Indeed, the lists of vices and virtues define the nature of love, offering negative and positive examples of self-seeking and caring conduct toward others within the community. As the summation of the law, love does not replace the law's commands, but is the lens for observing them.

# 8

# Ethics and the Disputed Letters of Paul

A new stage in the Pauline correspondence is evident in the letters written after Romans. New challenges confront the churches addressed in Colossians, Ephesians, and the Pastoral Epistles as old issues have diminished in importance. These letters assume rather than defend the mission to the gentiles (cf. Eph. 2:11–22; Col. 3:11), but now address other problems. Whereas in Romans Paul has argued for the sufficiency of the work of Christ in relation to the law, Galatians, Colossians, and Ephesians argue for the sufficiency of Christ in relation to cosmic powers. Similarly, each of the Pastoral Epistles seeks to ensure the Pauline gospel against heretical teachings that have not been confronted earlier. Thus these letters have both continuity and discontinuity with the earlier Pauline correspondence. While major Pauline themes—the saving significance of the cross of Jesus, the role of Paul in the divine plan, the incorporation of the gentile church into God's plan for Israel—are present in these letters, new challenges require both the adaptation of these themes and the introduction of new topics. Because of the discontinuity between the earlier and later Pauline letters, scholars in the last century have distinguished between the seven undisputable letters of Paul and the six letters that are regarded either as disputed or pseudepigraphic. My purpose in this chapter is not to argue the question of authorship, but to treat the disputed letters separately from the undisputed letters, assuming that they concern the issues of a stage of the Pauline tradition that is later than in the undisputed letters. Thus I shall explore the developments in the Pauline moral instruction.[1]

Among the criteria for dividing the Pauline corpus between undisputed and disputed (or pseudepigraphical) letters, none has received more attention than the moral instruction in the disputed letters. While the moral formation of the churches is a primary concern in all of the thirteen letters attributed to Paul, the disputed letters contain new features. For the first time in the Pauline corpus, these letters address the specific subgroups that compose the household (Col. 3:18–4:1; Eph. 5:21–6:9; 1 Tim. 6:1–2) within the house church. If one may assume that Colossians and Ephesians appeared before the Pastoral Epistles, the lists of duties in Ephesians and Colossians became expanded into duties for the wider circle of the congregation (cf. 1 Tim. 2:1–15; Titus 2:1–10). Interpreters have described this development as evidence of a decline from the freedom expressed in the Pauline corpus to the domestication and adaptation of Paul's moral instruction to conventional morality. Most of the scholarly discussion of these lists of duties has involved the search for the origins of the household codes in antiquity with the assumption that they are a foreign body in the Pauline letters. Consequently, most interpreters have treated the household codes in isolation from the argument of their respective books. This conversation fails to discuss the place of this form of moral instruction within the context of the respective letters. In this chapter, I will examine these letters to determine their continuity and discontinuity with the moral vision in Paul's undisputed letters.

## Moral Instruction in Colossians and Ephesians

Although both Ephesians and Colossians devote the first half of their arguments to the cosmic significance of the exalted Lord (Eph. 1–3; Col. 1–2), the moral transformation of the readers is their central concern. Despite the apparent division of the letters into doctrinal and ethical sections, this distinction is appropriate for neither of them, for both are essentially letters of moral advice. The prayer at the beginning of Colossians that the readers "walk worthily of the Lord in everything that is pleasing, bearing fruit in every good work" (Col. 1:10) echoes earlier correspondence and states the theme,[2] functioning as

---

1. I have chosen to refer to the author as Paul throughout this chapter because he is the implied, if not the actual, author of Colossians, Ephesians, and the Pastoral Epistles. I treat these letters as a second stage of the Pauline correspondence, and thus my argument does not require a demarcation between the actual voice of Paul and that of his interpreters.

2. See Meeks, "'To Walk Worthily of the Lord,'" 39. For moral conduct "worthy of the Lord," cf. 1 Thess. 2:12; cf. also Phil. 1:27 for conduct "worthy of the gospel." On moral conduct as "pleasing God" rather than humankind, cf. Rom. 8:8; 1 Cor. 7:32; Gal. 1:10; 1 Thess. 2:4. For bearing fruit as a metaphor for moral conduct, see Rom. 6:21–22; 7:4; Gal. 5:22; Phil. 1:11. The exordium of a speech introduced the major topic and made the audience favorably disposed.

the exordium of the letter. Using the familiar Jewish image of walking that is also employed in the earlier Pauline letters,[3] both letters contrast the "walk" prior to conversion with the current conduct and plead for the readers to make moral progress (cf. Eph. 2:2; Col. 2:6; 3:7, 10; 4:1, 5, 17). The ultimate goal for the readers is that they be "holy and blameless" (*hagious kai amōmous*) in God's sight (Eph. 1:4; cf. Col. 1:22, "holy and blameless and blameless," *hagious kai amōmous kai anenklētous*), as in the undisputed Pauline letters (1 Cor. 1:8; Phil. 2:15). Thus both maintain the familiar Pauline moral vision in terms borrowed from Israel's story.[4] Paul's concern to "present everyone perfect in Christ" (Col. 1:28) indicates that his purpose, as in the undisputed letters, is the eschatological presentation of his converts (cf. 2 Cor. 11:2) as morally transformed people.

### Identity and Morality

Just as the earlier Pauline letters establish the identity of the readers as a basis for their moral endeavor (cf. ch. 3), Ephesians and Colossians establish the identity of the readers, reflecting both continuity and discontinuity with the identity developed in the undisputed letters. Continuity with the undisputed letters is evident in two features. First, both Ephesians and Colossians contrast the new existence of the readers with their former existence in the familiar once-now pattern (cf. Eph. 2:1–6, 11–13, 19; Col. 1:21–22; 2:12–13, 20; 3:1, 3, 5, 7–8) that is common in the undisputed letters (cf. Rom. 7:5–6; 1 Cor. 6:11; Gal. 4:8–9). Adapting the imagery of Romans, Colossians employs the imagery of death and new life, associating this transition with baptism (Rom. 6:1–10; Col. 2:12–13). Both Ephesians and Colossians employ the terminology of the change of clothes (Eph. 4:22, 24–25; Col. 3:8, 12), employed also in the undisputed letters (Rom. 13:12; Gal. 3:27), maintaining imagery that is employed by the Old Testament (cf. Isa. 61:10; Zech. 3:3–4), Plato,[5] and Philo.[6]

Second, like the recipients of the undisputed letters, the readers of Ephesians and Colossians find their new identity within Israel's story. God "elected" (*exelexato*) them to be "holy and blameless" (Eph. 1:4), just as God once elected Israel to receive the inheritance (*klēronomia*, Eph. 1:14; cf. *klēros*, Col. 1:12).[7] In both letters the community lives at the turn of the ages (cf. Eph. 1:9) and is the recipient of the mystery that had been hidden until the revelation

---

3. On "walking" as the Pauline image for moral conduct, see Rom. 6:4; 8:4; 13:13; 1 Cor. 3:3; Gal. 5:16; Phil. 3:17; 1 Thess. 4:1, 12, and the discussion in ch. 2.

4. See ch. 2 for this language for Israel's identity.

5. Plato, *Resp.* 457A: "wearing a virtue of excellence or excellence instead of clothes."

6. Philo, *Flight* 110: "The mind of the wise is clothed with virtues." Cited in Darko, *No Longer Living as the Gentiles*, 43.

7. On Israel's hope for the inheritance, see Friedrich, "*Klēronomia ktl*," *EDNT* 2:298. In the Old Testament, the inheritance was the land promised to Abraham (cf. Exod. 32:13; Num. 26:42–56). This promise takes on an eschatological dimension during the exile. The "lot" (*klēros*)

in Christ (Eph. 1:9; Col. 1:26). Thus they have been incorporated into Israel
as "saints" (*hagioi*, Eph. 1:18; 2:19; 4:12; 5:3; Col. 1:26) and the "elect" (Col.
3:12). Paradoxically, God has both incorporated them into Israel (Eph. 2:11–22)
and placed them in a new humanity (Eph. 2:14–22; Col. 3:10–11) that has no
distinction between Jews and Greeks (Col. 3:11; cf. Gal. 3:28). As in ancient
Israel (cf. Deut. 7:7–11), the community's identity as "elect" and "beloved"
is the basis for the moral conduct that distinguishes it from its surroundings.

The discontinuity from the earlier correspondence is present in the cosmic
language of Ephesians and Colossians, which develops the theme of the exalta-
tion of Christ from the earlier tradition (cf. Rom. 8:32; 1 Cor. 15:23–28) into
the victory over cosmic powers. This cosmic victory is a central feature of the
community's identity, for the victorious one has rescued the readers from the
cosmic powers that once enslaved them (cf. Eph. 2:3; Col. 1:12). Not only is
the community the culmination of God's plan at the end of the ages; it shares
in the cosmic victory of Christ as it sits "in heavenly places" (Eph. 2:6). As
head of the universe (Eph. 1:10; cf. Col. 1:15–17) and head of his body, the
church (Eph. 1:22–23; Col. 1:18), Christ empowers the believers (Eph. 1:23;
Col. 2:10), who find their identity "in him" (Col. 2:10, 19), the cosmic Lord.
Whereas the body of Christ in Romans and 1 Corinthians is the local community, in Colossians and Ephesians it is the cosmic body that is empowered
by the head, Jesus Christ.

As in the earlier correspondence, Paul reminds the readers of their identity before he announces the alternative ethos. Indeed, the description of the
cosmic process provides the readers with the insight and symbolic world that
determine their perceptions of what they should do and empower them for
moral living.[8] The letters consistently refer to the insight that is the presupposition for their moral conduct. In the opening prayer of Colossians, Paul
prefaces his petition that the readers' conduct will be "worthy of the Lord"
with the prayer that they "be filled with the full knowledge of [God's] will in
all wisdom and spiritual understanding" (Col. 1:9). In Ephesians, Paul prays
for the community's "wisdom and revelation in the full knowledge" of the
exalted Lord (1:17), so that they will know the hope of their calling (1:18).
Whereas the community was once "darkened" (Eph. 4:18) and alienated (Col.
1:21) in its mind (*dianoia*), the new humanity now has the knowledge of God's
mystery (Col. 3:10). Consequently, Paul urges the readers not to be foolish
(*aphrones*, Eph. 5:17), and the author of Colossians summarizes the moral
instructions by urging the readers to "walk in wisdom" (4:5).

The victory of Christ over cosmic powers, announced in the Colossian
hymn (1:15–20; cf. Eph. 1:10, 20–23), empowers the community for the new

---

is the possession of the inheritance (Num. 16:14; 18:21) and later becomes the eschatological
inheritance (Isa. 57:6; Dan. 12:13; 1QS 2:17; *1 En.* 34:4; Wis. 3:14).

8. Meeks, "'To Walk Worthily of the Lord,'" 44.

existence. The fullness of deity dwells "in him" (2:9)—the exalted Lord—and the listeners are also "in him being filled" (2:10). The cross was the occasion for the triumph over cosmic powers and the cancellation of the debts of the community (Col. 2:14–15). In their baptism, they have been raised and made alive (Col. 2:12–13). Thus their cosmic existence releases them from obligations to other powers. They are "elect" (Col. 3:12).

This cosmic dimension to the church's identity is a determining factor in its moral life. Whereas their previous existence, characterized by enslavement to cosmic powers (Eph. 2:2), resulted in enslavement to the lusts (Eph. 2:3), the new existence is determined by the community's role as recipient of cosmic power (Eph. 4:4–16; Col. 2:12–15). According to Colossians, the cosmic victory liberates the community from adherence to ascetic rules (2:16–18, 20–23) and human commandments, the alternative to the new moral life described in 3:1–4:5.

### Becoming Holy and Blameless

Moral instruction does not begin in the second half of Ephesians and Colossians, for it is a theme from the beginning, as suggested by the employment in both letters of the terminology of "walking," which is present in the earlier Pauline letters and derived from traditional Jewish instruction. Colossians 2:6–7 functions as the thesis statement (*propositio*) of the letter, summoning the readers to appropriate conduct. Using the language of Jewish paraenesis, the author encourages the listeners, "As therefore you received Christ, walk in him." Colossians 2 suggests that the readers confront dangerous alternatives to this way of life. These include both philosophical speculation about cosmic powers (2:8) and worship of angelic powers (2:18, 23), accompanied by legal observances (2:16) and ascetic practices (2:21). Similarly, Ephesians describes the former existence of the readers as enslavement to cosmic powers resulting in submission to the lusts (Eph. 2:2–3). Although we know neither the immediacy of the danger nor precisely the nature of this threat, we may assume that the new converts faced a challenge similar to that of new converts everywhere: to determine a coherent view of the world and a way of life consistent with their symbolic world. To have a deficient symbolic world is to undermine the goal of moral transformation, according to which the readers would be "holy and without blemish and blameless."

For both Ephesians and Colossians, the life that is "holy and blameless" is the alternative to the existence determined by the cosmic powers that have been defeated by the exalted Christ. The former existence was characterized by enslavement either to the lusts (Eph. 2:3) or to human ascetic commandments (Col. 2:16–23), while the new life conforms to the heavenly existence of the believers, who "seek the things that are above" (Col. 3:2) and "sit in heavenly places" (Eph. 2:6). The specific instructions in Ephesians 4:17–6:9 and Colossians 3:5–4:5 depict the moral life of the new humanity that will be "holy and blameless." Having a new identity as the ones who have been "raised with Christ" (Col. 3:1; cf. 2:12–13) and whose life is "hidden with Christ in God" (3:3), they must see their task as to "seek the things that are above" (Col. 3:1 NRSV).

Both Ephesians (4:1–6:9) and Colossians (3:5–4:5) distinguish two alternative modes of existence. As in the earlier Pauline letters (cf. Rom. 7:5–6; 1 Cor. 6:9–11; Gal. 5:16–25), the author contrasts the previous conduct of the listeners with the new existence (3:7–8), using the metaphor of the change of clothes (Eph. 4:22–25; Col. 3:8, 10, 12), to which Colossians adds the metaphor of death-life (3:5), both of which are familiar in the earlier Pauline correspondence (cf. Rom. 6:11, 13; 13:13–14; Gal. 3:27). This sharp contrast between the way in which the readers once "walked" (Eph. 2:2; Col. 3:7) and the new existence suggests that the author envisions a similar contrast between the mores of the community and those of the surrounding society (cf. Eph. 5:11; Col. 4:5). The author thus employs the "rhetoric of differentiation" that distinguishes the readers from their environment.[9] This differentiation recalls Paul's demand that his converts not behave "like the gentiles" (1 Thess. 4:5), and it ultimately depends on the requirement in the Holiness Code that Israel not conduct themselves in the same way as the nations surrounding them (Lev. 18:1–5).

In Colossians, the lists of vices and virtues are arranged in groups of five and are augmented by additional injunctions that supplement both lists (3:5–9). Five vices should be "put to death" (3:5) and five are to be "put off" (3:8), while Ephesians lists the vices which are to be "put off" (4:25), to be "put away" (4:31), and "not to be mentioned" (5:3) by the community. The two letters differ only slightly from each other on the vices that are to be "put away" or "put to death." Almost all of these appear in the lists in the undisputed Pauline letters. "Fornication" (*porneia*) and "uncleanness" (*akatharsia*), both of which are derived ultimately from the Holiness Code (see chs. 1, 3), appear together in both Colossians and Ephesians (Eph. 5:3; Col. 3:5), as well as in the undisputed Pauline letters. "Passion" (*pathos*) and "evil desire" (*epithymia kakē*, Eph. 2:3; 4:22; Col. 3:5), which belong to the readers' former way of life, are reminiscent of Paul's earlier prohibition of the "passion of desire" (*pathos epithymias*) in 1 Thessalonians 4:5 and his pervasive encouragement to overcome the desires (*epithymiai*, cf. Rom. 1:24–26; 6:12; Gal. 5:17) of the flesh. The focus on sexual vices continues the early Christian appropriation of the sexual ethics of the Torah and Jewish moral instruction.

In addition to the sexual vices, "greed" (*pleonexia*) also appears in the Pauline vice lists (cf. 1 Cor. 5:11; 6:10) and Jewish paraenesis. Indeed, the term is used with a sexual connotation (cf. 1 Thess. 4:6). The equation of greed

9. See Darko, *No Longer Living as the Gentiles*, 31.

and idolatry (Eph. 5:5; Col. 3:5) echoes the Jewish ethical tradition.[10] These vices all have analogues in the Decalogue and are commonplace in the Jewish paraenetic tradition.[11]

Ephesians and Colossians also share the naming of other vices that community members must "put off," which also repeat earlier Pauline paraenesis (Eph. 4:31; Col. 3:8). "Wrath" (*orgē*), "anger" (*thymos*), and "evil" (*kakia*) appear in earlier letters (cf. 2 Cor. 12:20; Gal. 5:20). Ephesians adds clamoring (*kraugē*) and bitterness (*pikria*) to the anticommunal vices. These vices are common topics in both Hellenistic and Jewish moral instruction.

Colossians and Ephesians add to the familiar paraenesis prohibitions against lying, placing them within a communal context. In Colossians, the author encourages the listeners, "Do not lie to one another" (3:9 NRSV), an apparent allusion to the ninth commandment,[12] and in Ephesians the author encourages the readers to speak the truth because "we are members of one another" (4:25 NRSV). Ephesians actually cites Zechariah 8:16 (NRSV), "Speak the truth to one another," indicating the continuity of the instructions with the Old Testament. While injunctions against lying are commonplace in any culture, those in Colossians and Ephesians fit well with the traditional Jewish paraenesis. The prohibition against stealing (Eph. 4:28) also belongs to moral discourse of any culture, including the Jewish community.

In addition to the familiar themes from the undisputed letters, these two letters focus heavily on inappropriate speech that undermines community life. Both list blasphemy as a vice to be put away (Eph. 4:31; Col. 3:8). As a term for slander or defamation,[13] *blasphēmia* appears alongside anger and wrath as one of the anticommunal vices. It appears alongside "shameful speech" (*aischrologia* [*aischrotēs*, "obscenity" in Eph. 5:4]), a term that was used for speech that is either obscene or in bad taste.[14] Ephesians instructs the listeners, "Do not let any evil word come out of your mouth, but only what is useful for building up" (4:29). It later (Eph. 5:4) contrasts thankful speech with foolish speaking (*mōrologia*) and vulgar talk (*eutrapelia*).[15]

The vices involving appropriate speech develop both the sexual and antisocial themes in the vice lists, for they involve both slanderous speech and sexually charged conversation within the community. A community that shares

10. Rosner, *Greed as Idolatry*, 69–88.

11. See ch. 1. Rosner, *Greed as Idolatry*, 53–54.

12. Ibid., 54.

13. BDAG 178.

14. BDAG 29. Aristotle contrasts the preference for obscenity in older drama with the more refined taste of cultured gentlemen. According to Clement of Alexandria, the term includes stories about adultery and pederasty. It can also be used for derogatory comments about others or scurrilous talk (Polybius, *Histories* 8.11.8; 3.6.4).

15. *Eutrapelia* can refer to wittiness, course jesting, or risqué speech. BDAG 414.

the common life of sexual purity and avoidance of antisocial behavior will not engage in conversation that undermines these basic values.

While some of the vices to be "put away" have parallels in Hellenistic literature, all of them have parallels in the Jewish moral tradition. Indeed, as Lars Hartmann has argued, the Decalogue provides an important background to the moral instructions in Colossians 3:5–17, an insight that also applies to Ephesians. The sexual vices mentioned are expansions of the sin prohibited by the seventh commandment, against adultery (Exod. 20:14), and the tenth, against coveting of the neighbor's wife (Exod. 20:17). The references to greed as idolatry (Eph. 5:5; Col. 3:5) recall the second and tenth commandments (Exod. 20:4, 17). The prohibition of lying (Eph. 4:25; Col. 3:9) recalls the ninth commandment, against false witness (Exod. 20:16). In addition, Ephesians adds the prohibition of stealing (Eph. 4:28). Even the commands against anger and wrath may belong to the interpretative tradition of the sixth commandment, against murder.

These vices not only reflect the impact of the Decalogue, but also show the influence of the wisdom tradition. As I demonstrated in chapter 1, warnings against both the sexual and anticommunal vices are commonplace in the Wisdom literature. Moreover, the focus on inappropriate and injurious speech is common in the Wisdom literature. Sirach condemns reckless speech (4:29), gossip and slander (19:6; 28:13–26), mockery and abusive speech (27:17), and coarse or foul language (23:13).

Both Colossians and Ephesians contrast the vices of the old humanity that the readers "put away" with the positive attributes of the new humanity (literally "new man," Eph. 2:15; 4:24; cf. Col. 2:11), which they "put on" (Eph. 4:24; cf. Col. 2:10, 12). This community has no distinctions between "Greek and Jew, circumcision and uncircumcision, barbarian, Scythian, slave, free," because "Christ is all and in all" (Col. 3:11 NRSV; cf. Eph. 2:11–21). These categories undoubtedly reflect a Jewish perspective. Christ has not only reconciled humanity to himself (1:22), but also reconciled the peoples into one new humanity, which shares a common ethos.

The new humanity, which shares the identity of Israel as "the elect and holy and beloved" (3:12), is distinguished by the qualities that Paul inculcated in the earlier letters.[16] "Compassion" (*splanchna oiktirmou*, Col. 3:12) recalls Paul's commendation of "compassion and sympathy" (*splanchna kai oiktirmoi*) in Philippians 2:1 (cf. 2 Cor. 6:12; 7:15; Phil. 1:8; Philem. 7, 12). "Kindness" (*chrēstotēs*, Col. 3:12), "humility" (*tapeinophrosynē*, Col. 3:12; cf. Eph. 4:2), "meekness" (*praytēs*, Col. 3:12; Eph. 4:2), and "patience" (*makrothymia*, Col. 3:12; Eph. 4:2) all belong to traditional Pauline paraenesis and have roots in the Jewish paraenetic tradition. As the alternative to the vices in 3:5–9, they

---

16. For the indebtedness of the Colossian moral precepts to traditional Pauline paraenesis, see Frank, *Kolosserbrief*, 253–75.

may also depict the behavior of those who do not violate the commandments of the Decalogue.[17]

As with the vice lists, Paul adds injunctions to the list, reinforcing the communal nature of the moral instruction. Paul's frequent use of *allēlōn* to describe community solidarity is evident in the fact that members do not "lie to each other" (Col. 3:9), but "bear with one another" and "forgive each other" (Col. 3:13). At the apex of the injunctions is "love, the bond of perfection" (Col. 3:14; Eph. 4:2; 5:2), which maintains the focus of Pauline ethics (Gal. 5:14–15, 22). These instructions correspond to the moral instructions of the earlier letters, which are indebted to the focus of the Holiness Code (Lev. 17–26) on matters of both sexual morality and love for the other (Lev. 19:18).

Neither Ephesians nor Colossians distinguishes between ethics and other dimensions of the believers' existence. Ephesians instructs the readers, "Walk not as unwise but as wise" (Eph. 5:15), adding, "Do not be foolish" (5:17). Both letters use the common term "the will of God/the Lord" (Eph. 5:17; cf. Col. 1:9; 4:12). Both letters include instructions for corporate worship in which the readers admonish one another in "psalms, hymns, and spiritual songs" (Eph. 5:19; Col. 3:16) and give thanks (Eph. 5:20; Col. 3:15).

### The Household Code

The exhortation in both letters moves from the reciprocal responsibilities of members of the community to each other in worship (Eph. 5:19; Col. 3:16) to the reciprocal responsibilities of members of the household to each other. While the preceding moral instructions resemble the paraenesis of the earlier letters, the address to all members of the household is unprecedented in Pauline literature. The succinct form in which the writer expresses the reciprocal duties of the three pairs that composed the ancient household (wives and husbands, children and parents, slaves and masters) in Colossians (3:18–4:1) is expanded significantly in Ephesians (5:21–6:9) and appears in a variety of forms in subsequent literature (cf. 1 Pet. 2:18–3:7; 1 Tim. 6:1–2; cf. *Did.* 4:9–11; *Barn.* 19:5–7; *1 Clem.* 1:3; 21:6–9; Ign. *Pol.* 4:1–6; Pol. *Phil.* 4:2–6:3). In the Pastoral Epistles it is expanded to include other members of the house church (1 Tim. 2:1–15; 5:3–16; Titus 2:1–10). Because of the simplicity of the Colossian household code and the presumed sequence of the letters, most interpreters have argued for a development of the household code from Colossians, which was the source of the longer form in Ephesians. According to this view, the household code was adapted into the more extended household code in the Pastoral Epistles (cf. Titus 2:1–10; cf. 1 Tim. 2:1–15; 5:3–16) and the variant form in 1 Peter.[18]

17. Rosner, *Greed as Idolatry*, 55.
18. Boring, "Household Codes," *NIDB* 2:905; Woyke, *Die neutestamentlichen Haustafeln.* Berger argues for the opposite development, maintaining that the process began with the

## THE SEARCH FOR ORIGINS

Because the household code does not appear in undisputed letters of Paul and has a distinctive form and style in Colossians and Ephesians,[19] interpreters have treated it in isolation from both contexts. Since Martin Dibelius identified the household code with an ancient topos,[20] interpreters have regarded it as a foreign body appropriated into Christian paraenesis. Thus scholars have devoted their attention to searching for the origins of the household code, pointing out that it has no antecedents in the Old Testament, the teachings of Jesus, or the writings of Paul.[21] Dibelius, followed by Karl Weidinger,[22] pointed to Stoic parallels to the household code. Others have claimed that the topos originated in the moral instruction of Hellenistic Judaism.[23] More recently, scholars argue that the household code is indebted to discussions of household management among Greek philosophers.[24] In observing the parallels between the household code in the New Testament and those in the ancient philosophical tradition, interpreters have noted that the household code in the New Testament consists of only the conventional morality of the day. While scholars disagree over the circumstances that led to the development of rules for the household, the consensus remains that they represent a decline from the countercultural and egalitarian moral instruction of Paul toward the conventional morality of the Greco-Roman world.[25]

The search for the origin and *Sitz im Leben* of the household code rests on assumptions that do not fit well with all of the evidence. While the household was a common topic of philosophical and popular morality, no precise parallel exists for the form of the household code in Ephesians and Colossians.[26]

---

household codes that lacked reciprocal duties (1 Pet. 2:18–3:7; 1 Tim. 5:1–16) and concluded with the succinct and tightly organized version in Colossians (Berger, *Formen und Gattungen*, 199).

19. In addition to the movement to direct address to specific groups, the household codes are written in terse sentences, unlike the long sentences in chs. 1 and 2 (Bevere, *Sharing in the Inheritance*, 227–28).

20. Dibelius, *An die Kolosser, an die Epheser, an Philemon*, 36.

21. Boring, "Household Code," 905.

22. Weidinger, *Die Haustafeln*.

23. Crouch, *Origin of the Colossian Haustafel*.

24. See Balch, *Let Wives Be Submissive*. Balch traces the topos *peri oikonomias* from Plato and Aristotle through the Middle Platonists and Peripatetics to Stoics, Epicureans, Hellenistic Jews, and neo-Pythathoreans. The major texts included for comparison are Aristotle, *Pol.* 1.1253–54, 1–14; Dio Chrysostom, *Or.* 5.348–51; Seneca, *Ep.* 94.1; Dionysius of Halicarnassus, *Ant. rom.* 2.25.4–26.4; *Ps.-Phoc.* 175–227; Philo, *Decalogue* 165–67; *Spec. Laws* 2.224–41; Josephus, *Ag. Ap.* 2.199–208. See also Balch, "Neopythagorean Moralists and the New Testament Household Codes," 1.389–404. Balch calls attention to Hellenistic street philosophy as represented by a text in Stobaeus (*Ecl.* 4.2.19.24) containing a list of duties of social groups, including members of the household.

25. Gielen, *Tradition und Theologie*, 2.

26. See Barclay, *Colossians and Philemon*, 70–71.

Whereas ancient household codes primarily addressed those in authority over the proper treatment of their subordinates, the household code in these letters addresses each member of the household, including those who have the inferior status, in the vocative followed by the imperative and a motivation.[27] The use of the plural address reinforces the corporate nature of the community's hearing of the instructions. Having addressed the entire community in the preceding paraenesis, the author envisions a community composed of families who both hear the imperatives addressed to themselves and "overhear" the address to other family members.[28] Thus the reciprocal responsibility of members of the congregation extends to the entire household. Furthermore, in contrast to the ancient topos on household management, the household code appears in an apodictic style that recalls the legal tradition of the Old Testament and the direct address and imperatival discourse of the Wisdom literature. The imperatives connect the instructions to the preceding moral instruction in Colossians and Ephesians. Finally, the variety of forms of the household code in the New Testament suggests that it did not develop in a linear way from a single model, but emerged in a variety of ways to fit the needs of the congregations.

Because the household is fundamental in human society, rules for household management appeared not only in the philosophical literature, but in a variety of settings and cultures.[29] The *Delphic Precepts*, composed of 145 commandments representing popular morality, included instructions for the honor that children owe to parents ("respect your parents," 4), the proper treatment of children ("Do not curse your sons," 94), and the husband's rule over the wife ("Rule your wife," 94), all in the apodictic form. Thus the commonplace values of antiquity called for the submission of wives, the obedience of children, and the obedience of slaves.

These assumptions about the household are also reflected in the Pentateuch and the Wisdom literature. Three of the Ten Commandments address matters involving the household. The family is a major topic in the Wisdom literature (cf. Prov. 13:24; 17:17; 19:18, 26; 20:20; 23:13; 27:10, 29).[30] For example, Sirach elaborates on the fifth commandment in an extended section on the honor due to one's father (Sir. 3:2–16). All three of the relationships mentioned in the household code of Colossians and Ephesians appear in Sirach 7:19–28. The author addresses the husband's treatment of the wife (7:19, 26), the master's treatment of the slave (7:20–21), the parent's treatment of the children (7:23–25), and the adult children's treatment of fathers and mothers (7:27–28). *Sentences of Pseudo-Phocylides* also has an extended section on family duties,

27. Berger, *Formen und Gattungen*, 196–97.
28. Hering, *The Colossian and Ephesian* Haustafeln *in Theological Context*, 79.
29. See Berger, *Formen und Gattungen*, 197.
30. Bevere, *Sharing in the Inheritance*, 234.

addressing husbands, fathers, and slave owners in the imperative (207) about the proper treatment of those who are in their care.

Since the management of the household was a common theme in antiquity, the early Christian household codes had numerous antecedents. In Jewish literature, according to which the rules for the household were derived from the Torah, these rules from the Torah were cited and interpreted in the summaries of the law, which give instructions for the submission of wives, raising of children, honor to parents, and care of slaves (Philo, *Hypothetica* 7.2–4; Josephus, *Ag. Ap.* 2.201–2; *Ps.-Phoc.* 207–27; see ch. 1).[31] In his elaboration on the fifth commandment, Philo expands on the command to honor parents, indicating that the Jews recognize "many necessary laws drawn up to deal with the relations of old to young, rulers to subjects, benefactors to benefitted, slaves to masters" (*Decalogue* 165). He indicates that "parents belong to the superior class of the above-mentioned pairs, that which comprises seniors, rulers, benefactors and masters" (166). He includes other instructions "to the young on courtesy to the old, to the old on taking care of the young, to subjects on obeying their rulers, . . . to servants on rendering an affectionate loyalty to their masters, to masters on showing the gentleness and kindness by which inequality is equalized" (167). Thus Philo elaborates on the fifth commandment by including other regulations, including instructions to the young and to the slaves. In contrast to the common topos on household management, Philo describes the reciprocal duties of members of the household.

Interpreters have maintained that Philo derived his family ethic ultimately from the Greek household code, using the fifth commandment as a point of departure for a statement of Hellenistic ideals.[32] Benjamin G. Wold demonstrates, however, that 4Q415 Instruction has numerous parallels to Philo's treatment of the fifth commandment, concluding that interpretations of the fifth commandment as rules for the household were also rooted in Palestinian Judaism.[33] In interpreting the fifth commandment, this scroll includes not only instructions for the honoring of parents, but also instructions for husbands and wives, including a rare second-person address teaching women to honor their husbands.[34] Similarly, the summaries of the law (see ch. 1) included instructions for the submission of wives, the honoring of parents, the raising of children, and the treatment of slaves.

Interpreters have also looked for an occasion for the appropriation of the ancient household code into Christian exhortation. Dibelius suggested that the delay of the parousia resulted in the appropriation of the household code.[35]

---

31. Submission of wives is missing in *Pseudo-Phocylides*.
32. Balch, *Let Wives Be Submissive*, 117; Strecker, "Die neutestamentlichen Haustafeln," 358.
33. Wold, "Family Ethics in 4Q *Instruction* and the New Testament," 290–97.
34. Ibid., 291.
35. Dibelius, *An die Kolosser, an die Epheser, an Philemon*, 36.

Others have suggested that both the household and congregational codes (1 Tim. 2:1–15) were responses to liberation movements among women in Corinth and elsewhere, movements accompanied by egalitarianism within communities (cf. Gal. 3:28).[36] Others have argued that egalitarian movements within Christianity created a crisis in the public image of the congregations and that the writers responded by urging readers to adapt to their social environment.[37] However, the evidence in Colossians does not support any of these suggestions. Nowhere in the context of any of the household codes do the letters mention that the delay of the parousia is a precipitating factor in the moral advice. The idea of a primitive golden age of egalitarianism is the creation of those who engage in extensive mirror reading of 1 Corinthians. Paul does not say that the discussion of the roles of men and women in the assembly is a response to a liberation movement or to an appeal to Galatians 3:28 among those who advanced the freedom of women and slaves. This advice belongs to the traditions (1 Cor. 11:2) that he inculcates in all of the churches (1 Cor. 14:33).

That the household codes address three different relationships in the home is further evidence that they are not a response to primitive egalitarianism. For example, while the status of slaves was a major question, no evidence exists that a liberation movement among slaves evoked the advice in the household code. This fact is particularly noteworthy when one considers that the most extended advice is given to slaves. Furthermore, egalitarianism involving children was not an issue.

Rather than search for the "big bang" of the origins of the household codes in Christian moral instruction, we may observe the natural developments of early Christian discourse. The baptism of entire households (cf. Acts 11:14; 16:15; 18:8; 1 Cor. 1:16) and the important place of the household for congregational life and missionary activity undoubtedly raised questions about status in the new humanity (cf. Col. 3:11),[38] which had obliterated the distinctions between "slave and free" (3:11). Indeed, the claim that there is no longer "slave or free" (3:11; cf. Gal. 3:28) evoked questions in households about the relationships between slaves and masters, as the letter to Philemon indicates.

Paul's moral instructions led to questions about the status of specific groups within the community (1 Cor. 7:1). In response to the Corinthians' questions about family life in the new order, Paul responds with instructions involving marital relationships (1 Cor. 7:1–7), the status of children (1 Cor. 7:14), and the status of slaves (1 Cor. 7:20–21), speaking directly to the specific groups (1 Cor. 7:8, 10, 12, 21). When questions emerge about the relationship between

<hr />

36. See Crouch, *Origin of the Colossian Haustafel*, 124. Schüssler-Fiorenza, *In Memory of Her*, 253–54.

37. Balch, *Let Wives Be Submissive*, 80.

38. See Gielen, *Tradition und Theologie*, 68–86.

men and women in the assembly (1 Cor. 11:2–16; 14:34–36) of the house church, Paul answers with an appeal to his interpretation of the law. In 1 Corinthians 11:2–16 he delineates an order of creation, according to which the "head of the man is Christ and the head of the woman is the man" (1 Cor. 11:3), providing a warrant for requiring the differing attire of men and women who pray and prophesy. The argument from the creation story (1 Cor. 11:7–9) and from nature (1 Cor. 11:13–14), as I argued in chapter 5, reflects Paul's interpretation of the Torah as consistent with the law of nature. Similarly, he regulates the speech of women in Christian worship with the words, "Let them be submissive, as the law says" (1 Cor. 14:34). Although Paul does not indicate what text from Torah he has in mind, his words correspond to common interpretations of the law (see ch. 5).

Although the form of the household code in Colossians and Ephesians is unprecedented in Pauline correspondence, it is scarcely a radical departure from the earlier letters. Nor is it a conservative reaction to the liberation movements of the first century. The household codes of Colossians and Ephesians codify succinctly many of Paul's earlier instructions. Like the instructions that precede the household code in these letters (Eph. 4:17–5:20; Col. 3:5–17), they catechize converts regarding the moral existence of the new humanity. The closest analogies to the household code are found in the legal and wisdom traditions.[39] While the earlier paraenesis alludes to the Decalogue's prohibition against idolatry, false witness ("lying" in Eph. 4:25; Col. 3:9), theft (Eph. 4:28), and adultery (Eph. 5:3; Col. 3:5), the household codes in Colossians and Ephesians allude to the fifth commandment (Exod. 20:12) and follow the paraenetic tradition in Hellenistic Judaism by expanding the household code to include other familial relationships.

While the form of the household code is distinctive within the moral instructions, it nevertheless connects with the context and is consistent with the Jewish paraenetic tradition. Both the summaries of the law and the wisdom tradition contain the warnings against the antisocial vices (cf. Col. 3:5–17; Eph. 4:17–31) and the encouragement of appropriate family life (see ch. 4). The imperative in Colossians 3:17, "Whatever you do in word and deed, do all in the name of the Lord," is a bridge from the instructions of Colossians 3:5–16 to the household code (3:18–4:1) and is an appropriate introduction to the code, anticipating the focus on service in and to the Lord (*kyrios*). The Ephesian code has the transitional phrase, "Being subject to one another in reverence for Christ" (5:21), which belongs to one long sentence extending from 5:18 to 5:24. Thus the phrase is a transition from the description of mutual submission within the whole church to the submission within the family.[40]

39. Lincoln, "The Household Code and Wisdom Mode of Colossians," 104.
40. Darko, *No Longer Living as the Gentiles*, 83–84.

### SPECIFIC INSTRUCTIONS FOR FAMILY MEMBERS

That wives should submit[41] to their husbands was a commonplace in philosophical literature (see below), in common folk wisdom,[42] and in popular moral advice.[43] The Ephesian interpretation adds the rationale, "For the husband is the head (*kephalē*) of the wife, as Christ is the head of the church" (Eph. 5:23), echoing the language of 1 Corinthians 11:3. Indeed, inasmuch as it has been a common value in many cultures since antiquity, one can scarcely identify a particular source for the instruction to wives in Colossians 3:18. This advice also belongs to the tradition of Jewish summaries of the law. One may see this in Josephus's *Against Apion*, a book intended to counter anti-Jewish slander and present Jewish law as conforming to the highest ethical ideals of the time (cf. especially *Ag. Ap.* 2.184–87). In a discussion of Jewish marriage laws, Josephus says, "The woman is in all things inferior to the man. Let her accordingly be submissive, not for her humiliation, but that she may be directed" (2.201). Philo also lists the submission of women in his summary of the law in his *Hypothetica*, recalling that the lawgiver had said "that wives shall serve their husbands, not indeed in any particular so as to be insulted by them, but in the spirit of reasonable obedience in all things." Thus Paul's advice to wives does not reflect an appropriation of common Greek morality, but continues his common use of the Jewish paraenetic tradition.

The advice to wives reflects no radical departure either from the undisputed letters or from the instructions that have preceded the household code in Ephesians and Colossians. Paul has previously delineated an order of creation, indicating that the "head of the woman is man" (1 Cor. 11:3), and instructed women to be submissive in the assembly. He has encouraged the entire community to "be submissive" to those who serve (1 Cor. 16:16). Moreover, he has encouraged his readers to adopt the mind-set of the one who did not look out for his own interests, but "humbled himself" (Phil. 2:6–8). Consequently, Paul regards both humility and "counting others better than ourselves" (Phil. 2:3) as positive values within a community that does not seek power. This theme continues in the instructions in Ephesians and Colossians for the whole community to live in humility (*tapeinophrosynē*, Eph. 4:2; Col. 3:12). Thus, while the advice for wives to submit to their husbands corresponds to conventional

---

41. Interpreters have attempted to distinguish between "be submissive" (*hypotassesthe*), addressed to wives, and "obey" (*hypakouete*), addressed to the children and slaves. The words are scarcely distinguishable. Titus 2:9 and 1 Pet. 2:18 use *hypotassein* for slaves as well as for wives. The words are used interchangeably in 1 Pet. 3:1, 5–6. See Talbert, *Ephesians and Colossians*, 141.

42. See the numerous gnomic sentences listed by Berger, *Formen und Gattungen*, 197. *Sentences of Sextus* 236: "The man who sends his wife away admits that he cannot rule over his wife"; 508: "The prudent man is able to rule over the wife"; 514: "The man is the law for the wife"; 515: "The man should bring the wife to obedience."

43. Cf. Plutarch, *Conj. praec.* 142E: "So is it with women also; if they subordinate (*hypotattousai*) themselves to their husbands, they are commended; but if they want to have control, they cut a sorrier figure than the subjects of their control" (LCL 2, trans. Babbit).

morality, it takes on a new dimension within a community shaped by the re-evaluation of humility and concern for the welfare of others. The wives are the exemplars of the humility that characterizes the entire community of believers.

The reciprocal advice, "Husbands, love your wives," also repeats com-monplace moral values. The love of family members for each other, including both the husband's love for the wife and the wife's love for the husband, was a common value in antiquity[44] and in Jewish literature. Proverbs 5:18–20 instructs husbands in the proper treatment of wives. The author of 4 Mac-cabees assumes that "love (*philia*) for one's wife" (2:11) and "love (*philia*) for children" (2:12) are natural emotions. Among the numerous instructions on family life in the *Sentences of Pseudo-Phocylides* is the demand to husbands, "Love your own wife" (195). The author elaborates in concrete terms on the meaning of the husband's love for the wife, instructing husbands to avoid shameful ways of intercourse (189) and "unbridled sensuality" toward the wife (193), concluding that the wife should be kindly disposed to the husband and the husband should be kindly disposed to the wife (196).

Although Sirach's advice to husbands does not specifically include the com-mand to love their wives, the author includes numerous rules for the kindly treatment of wives. He recognizes the reciprocal responsibilities of husbands and wives, instructing husbands not to sin against the marriage bed (23:16; cf. 41:21–22) or dismiss a good wife (7:19, 26). Thus when Paul formulates the demand to love in negative terms, "Do not be bitter toward them," he reflects the common values of the wisdom tradition.

The reciprocal duties of children and parents in the household code have antecedents in popular morality, the Torah, and Wisdom literature. Summa-ries of the law listed duties of both parents and children (see ch. 1). Sirach gives instructions for both parents and children (Sir. 3:1–10; 16:1–4; 30:1–13), describing the responsibilities of both.

That children should obey their parents is also commonplace wisdom in Greco-Roman antiquity,[45] the Torah, and subsequent Jewish interpretation. The command, "Children, obey your parents in all things" (Col. 3:20), may be a paraphrase of the fifth commandment (Exod. 20:12), "Honor your fa-ther and mother," as the Ephesian parallel specifically indicates (Eph. 6:2). Regulations in the Torah elaborate on this commandment, condemning those who strike or curse father or mother (Exod. 21:25, 27; Lev. 20:9; Deut. 27:16) and the "stubborn and rebellious son" (Deut. 21:18–20). The Jewish sum-maries of the law included references to honor due to parents and the aged. Philo, in the *Hypothetica*, summarizes the law's requirements on the subject by declaring "that parents shall govern their children for their preservation

44. See ch. 7.
45. See Balla, *The Child-Parent Relationship*, 63. Diogenes Laertius, *Vit.* 7.120: "The Stoics approve also of honouring parents and brothers in the second place next after the gods."

and benefit." Josephus summarized the fifth commandment, indicating that "honor to parents is second only to honor to God" (*Ag. Ap.* 2.206). The age of the children is not indicated in Ephesians and Colossians; *teknon* defines the relationship rather than the age of those who are addressed. The instructions in the Torah and Wisdom literature describing different forms of disobedience[46] indicate that obedience to parents was a requirement for adult as well as minor children. The reciprocal advice given to fathers suggests that the advice in the household code is directed to children within the household.

The reciprocal responsibilities of fathers, "Do not irritate (*mē erithizete*) your children, lest they become discouraged" (Col. 3:21), and, "Do not provoke (*mē parorgizete*) your children, but train them in the discipline and instruction of the Lord" (Eph. 6:4), have parallels in Greco-Roman antiquity and Jewish literature. Pseudo-Plutarch explains that blows and torture are suitable for slaves, but not for children (*Lib. ed.* 12 [2.8F]). Menander advises fathers to reason rather than be angry with the child (Stobaeus, *Ecl.* 4.26.3–5).[47] The primary focus of the Pentateuch and Wisdom literature is the authority of the parents over the children. The Wisdom literature recommends harsh discipline, but rarely offers mediating counsel on the limitations on punishment. Only the *Sentences of Pseudo-Phocylides* warns fathers against abusing their children, instructing them, "Do not be harsh with your children, but be gentle" (207). The imperative, "Train them in the discipline and instruction of the Lord," echoes common perspectives in Jewish literature (cf. Deut. 6:4–9; Prov. 3:11; 4:1–9; 6:20–23; 13:1).

Although the proper treatment of slaves was a common topic in ancient literature (see below), the address to the slaves in Colossians 3:22 and elsewhere in the New Testament (cf. Eph. 6:5; 1 Tim. 6:1–2; 1 Pet. 2:18–25) is without parallel. Philo, however, provides the closest analogy to the address to slaves and the reciprocal duties of slaves and masters in his elaboration on the fifth commandment. Here he lists the reciprocal duties of rulers and subjects, the old and the young, adding instructions to both masters and slaves: "to servants on rendering an affectionate loyalty to their masters, to masters on showing the gentleness and kindness by which inequality is equalized" (*Decalogue* 167).

Paul has addressed slaves previously (1 Cor. 7:21), and he advises Philemon, a slave owner in Colossae, about his relationship to his slave Onesimus, indicating that the latter should now be recognized as Paul's child (Philem. 10) and Philemon's brother (Philem. 16). Thus the direct address to slaves is consistent with their new status as members of the family and of the Christian community. Indeed, the instruction, "Slaves, obey your earthly masters" (3:22 NRSV), is parallel to the advice to children to obey their parents (Col. 3:20). As in Philemon and 1 Corinthians, the slaves are members of the community.

46. Cf. Deut. 21:18–21; Sir. 3:2–16.
47. See Schweizer, *Letter to the Colossians*, 224.

The novelty of direct address to the slaves may explain why the writer breaks the pattern of the brief motivation for the commands, elaborating at length in Colossians 3:22b–25. The parallel between "children, obey your parents in all things" (3:20) and "slaves, obey your masters"[48] reflects the concern to include the disadvantaged among the members of the community.[49] Parallel to "in all things" (*kata panta*) in the advice to children, the instructions to slaves are elaborated with the words "not with eye service, as men-pleasers, but in singleness of heart, fearing the Lord" (3:22 NRSV).

The distinction between earthly (*kata sarka*) and heavenly masters (*kyrioi*) dominates the instructions to slaves, recalling the opening prayer that the readers "walk worthily of the Lord" (1:10) and the reminder that they are being filled "in him" (2:10), the one who has triumphed over cosmic powers. Consequently, the instruction to slaves, "Whatever you do, work as to the Lord" (3:23), seems to be paradigmatic for all members of the community, who "do everything in the name of the Lord" (3:17 NRSV), despite their earthly status. Like all members of the community, slaves fear the Lord (3:22), not other powers. That they "serve the Lord" (3:24) is consistent with Paul's general directive to "serve the Lord" (Rom. 12:11) and the community's call to serve one another.

While the direct address to slaves is new, the advice draws heavily on the Jewish paraenetic tradition. Only the word "eye service" (*ophthalmodoulia*) is without parallel in either Jewish or Greek texts prior to Paul. Psalm 52:6 LXX (53:6 Eng. translation "ungodly") speaks negatively of "men-pleasers" (*anthropareskoi*), which is used here in contrast to the opening prayer that all members "please God" (1:10). To live in "singleness of heart" is an ideal in the Jewish paraenetic tradition (Wis. 1:1; *T. Reub.* 4:1; *T. Iss.* 3:8; 4:1), which also speaks consistently of "fearing the Lord" (Ps. 111:10; Prov. 1:7; Sir. 1:14, 16, 18, 20, 27). The motivation of recompense for our deeds is also common in the Jewish paraenetic tradition and in the Pauline correspondence (cf. 2 Cor. 5:10).

That there is "no partiality" (*prosōpolēmpsia*) with God is also a major theme in Jewish literature. God is "not partial and takes no bribes" (Deut. 10:17); God sets the standard for all human judges (Lev. 19:15; Deut. 1:17). The advice to slaves may be, as Lohmeyer suggested,[50] an allusion to Sirach 35:11–15, which declares that God is the one who repays those who give generously, concluding that "with him there is no partiality." In the Ephesian parallel, the reminder that there is no partiality with God appears in the advice to the masters (Eph. 6:9), cautioning those in power against abuse of the slaves.

The address to slaves appears not only in Colossians and Ephesians, but also in 1 Timothy (6:1–2), Titus (2:9–10), and 1 Peter (2:18–25), whereas the

---

48. "In all things" (*kata panta*) in 3:22 is probably a scribal addition, based on the reading of the phrase in 3:20.

49. See Dunn, *Colossians*, 253.

50. Lohmeyer, *Die Briefe an die Philipper, an die Kolosser und an Philemon*, 158–59.

reciprocal address to masters appears only in Colossians and Ephesians. In both instances the advice to slaves is more extended than the advice to masters. The predominance of address to slaves probably reflects their role in the house churches and the new questions that emerged about their status in both the household and the church. The household codes in the New Testament thus reverse the ancient practice, according to which the advice is given only to the masters. Indeed, in view of the extended advice to masters in the Old Testament and Jewish literature, the brevity of the advice to masters here is noteworthy.

Whereas the direct address to slaves is unusual in ancient moral instruction, the address to masters is commonplace in the Old Testament and Greco-Roman literature. In Colossians, Paul instructs masters, "Grant what is just (*to dikaion*) and fair (*ten isotēta*) to the slaves," while the interpretation in Ephesians has, "Masters, do the same to them, cease threatening." The Torah instructs concerning the proper treatment of slaves (Exod. 21:20–21) and provides for their rest (Exod. 23:12; Deut. 5:14). Sirach also warns against the abuse of slaves (7:20–21). A common theme in Greco-Roman literature was the proper treatment of slaves. Indeed, the instruction for masters in Colossians 4:1 to "grant what is just and fair" to the slaves appeals to values that were fundamental for ancient civic life. According to Plato (*Leg.* 4.231), "fairness (*isotēs*) is the mother of justice (*dikaiosynē*)." The just judge (*isos dikastēs*) metes out impartial justice (*Leg.* 12.957). According to Aristotle, the just person is the one who safeguards equality (*isotēs*, *Eth. nic.* 5.2.1129a). In explaining Stoic thought, Diogenes Laertius (*Vit.* 7.126) regards *isotēs* as a subcategory of *dikaiosynē*. Thus what is "just" and what is "fair" (or equal) are consistently associated with each other in ancient literature.

Ancient writers applied the values of justice and fairness to the treatment of slaves. According to Plato's *Leges*, one should punish slaves justly (*en dikē*) and not make them conceited by merely admonishing them as if they were free people (6.777d–778). "Just" and "equal" means that they should be fed (but in smaller rations).[51] Aristotle defined "just" and "equal" as the distribution of goods in proportion to one's social rank (*Eth. nic.* 5.1131b–1133b; 1134a–1135a; 1137a–1138a). This instruction would resonate with the values of other ancient writers, for whom justice and fairness were central themes in ethical instruction. Plato's *Leges* discusses slave management at length (6.777–778). "Proper treatment of men in that position is to use no violence toward a servant but to wrong him—if such a thing could be—with even more reluctance than an equal" (6.777d).

The address to masters is noteworthy in Colossians and Ephesians for its brevity in comparison with the lengthy instructions to slaves. Although instructions for slaves appear elsewhere in the New Testament (cf. 1 Tim. 6:1–2; Titus 2:9; 1 Pet. 2:18–25), instructions to masters appear only in these two

51. Harrill, *Slaves in the New Testament*, 95.

epistles and in Philemon. The preponderance of instructions to slaves may reflect the demographics of early Christians and the kinds of questions that Paul answered earlier (1 Cor. 7:17–21).

Philo consistently associates equality with justice, maintaining that the law inculcates these values.[52] He connects this idea to slave management, indicating that the rules he sets forth are derived from the law. The law teaches "masters on showing the gentleness (*ēpiotēta*) and kindness (*praotēta*), by which inequality is equalized" (*Decalogue* 167). He indicates that the law teaches justice toward slaves, the practice of self-control, and restraint in harsh commands (*Spec. Laws* 2.90–92).

Both justice and equality played a role in Paul's instruction in the undisputed letters. He encouraged the Philippians to "think on" matters that are just (*ta dikaia*) (4:8). He encouraged the Corinthians to participate in the collection for the saints at Jerusalem for the sake of equality (2 Cor. 8:13).

Ephesians and Colossians share both the form and the basic content of the instructions for members of the household. In giving the motivation to each member of the household, the authors integrate the household instructions into the larger theological agenda of the work. Having announced the primacy of Jesus Christ as cosmic Lord from the beginning, the authors of these letters insist that people serve the *kyrios* within the ordinary roles of the household. Wives submit to their husbands "as is fitting in the Lord" (Col. 3:18 NRSV) and "to the Lord" (Eph. 5:22). Children obey "as is well pleasing in the Lord" (Col. 3:20), while slaves distinguish between the earthly and heavenly *kyrios*, recognizing that all work is to Christ (Eph. 6:5; "the Lord Christ," Col. 3:24). Even masters (*kyrioi*) recognize that they are subject to the ultimate *kyrios* (Eph. 6:9; Col. 4:1). The author of Ephesians further integrates the household into the theology of the book by describing the exalted Lord as the ultimate husband and model for earthly husbands.

## Moral Advice in the Pastoral Epistles

The challenge facing the author of the Pastoral Epistles is the preservation of healthy teaching (*hygiainousa didaskalia*) from the "disease" (1 Tim. 6:4; 2 Tim. 2:17) of false teaching (1 Tim. 1:10; 6:3; 2 Tim. 4:3; Titus 1:9; cf. 1 Tim. 1:3; 4:1–6). Despite the numerous scholarly attempts to ascertain both the nature of the disease and the author's precise definition of "healthy teaching," the issue remains unresolved because the author's purpose was not to draw a profile of this disease, but to warn against it.[53] The primary focus is not the nature of the heresy, but the moral consequences of both healthy and unhealthy

---

52. Cf. *Creation* 51; *Sacrifices* 27; *Dreams* 2.40; *Moses* 1.328; *Spec. Laws* 2.204; *Good Person* 84.4.231.

53. Johnson, "II Timothy," 1–3.

instruction.[54] The author insists that the goal of healthy teaching is "love from a pure heart and a good conscience and a genuine faith" (1 Tim. 1:5), while unhealthy teaching results in moral corruption (cf. 1 Tim. 1:10; 6:3–5; 2 Tim. 3:1–9; Titus 2:12; 3:3). Consequently, the author encourages his emissaries to teach conduct that is "consistent with healthy teaching" (Titus 2:1). In contrast to the moral corruption of the false teachers, Timothy and Titus should become models of proper behavior (1 Tim. 4:12; Titus 2:7) and ensure that both the leaders (1 Tim. 3:1–15; Titus 1:5–16) and the entire congregation (Titus 2:1–10) exhibit moral conduct that is consistent with healthy teaching.

The moral vision of the Pastoral Epistles has elements of both continuity and discontinuity with that of the undisputed Pauline letters. The Pauline emphasis on faith and love (cf. 1 Thess. 1:3; 3:6) continues in the Pastoral Epistles (1 Tim. 1:5). Timothy's task is to live in faith and love and to teach others to do so also (1 Tim. 2:15; 4:12; 6:11). Like the undisputed Pauline letters, the Pastoral Epistles frequently use lists of vices and virtues, condemning some of the same vices that are condemned in the undisputed Pauline letters. Sexual vices continue to play a significant role, as the author condemns fornicators (1 Tim. 1:10; cf. 1 Cor. 1:9), those involved in homosexual practices (*arsenokoitai*, 1 Tim. 1:10; cf. 1 Cor. 6:9), and those who are subservient to the lusts (1 Tim. 6:9; 2 Tim. 2:22; 3:6; Titus 2:12; cf. Rom. 1:24–26). He also includes other vices first mentioned in the undisputed letters, deriving several from the vice list of Romans 1:29–31, including the love of money (*philargyria*, 1 Tim. 6:10; 2 Tim. 3:2; cf. *pleonektēs*, 1 Cor. 5:10; *pleonexia* in Rom. 1:29; 1 Cor. 6:10), disobedience to parents (2 Tim. 3:2; cf. Rom. 1:29), and arrogance (2 Tim. 3:2; cf. Rom. 1:29). As in the undisputed Pauline letters, the Pastoral Epistles demarcate the morality of the community of believers from that of the unbeliever (cf. 1 Tim. 5:8), the false teacher (1 Tim. 1:3), and the adversary (1 Tim. 5:14; Titus 2:8). Distinguishing sharply between insiders and outsiders, the writer urges conduct that will not cause the latter to blaspheme God's name (1 Tim. 6:1; cf. Titus 2:5; 1 Thess. 4:12). The letter to Titus echoes the familiar Pauline once-now pattern, describing the sharp contrast between the community's former behavior (cf. Titus 3:3) and the new existence (Titus 3:4–6; cf. 2:11–14), which is antithetical to the conduct of those in their surroundings (cf. Titus 1:12).

The moral instructions of the Pastoral Epistles also continue some of the topics in Ephesians and Colossians that have no precedent in the undisputed letters of Paul. Continuity and discontinuity are especially evident in the author's expansion of the instructions to the specific members of the household to include the wider circle of the house church. The instructions that slaves be submissive to their masters (1 Tim. 6:1–2; Titus 2:9) and young wives be submissive to their husbands (2:5) echo the instruction of the earlier letters.

54. De Villiers, "Heroes at Home," 365.

The author envisions not only the familiar threefold relationships of Colossians and Ephesians, however, but a community composed also of widows (1 Tim. 5:3–16), old men and women (Titus 2:2–3; cf. 1 Tim. 5:1–2), and young men and women (Titus 2:4–8), and he instructs each group in appropriate conduct. In 1 Timothy and Titus, the paterfamilias of the household serves a similar function in the house church (1 Tim. 3:4; Titus 1:6). According to 1 Timothy, the women of the house church practice the submissiveness that they first demonstrated in the household (2:9–15; cf. 1 Cor. 11:1–16; 14:33–36), which was also the norm in the Pauline assemblies. The emphasis on the family is in sharp contrast to the practice of heretics who forbid marriage (1 Tim. 4:3) and the environment in which sexual vices (cf. 1 Tim. 1:10) and disobedience to parents become common (cf. 2 Tim. 3:2). Indeed, proper management of the household is a qualification for those who exercise leadership roles in the house church (1 Tim. 3:2, 4–5, 12; 5:4, 8; Titus 1:6). These family values would have resonated in both the Jewish and Greco-Roman environment.[55]

While the Pastoral Epistles echo some of the moral instruction from the undisputed letters, they are most notable for their discontinuity from the earlier letters, as the expansion of the rules for the household indicates. Not only are numerous vices listed in the Pastoral Epistles for the first time; the author expresses a positive moral vision with a complex of terms that have little or no role in either undisputed Pauline letters or Colossians and Ephesians. This moral vision is most succinctly summarized in the description, by the author of Titus, of the results of the epiphany of God's grace, "teaching us so that, denying ungodliness (*asebeian*) and worldly lusts (*kosmikas epithymias*), we may live soberly (*sōphronōs*), righteously (*dikaiōs*), and godly (*eusebōs*) in this present age" (Titus 2:12). This contrast between two modes of existence is fundamental to the author's attempt to inculcate the proper moral life among the churches. In 3:3–7 the author continues with a similar contrast between the readers' former existence (3:3) and the new moral life (3:1–2). These summaries provide the framework for our understanding of the vices and virtues that appear frequently in the Pastoral Epistles.

Here the Christ event was educational ("teaching us," Titus 2:12) in a way that is reminiscent of the educational value of the Torah in Jewish literature (cf. 4 Macc. 1:17; 5:23–24; 13:22). The author describes the believers' moral life in three adverbs that contrast the community to its local environment (cf. Titus 1:12; cf. 3:3). These terms approximate the Greek cardinal virtues more than any other list in the New Testament. *Sōphrosynē* (rationality, prudence) and *dikaiosynē* (righteousness, justice) commonly appear in the lists of cardinal virtues (see ch. 4), and so does *eusebeia* (reverence; godliness; Latin *pietas*).[56] These words pervade the Pastoral Epistles. Thus the three adverbs in Titus

---

55. D'Angelo, "Eusebeia: Roman Imperial Family Values."
56. Ibid., 143. See also Mott, "Greek Ethics and Christian Conversion," 23.

2:12 state in summary form what the author articulates in the numerous lists of attributes for members of the community.

"Soberly" (*sōphronōs*) is the adverb form of *sōphrosynē*, one of the cardinal virtues. The term connotes prudence, moderation, and being of sound mind.[57] In 4 Maccabees 2:2 Joseph is the exemplar of this virtue when he resists sexual temptation. The Pastoral Epistles use noun, verb, and adjective forms of the same word to describe the modesty of women (1 Tim. 2:9) and the demeanor of younger men (Titus 2:6), older men, and older women (Titus 2:2, 5). It is also used for the quality to be sought in a bishop (1 Tim. 3:2). Closely related to *sōphrōn* is *nēphalios* (temperate), which can refer especially to moderation in drinking or self-control or levelheadedness.[58] The term appears alongside *sōphrōn* (1 Tim. 3:2; Titus 2:2) to describe the bishop and the qualities of old men, but does not appear outside the Pastoral Epistles. Similarly, "respectable" (*semnos*) appears only once in the undisputed letters of Paul (Phil. 4:8), but in the Pastoral Epistles is the quality to be sought in deacons (1 Tim. 3:8), women (1 Tim. 3:11), and old men (Titus 2:2).

To live "righteously" (*dikaiōs*)—the second adverb in Titus 2:12—was also an ideal of the Pastoral Epistles. The author encourages Timothy to "pursue righteousness" (*dikaiosynē*) along with the other virtues (1 Tim. 6:11). As one of the cardinal virtues, here placed alongside *sōphrōn*, it would have resonated in Greco-Roman circles. The word was also a term commonly used in the Jewish tradition for fulfilling the obligations of the law. Thus the author indicates that Scripture provides "training (*paideia*) in righteousness" (2 Tim. 3:16).

The third adverb in Titus 2:12 is *eusebōs*. *Eusebeia* is the most comprehensive term for moral conduct; forms of this word are used nowhere else in the Pauline correspondence and only rarely elsewhere in the New Testament (cf. Acts 3:12; 17:23; 2 Pet. 1:3, 6; 2:9; 3:11). As the opposite of *asebeia* (ungodliness, irreverence, 2 Tim. 2:16; Titus 2:12),[59] *eusebeia* connotes reverence for the deity in classical literature (cf. Pseudo-Plato, *Def.* 412–13a).[60] It also includes reverence for parents, ancestors, rulers, and the social order.[61] The Latin equivalent *pietas* played a significant role in Roman life as the basis of human society and the highest virtue (Cicero, *Nat. d.* 1.3–4). From the time of Augustus, it was the central virtue cultivated by a series of emperors, especially in their attempt to restore the stability of the family.[62]

The inseparability of theology and ethics is evident in the use of *eusebeia* in the Pastoral Epistles. The term encompasses both the content of the Christian

---

57. BDAG 986.
58. BDAG 672.
59. BDAG 141.
60. BDAG 413.
61. See the discussion in Standhartinger, "*Eusebeia* in den Pastoralbriefen," 55–68.
62. D'Angelo, "Eusebeia: Roman Imperial Family Values," 141; Standhartinger, "*Eusebeia* in den Pastoralbriefen," 67–68.

faith and the manner of life that corresponds to it. The "mystery of godliness" (*eusebeia*) is the christological hymn in 1 Timothy 3:16. The "teaching that is in accordance with *eusebeia*" is the equivalent of the "sound words of our Lord Jesus Christ" (1 Tim. 6:3 NRSV). Similarly, the "truth that is in accord with *eusebeia*" (Titus 1:1) is the Christian message. The ethical dimension is evident in the author's desire that believers live a godly life (1 Tim. 2:2; 2 Tim. 3:12) and pursue godliness (1 Tim. 4:7–8; 6:11).

Although *eusebeia* is the basic term for moral conduct, the Pastoral Epistles offer few glimpses into its actual content. It includes the care for one's family (1 Tim. 5:4) and the appropriate conduct of women (1 Tim. 2:8–15). The instructions for women to wear modest attire suitable for those who profess godliness (*theosebeia*) presupposes a common understanding of appropriate dress for women. The content of *eusebeia* becomes more evident in the sharp contrasts that the author draws to the immoral conduct of the heretics. Timothy's task is to devote himself to *eusebeia* rather than profane myths and old wives' tales (4:7–8). The opposition has a "form of godliness" (2 Tim. 3:5) and thinks "godliness is a means of gain" (1 Tim. 6:5). The result of their false *eusebeia* is evident in the lists of vices that are the alternative to true godliness (cf. 1 Tim. 1:9–10; 6:4; 2 Tim. 3:1–4). While some of the vices echo Pauline themes, the most remarkable fact is that only eleven vices out of forty-one appear in the other New Testament lists.[63] Thus, while the Christian message results in a life of *eusebeia*, unhealthy instruction leads to the existence portrayed as *asebeia* (cf. Titus 2:12).

If the vice lists describe ungodliness, the lists of virtues may be placed under the general heading of the life in godliness (cf. 1 Tim. 2:2; 4:7; 2 Tim. 3:12). The virtues of church leaders (1 Tim. 3:1–12; 5:3–17; Titus 1:5–16) have numerous parallels to the virtues of all of the members of the house church (Titus 2:1–10). Dibelius observed that the qualifications for leaders resemble Onasander's list of qualifications for a good general.[64] The lists also include qualities that are commonplace in the Jewish tradition and early Christian moral instruction. As the inclusio in the qualifications for bishop indicates in

---

63. Wibbing lists thirty vices/offenders that are new to the Pastoral Epistles (*Tugend- und Lasterkataloge*, 89). The offenders in 1 Tim. 1:9–10 include the lawless (*anomos*), disobedient (*anypotaktos*), godless (*asebēs*), sinner (*hamartōlos*), unholy (*anosios*), profane (*bebēlos*), one who kills father (*patrolōas*) or mother (*mētrolōas*), murderer (*androphonos*), slave-dealer (*andrapodistēs*), perjurer (*epiorkos*). The following offenders appear in the list in 2 Tim. 3:2–5: the lover of self (*philautos*), lover of money (*philargyros*), ungrateful (*acharistos*), implacable (*aspondos*), slanderer (*diabolos*), one who is without self-control (*akratēs*), brute (*anēmeros*), hater of good (*aphilagathos*), traitor (*prodotēs*), reckless person (*propetēs*), one who is swollen with conceit (*tetyphomenos*), lover of pleasure (*philēdonos*). Offenders in Titus 3:3 include the foolish (*anoētos*), disobedient (*apeithēs*), one who is led astray (*planomenos*), one who is enslaved to pleasure (*hēdonē*), one who is despicable (*stygētos*). Vices listed in 1 Tim. 6:4 include frictional wrangling (*diaparatribē*; cf. BDAG 235) and base suspicion (*hyponoia*).

64. See Dibelius and Conzelmann, *The Pastoral Epistles*, 158.

1 Timothy 3:1, 7, the portrayal of a life in godliness largely corresponds to public perceptions of positive moral qualities.

Scholars have frequently maintained that the portrayal of the life in godliness corresponds to the "family values" inculcated by Augustus and his successors under the heading of *pietas*.[65] While parallels with the Roman understanding of *pietas* are evident, to identify the moral instruction of the Pastoral Epistles with Roman values is reductionistic. *Eusebeia* in these letters involves more than domestic rules. While the vices of the heretics and virtues of members correspond to common expectations in Roman society, they also reflect expectations in the previous Pauline tradition and in Jewish moral instruction that is based on the Torah. The Jewish moral tradition preceded the Pastoral Epistles in combining the instructions of Torah with the cardinal virtues. *Eusebeia*, a term that appears only in the later works of the LXX, is used frequently in 4 Maccabees for the life in accordance with Torah. Both 4 Maccabees and the Pastoral Epistles indicate that those who pursue *eusebeia* will suffer persecution. While 4 Maccabees maintains that the law teaches the cardinal virtues and *eusebeia*, the Pastoral Epistles indicate that the Christian message educates in *eusebeia*. Both Philo and the Pastoral Epistles urge that one "train in *eusebeia*." Thus the Pastoral Epistles follow the tradition of Hellenistic Judaism in describing the Christian life with the language of Hellenism. While Hellenistic Jewish writers employ *eusebeia* as the comprehensive term for life under the law, the Pastoral Epistles use it for life in accordance with the Christian message. As in the works of Philo, Josephus, and the author of 4 Maccabees, these letters are consistent in appealing to the Jewish values while interpreting them with the language of Hellenism. Unlike the undisputed Pauline letters, the Pastoral Epistles employ the language of the cardinal virtues.

### Conclusion: Developments among the Disputed Letters

Colossians, Ephesians, and the Pastoral Epistles, like the undisputed Pauline letters, call for a countercultural ethic that distinguishes the life of converts from their previous life and from the surrounding culture. The moral instruction of Colossians and Ephesians continues the Pauline emphasis on sexual conduct and love for others within the community while adding specific instructions for members of the household. As in the undisputed letters, despite the calls for a countercultural ethic, much of the moral advice is consistent with surrounding cultures. Although some of the moral values correspond to Greco-Roman moral advice, all the instructions are consistent with Jewish interpretations of the law. The hierarchical relationship between men and

---

65. D'Angelo, "Eusebeia: Roman Imperial Family Values," 139; Standhartinger, "*Eusebeia* in den Pastoralbriefen," 81–82; Quinn, *Letter to Titus*, 289.

women in the undisputed letters (1 Cor. 11:2–16) continues in the disputed letters. Like the moral advice of the undisputed Pauline letters, they are consistent with Diaspora teachings.

The Pastoral Epistles maintain continuity with traditional Pauline ethics, including rules for sexual behavior. However, they also abandon some aspects of Pauline ethics and introduce others. The strong Pauline communal emphasis on "one another" disappears. For the first time in the Pauline tradition, the Greek cardinal virtues are equated with Christian conduct. The works of Philo and Josephus and the unknown author of 4 Maccabees provided the precedent for this moral vision. Just as they had equated life according to the law with the cardinal virtues, the Pastoral Epistles depict the Christian message as the source of the life in godliness. Yet the vices and virtues are not distinctively Christian insofar as many are commonplace in many cultures, including both Greco-Roman society and the tradition of Hellenistic Judaism.

# Conclusion

## The Coherence of Paul's Moral Teaching

Paul's major challenge as a missionary and planter of churches was to ensure the moral transformation of his communities. His task was not only to make converts, but to resocialize them and provide a common ethos and shared practices. He envisioned a corporate narrative in which his communities began as slaves of various vices and then pursued the goal of their transformed existence. He writes in the middle of that narrative to reaffirm previous teaching and to confront those who have relapsed into previous practices. Paul's moral instruction was not only an ad hoc response to the crises in his communities, but a coherent vision of the formation of his converts. Although he did not offer a comprehensive ethical guide, his instructions indicate the most important aspects of moral conduct. As his catechesis indicates, he established traditions that were normative in all of his churches (cf. 1 Cor. 11:16).

### Paul's Teaching in Hellenistic and Jewish Context

As a repetition of his original catechesis, 1 Thessalonians offers a window into Paul's teaching to new converts. This catechesis involved, first, the memory of the death and resurrection of Jesus (4:14). Indeed, Paul regularly appealed to the readers' knowledge of the story of Jesus as a warrant for behavior in the letters. In subsequent letters, he shapes the moral values of the readers by insisting that they die to themselves (cf. Rom. 6:1–11; 1 Cor. 11:17–34; 2 Cor. 5:14–15) and imitate Christ (cf. Rom. 15:1–3; 1 Cor. 11:1; 2 Cor. 8:9; Phil. 2:1–11; 3:17). He elaborates on the basic catechesis in responses to specific circumstances.

Second, Paul consistently places the story of Jesus and the readers' own experience within the narrative of Israel, providing a symbolic world and an identity. The community's knowledge of what "is" is the basis for its knowledge of the "ought." The members' identity as the elect and holy ones of Israel separates them from "the gentiles" (cf. 1 Thess. 4:5) and requires moral conduct that distinguishes them from their surroundings. Paul's moral exhortations define this new moral conduct.

Third, Paul appeals not only to the story of Jesus to shape the moral conduct of his communities, but also to the Torah. While he does not insist that his converts keep commandments that serve as boundary markers of Jewish identity (circumcision, the Sabbath, and food laws), he gives moral instructions that are derived from the Torah and correspond largely to the summaries of the law that Jews in the Diaspora had developed. Although he does not cite specific laws in many instances, he nevertheless follows common interpretations of the law. His primary focus on sexual laws and love for others within the community indicates the special importance of the Holiness Code (Lev. 17–26) for his moral instruction. His special attention to this portion of Scripture is consistent with the teachings of Jews in the Diaspora.[1]

Paul appeals to the law to shape the moral imagination in all of the letters. Not only does the Torah provide the basic narrative; its moral precepts were "for our instruction" (Rom. 15:4). It was always the interpreted law that was normative, and the Christ event provided the lenses for interpretation. Like Philo of Alexandria, he assumed the agreement between the law of nature and the Torah.

Paul provides moral instructions within the context of two traditions of moral discourse that intersected in a variety of ways in the Hellenistic Age. Because many ethical values are commonplace in all cultures, Greek philosophical and popular morality on the one hand and the Jewish tradition on the other held many values in common. Some Diaspora Jews also borrowed from the Greek ethical tradition, arguing that the cardinal virtues were consistent with the Torah. While Paul occasionally echoes Stoic ethical teaching (cf. Rom. 1:18–25; 12:3; 1 Cor. 11:13–14; Phil. 1:9–11), the absence of the cardinal virtues in his letters indicates that he is less dependent on the Greek ethical tradition than Philo, 4 Maccabees, or the Wisdom of Solomon. The evidence of his letters suggests that Paul relies primarily, if not exclusively, on the Jewish interpretation of the Torah in giving specific instructions to his communities. His Jewish predecessors had already provided the model for using Greek ethical thought to elaborate on the teaching of Torah.

Paul differs from both the Greek and Jewish traditions on the human capacity to do the good, as he suggests in the claim that "no one is righteous" (Rom. 3:10). In contrast to the Greek focus on knowledge as the basis of the

---

1. Niebuhr, "Tora ohne Tempel," 427–31.

moral life and the Jewish insistence that the keeping of the law is a possibility, Paul spoke with pessimism about human potential for doing the good. However, he speaks with great optimism about the potential of his communities to do the will of God, relying on the exilic prophets' hope for a new covenant when God would place the law within the hearts of the people and empower them with the Spirit (cf. Jer. 31:31–34; Ezek. 11:19; 36:26). Paul assumes that his gentile communities are living at the turn of the ages when God will act to ensure the obedience of the people. Thus he gives moral instructions that he assumes the communities can keep. The "just requirement of the law" is fulfilled among his churches (Rom. 8:4).

The centrality of love is a distinguishing, and the most consistent, feature of Paul's moral instruction. While love plays a minor role in Greek ethical theory and a significant role in Jewish paraenesis, the centrality of this theme is unique to Paul, who maintains that love is the fulfillment of the law (Rom. 13:8, 10; Gal. 5:14). Furthermore, love has a new dimension in Paul that is unparalleled. Unlike other interpreters of Leviticus 19:18, Paul does not limit love to the fellow Israelite, but extends it primarily to the multiethnic community of faith. For him, love is a familial term. Indeed, he interprets Leviticus 19:18, a passage originally aimed at the proper treatment of fellow Israelites and resident aliens (19:34), as the summation of the law and the bond that unites disparate people within the Christian community. Unlike Philo and Greek philosophers, Paul never speaks of *philanthrōpia*, the love for humankind, but instructs readers to "love one another." He employs the Greek ideal of *philadelphia*—which in Greek writings, 4 Maccabees, and the *Testaments of the Twelve Patriarchs* was used for the relationship of siblings to each other—for the love of members of the community for each other. Undoubtedly, Paul derived the focus on love from Leviticus 19:18, but he also recognized the deepest paradigmatic expression of it in the love of God and the sacrificial death of Christ (cf. 2 Cor. 5:14–15). He elaborates on the concrete meaning of love in 1 Corinthians 8–14 and Romans 12:1–15:13, demonstrating that he does not speak in vague generalities about the importance of love. Paul envisions the church as a family that provides the emotional support, general welfare, protection, and sacrifice that correspond with the larger society's ideals about the family.

One may observe both continuity and discontinuity in the moral focus of the disputed letters of Paul as the earlier Pauline instructions are adapted to new situations. Both Colossians and Ephesians address gentile churches and assume that the readers are no longer subject to the demands of the law (Eph. 2:14–18; Col. 2:14). However, they reiterate the moral requirements of the undisputed letters and the call for the converts to separate themselves radically from their former existence (cf. Eph. 4:20–24; Col. 3:8–12) and the surrounding environment. Moral requirements continue to include a separation from the sexual practices of nonbelievers and a communal ethic in which the readers put away the vices that disrupt community life (Eph. 4:31; Col. 3:6–9) and adopt loving practices toward each other (Eph. 4:2; Col. 3:9). As in the earlier paraeneses, specific vices and virtues have parallels in both Greek moral instruction and Jewish paraenesis. While some of the vices and virtues have precedents in Greek moral instruction, all of them belong to traditional Jewish paraenesis. Only the latter prohibits idolatry (cf. Eph. 5:5; Col. 3:5), sexual immorality (*porneia*, Eph. 5:3; Col. 3:5), and uncleanness (*akatharsia*, Eph. 4:19; cf. 5:5). As in the undisputed letters, the instructions are consistent with Jewish summaries of the law.

Interpreters have noted that the unprecedented appearance of the household codes in Colossians and Ephesians is evidence of discontinuity from Pauline paraenesis and the adoption of Greek popular ethics. However, as we have observed, the presence of partial parallels in Greek popular ethics scarcely distinguishes the household code from other Pauline paraeneses, for Paul's paraenesis has numerous parallels to popular morality. Moreover, the Jewish summaries of the law, on which Paul depends in other paraeneses, also contain much of the content of the household code. The household codes state succinctly much of what Paul has said in the undisputed letters (cf. 1 Cor. 11:2–16; 14:34–36; Philemon). Thus the presence of the household code does not reflect major discontinuity from the earlier letters. Early Christians probably developed the household code, like the other lists, for catechetical purposes, relying on summaries of the law developed among Diaspora Jews.

Insofar as the Pastoral Epistles contain less sustained argument than the earlier epistles, they focus more on the morality of believers, drawing a sharp contrast between the immorality of the surrounding society (cf. Titus 1:9–12), including the false teachers (cf. 2 Tim. 3:1–9), and the conduct of believers (cf. Titus 2:1–10). Thus the Pastoral Epistles continue the familiar Pauline distinction between the morality of insiders and that of outsiders (cf. 1 Tim. 5:8, 14). Continuity with the earlier correspondence is especially evident in the emphasis on faith and love as the primary attributes of believers. According to 1 Timothy, the goal of instruction is "love from a pure heart and a good conscience and sincere faith" (1 Tim. 1:5). The combination of love and faith, a common feature in the Pastoral Epistles (cf. 1 Tim. 1:14; 2:15; 4:12; 6:11; 2 Tim. 1:13; 2:22; Titus 2:2), recalls the attributes Paul mentioned in his first letter (cf. 1 Thess. 1:3; 3:6; 5:8).

Discontinuity between the Pastoral Epistles and earlier Pauline correspondence is evident in the extraordinary number of vices and virtues that appear in the Pauline correspondence for the first time.[2] The important place of *eusebeia* (piety) in the Pastoral Epistles (1 Tim. 2:2; 3:16; 4:7–8; 6:3, 5–6; 2 Tim. 3:5; Titus 1:1), as the umbrella term for Christian teaching and conduct, appeals to an important ethical value among Greco-Roman moralists. In each of the

---

2. See the list in Wibbing, *Tugend- und Lasterkataloge*, 88.

Pastoral Epistles, the writer follows the precedent of Diaspora Jewish teachers, including Philo and the author of 4 Maccabees, who equated *eusebeia* with the observance of the law. The Pastoral Epistles adapt this precedent, equating *eusebeia* with the moral life. The instructions for church leaders (1 Tim. 3:1–13) and the entire community (Titus 2:1–10) are drawn from popular morality and reflect the church's desire to hold to moral standards that are compatible with the values of the larger society (cf. Titus 2:4, 8, 10). Thus the Pastoral Epistles, like the earlier correspondence, call for a paradoxical communal ethic that both accommodates popular morality and calls for separation from its vices. Although all of Paul's moral instructions correspond to popular morality to some extent, the unusual number of vices and virtues that appear in the Pastoral Epistles suggests that they reflect increasing openness to those aspects of Greco-Roman morality that are reconcilable with the traditional Jewish morality in Paul's letters.

The constant thread throughout the moral instruction of all the Pauline literature is the concern for communal formation. Letters written to churches created a communal consciousness and a shared ethos that separated the converts from their past and from the society in which they lived. Instructions were not addressed to isolated individuals, but to those who shared a common story. The vices and virtues called for the united stance of the community toward possessions, sexuality, and their neighbors and a demarcation between insiders and outsiders. Paul prohibited anticommunal behaviors involving strife, jealousy, and division, and encouraged loving behavior toward the new fictive family.

In shaping communities who lived as minorities within an often hostile culture, Paul did not speak to the larger problems of society or engage in public ethics. While he addressed the love command to the new fictive families, he also extended it to include relationships with outsiders, insisting that believers "do good to all" (Gal. 6:10), repay evil with good (Rom. 12:17–21), submit to those who maintain order (Rom. 13:1), and pay taxes (Rom. 13:6–7). Thus he envisioned communities that were committed to the common good of everyone.

### The Continuing Relevance of Paul's Moral Instruction

The distance between the house churches founded by Paul and modern readers raises the question of the relevance of his moral instructions for our own time. Paul worked within socioeconomic structures, including slavery, that are not relevant to us. He did not address multiple moral issues that confront us today. Indeed, he offered no comprehensive code to guide us on the most pressing issues of the day, including such issues as when life begins or ends. The absence of a public ethic in Paul raises further issues concerning the Christian's response to matters of public debate. Nevertheless, we continue to turn to Paul for guidance. Although we must acknowledge the distance between Paul's context and ours, I am convinced that he offers guidance in the contemporary situation.

Paul's moral guidance is relevant only for those who live within communities that share the corporate narrative of transformation into the image of Christ. If an ethic that was not "conformed to this age" was not widely accepted in the first century, it is not likely to be widely accepted in the culture of today. The Pauline ethic thus functions in a context in which members of the Christian family unite in a cohesive moral community, rejecting many of the values of their culture while living together in harmony, holding one another accountable and supporting one another. Thus this ethic of community cohesion is irreconcilable with the focus on individual autonomy in our culture and relevant only for those who live within the corporate identity of the believing community.

Although Paul did not provide a comprehensive code of ethics, he provided an important model for ethical reflection as he interpreted the Old Testament through the lenses of the Christ event. He cited the legal traditions of the Old Testament and engaged the interpretative tradition of Hellenistic Judaism, applying ancient legal materials for the new situation. He was so shaped by the Christ event that he interpreted the new situation through a process of dialogue with the ancient traditions and the Christ event. His exhortation to "discern the will of God" (Rom. 12:2) was not an open-ended process. It was determined by reflection on Scripture and the story of Christ.

The central feature of Paul's ethic, drawn from the Old Testament (Lev. 19:18) and the story of Christ (Rom. 5:7–8), was love within the community of faith. As he indicates on numerous occasions, the sacrifice of Christ was the ultimate expression of love and the continuing norm within the community. Those who identify with the crucified Christ seek the good of the other rather than their own self-fulfillment. To have the mind of Christ (Phil. 2:5) is to humble oneself for others. Love extends not only to those from one social class or ethnic group, but to all for whom Christ died. While the Pauline ideal has seldom been practiced, it offers a vision of a humanity not torn by selfish ambition, racism, or exploitation, but united by the love demonstrated by the crucified Christ.

The positive side of Paul's consistent prohibition of sexual immorality is the establishment of communities that are free of sexual exploitation in which women were the primary victims. Drawing on the Old Testament heritage, he shaped communities that rejected their society's acceptance of sexual immorality. They lived in house churches where men and women could come together in an atmosphere of trust. Paul's instructions for married people to have regular sexual intercourse (1 Cor. 7:1–7) indicates that he shares the positive view of sex with the Jewish tradition. His insistence on self-control (Gal. 5:23), mastery of the desires (1 Thess. 4:5), and care for the other shaped his communities, providing an appropriate model for Christian approaches to sexuality today. To follow the Pauline model is to reject the treatment of others as objects of one's own gratification.

Paul's instructions, addressed to minority communities, may be especially relevant for Christians who now have little voice in the public square. While minority voices do not shape public policy, they contribute to society by offering an alternative answer to the issues that confront it. Paul's statement that the Philippians "shine as lights in the world" (Phil. 2:15) suggests the possible impact of cohesive moral communities on the public. Those who are not "conformed to this world" do not retreat from it, but offer an example of a new humanity that has torn down barriers between peoples, demonstrated love for the weak, and provided a common ethos based on a shared story.

# Works Cited

Aasgaard, Reidar. "'Brotherly Advice': Christian Siblingship and New Testament Pa-
raenesis." Pages 237–65 in *Early Christian Paraenesis in Context*. Edited by James
Starr and Troels Engberg-Pedersen. Beihefte zur Zeitschrift für die neutestamentliche
Wissenschaft 125. Berlin: De Gruyter, 2004.

———. *'My Beloved Brothers and Sisters!' Christian Siblingship in Paul*. Journal for the
Study of the New Testament: Supplement Series 265. London: T&T Clark, 2004.

———. "'Role Ethics' in Paul: The Significance of the Sibling Role for Paul's Ethical
Thinking." *New Testament Studies* 48 (2002): 513–30.

Aristotle. *Ethica Nicomachea*. Translated by H. Rackham. Loeb Classical Library.
Cambridge: Harvard University Press, 1939–2003.

Aune, David E. "Mastery of the Passions: Philo, 4 Maccabees and Earliest Christianity."
Pages 125–58 in *Hellenization Revisited: Shaping a Christian Response within the
Greco-Roman World*. Edited by Wendy E. Helleman. Christian Studies Today. New
York: University Press of America, 1994.

Avemarie, Friedrich. "The Tension between God's Command and Israel's Obedience
as Reflected in the Early Rabbinic Literature." Pages 50–70 in *Divine and Human
Agency in Paul and His Cultural Environment*. Edited by John M. Barclay and
Simon J. Gathercole. London: T&T Clark, 2008.

Balch, David. *Let Wives Be Submissive: The Domestic Code in 1 Peter*. Society of Biblical Literature Monograph Series 26. Chico, CA: Scholars Press, 1981.

———. "Neopythagorean Moralists and the New Testament Household Codes."
Pages 2.26.1.380–411 in *Aufstieg und Niedergang der römischen Welt: Geschichte
und Kultur Roms im Spiegel der neueren Forschung*. Edited by H. Temporini and
W. Haase. Berlin: De Gruyter, 1992–.

Balla, Peter. *The Child-Parent Relationship in the New Testament and Its Environment*. Peabody, MA: Hendrickson, 2005.

Balz, Horst Robert. "*Hagios ktl.*" Pages 16–20 in vol. 1 of Balz and Schneider, *Exegetical Dictionary of the New Testament*.

———, ed. *Theologische Realenzyklopädie*. 36 vols. Berlin: de Gruyter, 1993–2006.

Balz, Horst, and Gerhard Schneider, eds. *Exegetical Dictionary of the New Testament.* 3 vols. Grand Rapids: Eerdmans, 1990–1993.

Banks, Robert. "'Walking' as a Metaphor of the Christian Life: The Origins of a Significant Pauline Usage." Pages 303–13 in *Perspectives on Language and Text.* Edited by Edgar W. Conrad and Edward G. Newing. Winona Lake, IN: Eisenbrauns, 1987.

Barclay, John. *Colossians and Philemon.* Sheffield: Sheffield Academic Press, 1997.

———. *Obeying the Truth: Paul's Ethics in Galatians.* Minneapolis: Fortress, 1991.

Barclay, John M. G., and Simon J. Gathercole, eds. *Divine and Human Agency in Paul and His Cultural Environment.* London: T&T Clark, 2008.

Barr, James. "Words for Love in Biblical Greek." Pages 3–18 in *The Glory of Christ in the New Testament: Studies in Christology in Memory of George Bradford Caird.* Edited by L. D. Hurst and N. T. Wright. Oxford: Clarendon, 1987.

Berger, Klaus. *Formen und Gattungen im Neuen Testament.* Uni-Taschenbücher 2532. Tübingen: Francke, 2005.

———. *Die Gesetzesauslegung Jesu: Ihr historischer Hintergrund im Judentum und im Alten Testament. 1. Markus und Parallelen.* Neukirchen: Neukirchener Verlag, 1972.

Berger, Peter, and Thomas Luckmann. *The Social Construction of Reality: A Treatise on the Sociology of Knowledge.* Garden City, NY: Doubleday, 1967.

Bertram, G. "*Phrēn.*" Pages 220–35 in vol. 9 of Kittel and Friedrich, *Theological Dictionary of the New Testament.*

Best, E. *The 1st and 2nd Epistles to the Thessalonians.* Black's New Testament Commentaries 13. London: Black, 1972.

Betz, Hans Dieter. "The Foundations of Christian Ethics according to Romans 12:1–2." Pages 55–72 in *Witness and Existence.* Edited by Philip E. Devenish and George L. Goodwin. Chicago: University of Chicago Press, 1989.

———. *Galatians.* Hermeneia. Philadelphia: Fortress, 1979.

Beutler, J., ed. *Der neue Mensch in Christus: Hellenistische Anthropologie und Ethik im Neuen Testament.* Freiburg, Germany: Herder, 2001.

Bevere, Allan R. *Sharing in the Inheritance: Identity and the Moral Life in Colossians.* Journal for the Study of the New Testament: Supplement Series 226. London: Sheffield Academic Press, 2003.

Blischke, Folker. *Die Begründung und die Durchsetzung der Ethik bei Paulus.* Arbeiten zur Bibel und ihrer Geschichte 25. Leipzig: Evangelische Verlagsanstalt, 2007.

Bockmuehl, Markus. *Jewish Law in Gentile Churches: Halakhah and the Beginning of Christian Public Ethics.* Grand Rapids: Baker Academic, 2000.

Boring, Eugene. "Household Codes." Pages 905–6 in vol. 2 of *The New Interpreter's Dictionary of the Bible.* Edited by Katharine Doob Sakenfeld. 5 vols. Nashville: Abingdon, 2007.

Brown, Alexandra R. *The Cross and Human Transformation: Paul's Apocalyptic Word in 1 Corinthians.* Minneapolis: Fortress, 1995.

Bruce, F. F. *1 & 2 Thessalonians.* Word Biblical Commentary 45. Waco: Word, 1982.

Bultmann, Rudolf. *Glaube und Verstehen: Gesammelte Aufsätze.* Tübingen: J. C. B. Mohr (Paul Siebeck), 1954.

———. "Das Problem der Ethik bei Paulus." *Zeitschrift für die neutestamentliche Wissenschaft und die Kunde der älteren Kirche* 23 (1924): 123–40. Translated by Christoph W. Stenschke as "The Problem of Ethics in Paul." Pages 195–216 in Rosner, *Understanding Paul's Ethics*.

———. *Theology of the New Testament*. 2 vols. London: SCM, 1952–1955.

Burke, Trevor J. *Family Matters: A Socio-Historical Study of Kinship Metaphors in 1 Thessalonians*. Journal for the Study of the New Testament: Supplement Series 247. London: T&T Clark, 2003.

Byrne, Brendan, SJ. *Romans*. Sacra pagina. Collegeville, MN: Liturgical Press, 1996.

Carras, George P. "Jewish Ethics and Gentile Converts: Remarks on 1 Thess 4,3–8." Pages 306–15 in *The Thessalonian Correspondence*. Edited by Raymond Collins. Bibliotheca ephemeridum theologicarum lovaniensium 87. Leuven, Belgium: Leuven University Press, 1990.

Chadwick, Henry. *The Sentences of Sextus*. Cambridge: Cambridge University Press, 1959.

Cohen, Naomi. "The Greek Virtues and the Mosaic Laws in Philo: An Elucidation of *De Specialibus legibus* IV 133–135," *Studia philonica Annual* 5 (1993): 9–23.

Collins, John J. *Between Athens and Jerusalem: Jewish Identity in the Hellenistic Diaspora*. New York: Crossroad, 1986.

Collins, Raymond F. *Sexual Ethics and the New Testament: Behavior and Belief*. New York: Herder and Herder, 2000.

———. "'This Is the Will of God: Your Sanctification' (1 Thess. 4:3)." Pages 299–325 in *Studies on the First Letter to the Thessalonians*. Edited by Raymond F. Collins. Leuven, Belgium: Leuven University Press, 1984.

Crouch, James E. *The Origin of the Colossian Haustafel*. Forschungen zur Religion und Literatur des Alten und Neuen Testaments 109. Göttingen: Vandenhoeck & Ruprecht, 1972.

D'Angelo, Mary. "Eusebeia: Roman Imperial Family Values and the Sexual Politics of 4 Maccabees and the Pastorals." *Biblical Interpretation* 11 (2003): 139–65.

Darko, Daniel K. *No Longer Living as the Gentiles: Differentiation and Shared Ethical Values in Ephesians 4:17–6:9*. Library of New Testament Studies 375. Edinburgh: T&T Clark, 2008.

Dautzenberg, Gerhard. "Φεύγετε τὴν πορνείαν (1 Kor 6:18): Eine Fallstudie zur paulinischen Sexualethik in ihrem Verhältnis zur Sexualethik des Frühjudentums." Pages 271–98 in *Neues Testament und Ethik für Rudolf Schnackenburg*. Edited by H. Merklein. Freiburg: Herder, 1989.

De Villiers, Pieter G. R. "Heroes at Home: Identity, Ethos, and Ethics in 1 Timothy within the Context of the Pastoral Epistles." Pages 357–86 in van der Watt and Malan, *Identity, Ethics, and Ethos*.

———. "'A Life Worthy of God': Identity and Ethics in the Thessalonian Correspondence." Pages 335–55 in van der Watt and Malan, *Identity, Ethics, and Ethos*.

Deidun, Thomas J. *New Covenant Morality in Paul*. Rome: Biblical Institute Press, 1981.

Deming, Will. *Paul on Marriage and Celibacy: The Hellenistic Background of 1 Corinthians 7*. Society for New Testament Studies Monograph Series 83. Cambridge: Cambridge University Press, 1995.

Dibelius, Martin. *An die Kolosser, an die Epheser, an Philemon*. 3rd ed. Handbuch zum Neuen Testament 12. Tübingen: J. C. B. Mohr, 1927.

———. *An die Thessalonicher I–II und die Philipper*. 3rd ed. Handbuch zum Neuen Testament 11. Tübingen: J. C. B. Mohr (Paul Siebeck), 1937.

———. *From Tradition to Gospel*. London: Nicholson and Watson, 1934.

Dibelius, Martin, and Hans Conzelmann. *The Pastoral Epistles*. Hermeneia. Philadelphia: Fortress, 1972.

Dihle, A. "Ethik." Pages 646–796 in vol. 6 of *Reallexikon für Antike und Christentum*. Edited by T. Klauser et al. 23 vols. Stuttgart: Hiersemann, 1950–.

Donaldson, Terence L. *Paul and the Gentiles: Remapping the Apostle's Convictional World*. Minneapolis: Fortress, 1997.

Doty, William. *Letters in Primitive Christianity*. Philadelphia: Fortress, 1979.

Dunn, James D. G. *The Epistles to the Colossians and to Philemon: A Commentary on the Greek Text*. The New International Greek Testament Commentary. Grand Rapids: Eerdmans, 1996.

———. *Romans 9–16*. Word Biblical Commentary 38B. Dallas: Word, 1988.

———. *The Theology of Paul's Letter to the Galatians*. New Testament Theology. Cambridge: Cambridge University Press, 1993.

———. *Unity and Diversity in the New Testament: An Inquiry into the Character of Earliest Christianity*. Philadelphia: Westminster, 1977.

Elgvin, Torleif. "'To Master His Own Vessel': 1 Thess 4:4 in Light of New Qumran Evidence." *New Testament Studies* 43 (1997): 604–19.

Elliott, J. H. "No Kingdom for Softies? or, What Was Paul Really Saying? 1 Corinthians 6:9–10 in Context." *Biblical Theology Bulletin* 34 (2004): 17–40.

Ellis, E. Earle. "Traditions in 1 Corinthians." *New Testament Studies* 32 (1986): 481–502.

Engberg-Pedersen, Troels. "The Concept of Paraenesis." Pages 47–72 in *Early Christian Paraenesis in Context*. Edited by James Starr and Troels Engberg-Pedersen. Beihefte zur Zeitschrift für die neutestamentliche Wissenschaft 125. Berlin: De Gruyter, 2006.

———. *Paul and the Stoics*. Edinburgh: T&T Clark, 2000.

———. "Paul, Virtues, and Vices." In *Paul in the Greco-Roman World: A Sourcebook*. Edited by J. Paul Sampley. Harrisburg, PA: Trinity Press International, 2003.

———. "Paul's Stoicizing Politics in Romans 12–13: The Role of 13.1–10 in the Argument." *Journal for the Study of the New Testament* 29 (2006): 163–72.

Esler, Philip F. "Family Imagery and Christian Identity in Gal 5:13 to 6:10." Pages 121–49 in Moxnes, *Constructing Early Christian Families*.

———. "Keeping It in the Family: Culture, Kinship and Identity in 1 Thessalonians and Galatians." Pages 145–84 in *Families and Family Relations as Represented in Early Judaisms and Early Christianities: Texts and Fictions*. Edited by Jan Willem van Henden and Athalya Brenner. Leiden: Deo, 2000.

———. "Paul and Stoicism: Romans 12 as a Test Case." *New Testament Studies* 50 (2004): 106–24.

Euripides. *Euripides: Cyclops, Alcestis, Medea.* Translated and edited by David Kovacs. Loeb Classical Library. Cambridge: Harvard University Press, 1994. Reprinted and revised, 2001.

———. "Medea." In *Euripides: Alcestis, Medea, the Heracleidae, Hippolytus.* Vol. 1 of *The Complete Tragedies.* Translated by Rex Warren. Edited by David Grene and Richard Lattimore. 5 vols. Chicago: University of Chicago Press, 1955.

Finsterbusch, Karin. *Die Thora als Lebensweisung für Heidenchristen. Studien zur Bedeutung der Thora für die paulinische Ethik.* Forschungen zur Religion und Literatur des Alten und Neuen Testaments 20. Göttingen: Vandenhoeck & Ruprecht, 1995.

Fitzgerald, John. "The Passions and Moral Progress: An Introduction." Pages 1–25 in *Passions and Moral Progress in Greco-Roman Thought.* Edited by John Fitzgerald. London: Routledge, 2008.

———. "Virtue/Vice Lists." Pages 857–59 in vol. 6 of Freedman, *Anchor Bible Dictionary.*

Frank, Nicole. *Der Kolosserbrief im Kontext des paulinischen Erbes.* Wissenschaftliche Untersuchungen zum Neuen Testament 271. Tübingen: Mohr Siebeck, 2009.

Freedman, D. N., ed. *Anchor Bible Dictionary.* 6 vols. New York: Doubleday, 1992.

Friedrich, J. H. "*Kleronomia ktl.*" Page 298 in vol. 2 of Balz and Schneider, *Exegetical Dictionary of the New Testament.*

Furnish, Victor. *Theology and Ethics in Paul.* Nashville: Abingdon, 1968.

Gathercole, Simon. "Sin in God's Economy: Agencies in Romans 1 and 7." Pages 158–72 in Barclay and Gathercole, *Divine and Human Agency in Paul and His Cultural Environment.*

Geertz, Clifford. *The Interpretation of Cultures.* New York: Basic Books, 1973.

Gemünden, Petra von. "Der Affekt der *Epithumia* und der *Nomos*: Affektkontrolle und soziale Identitätsbildung im 4. Makkabäerbuch mit einem Ausblick auf den Römerbrief." Pages 55–74 in *Das Gesetz im frühen Judentum und im Neuen Testament: Festschrift für Christoph Burchard zum 75. Geburtstag.* Edited by Dieter Sänger and Mattias Konradt. Novum Testamentum et Orbis Antiquus/Studien zur Umwelt des Neuen Testaments 57. Freiburg, Germany: Vandenhoeck & Ruprecht, 2006.

Gielen, M. *Tradition und Theologie neutestamentlicher Haustafelethik: Ein Beitrag zur Frage einer christlichen Auseinandersetzung mit gesellschaftlichen Normen.* Bonner biblische Beiträge 75. Frankfurt am Main, Germany: Hain, 1990.

Goldstein, H. "*Aselgeia.*" Page 169 in vol. 1 of Balz and Schneider, *Exegetical Dictionary of the New Testament.*

Grundmann, W. "*Tapeinos.*" Pages 1–27 in vol. 8 of Kittel and Friedrich, *Theological Dictionary of the New Testament.*

Gupta, Nijay K. "Which 'Body' Is a Temple (1 Corinthians 6:19)? Paul beyond the Individual/Communal Divide." *Catholic Biblical Quarterly* 72 (2010): 518–36.

Hägerland, Tobias. "Rituals of (Ex-)Communication and Identity: 1 Cor 5 and 4Q266 11; 4Q270 7." Pages 43–60 in *Identity Formation in the New Testament.* Edited by Bengt Holmberg and Mikael Winninge. Wissenschaftliche Untersuchungen zum Neuen Testament 227. Tübingen: Mohr Siebeck, 2008.

Hahn, Ferdinand. *Theologie des Neuen Testaments. I. Die Vielfalt des Neuen Testaments: Theologiegeschichte des Urchristentums*. Tübingen: J. C. B. Mohr, 2002.

Harnack, Adolf. "The Old Testament in the Pauline Letters and in the Pauline Churches." Pages 27–49 in Rosner, *Understanding Paul's Ethics* (Eng. translation of "Das Alte Testament in den paulinischen Briefen und in den paulinischen Gemeinden." In *Sitzungsberichte der Preussischen Akademie der Wissenschaften*. Berlin: De Gruyter, 1928).

Harrill, J. Albert. *Slaves in the New Testament: Literary, Social, and Moral Dimensions*. Minneapolis: Fortress, 2006.

Hartmann, Lars. "Code and Context: A Few Reflections on the Paraenesis of Col. 3:6–4:1." Pages 237–47 in *Tradition and Interpretation of the New Testament*. Edited by G. F. Hawthorne and O. Betz. Grand Rapids: Eerdmans, 1987.

Hays, Richard B. *The Conversion of the Imagination: Paul as Interpreter of Israel's Scripture*. Grand Rapids: Eerdmans, 2005.

———. *The Moral Vision of the New Testament: A Contemporary Introduction to Christian Ethics*. San Francisco: HarperCollins, 1996.

———. "Relations Natural and Unnatural: A Response to John Boswell's Exegesis of Romans 1." *Journal of Religious Ethics* 14 (1986): 184–215.

———. "The Role of Scripture in Paul's Ethics." Pages 30–47 in *Theology and Ethics in Paul and His Interpreters: Essays in Honor of Victor Paul Furnish*. Edited by Eugene H. Lovering Jr. and Jerry L. Sumney. Nashville: Abingdon, 1996.

Hense, Otto, ed. *Ioannis Stobaei Anthologium*. 5 vols. Berlin: Weidmannos, 1956.

Hering, James P. *The Colossian and Ephesian* Haustafeln *in Theological Context: An Analysis of Their Origins, Relationship, and Message*. American University Studies 7. New York: Peter Lang, 2007.

Holtz, Traugott. *Der erste Brief an die Thessalonicher*. Evangelisch-katholischer Kommentar zum Neuen Testament. Zürich: Benziger, 1986.

———. "Zur Frage der inhaltlichen Weisungen bei Paulus." *Theologische Literaturzeitung* 106 (1981): 385–400.

———. "The Question of the Content of Paul's Instructions." Pages 51–71 in Rosner, *Understanding Paul's Ethics*.

Hooker, Morna D. "Interchange in Christ and Ethics." *Journal for the Study of the New Testament* 25 (1985): 3–17.

Horrell, David G. "Particular Identity and Common Ethics: Reflections on the Foundations and Content of Pauline Ethics in 1 Corinthians 5." Pages 197–212 in *Jenseits von Indikativ und Imperativ*. Edited by Friedrich Wilhelm Horn and Ruben Zimmermann. Wissenschaftliche Untersuchungen zum Neuen Testament 238. Tübingen: Mohr Siebeck, 2009.

———. *Solidarity and Difference: A Contemporary Reading of Paul's Ethics*. London: T&T Clark, 2005.

Horsley, G. H. R. *New Documents Illustrating Early Christianity: A Review of Inscriptions and Papyri Published in 1977*. Sydney, Australia: MacQuarie University, 1982.

Horsley, Richard. "The Law of Nature in Philo and Cicero." *Harvard Theological Review* 71 (1978): 35–59.

Hübner, Hans. *Corpus Paulinum.* Vol. 2 of *Vetus Testamentum in Novo.* Göttingen: Vandenhoeck & Ruprecht, 1997.

———. "Zur Ethik der Sapientia Salomonis." Pages 166–87 in *Studien zum Text und zur Ethik des Neuen Testaments.* Edited by W. Schrage. Beihefte zur Zeitschrift für die neutestamentliche Wissenschaft 47. Berlin: De Gruyter, 1986.

Inwood, Brad. "Ethics." Pages 82–83 in vol. 5 of *Brill's New Pauly.* Edited by Herbert Cancik, Helmut Schneider, and Manfred Landfester. 16 vols. Leiden: Brill, 2004.

Jensen, Joseph. "Does *Porneia* Mean Fornication? A Critique of Bruce Malina." *Novum Testamentum* 20 (1978): 161–84.

Johnson, Luke Timothy. "II Timothy and the Polemic against the False Teachers: A Re-examination." *Journal of Religious Studies* 6–7 (1978/1979): 1–26.

*Josephus.* Translated by H. St. J. Thackeray et al. 10 vols. Loeb Classical Library. Cambridge: Harvard University Press, 1926–65.

Judge, E. A. "St. Paul as a Radical Critic of Society." Pages 99–115 in *Social Distinctives of the Christians in the First Century.* Peabody, MA: Hendrickson, 2008.

Keck, Leander. "What Makes Romans Tick?" Pages 3–29 in vol. 3 of *Pauline Theology.* Edited by Jouette M. Bassler, David M. Hay, and E. Elizabeth Johnson. 4 vols. Minneapolis: Fortress, 1991–1997.

Keesmaat, Sylvia C. "If Your Enemy Is Hungry: Love and Subversive Politics in Romans 12–13." Pages 141–58 in *Character Ethics and the New Testament: Moral Dimensions of Scripture.* Edited by Robert L. Brawley. Louisville: Westminster John Knox, 2007.

Kittel, G., and G. Friedrich, eds. *Theological Dictionary of the New Testament.* Translated by G. W. Bromiley. 10 vols. Grand Rapids: Eerdmans, 1964–1976.

Klassen, W. "Musonius Rufus, Jesus and Paul: Three First-Century Feminists." Pages 185–206 in *From Jesus to Paul: Studies in Honor of Francis Wright Beare.* Edited by P. Richardson and J. C. Hurd. Waterloo, ON: Wilfrid Laurier University Press, 1984.

Klauck, Hans-Josef. *Alte Welt und neuer Glaube.* Novum Testamentum et Orbis Antiquus 29. Göttingen: Vandenhoeck & Ruprecht, 1994.

———. "Die Bruderliebe bei Plutarch und im vierten Makkabäerbuch." Pages 83–98 in Klauck, *Alte Welt und neuer Glaube.*

Klauser, T., et al. *Reallexikon für Antike und Christentum.* Stuttgart: Hiersemann, 1950–.

Koester, Helmut. "*Physis.*" Page 269 in vol. 9 of Kittel and Friedrich, *Theological Dictionary of the New Testament.*

Kremer, J. "*Thlipsis.*" Pages 152–53 in vol. 2 of Balz and Schneider, *Exegetical Dictionary of the New Testament.*

Krentz, Edgar M. "Πάθη and Ἀπάθεια in Early Roman Empire Stoics." Pages 122–35 in *Passions and Moral Progress in Greco-Roman Thought.* Edited by John T. Fitzgerald. London: Routledge, 2008.

Kretzer, A. "*Paralambanō.*" Pages 29–33 in vol. 3 of Balz and Schneider, *Exegetical Dictionary of the New Testament.*

Laato, Timo. *Paul and Judaism: An Anthropological Approach.* Atlanta: Scholars Press, 1995.

Lang, F. "*Sainō*." Pages 55–56 in vol. 7 of Kittel and Friedrich, *Theological Dictionary of the New Testament*.

Liddell, Henry George, Robert Scott, and Henry Stuart Jones. *A Greek-English Lexicon*. 9th ed. Oxford: Clarendon, 1968.

Lincoln, Andrew T. "The Household Code and Wisdom Mode of Colossians." *Journal for the Study of the New Testament* 74 (1999): 93–112.

Lindbeck, George. *The Nature of Doctrine*. Philadelphia: Westminster, 1984.

Lindemann, Andreas. "Die biblischen Toragebote und die paulinische Ethik." Pages 242–65 in *Studien zum Text und zur Ethik des Neuen Testaments: Festschrift zum 80. Geburtstag von Heinrich Greeven*. Beihefte zur Zeitschrift für die neutestamentliche Wissenschaft 47. Berlin: De Gruyter, 1986.

Lips, Herman von. "Heiligkeit und Liebe: Kriterien christlicher Ethik am Beispiel des 1. Korintherbriefes." Pages 169–80 in *Eschatologie und Ethik im frühen Christentum*. Edited by Christfried Böttrich. Greifswalder theologische Forschungen 11: Für Günther Haufe. Frankfurt am Main, Germany: Peter Lang, 2006.

Loader, William R. G. "Sexuality in *The Testaments of the Twelve Patriarchs* and the New Testament." Pages 293–309 in *Transcending Boundaries: Contemporary Readings of the New Testament*. Edited by Rekha M. Chennattu and Mary L. Coloe. Rome: LAS, 2005.

Lohmeyer, Ernst. *Die Briefe an die Philipper, an die Kolosser und an Philemon*. Kritisch-exegetischer Kommentar über das Neue Testament. 13th ed. Göttingen: Vandenhoeck and Ruprecht, 1964.

Lohse, Eduard. "Das Gesetz Christi: Zur theologischen Begründung christlicher Ethik im Galaterbrief." Pages 378–89 in *Ekklesiologie des Neuen Testaments für Karl Kertelge*. Edited by Rainer Kampling and Thomas Söding. Freiburg, Germany: Herder, 1996.

———. *Theological Ethics of the New Testament*. Minneapolis: Fortress, 1988.

Mafico, Temba L. J. "Ethics (OT)." Page 646 in vol. 2 of Freedman, *Anchor Bible Dictionary*.

Malherbe, Abraham J. "Hellenistic Moralists and the New Testament." Pages 2.26.1.267–333 in *Aufstieg und Niedergang der römischen Welt: Geschichte und Kultur Roms im Spiegel der neueren Forschung*. Edited by H. Temporini and W. Haase. Berlin: De Gruyter, 1992–.

———. *The Letters to the Thessalonians*. Anchor Bible 32B. Garden City, NY: Doubleday, 2000.

———. *Moral Exhortation: A Greco-Roman Sourcebook*. Library of Early Christianity. Philadelphia: Westminster, 1986.

Martin, Dale. "*Arsenokoitēs* and *Malakos*: Meanings and Consequences." Pages 117–36 in *Biblical Ethics and Homosexuality: Listening to Scripture*. Edited by Robert L. Brawley. Louisville: Westminster John Knox, 1996.

———. *The Corinthian Body*. New Haven: Yale University Press, 1995.

———. "Paul without Passion: On Paul's Rejection of Desire in Sex and Marriage." Pages 201–15 in Moxnes, *Constructing Early Christian Families*.

Meeks, Wayne. "The Image of the Androgyne: Some Uses of a Symbol in Earliest Christianity." *History of Religions* 13 (1974): 165–208.

————. *The Moral World of the First Christians*. Philadelphia: Westminster, 1986.

————. *The Origins of Christian Morality: The First Two Centuries*. New Haven: Yale University Press, 1993.

————. "'To Walk Worthily of the Lord': Moral Formation in the Pauline School Exemplified by the Letter to Colossians." Pages 37–58 in *Hermes and Athena: Biblical Exegesis and Philosophical Theology*. Edited by Eleonore Stump and Thomas P. Flint. Notre Dame, IN: University of Notre Dame Press, 1993.

Meyers, Carol. "Temple, Jerusalem." Pages 350–69 in vol. 6 of Freedman, *Anchor Bible Dictionary*.

Mitchell, Margaret M. *Paul and the Rhetoric of Reconciliation: An Exegetical Investigation of the Language and Composition of 1 Corinthians*. Louisville: Westminster John Knox, 1991.

Morgan, Teresa. *Popular Morality in the Early Roman Empire*. Cambridge: Cambridge University Press, 2007.

Mott, Stephen Charles. "Greek Ethics and Christian Conversion: The Philonic Background of Titus II 10–14 and III 3–7." *Novum Testamentum* 20 (1978): 22–48.

Moxnes, Halvor. *Constructing Early Christian Families: Family as Social Reality and Metaphor*. London: Routledge, 1997.

————. "The Quest for Honor and the Unity of the Community in Romans 12 and in the Orations of Dio Chrysostom." Pages 203–30 in *Paul in His Hellenistic Context*. Edited by Troels Engberg-Pedersen. Minneapolis: Fortress, 1995.

Najman, Hindy. "The Law of Nature and the Authority of Mosaic Law." *Studia philonica Annual* 11 (1999): 55–73.

Newton, Michael. *The Concept of Purity at Qumran and in the Letters of Paul*. Cambridge: Cambridge University Press, 1985.

Niccum, Curt. "The Voice of the Manuscripts on the Silence of Women: The External Evidence for 1 Cor 14:34–5." *New Testament Studies* 43 (1997): 242–55.

Niebuhr, Karl-Wilhelm. *Gesetz und Paränese: Katechismusartige Weisungsreihen in der frühjüdischen Literatur*. Wissenschaftliche Untersuchungen zum Neuen Testament. Second Series 28. Tübingen: J. C. B. Mohr (Paul Siebeck), 1987.

————. "Tora ohne Tempel: Paulus und der Jakobusbrief im Zusammenhang frühjüdischer Torarezeption für die Diaspora." Pages 427–60 in *Gemeinde ohne Tempel: Zur Substituierung und Transformation des Jerusalemer Tempels und seines Kults im Alten Testament, Judentum und frühen Christentum*. Edited by Beate Ego, Armin Lange, and Peter Pilhofer with Kathrin Ehlers. Tübingen: Mohr Siebeck, 1999.

Nussbaum, Martha C. *The Therapy of Desire: Theory and Practice in Hellenistic Ethics*. Princeton: Princeton University Press, 1994.

O'Day, Gail. "Jeremiah 9:22 and 1 Corinthians 1:26–31: A Study in Intertextuality." *Journal of Biblical Literature* 109 (1990): 259–67.

Ovid. *Metamorphoses*. Translated by Frank Justus Miller. Loeb Classical Library. 2 vols. Cambridge: Harvard University Press, 1960.

Paschke, Bori A. "Ambiguity in Paul's References to Greco-Roman Sexual Ethics." *Ephemerides theologicae lovanienses* 83 (2007): 169–92.

Peng, Kuo-Wei. *Hate the Evil, Hold Fast to the Good: Structuring Romans 12.1–15.1.* Library of New Testament Studies 300. Edinburgh: T&T Clark, 2006.

Peterman, Gerald W. "Marriage and Sexual Fidelity in the Papyri, Plutarch and Paul." *Tyndale Bulletin* 50, no. 2 (1999): 163–72.

*Philo*. Translated by F. H. Cooper and G. H. Whitaker. Loeb Classical Library. 10 vols. Cambridge: Harvard University Press, 1929–62.

Plutarch. *Moralia*. Translated by Frank Cole Babbit. 16 vols. Loeb Classical Library. Cambridge: Harvard University Press, 1928–71.

Pohlenz, Max. *Die Stoa: Geschichte einer geistigen Bewegung*. Göttingen: Vandenhoeck & Ruprecht, 1948.

Popkes, W. *Paränese und das Neue Testament*. Stuttgarter Bibelstudien 168. Stuttgart: Katholisches Bibelwerk, 1996.

Preisker, H. *Das Ethos des Urchristentums*. Gütersloh, Germany: Gerd Mohn, 1949.

Quinn, Jerome. *The Letter to Titus*. Anchor Bible 35. New York: Doubleday, 1990.

Ranieri, Filippo. "Virtue." Pages 458–59 in vol. 15 of *Brill's New Pauly*. Edited by Hubert Cancik and Helmut Schneider. 15 vols. Leiden: Brill, 2010.

Reddit, Paul. "The Concept of *Nomos* in Fourth Maccabees." *Catholic Biblical Quarterly* 45 (1983): 245–70.

Reese, J. *1 and 2 Thessalonians*. Wilmington, DE: Michael Glazier, 1979.

Rehrl, S. *Das Problem der Demut in der profan-griechischen Literatur im Vergleich zu Septuaginta im Neuen Testament*. Münster: Aschendorf, 1961.

Reinmuth, Eckart. *Geist und Gesetz: Studien zu Voraussetzungen und Inhalt der paulinischen Paränese*. Theologische Arbeiten 44. Berlin: Evangelische Verlagsanstalt, 1985.

Roloff, J. "*Ekklēsia*." Pages 410–15 in vol. 1 of Balz and Schneider, *Exegetical Dictionary of the New Testament*.

Rosner, Brian S. *Greed as Idolatry: The Origin and Meaning of a Pauline Metaphor*. Grand Rapids: Eerdmans, 2007.

———. *Paul, Scripture, and Ethics: A Study of 1 Corinthians 5–7*. Arbeiten zur Geschichte des antiken Judentums und des Urchristentums. Leiden, Netherlands: Brill, 1994.

———, ed. *Understanding Paul's Ethics: Twentieth-Century Approaches*. Grand Rapids: Eerdmans, 1995.

Sanders, E. P. *Paul, the Law, and the Jewish People*. Philadelphia: Fortress, 1983.

Sandnes, Karl Olav. *A New Family: Conversion and Ecclesiology in the Early Church with Cross-Cultural Comparisons*. New York: Peter Lang, 1993.

Schäfer, Peter. *Gemeinde als "Bruderschaft": Ein Beitrag zum Kirchenverständnis des Paulus*. Europäische Hochschulschriften. New York: Peter Lang, 1989.

Schlier, H. *Der Apostel und seine Gemeinde: Auslegung des ersten Briefes an die Thessalonicher*. Freiburg, Germany: Herder, 1972.

Schmeller, T. "Neutestamentliches Gruppenethos." Pages 120–34 in Beutler, *Der neue Mensch in Christus*.

Schnelle, Udo. *Apostle Paul: His Life and Theology*. Translated by M. Eugene Boring. Grand Rapids: Baker Academic, 2003.

———. "Die Ethik des 1. Thessalonicherbriefes." Pages 295–305 in *The Thessalonian Correspondence*. Edited by Raymond Collins. Leuven, Belgium: Leuven University Press, 1990.

———. "Das Liebesgebot im Neuen Testament: Jesus, Paulus und Johannes." Pages 21–34 in *"Liebe" im Wandel der Zeiten: Kulturwissenschaftliche Perspektiven*. Edited by Klaus Tanner. Leipzig, Germany: Evangelische Verlagsanstalt, 2005.

———. "Transformation und Partizipation als Grundgedanken paulinischer Theologie." *New Testament Studies* 47 (2001): 58–75.

Schrage, W. *Der erste Brief an die Korinther*. Evangelisch-Katholischer Kommentar zum Neuen Testament. 3 vols. Zürich: Benziger, 1991.

———. *The Ethics of the New Testament*. Translated by David Green. Philadelphia: Fortress, 1982.

———. *Ethik des Neuen Testaments*. Das Neue Testament Deutsch Ergänzungsreihe 4. Göttingen: Vandenhoeck & Ruprecht, 1982.

———. "The Formal Ethical Interpretation of Pauline Paraenesis." Pages 301–35 in Rosner, *Understanding Paul's Ethics*.

———. "Heiligung als Prozess bei Paulus." Pages 203–15 in Schrage, *Kreuzestheologie und Ethik im Neuen Testament*.

———. *Die konkreten Einzelgebote in der paulinischen Paränese*. Gütersloh, Germany: Gerd Mohn, 1961.

———. *Kreuzestheologie und Ethik im Neuen Testament: Gesammelte Studien*. Edited by Dietrich-Alex Koch and Mattias Köchert. Forschungen zur Religion und Literatur des Alten und Neuen Testaments 205. Göttingen: Vandenhoeck & Ruprecht, 2004.

———. "Zur formalethischen Deutung der paulinischen Paränese." Pages 171–201 in Schrage, *Kreuzestheologie und Ethik im Neuen Testament*.

Schubert, Paul. *Form and Function of the Pauline Thanksgivings*. Beihefte zur Zeitschrift für die neutestamentliche Wissenschaft 20. Berlin: Töpelmann, 1939.

Schulz, S. *Neutestamentliche Ethik*. Zürcher Grundrisse zur Bibel. Zürich: Theologischer Verlag, 1987.

Schürmann, Heinz. "'Das Gesetz des Christus,' (Gal. 6,2)." Pages 282–300 in Söding, *Studien zur neutestamentliche Ethik*.

Schüssler-Fiorenza, Elisabeth. *In Memory of Her: A Feminist Theological Reconstruction of Christian Origins*. London: SCM, 1983.

Schweizer, Eduard. *The Letter to the Colossians*. Minneapolis: Augsburg, 1976.

Scroggs, Robin. "Paul and the Eschatological Woman." *Journal of the American Academy of Religion* 40 (1972): 283–303.

———. *Paul for a New Day*. Philadelphia: Fortress, 1977.

Seebass, Horst. "Liebe II." Pages 128–33 in vol. 21 of Balz, *Theologische Realenzyklopädie*.

Seesemann, H. "Pateō." Pages 943–45 in vol. 5 of Kittel and Friedrich, *Theological Dictionary of the New Testament*.

Smith, Jay E. "Another Look at 4Q416 2 ii.21, a Critical Parallel to First Thessalonians 4:4." *Catholic Biblical Quarterly* 63 (2001): 499–504.

Söding, Thomas. *Das Liebesgebot bei Paulus: Die Mahnung zur Agape im Rahmen der paulinischen Ethik*. Neutestamentliche Abhandlungen 26. Münster, Germany: Aschendorf, 1995.

———. *Die Trias Glaube, Hoffnung, Liebe bei Paulus: Eine exegetische Studie*. Stuttgarter Bibelstudien 150. Stuttgart: Katholisches Bibelwerk, 1992.

———. "Das Wortfeld der Liebe im paganen und biblischen Griechisch: Philologische Beobachtungen an der Wurzel ΑΓΑΠ-." *Ephemerides theologicae lovanienses* 68 (1992): 284–330.

———, ed. *Studien zur neutestamentliche Ethik*. Stuttgarter biblische Aufsatzbände Neues Testament 7. Stuttgart: Katholisches Bibelwerk, 1990.

Speyer, Wolfgang. "Hellenistisch-römische Voraussetzungen der Verbreitung des Christentums." Pages 11–38 in Beutler, *Der neue Mensch in Christus*.

Spicq, C. "*Agathopoieō*." Pages 1–4 in vol. 1 of Spicq, *Theological Lexicon of the New Testament*.

———. "*Alētheia*." Pages 66–86 in vol. 1 of Spicq, *Theological Lexicon of the New Testament*.

———. "*Atakteō*." Pages 223–26 in vol. 1 of Spicq, *Theological Lexicon of the New Testament*.

———. "*Chara*." Pages 498–99 in vol. 3 of Spicq, *Theological Lexicon of the New Testament*.

———. "*Chrēsteuomai*." Pages 511–16 in vol. 3 of Spicq, *Theological Lexicon of the New Testament*.

———. "*Erethizō*." Pages 69–72 in vol. 2 of Spicq, *Theological Lexicon of the New Testament*.

———. "*Hēsychazō*." Pages 178–83 in vol. 2 of Spicq, *Theological Lexicon of the New Testament*.

———. "*Loidoreō*." Pages 407–9 in vol. 2 of Spicq, *Theological Lexicon of the New Testament*.

———. "*Nouthesia*." Pages 548–51 in vol. 2 of Spicq, *Theological Lexicon of the New Testament*.

———. "*Praypatheia*." Pages 160–71 in vol. 3 of Spicq, *Theological Lexicon of the New Testament*.

———. "*Tapeinos*." Pages 369–71 in vol. 3 of Spicq, *Theological Lexicon of the New Testament*.

———. *Theological Lexicon of the New Testament*. 3 vols. Translated by James D. Ernest. Peabody, MA: Hendrickson, 1994.

Standhartinger, Angela. "*Eusebeia* in den Pastoralbriefen: Ein Beitrag zum Einfluss römischen Denkens auf das Entstehende Christentum." *Novum Testamentum* 48 (2006): 51–82.

Sterling, Gregory. "Universalizing the Particular: Natural Law in Second Temple Jewish Ethics." Pages 64–80 in *Laws Stamped with the Seals of Nature: Law and Nature in Hellenistic Philosophy and Philo of Alexandria*. Edited by David T. Runia, Gregory E. Sterling, and Hindy Najman. *Studia philonica Annual* 15. Brown Judaic Series 337. Providence: Brown University Press, 2003.

Stowers, Stanley K. *A Rereading of Romans: Justice, Jews, and Gentiles*. New Haven: Yale University Press, 1994.

Strecker, Georg. "Autonome Sittlichkeit und das Proprium der christlichen Ethik bei Paulus." *Theologische Literaturzeitung* 104 (1979): 866–72.

———. "Die neutestamentlichen Haustafeln (Kol 3,18–4,1 und Eph 5,22–6,9)." Pages 349–75 in *Neues Testament und Ethik: Für Rudolf Schnackenburg*. Edited by Helmut Merklein. Freiburg, Germany: Herder, 1989.

Stuhlmacher, Peter. *Paul's Letter to the Romans: A Commentary*. Louisville: Westminster John Knox, 1994.

———. *Revisiting Paul's Doctrine of Justification: A Challenge to the New Perspective*. Downers Grove, IL: InterVarsity, 2001.

Talbert, Charles H. *Ephesians and Colossians*. Paideia. Grand Rapids: Baker Academic, 2007.

Theissen, Gerd. "Urchristliches Ethos: Eine Synthese aus biblischer und griechischer Tradition." Pages 209–22 in *Kontexte der Schrift*. Vol. 2 of *Kultur, Politik, Religion, Sprache-Text: Für Wolfgang Stegemann*. Edited by Christian Strecker. Stuttgart: Kohlhammer, 2005.

Thompson, James W. "Creation, Shame and Nature in 1 Cor 11:2–16: The Background and Coherence of Paul's Argument." Pages 237–57 in *Early Christianity and Classical Culture: Comparative Studies in Honor of Abraham J. Malherbe*. Edited by John T. Fitzgerald, Thomas H. Olbricht, and L. Michael White. Novum Testamentum Supplements 110. Leiden, Netherlands: Brill, 2003.

———. *Pastoral Ministry according to Paul*. Grand Rapids: Baker Academic, 2006.

———. "Reading the Letters as Narrative." Pages 81–106 in *Narrative Reading, Narrative Preaching: Reuniting New Testament Interpretation and Proclamation*. Edited by Joel Green and Michael Pasquarello III. Grand Rapids: Baker Academic, 2003.

Thorsteinsson, Runar M. "Paul and Roman Stoicism: Romans 12 and Contemporary Stoic Ethics." *Journal for the Study of the New Testament* 29 (2006): 139–61.

Tomson, Peter. *Paul and the Jewish Law: Halakha in the Letters of the Apostle to the Gentiles*. Compendia rerum iudaicarum ad Novum Testamentum. Minneapolis: Fortress, 1990.

Van der Horst, P. W. "Musonius Rufus and the New Testament: A Contribution to the Corpus Hellenisticum." *Novum Testamentum* 16 (1974): 306–15.

———. *The Sentences of Pseudo-Phocylides*. Studia in Veteris Testamenti pseudepigraphica 4. Leiden, Netherlands: Brill, 1978.

Van der Watt, Jan G., and François S. Malen, eds. *Identity, Ethics, and Ethos in the New Testament*. Beihefte zur Zeitschrift für die neutestamentliche Wissenschaft 141. Berlin: De Gruyter, 2006.

Vögtle, A. "Affekt." Pages 160–73 in vol. 1 of Balz, *Theologische Realenzyklopädie*.

———. *Die Tugend- und Lasterkataloge im Neuen Testament*. Neutestamentliche Abhandlungen. Münster, Germany: Aschendorf, 1936.

Volf, Miroslav. "Christliche Identität und Differenz." *Zeitschrift für Theologie und Kirche* 92 (1995): 357–75.

Wagner, J. Ross. "Not beyond the Things Which Are Written: A Call to Boast Only in the Lord (1 Cor. 4.6)." *New Testament Studies* 44 (1998): 279–87.

Ward, Roy Bowen. "Musonius and Paul on Marriage." *New Testament Studies* 36 (1990): 281–89.

Warner, R., trans. *Medea*. In vol. 1 of *Euripides*, edited by R. A. Lattimore. Chicago: University of Chicago Press, 1955.

Watson, Francis. "Constructing an Antithesis: Pauline and Other Jewish Perspectives on Divine and Human Agency." Pages 99–116 in Barclay and Gathercole, *Divine and Human Agency in Paul and His Cultural Environment*.

Webb, William J. *Returning Home: New Covenant and Second Exodus as the Context for 2 Corinthians 6:14–7:1*. Journal for the Study of the New Testament: Supplement Series 85. Sheffield: JSOT, 1993.

Weber, Reinhard. *Das Gesetz im hellenistischen Judentum: Studien zum Verständnis und zur Funktion der Thora von Demetrios bis Pseudo-Phokylides*. Arbeiten zur Religion und Geschichte des Urchristentums 10. Frankfurt am Main: Peter Lang, 2000.

Weder, Hans. "Die Normativität der Freiheit: Eine Überlegung zu Gal 5,1.13–25." Pages 129–45 in *Paulus, Apostel Jesu Christi: Für Günther Klein*. Edited by Michael Trowitzsch. Tübingen: Mohr Siebeck, 1998.

Wegenast, K. *Das Verständnis der Tradition bei Paulus und in den Deuteropaulinen*. Wissenschaftliche Monographien zum Alten und Neuen Testament 8. Neukirchen-Vluyn, Germany: Neukirchener Verlag, 1962.

Weidinger, Karl. *Die Haustafeln: Ein Stück urchristlicher Paraenese*. Leipzig: Heinrich, 1928.

Weima, Jeffrey A. D. "How You Must Walk to Please God: Holiness and Discipleship in 1 Thessalonians." Pages 98–119 in *Patterns of Discipleship in the New Testament*. Edited by Richard N. Longenecker. Grand Rapids: Eerdmans, 1996.

Welborn, Lawrence. *Politics and Rhetoric in the Corinthian Epistles*. Macon, GA: Mercer University Press, 1997.

Westerholm, Stephen. "Paul's Anthropological 'Pessimism' in Its Jewish Context." Pages 71–98 in Barclay and Gathercole, *Divine and Human Agency in Paul and His Cultural Environment*.

Whitton, J. "A Neglected Meaning of *SKEUOS* in 1 Thessalonians 4.4." *New Testament Studies* 28 (1982): 142–43.

Wibbing, S. *Die Tugend- und Lasterkataloge im Neuen Testament und ihre Traditionsgeschichte unter Berücksichtigung der Qumram-Texte*. Berlin: Töpelmann, 1959.

Wilson, Walter T. *Love without Pretense: Romans 12:9–21 and Hellenistic-Jewish Wisdom Literature*. Wissenschaftliche Untersuchungen zum Neuen Testament. Second Series 46. Tübingen: J. C. B. Mohr, 1991.

Winston, David. *The Wisdom of Solomon: A New Translation and Commentary*. Anchor Bible 43. Garden City, NY: Doubleday, 1979.

Winter, Bruce W. *After Paul Left Corinth: The Influence of Secular Ethics and Social Change*. Grand Rapids: Eerdmans, 2001.

———. "Theological and Ethical Responses to Religious Pluralism—1 Corinthians 8–10." *Tyndale Bulletin* 41, no. 2 (1990): 209–26.

Wischmeyer, O. "Das Gebot der Nächstenliebe bei Paulus: Eine traditionsgeschichtliche Untersuchung." *Biblische Zeitschrift*, n.s., 30 (1986): 161–87.

Wold, Benjamin G. "Family Ethics in 4Q *Instruction* and the New Testament." *Novum Testamentum* 50 (2008): 286–300.

Wolter, Michael. "Der Brief des sogenannten Unzuchtsünders." Pages 181–96 in Wolter, *Theologie und Ethos im frühen Christentum*.

———. "Die ethische Identität christlicher Gemeinden in neutestamentlicher Zeit." Pages 61–90 in *Woran orientiert sich Ethik*. Edited by Wilfried Härle and Reiner Preul. Marburger Jahrbuch Theologie 13. Marburg, Germany: Elwert, 2001.

———. "Ethos und Identität in paulinischen Gemeinden." *New Testament Studies* 43, no. 3 (1997): 430–44.

———. "Identität und Ethos bei Paulus." Pages 121–69 in Wolter, *Theologie und Ethos im frühen Christentum*.

———. *Theologie und Ethos im frühen Christentum*. Wissenschaftliche Untersuchungen zum Neuen Testament 236. Tübingen: Mohr Siebeck, 2009.

Woyke, J. *Die neutestamentlichen Haustafeln: Ein kritischer und konstructiver Forschungsüberblick*. Stuttgarter Bibelstudien 184. Stuttgart: Katholisches Bibelwerk, 2000.

Wright, David. "Homosexuals or Prostitutes? The Meaning of *Arsenokoitai* (1 Cor. 6:9, 1 Tim. 1:10)." *Vigiliae christianae* 38 (1984): 125–53.

Wright, N. T. *The New Testament and the People of God*. Minneapolis: Fortress, 1992.

Yarbrough, O. Larry. *Not Like the Gentiles: Marriage Rules in the Letters of Paul*. Society of Biblical Literature Dissertation Series 80. Atlanta: Scholars Press, 1984.

Zeller, Dieter. "Konkrete Ethik im hellenistischen Kontext." Pages 82–98 in Beutler, *Der neue Mensch in Christus*.

Zimmermann, Ruben. "Jenseits von Indikativ und Imperativ: Entwurf einer 'impliziten Ethic' des Paulus am Beispiel des 1. Korintherbriefes." *Theologische Literaturzeitung* 132 (2007): 259–84.

Zmijewski, J. "*Chrēstotēs*." Pages 475–77 in vol. 3 of Balz and Schneider, *Exegetical Dictionary of the New Testament*.

# Index of Subjects

# Index of Modern Authors

# Index of Ancient Sources